MC MASTER UNIVERSITY
1 / THE TORONTO YEARS

CHARLES M. JOHNSTON

McMaster University

VOLUME 1 / THE TORONTO YEARS

PUBLISHED FOR McMASTER UNIVERSITY BY

UNIVERSITY OF TORONTO PRESS

TORONTO AND BUFFALO

© University of Toronto Press 1976
Toronto and Buffalo
Printed in Canada

Library of Congress Cataloging in Publication Data

Johnston, Charles Murray, 1926–
    McMaster University.

    Includes bibliographical references and index.
    Contents: v.   1. The Toronto years.
    1. McMaster University, Hamilton, Ont. – History.
    LE3M32J64   378.713'52   75-33006
    ISBN 0-8020-3332-6

In memory of H.W. McCready

Contents

Illustrations

These illustrations appear between pages 156 and 157.

John Gilmour
Robert Fyfe
William McMaster
Susan Moulton McMaster
John Castle
D.E. Thomson
Malcolm MacVicar
T.H. Rand
James Ten Broeke
J.L. Gilmour
A.C. McKay
W.J. McKay
W.P. Cohoe
J.H. Farmer
Science class, 1896. William Piersol
   and A.B. Willmott instructing
Chancellor O.C.S. Wallace
   addressing a class, 1904
R.W. Smith's biology class, ca 1900
William Findlay

George Cross
I.G. Matthews
Elmore Harris
J.B. Tingle
H.F. Dawes
C.W. New
A.L. McCrimmon
McMaster OTC platoon on parade
McMaster Hall (etching by
   Owen Staples, ca 1923)
McMasterrifics, 1923
Girls' field hockey team outside
   Wallingford Hall, 1923
H.P. Whidden
L.H. Marshall
W.S.W. McLay
T.T. Shields
Albert Matthews
John MacNeill

Preface

The city of Hamilton is McMaster University's second home. The institution was originally located in Toronto where it functioned for forty years after it was chartered by an Act of the provincial legislature in 1887 and endowed with funds from the estate of Senator William McMaster. A prominent Toronto businessman and financier, the Irish-born McMaster had long sought to provide for an educated Baptist clergy and a 'practical Christian school of learning.' The application for the charter was made on behalf of the Baptist denomination of central Canada in keeping with the senator's wish that the enterprise be given as a trust to all the churches in that constituency. From the outset the latter, through its successive co-ordinating bodies, including the present Baptist Convention of Ontario and Quebec, formed in 1888, accepted full responsibility for the new university's affairs.

This arrangement, as the following pages will attempt to demonstrate, was destined to have a profound influence on the institution and proved to have both advantages and disadvantages. Most notably, accountability to the Convention, which kept the university in close touch with the denominational community whose financial and moral support was vital for its development, also meant that if some delegates at the annual assemblies of the Baptist Convention were so disposed the university's affairs could be made the subject of prolonged and bitter public debate. On a number of occasions ugly confrontations on the floor of the Convention threatened the very life of McMaster. During one such crisis, precipitated in the 1920s by the Rev. T.T. Shields's attacks on the institution and its instructional policies, serious negotiations were begun to remove it from its original home in Toronto to nearby Hamilton, so that it might enjoy what a relieved contemporary called a 'fresh start.'

In the light of this development the history of McMaster University seems to divide itself naturally into two segments. The present volume, which is concerned with the first segment, deals briefly with McMaster's Baptist forerunners and then turns to the founding of the university and its subsequent career during its years on the Bloor Street campus in Toronto. In 1928, following protracted discussions and negotiations, the 'New McMaster Campaign' was launched which resulted two years later in the physical re-establishment of the institution in its new setting in Hamilton. That year seemed an appropriate point at which to close the first volume of the history, because once the decision was made to move elsewhere and a financial drive mounted to achieve that object, the Toronto phase of the university's operations virtually came to an end. Over the next two years, until the Hamilton campus actually materialized, the institution's leaders were engrossed in the details and mechanics of the transfer and already orienting themselves to their new home and responding to the challenge of their enlarged responsibilities.

The second and concluding volume of the history will open with an account of the progress of the 'New McMaster Campaign' and of the steps taken to transplant McMaster in its new surroundings. It will relate the university's subsequent career down to 1957 when, bowing to changing circumstances, the Baptist Convention regretfully relinquished control to enable it to become a non-denominational private institution eligible for public funding. This was a landmark as significant for McMaster as its move from Toronto over a quarter of a century before and brought to an end the second phase in its history.

An effort has been made throughout the study to explain and assess the principles and ideals that shaped McMaster University and to examine how it discharged its obligations to the Baptist constituency and to society at large. Problems arising from the university's reluctance to federate with the 'Provincial University' are examined. Also discussed is the close relationship forged between the central Canadian branch of the Baptist denomination and its counterparts elsewhere in the Atlantic world, a relationship that frequently stood McMaster in good stead when it came to setting goals and recruiting personnel. At the same time, however, the record reflects the strife of the university's involvement in doctrinal conflicts, especially in the struggle between modernism and fundamentalism.

But this study is also one of individuals, of the people who helped to found and then sustain the institution over the years as instructors, administrators, students, and benefactors. As an earlier historical review of McMaster put it:

'Few institutions are more difficult to bring to birth and to maintain in vigorous life than a university [and] it must be founded by men who hope to reap nothing from it for themselves.' This statement could apply to all such founders and not least to those who established McMaster and championed, as 'a matter of principle,' its independent course and its function as a 'practical Christian school of learning.'

Acknowledgments

To begin with, I wish to commend the administration of McMaster University, who commissioned this history, for their extraordinary patience and forbearance while the work was in progress. And on behalf of myself and the university I gratefully acknowledge the generosity of the McMaster Alumni Association whose financial support helped make its publication possible.

Over the years the congenial staff of the Canadian Baptist Archives at the McMaster Divinity College, my principal source, made the preparation of this history as painless as it was in their power to arrange. These helpful people were in turn Ethelyn Harlow, Dr Marget Meikleham, Gwen Laurie, Suzanne McEachnie, and Joan Oliphant, the present librarian. Miss Oliphant's cheerful assistant, Maxine Soble, could also be counted upon to track down sources and locate illustrative material.

I owe a special debt of gratitude to Dr Meikleham, former head of the McMaster University Library, who, following her retirement from that post, presided expertly and graciously over the Canadian Baptist Archives. Through her efforts and those of Professor G.P. Albaugh of the Divinity College, many vital manuscripts were salvaged when storerooms were flooded some years ago.

Professor Albaugh also extended me many courtesies, from sorting out complex theological questions to reading and commenting constructively upon the manuscript. I benefited as well from many conversations with his colleagues in the pleasant surroundings of the Divinity College faculty lounge. And I very much appreciate the kindness of Principal Ivan Morgan and Professor Murray Ford in providing me with comfortable working quarters in the college.

The staffs of other repositories and colleges also eased the task of research, notably those of the Mills Memorial Library, the Registrar's Office, and the President's Office at McMaster, the Rare Book Room of the University of Toronto, the Hamilton Public Library, and the Toronto Public Library. In addition, the many alumni and friends of McMaster who answered my pleas for help, either by submitting to interviews or by forwarding recollections, documents, and photographs, made their own valuable contribution to the undertaking. I wish to thank Mr and Mrs Colin Farmer for their assistance, Jarvis Street Baptist Church for permission to reproduce the picture of Dr T.T. Shields, the Staples family for furnishing the etching of McMaster University by Owen Staples, and R.H. McNairn for providing materials on and the photograph of the COTC contingent. Most of the remaining illustrations were kindly supplied by the Canadian Baptist Archives.

I also welcome the opportunity to thank Regina MacLean for reading the manuscript and offering sound suggestions for improving it, Bruce Hill for his assistance in the early stages of the research, and Margaret Belec for her excellent typing services. Next, I want to record my appreciation of the skilful editorial labours of Larry MacDonald of the University of Toronto Press, who readied the manuscript for publication.

As usual, my wife's assistance was invaluable. For hours on end she listened patiently and responded helpfully when I read out freshly written material or discussed how I might organize and present it. Then, when it was all over, she helped me to prepare the index.

CMJ

MCMASTER UNIVERSITY
1/THE TORONTO YEARS

1

The forerunners

The chartering of McMaster University in 1887 was the culmination of Baptist educational ventures that reached far back into pre-Confederation Canada. All of them were ambitious, whether, to put them in sequence, the Canada Baptist College in Montreal, the Canadian Literary Institute in Woodstock, the Toronto Baptist College and Moulton College in Toronto, or the university itself. The Montreal enterprise is closely linked with the name of the Scotsman John Gilmour, a former seaman and schoolmaster who had started his preaching career at Greenock in 1820.[1] He had emigrated to Lower Canada a decade later and organized a congregation – the St Helen Street Church – in response to requests from compatriots who had settled in the city and along the lower Ottawa Valley. Anticipating the role of its future rival, Toronto, Montreal in the 1830s served as a natural focal point for many undertakings, including the pioneering Baptist educational experiments in the sprawling Laurentian portion of British America. Gilmour, who had visited the place years before as a seafarer, was only repeating what long-established enthusiasts had already said of Montreal, the 'entrepot of the Northern World,' when he remarked that it was 'the emporium of Canada ... the point whence radiate in every direction roads and con-veyances.' Until mid-century, when immigration and commercial expansion had shifted the demographic and economic centre of gravity westward into Upper Canada, Montreal remained the most strategically located community for the educational campaigns undertaken by Gilmour and other eager Protestant missionaries.

Before drawing up plans for the institution that would shortly materialize as the Canada Baptist College, Gilmour actively collaborated for a time with a Presbyterian group, the Canada Education and Home Missionary Society, whose objective was the establishment of an interdenominational seminary for the training of a colonial clergy. Gilmour's ecumenical commitment owed much to the effect, during his early years in Scotland, of the liberal teaching of the Haldanes, and something as well to the practical and financial difficulties that any one sect faced in organizing on its own such an educational facility. The interests of the Society, as its historian has indicated, throw light 'on the characteristics and activities of the Montreal English-speaking community [which] sought to mitigate its difficulties as a minority group in [a large French-speaking population].'[2]

The Society was forced in 1835 to give up its educational experiment when it was rocked by serious dissension through the hostility of many newly arrived Scots who volubly protested what they felt was its preposterous interdenominationalism. At this juncture, apparently, Gilmour turned to the alternative plan for a Baptist theological school, one to be supervised, he was careful to point out, by mentors from the Old Country. For Gilmour and his fellow planners the stipulation was an imperative. On theological as well as practical grounds they were anxious to sever the connection with those American institutions that had hitherto been relied upon to supply so many of their scattered pulpits in the absence of British support and a local seminary.

Theologically, as 'open communionists,' they were opposed to the restrictive and less tolerant 'closed communion' views of American Baptists. As practical men of affairs they also realized that their brightest hopefuls might never return from the greener academic fields of the United States where pastoral services were more richly rewarded. Yet ironically it was this strong subscription to the principle of open communion that ultimately deprived the projected Canada Baptist College of vital assistance from other sections of the Laurentian community. As so often the case in their Canadian experience, Baptists would dramatically fall out, invariably in full public view, over crucial doctrinal issues. The plain fact of the matter was that many Baptists who emigrated from the United States to the sister colony of Upper Canada before mid-century clung to the more restrictive practice and refused to support what they considered to be the unorthodoxy of open communion at the school in Montreal.

This, however, was a problem for the future. The immediate task facing Gilmour and his group was to seek assistance locally and in Britain for the enterprise by which they had set so much store. As a fund-raiser, Gilmour displayed talents that matched his pulpit proficiency at St Helen Street, and he achieved impressive results. Through his efforts the Baptist Colonial Missionary Society in Britain and its offshoot, the Canada Baptist Missionary Society, whose driving spirit he predictably was, had by 1836 raised nearly £1800 for an endowment and a building fund.[3] An indispensable role on the local scene was played by wealthy Baptist members of Montreal's business community, notably the banker Joseph Wenham and the printer-publisher Rollo Campbell, who consistently afforded material aid and moral comfort. While Montreal might not have been able to boast the largest concentration of Baptists in the Canadas, it enjoyed metropolitan advantages which readily produced those men of affluence who could support such an educational undertaking. Again, this selection of a well established and influential centre with respectable commercial and cultural assets as a site for the Canada Baptist College would be recalled many years later by the founders of McMaster University when they cast about for an equally promising site in Ontario for their institution.

Although the selection of Montreal was understandable in view of its commanding locale, its historical momentum in trade and finance, and its wealthy enclave of interested Baptists, the actual timing of the college's organization was grotesque. If McMaster University a century later was delivered to Hamilton in the teeth of the Depression, the Canada Baptist College was founded on the very eve of rebellion. Political tension, already aggravated by ethnic conflict between *les Anglais* and *les Patriotes* under Louis-Joseph Papineau, was sharpened in 1836 by widespread commercial and agricultural distress. By the time the shooting started a year later, Montreal and its hinterland were already feeling the pinch of crop failures and plunging prices and experiencing an 'excessive languor that pervades nearly every branch of commerce.'[4] There is no reason to suppose that the Wenhams and the Campbells and other Baptist businessmen of Montreal escaped the slump that stopped so many building programs and blocked the flow of trade.

Yet in spite of the forbidding environment of depression and armed conflict, the college was successfully launched. By the time it opened its doors on 24 September 1838 in a stone house, 'among the green fields and farms' of the city's outskirts, the rebellion had been crushed, Papineau was in exile and a semblance of order had returned to the community. Arrangements went forward to enrol students and to devise a theological curriculum. During the first session seven students were admitted, a number that increased steadily over the years to seventeen in 1845, the largest annual theological enrolment that the school enjoyed. The curriculum embraced not only, as one might expect, such courses as natural philosophy, theology, philosophy, Euclid, and ecclesiastical and civil history, in which Gilmour had long had a consuming interest, but an impressive range of oriental and classical literatures, including the exotic Syriac and Chaldean.[5]

When more elaborate quarters were provided for the college in the summer of 1846, plans were also drawn up for an 'Academical Department,' a form of secondary school. This served to prepare 'younger gentlemen' for entrance to the college, for professional training, and for vocations in Montreal's marts of trade. Almost simultaneously, provision was made for enrolling in an expanded arts course those candidates who were not necessarily contemplating a career in the pulpit. These innovations made it possible for evangelical Christians other than Baptists to enrol. This situation understandably elicited the interest of Methodists and Congregationalists in the college's affairs, and raised the institution's hopes that a larger enrolment might ease the financial burden under which all seats of learning groaned in early Victorian Canada. In part, however, the decision to add secular subjects and a modest arts curriculum to the college's theological offerings was governed by important academic and political decisions taken elsewhere.

The academic decision was taken right under the nose of the Canada Baptist College; for it had to do with the early policies of its neighbour, McGill College. When it was first mooted, Gilmour had welcomed the new institution in the belief that it would make Montreal 'the Athens of Canada.' At the outset the Baptist leader may have hoped for some kind of academic division of labour whereby Baptist theological candidates would have the opportunity of taking arts courses at McGill. If this was, in fact, what Gilmour envisaged, it would have borne a striking resemblance to the relationship that a later generation of Baptists contemplated with the University of Toronto. But any hopes of this kind Gilmour may have entertained were not redeemed. Instead of co-operation, rivalry developed between the Canada Baptist College and McGill, caused in part by the rigidity of McGill's Anglican stance in the early years and its refusal to countenance the admission of other Protestants to its arts department.[6]

Aside from this local confrontation, a provincial one, brought on by the so-called university question, doubtless governed the decision of the Canada Baptist College to expand its curriculum to include arts and vocational subjects in the late 1840s. For years the question whether or not a provincial institution of higher learning should be established in Toronto under denominational control had seasoned parliamentary debates in Upper Canada. Spokesmen of the Church of England had insisted on the principle of denominational control of such an institution – already called King's College in anticipation – and in particular on its being entrusted to them. Their opponents, invariably evangelicals, just as vigorously campaigned for a university college free of all sectarian influences. The question for Baptists at mid-century was a critical one. Almost to a man they were disposed to champion a non-sectarian university in which secular subjects would be offered to all regardless of creed. Within this concept of a university they could nonetheless justify provision for the affiliation of denominational colleges in which, as in the case of the early curriculum of the Canada Baptist College, the theological courses would be the principal, indeed the exclusive, fare. A model to guide their thinking was the University of London, a non-sectarian facility with which a Baptist school, later named Regent's Park College, had already been affiliated.

The principles behind the Baptist concept of a university could be traced to the Reformation, when the Anabaptists, the radicals of that spiritual revolt, had, unlike the followers of Martin Luther and John Calvin, deliberately set the temporal off from the spiritual out of a revulsion for the excesses of the Renaissance papacy. Whatever the terms might have meant to other sectarians, 'church' and 'state' had a special meaning for the Anabaptists' ideological descendants. For them the church was not an elaborately structured entity comparable to the polity of the state. Rather, its distinctive feature was a loosely organized congregation of believers who were not manipulated by a higher power and who stressed the ideal of complete religious liberty.[7] It then followed that a church so conceived could not readily consort with the more complex arrangements that the state had devised to manage its affairs. But spiritually as well as structurally the Baptists had reason to shun an intimate association with the public authority. By its very nature the state was the antithesis of Christianity and ought not to be encouraged to mix with the sacred to the extent of supporting one sect to the exclusion of all others. For the Baptists of the Province of Canada the distressing case in point was the close working relationship between government and the Church of England, and the latter's attempt to control the proposed provincial university. The Baptists, however, went even further: they asserted that public funds should not be appropriated nor spent for any religious object, however charitably inspired or equitably distributed. This purist view, amongst denominations apparently strongest with Baptists, long remained a potent force in the considerations of those who shaped the decisions and directed the debates on Baptist educational policy in Canada. Flowing from the argument was the corollary, so dear to the voluntarist, that non-Christians in the community ought not to be taxed for denominational ends and that each sect, if it wished to keep alive traditions and to transmit beliefs, should support itself out of its own resources and not expect largesse from the ratepaying public at large.[8]

Not surprisingly, then, most Baptists supported legislation to establish a non-sectarian institution for teaching secular subjects and for providing the higher learning essential for meeting the professional and material needs of society. Baptists, along with ratepayers of other denominations, would aid this sort of undertaking simply because for them it recognized the vital division between the sacred and the secular. But they saw nothing implicit in this inconsistent with the notion that their own seminaries could, if necessary, be affiliated with such a state institution. The separation of church and state need not rule out healthy co-operation between them.

It became painfully clear, however, that successive attempts in the 1840s to legislate into existence what its critics called a 'godless' university were doomed to failure. In these circumstances the directors of the Canada Baptist College elected to go ahead with plans to furnish their own arts and vocational instruction and to invite the enrolment of persons of 'good moral character, of all classes and persuasions.' An amalgam of convictions, political and academic decisions, and a blending of the enlightened and the expedient combined to launch secular instruction in 'science and literary studies' alongside the offerings in theology. But this curricular expansion and the high hopes of survival that had accompanied it failed to avert the disaster of 1849, when a variety of circumstances, some new, others that had lain in wait for the college from the very beginning, conspired to close its doors.

The contributing factors beyond the institution's control were the common and unwanted property of the whole early Victorian generation in the St Lawrence Valley. Once again, as at the college's founding, commercial disorders convulsed the economy, this time as a consequence of policies formulated on the other side of the Atlantic. For two generations Montreal's and British America's commercial fortunes had been bound up with the old colonial system. That ramshackle structure of mercantilistic regulations, which had somehow afforded Britain safe markets and raw materials in her overseas dependencies, had also furnished those dependencies assured returns from the sale of their staple products in the protected metropolitan market and given Montreal its profitable role as the colony's forwarding agent. In the late 1840s these certitudes were dramatically destroyed when a rapidly industrializing Britain decided to embark upon free trade. Almost at once the props of the local economy were toppled by the repeal of colonial preferences and the other safeguards of the ancient commercial regime. When Montreal business sagged, the city's non-commercial institutions, including the Canada Baptist College, could not help but be affected. More than once the word 'ominous' was used to describe the dwindling enrolment produced by depression and to communicate the commercial and financial plight of those Baptist businessmen who had long been the college's mainstay.

Another decision taken overseas was even more deplorable because it occurred within the family. The English missionary society, also caught in a financial squeeze, announced its intention to cancel its support of the Canadian field and to leave the college to its own slender resources, prompting the prophecy that this would cause the sun of British Baptist influence to set on the Canadian scene.[9] Another account of the institution's misfortunes accused its principal of extravagant enthusiasms and political partisanship at a time when restraint and 'sober, well-disposed views' were clearly in demand.[10]

The business cycle and personalities aside, however, those basic doctrinal differences which had marred the college's founding doubtless hastened its end. Closed communionists of Canada West, many of whom were imbued with the doctrines of American Baptists, had always resented the manifestly English practices of the Montreal brethren and by and large had withheld their aid. As their numbers grew they openly began to wonder why Montreal should be permitted to continue to fill Canadian pulpits. Again, in spite of the abortive attempts to found a non-sectarian university in Toronto with which a Baptist seminary could have been affiliated, many in the west believed that such a facility would inevitably come and that a Baptist school in Toronto should therefore be planned with or without the approval of the Montreal institution.

Indeed, one aging graduate of the Canada Baptist College convinced himself years later that the major reason for his alma mater's collapse was the selection of Toronto as the site for a new Baptist educational institution. This was a clear indication to him that the rest of the country had grown jealous of the effort that had been made in Montreal. In any case, he probably spoke for many alumni when he emotionally reminisced in 1906 about the 'many tender scenes once centred in the B. Coll. in Montreal – 1840-5 – and now continued in McMaster,'[11] as though the latter place had been in Baptist plans all along. A powerful echo of the old conflict between the eastern and western wings of the constituency sounded in a letter from one of the original governors of McMaster and a life-long Montreal resident who had prospered as a provisioner. 'It is evident' he wrote at the turn of the century 'that McMaster does not and perhaps neither Toronto nor the leading Baptists of the West, understand or appreciate the struggle we [have made and] are making.'[12] The enmity, jealousy, and rivalry that frequently soured relations between the two Canadian metropolises were reflected in the dealings between the two Baptist spheres of influence centred on Montreal and Toronto.

One other factor must also be examined in any account of the decline and fall of the Canada Baptist College. With all the talk among the upper social echelons of the constituency of a need for an 'educated ministry,' many a Baptist in the rank and file of the back townships and the village streets distrusted any formula for creating 'man-made ministers.'[13] They challenged the very philosophy that had inspired the Canada Baptist College, complaining that it had not sprung from the 'heart sweat' of the people. The school had, moreover, made no effort to reach the Baptist home, particularly in Canada West. These accusations and misgivings, as recurrent in Baptist educational affairs as the issue of church and state, boded ill for the efforts of those who sought a replacement for the college when it closed in 1849. But a timely spur for such efforts came the same year in the form of Robert Baldwin's University Bill, which finally promised to succeed where earlier legislation had failed: to found that provincial institution upon which Baptist educational leaders had for so many years pinned their hopes.

Among those who took part in the endeavour to rebuild Baptist educational fortunes elsewhere in the province were, understandably, the people who had been prominent in the Canada Baptist College in the forties. One of the leading figures was the Rev. Robert Alexander Fyfe, a British American native of Laprairie, a Montreal suburb, who had once served briefly as principal of the Canada Baptist College.[14] Like so many Baptist youth who showed pastoral promise, Fyfe had furthered his education in the United States, the very process the school had been designed to obviate. After attending a number of institutions he ultimately graduated in 1842 from Newton Theological Seminary in Massachusetts and was ordained a Baptist pastor. Returning to Canada he served successively as a minister in Perth, as interim principal of the college, and as pastor of a church in Toronto. In the latter post he enjoyed the opportunity of entering into the debate then in progress on the future of the proposed provincial university, a question haunting politicians throughout the forties. Fyfe made no bones about his preference when the university bills were debated, coming out squarely for the endowment of a non-sectarian 'college of literature, science, and art,' with which a Baptist theological college could honourably be affiliated.

In the course of the discussions he stressed what numbers of other evangelical church leaders had also envisaged, that such an institution would be invaluable as a nation-building force. 'I cannot but lament a state of affairs in this country,' he wrote. 'Men come from Ireland, England, and Scotland retaining all their peculiarities, even their nationalities. We ought to look upon ourselves as Canadians and earnestly enquire by what means we can advance the interests of the country ... Now the great Provincial Institution ... would tend to remove this evil. It would form the nucleus for a national feeling in Canada.'[15] To reconcile what one prominent Baptist layman in

Toronto described as the 'rather irreconcilable elements ... of Yankees, English, Irish, Scotch, Welsh and Canadian ... who compose the Churches here'[16] was a goal that many evangelicals set for themselves long before the 'Canada First' movement was heard of in the land. Egerton Ryerson, the titan of the Methodists, may have put the case more elegantly than Fyfe and his coreligionists, but the message was the same. Their 'incipient nationalism,' to quote one recent study of the theme, expressed as a 'common feeling of identification with Canada ... arose naturally out of the experience of the churches in creating acceptable syntheses from imported and local materials.'[17] Fyfe's campaign to achieve some such synthesis in his own constituency was inspired in no small part by patriotic fervour and by the desire to heal the breach between the English open communionists of Montreal and their counterparts in Canada West.

Fyfe's sojourns in the United States, the first spent as a student, the second as a pastor in the early fifties, had only served to sharpen his sense of attachment to British America. A touch of homesickness, probably more acute during his student days, an ill-defined feeling that whatever the Americans had achieved might not be adaptable to Canadian circumstances, and the belief that he 'should not be drawn away from where I am more needed,'[18] all these factors had prompted him to return to Canada on two occasions and to spend time 'among his own.' During the first of these intervals he had learned, at first hand as its principal, of the problems facing the Canada Baptist College and of the strained relations between the Montreal brethren and the people in the west.

During his brief tenure at the college he had stressed the importance of diversifying the curriculum to provide the practical and literary as well as the philosophical and theological, a proposal that pointed the way to the course of studies he would seek to offer years later at the Literary Institute in Woodstock. Fyfe doubtless would have agreed with the view expressed by a fellow Baptist that the higher educational institutions of Canada 'ought to be practical. There should be less regard to the refined and recondite in classical or mathematical studies, and more to the useful, in every department. General knowledge should be acquired. History should be thoroughly studied. Natural Philosophy and Chemistry, and the application of the latter Science to Agriculture should engage a large share of the attention. The principles of Political Economy should be carefully taught.'[19] What the Montreal institution had lacked in these and other respects Fyfe would aim at including in the curriculum of any successor, particularly courses in history, because in his view this was the vital prerequisite to that understanding of shared traditions and sentiments without which no 'national feeling' could hope to emerge.[20]

But equally as important to Fyfe as curricular reform was the matter of relocation. Characteristically, he bluntly charged that the Canada Baptist College had never attempted to meet the needs of the faithful elsewhere in the province and went on to urge those neglected people to organize their own institution, this even before the Montreal college went out of existence in 1849. At least one pastor in Canada West had gone on record in favour of such an experiment as early as 1843, concluding that 'if there is no possibility of removing the College from Montreal to Hamilton, I trust the churches will move and have one for themselves either there or in Brantford.'[21] By this date the Baptist population of Upper Canada stood, according to reasonably reliable estimates, at the not unimpressive level of eighteen thousand out of a total population of 486,000.[22] Most of these Baptists were congregated in the region west of Toronto in the southwestern peninsula; hence the favourable situation of the Brantford and Hamilton district should plans ever go forward to found an institution in 'the West.'

With the passage of the Baldwin Bill in 1849, Baptists were provided with their 'providential' opportunity to found a successor to the Canada Baptist College that could be affiliated with the 'national' university. Fully three years passed, however, before anything like a viable scheme was promoted. In the interval, Baptists in Canada West had nonetheless organized their own Regular Baptist Missionary Society, a committee of which was entrusted with the task of setting up the theological school. Until the latter materialized it was hoped that the newly established Baptist seminary in Rochester, New York, would temporarily meet the Canadian need for ministerial training. Meanwhile, Dr MacLay, a highly regarded member of the American Bible Union, was recruited as a fund-raiser for the project in Canada West. Although this persuasive cleric raised some £6000, the scheme came to grief over an issue that had long plagued the Canada Baptist College's relations with western Baptists. The communion question was again bitterly debated when John Gilmour and other open communionists sought some control over the prospective institution after their financial aid was invited. The closed communionists resented the proposed bargain; no agreement was reached, and 'MacLay College' failed to progress beyond the paperwork that had gone into it.

The setback demoralized the entire constituency. Even so, some Baptists derived a kind of negative comfort from the fact that the Baldwin formula of 1849 had, in their view, been seriously modified, if not emasculated, by subsequent legislation the very year that the communion question had thwarted their own efforts. The Hincks Bill of 1852 had sought to mollify vested ecclesiastical interests that had been demanding a share of the original university endowment, the same demand that Fyfe and others had resisted a decade before. In practice, however, Francis Hincks's offer to grant the denominational colleges whatever was left over after the university's needs were met was an empty one because the remnant would have been negligible.

In any case, deprived by internal dissension of the opportunity to found a full-fledged 'Divinity Hall,' Baptists in Canada West proceeded with an alternative: the establishment of an institute that would combine coeducational grammar school training with theological instruction for prospective Baptist pastors. This venture enabled Fyfe to recapitulate and ultimately to implement the educational changes he had first promoted at the Canada Baptist College. In his opinion it had always been unrealistic to expect semi-literate farmers' sons to be rushed into theological studies without adequate preparation in 'literary and practical' subjects. Moreover, such sound preparation at the grammar school level would afford Baptist youth with more rewarding instruction than Fyfe believed was then available in the publicly supported schools in western Ontario. Finally, should graduates of the planned institution ever wish to pursue higher education in the arts and sciences, they could enrol in the provincial university where they would be free from sectarian control, the condition to which Fyfe had long attached so much importance.

These ideas Fyfe incorporated in a letter to the *Christian Messenger* late in 1855.[23] The document foreshadowed the constitution of the Canadian Literary Institute which was founded within two years in the town of Woodstock. The decision to go ahead with that undertaking overrode an invitation from the University of Rochester to support there the appointment of a Canadian professorship. To satisfy 'national' considerations, and to correct what Fyfe called a 'mortifying lack of Baptist institutions of any grade' in Canada West, he placed himself at the head of a committee to find a suitable location. Given their size and prominence it appears surprising that neither Toronto nor Hamilton were given serious consideration by Fyfe's committee. Possibly the disturbances about to disrupt some of the wealthier Baptist churches in the two cities, particularly in Toronto, might have had something to do with their being neglected; in such circumstances they would not likely be disposed to offer the kind of aid the new institution required. Moreover, when Fyfe was pastor at the Bond Street Church in Toronto, he had failed to excite the unqualified admiration of all those who had submitted to his sermons.[24] These factors may have joined with a sincere desire to start again in a less urbanized atmosphere, especially after the failure in Montreal less than a decade before. In a rural environment the promoters might have wished to convince the less worldly members of the constituency that the institute would belong as much to them as to the sophisticates.

In any event, of the three places ultimately considered, Woodstock, Fonthill, and Brantford, the first won out because it offered the largest guaranteed pledge (some $16,000), eminent accessibility, and the advantages that accrued to a county town. Well served by the newly completed Great Western Railway, Woodstock occupied a strategic point in southwestern Ontario. Admittedly, an English tourist of the time described the place less than enthusiastically in these terms: 'Woodstock stands on undulating ground and is a completely rural, straggling place, like a large village with a number of gentlemen's homes in it ... It contains six churches, a gaol, a court-house, a grammar school, a mechanics' institute, some mills and boasts of a newspaper.' But he concluded on a note that would have appealed strongly to Fyfe: 'All material improvements progress in the Canadian Peninsula. Full of promise, as is the whole land, that, after all, is the garden of the province — the heart, the soul of that great country. It should no longer be called a colony ... Canada is a mighty country, attached to England, though neither England's slave nor England's school-boy, but full of vast internal resources, prosperous, contented, and happy.'[25]

The school that Fyfe was planning for Woodstock was not for that community alone, nor even for its immediate hinterland, but for the whole country. It was to be, in short, the Canadian Literary Institute, a name obviously not to be taken lightly; as Fyfe proclaimed, 'there is not a corner in the land in which its blessings may not reach.'[26] For him it belonged to the whole Baptist constituency of Canada and would even extend a welcome to non-Baptists who might wish to have their children educated in a Christian setting dedicated to practical educational goals. In this manner he hoped that the sectional rivalry born of the doctrinal disputes that had hamstrung the Canada Baptist College would be avoided from the outset and that effective preparatory training would be provided for Baptist pastors into the bargain. The day the cornerstone was laid, 23 June 1857, augured well for these objectives. Hopeful administrators noted an 'amiable atmosphere and a keen interest in the welfare of the undertaking ... exhibited by all present regardless of name or sect, in contrast to the feeling toward the College in Montreal.'[27] Nor was it a display of empty rhetoric when the Grand River Association (North) resolved a year later that 'whereas the education of our sons and daughters is a matter of very great importance and whereas the progress of science and the march of intellect demand that we keep pace with the times we live in, *if we would not be left behind*, this Association hail with satisfaction the erection of the Literary Institute in the Town of Woodstock.'[28]

The times were indeed stimulating and challenging. The arrival of the iron horse and its capacity to annihilate distances, the organization of literary societies and mechanics' institutes (the forerunners of public library systems), and the heady discussions about the moral and material necessity for taking over the vast expanse of Rupert's Land in the Northwest, these were stirring happenings, unknown a brief generation before, in a community teetering precariously on the edge of a pioneer frontier.

Trying not to be left behind, the CLI sought to achieve the goals set for it by Fyfe and to preserve the optimism that had sponsored it. But throughout its career in Woodstock it was forced to endure financial disasters, physical calamities, and personal animosities. In 1861, for example, barely a year after its opening, the institute was wiped out by fire, only to be replaced almost at once as the result of a vigorous campaign which produced donations not only from the Baptists of British North America but also from denominational well-wishers in the United Kingdom and the neighbouring states of the Union. In keeping with one of their fundamental principles, the Baptists respectfully declined the civic aid offered by the hospitable town of Woodstock.[29]

In the meantime, Fyfe and his colleagues kept up their running battle to preserve the provincial university as the sort of institution to which they could send CLI graduates to take advanced work. For a period in the early sixties it appeared as though denominationalism might after all be introduced at this upper educational level. The provision for affiliation had practically become inoperative as first the Methodists and then other interested denominations virtually disavowed the Hincks settlement of 1853. The possibility then emerged that the university would fall under denominational control after a commission of inquiry proposed that University College be abolished and the original plan of King's College revived, including an arrangement that would have given the latter a larger portion of the original endowment.[30] In the same year that the commission reported, an enraged Fyfe was appointed to the university Senate and he may have played a crucial part in that body's refusal to give in on the matter. Although, to be sure, affiliation did remain a dead letter, an important Baptist objective had been attained with the preservation intact of University College. And among his other pursuits on the Senate, Fyfe seldom hesitated to suggest curricular reform even while he continued to preside painstakingly over all the manifold arrangements of his own creation in Woodstock.

After its rise, literally from the ashes, in 1862 the Literary Institute boasted two substantial buildings, a classroom and office structure, and a residence for female students. Over the next twenty years a refectory, an infirmary, a gymnasium, a manual training building, accommodations for a commercial department, and the requisite kitchens and related plumbing were progressively constructed, again exclusively with subsidies obtained from the denomination. The manual training facilities in particular were the clearest expression of the practical thrust of Fyfe's program at Woodstock.[31] Another was the arrangement made with the University of Toronto whereby qualified graduates of the CLI would be admitted to the second year of its arts course.

The backgrounds of the early students reflected the nature of that mid-Victorian society in western Ontario — still largely agrarian and pastoral — which posed for Fyfe the problem of transforming the raw farm hands who made up the bulk of the student population into useful tradesmen, competent professional people, and polished preachers. Some of the training to which newcomers were subjected was even more basic than the formal curriculum. One graduate recalled that many red-faced youngsters had to be taught the rudiments of proper table manners and given persistent instruction 'in the use and care of a flush toilet.'[32] At the same time a scrupulous concern for their off-campus diversions was predictably shown in the regulations; students caught drinking at a public bar, for example, would 'submit written pledges that they would not use liquor and would not leave the grounds in the evening hours for one month.'[33] Again, there was to be no consumption of tobacco and no excessive 'communication of a social nature' between male and female students (presumably in that order of importance).

Apart from the difficulties attendant upon curricular challenges, building programs, and student discipline, the work of Fyfe's institution was hampered by two fundamental problems which contributed to its recurring financial crises and to the enormous strain that led ultimately to the death of its principal in 1878. For one thing, the institute lacked an endowment and was obliged to rely upon subscription and tuition fees, which in turn depended upon the steady support of friends in the denomination. This support, however, was periodically endangered by sharp divisions within the constituency. In spite of the aid Fyfe received from many Baptists, others were, notwithstanding the failure of the Montreal school, still opposed to combining literary with theological education under one roof. When these people could not be won over, Fyfe's enterprise was denied vital assistance.

For that matter, Fyfe's conception of the role that the denomination ought to play in the management and control of the CLI further alienated this group. He did not regard the institute as an exclusive Baptist facility, a grave shortcoming in the eyes of many. Of the fifteen trustees who managed its affairs only ten had to be Baptists, unlike the arrangement made for McMaster University thirty years later. The trustees, moreover, were responsible, not to a Baptist convention or ruling body as such, but to the subscribers who had pledged the money for the school's construction and operation. Although 'it would appear' to quote an interested observer a century later 'that Fyfe had a wiser vision than ... [Senator] McMaster because he kept his institution free from denominational ties,'[34] this very freedom lost Fyfe the support of some affluent Baptists who otherwise might have offered essential aid. This fact doubtless influenced the senator's decisions with respect to the university's charter in 1887.

Division in the ranks was the first basic problem; the second arose from Fyfe's decision to restrict the site for the institute to the southwestern part of the province. Influential brethren in Toronto, evincing more interest in such a facility during the sixties than they had shown previously, periodically protested the neglect of their municipality.[35] Although Fyfe apparently sympathized with such complaints he came to feel that a move to Toronto would cause more harm than good and do virtually nothing to solve the institute's financial crises. In effect, the factors that had prescribed the geographical limits of 1857 still held good – local jealousies and divisiveness in Toronto[36] (though this seems to have subsided to a degree by the late sixties) and the advantages of a small-town setting. Finally, as long as Fyfe remained in charge at the CLI there was only the remotest prospect that Toronto's demands would ever be met. But his restraining influence was abruptly removed with his death in 1878. Almost at once plans were formulated to move, if not the whole institute then at least its theological department, to the 'Queen City.' It was at this juncture that Senator William McMaster made his influence felt and his money available. Another stage in the development of Baptist educational institutions in central Canada was about to begin.

2
William McMaster and the Toronto
Baptist College

If one account is to be believed, Senator McMaster largely engineered the transplant of the CLI theological department to Toronto. This he did, it seems, while conveying the impression, which apparently fooled few people, that he was merely ready to finance a scheme proposed by others more knowledgeable than he in such matters.[1] Judging the senator's actions in this instance by the dynamism he had exhibited in business and finance and his strong attachment to his denomination it is difficult to quarrel with the notion that he was back of it all. In 1881, two years after the decision to move the theological department had been made, McMaster, who obviously felt that he owed her an explanation, disclosed to Fyfe's widow that one of his reasons for promoting the move was that the denomination, for all its efforts at the CLI, had, in fact, no truly 'Chartered Theological College, but had instead, a Literary Institute, which generously admitted to the Board of Trustees gentlemen who were not Baptists at all.'[2] Although this was hardly news to the good lady, the senator went on to point out that while this procedure was appropriate for an arts institution it was grossly out of place in a theological school. Such an institution, he continued, ought to be under exclusive Baptist control. This argument, along with the advantages ensuing from Toronto's favourable location in the province, played a large role in shaping McMaster's decisions on the proposed changes in the structure of the CLI.

By the late seventies, McMaster, a native of Tyrone County, Ireland, had been in the country half a century, a period during which he had built up highly respectable and profitable concerns. He was indeed as good a personification as any entrepreneur at mid-century of the phenomenon known as metropolitanism. The urge had seized him and his well placed fellow citizens to transform Toronto from a severely circumscribed lake port and warehouse into an expansive community capable of dominating the raw materials and markets of a limitless hinterland.[3] Thus McMaster was in at the start of Toronto's adventures in the realm of informal imperialism, the effort to establish a commercial dominion at least the equal of Montreal's. This impressive attempt to invade Montreal's western domain and to reduce that metropolis's power appeared to be a kind of commercial analogue to the envy and distaste that western Baptists had once harboured for the pretensions of the Canada Baptist College.

When Toronto's expansionists sought to gain domination over the Northwest, McMaster was actively involved. Again, when that remarkable enterprise known as the Northwest Navigation and Transportation Company was chartered, McMaster was prominently listed among its supporters, visionaries in the city's business circles who anticipated by a quarter century the construction of a railway to the Pacific. McMaster's unabashed promotion of Toronto was inspired in large part by his activities as one of the city's leading drapers and traders. After his arrival in 1833 he had gained employment in the dry goods business owned by the pioneering Robert Cathcart.[4] According to an account prepared by a relative of McMaster, Cathcart, 'whose headquarters was Penetanguishene ... collected pelts from the Indians, and gave in exchange Trade Goods furnished by Uncle William. As time wore on, more sophisticated goods were required, leading to a considerable import business in dry goods, and the establishment of the wholesale business located on Front Street.'[5]

In the following year the energetic immigrant had become a partner in the firm, and when Cathcart retired in the forties an eager McMaster took over the business and expanded its operations.[6] By this time he was actively assisted by his two Irish nephews, Arthur R. and J. Short McMaster, whom he had taken in as partners. Using his company as a springboard McMaster next ventured into the world of finance. One scholar has credited his banking acumen with having rehabilitated the hard-pressed financial structure of Canada West following the disastrous depression of 1857.[7] From this accomplishment McMaster went on to help found, and in April 1867 to become the first president of, the Bank of Commerce.

This apparently singleminded approach to economic attainment has been explained by one historian in terms of the peculiar limitations to which McMaster and other Baptists were subjected in nineteenth-century Canada. Excluded from the factional bitterness generated by the struggle of the larger and wealthier denominations for power and patronage, Canadian Baptists, according to this argument, were forced, like the Jews in the Middle Ages, to concentrate on activities in the marketplace.[8] But for many of them this was not a matter for regret but a free choice, one formed by their conception of the relationship between church and state, according to which, in effect, it was mischievous and compromising for Baptists to become involved in a scramble for political spoils. Not that entrepreneurs of the larger denominations were unsuccessful in their own commercial avocations: John Macdonald, for example, a business rival and political associate of William McMaster, was an active Methodist layman and a large-scale importer in Toronto.

Nonetheless, the potent individualism for which Baptists were noted, and which had been dramatically exemplified in Robert Fyfe, doubtless invested McMaster's career with a unique flavour. Furthermore, it led him into the ranks of the Reform alliance by making him a natural supporter of those who, like George Brown and Alexander Mackenzie, the Grit leaders, opposed the pretensions of the Church of England and its political allies and sought a better deal for evangelical non-conformists in the community. In the same month that he attained the presidency of the Bank of Commerce – Toronto's answer to the Bank of Montreal – McMaster was active on behalf of the Central Executive Committee of the Reform Association of Upper Canada and directing the activities of its vital Toronto branch.[9] For his political pains he was called in 1867 to the newly formed Dominion Senate, the successor to the Legislative Council of the Province of Canada, a body on which he had also served.

While one historian has lamented the way in which the province's agrarian democracy was shamelessly seduced by urban businessmen like George Brown and William McMaster,[10] these men doubtless congratulated themselves on the way in which their Reform Party had so cleverly associated itself with the forces of political reform and commercial progress. Nevertheless, some of McMaster's more humble coreligionists might have shared the misgivings of those rural democrats for the disturbingly sophisticated and, by implication, hypocritical ways of their urbanized lay leaders. 'I have been told by customers of the Bank of Commerce' a McMaster alumnus once wrote 'that [McMaster] could be found in his office reading the Bible, but it was said that many of his decisions did not partake in any large measure [of] the altruistic teachings of the New Testament.'[11]

Even the relatively worldly George Brown, McMaster's business associate and political confederate, could himself marvel at the 'awful splurge' of a party laid on by the senator in 1868.[12] At times McMaster seemed to display an ostentation and a pushiness that alienated some of his friends and confirmed his ill-wishers' suspicions of his ways and motives. Yet for other people, Baptist and non-Baptist alike, McMaster was regarded as an inspiration to all those seeking material success on a grand scale. Egerton Ryerson, who saw a good deal of the senator socially, thought him the embodiment of the Protestant ethic, the Christian person who had clearly achieved salvation in the next world through the rigorous and successful application of his enviable talents in this one.[13]

Ryerson, long the guardian of educational values in the province, had good cause to praise McMaster on other grounds. He came to respect the senator's perceptive assessment of problems as the Baptist representative on the provincial Council of Public Instruction and as a member of the University of Toronto Senate and to acclaim his direction of well attended public prayer meetings. Unquestionably, McMaster attached great importance to the need for improved educational facilities for the country in general, as well as for Baptists in particular, a concern that he had shared for years with Robert Fyfe. It would appear that one of the reasons for McMaster's departure from the sect known as the Disciples of Christ was their avowed opposition to an educated ministry,[14] a goal as precious to McMaster as the promotion of his business interests.[15]

As so often in the past, however, talk of an 'educated ministry' alienated those Baptists who had always belittled the need for a book-trained pastorate and who were making life difficult for Fyfe and the Canadian Literary Institute in Woodstock. Some of McMaster's coreligionists in the Toronto business community also took exception not only to his reputedly lavish 'splurges' but to what appeared to them to be the ostentatious fashion in which he had sponsored the construction of a Victorian Toronto landmark, the Jarvis Street Church, the successor to a smaller Baptist church on Bond Street. 'There has been built recently' grumbled William Davies, the Baptist founder of a packing firm, in the summer of 1876

this large Baptist Chapel, gothic, brown stone, spire pointing upward if not heavenward, marble baptistry &c &c Cost $100.000 & odd, & the organ $7000 besides, & I believe it is all paid for, but is has been built regardless of the needs of the city . . . One of the members . . . a Senator, very wealthy, married an American, natural result they soon had an American minister, then this new building also American, then the Lady & the minister lay their heads together & get a professional singer a sort of *prima donna* & she is paid $300.00 per year and many are very much hurt about it . . . This building was erected to the N.E. of its former site which has left the s.w. part of the city without any Baptist church, while they have gone into a district that was pretty well served. There appears to have been a spirit of centralization & aggrandizement abt. it which is hateful.[16]

Admittedly Davies's resentment might reveal more about his personal feelings than about the matters and the personalities discussed. Even so, his letters might help to explain why McMaster and his varied architectural, social, and educational promotions, including the removal of the CLI's theological department to Toronto, evoked something less than respect in certain quarters of the Baptist constituency. At one point Davies put into words what many then merely dared suspect, that at least some of the senator's decisions were influenced in a kind of conspiratorial way by his reportedly influential American wife, Susan Moulton, and by the American minister of the new Jarvis Street Church, John Harvard Castle.

Susan Moulton, the senator's second spouse, was a native of Newburgh, New York, and the widow of an affluent Michigan lumberman. Long absorbed in the Home Missionary Work of the Northern Baptist Convention of the United States, she was anxious to infuse into Canadian Baptist life the unity and energy with which she felt the American body was amply endowed. Moved by these aspirations she was instrumental in landing Dr Castle, a solid representative of the Northern Convention, for the Bond Street church in 1873 and then for the imposing new pulpit her husband had helped to provide on Jarvis Street. For his part, Castle, a native of Philadelphia and a groomed product of the Rochester Seminary, seemed an appropriate choice for an expanding and challenging municipality like Toronto.[17]

Nevertheless Davies had believed in 1876 that the construction of Jarvis Street Church was not only unnecessary but an expression of 'hateful aggrandizement and centralization.' These strictures anticipated by three years some of the objections raised when it was learned that McMaster and Castle were about to play a decisive role in transferring the CLI's theological department to the city. In the minds of some it was Jarvis Street all over again: in this instance McMaster was going to use his money to buy the denomination or, at the very least, to bribe it. The advocates of the removal scheme understandably sought to dispel this impression in the discussions they duly launched with the people in Woodstock. And, as all were well aware, the merits of the removal to Toronto, finances aside, would have to be carefully examined.

The foundation for these critical discussions was laid in April 1879 when the trustees of the Literary Institute appointed a committee, to which McMaster was named, to investigate the question of removal. Plans were made to have this committee report to a special meeting of the school's subscribers and trustees and delegates from various Baptist churches, the upshot of which was an Educational Conference which met at Guelph on 17 July 1879. The one hundred or so who attended put in a full day discussing the varied arguments for and against the transfer to Toronto of the theological department. Because those arguments would be rethrashed eight years later when the question of the university's location came up for discussion they are worth examining at some length.

Several weeks before the delegates assembled in Guelph the main issue had already been aired in the denominational press and in student meetings at the Literary Institute. 'If the students were personally consulted,' wrote a contributor to *The Tyro*, the school's newspaper,

probably the majority would favour the movement, if they took into account personal considerations only. It cannot be denied that a city such as Toronto affords many opportunities for pleasure and improvement which are wanting in a town. Then, too, being within walking distance of the University [of Toronto, as though he had already been assured of the site] some who did not feel inclined to take a full course there might attend lectures in some special department.[18]

Then, however, the writer pointed out what many opponents of the project would repeatedly underscore: that 'the moral effect of the two departments [the literary and the theological] upon each other, as they now stand, is beneficial to both.'

The student editor had spotted some of the basic issues that would heatedly divide the meetings at Guelph. The advocates of removal never tired of extolling the cultural, academic, and social advantages of the 'Ontario metropolis' and the stimulus, the 'polish,' and the institutional amenities that only residence in a community like Toronto could afford a Canadian youth bent on a ministerial career. But the critics of the proposal were just as certain that life in Toronto would furnish unwholesome distractions and excitement. Clearly, as an American contributor to the *Canadian Baptist* put it, the big city was 'no place to study,' let alone to prepare for the pastorate. He went on to applaud the American example of locating colleges and seminaries in a rural environment. He made much of the point that such sister institutions as Newton Academy and Madison University, which Fyfe had attended, had evolved within the protective embrace of small towns. This Baptist obviously shared with many others the entirely repugnant image of the city so fashionable then in rural and small-town Canada. For these people 'city' was a mildly pejorative word in 1879.[19]

On the other hand, those won over to the removal scheme could retort, fittingly enough in the year of John A. Macdonald's National Policy, that Canadian and American approaches to many issues had often diverged, not least in the realm of higher education. The small liberal arts college, they pointed out, had never really taken root on the British American scene; instead, universities had been thrust into urban environments at the outset, as shown by the establishment of the provincial university in Toronto, McGill in Montreal, Laval in Quebec City, and Dalhousie in Halifax.[20] They readily conceded that while such municipalities were no match for the magnitude of, say, Chicago and New York City, they were assuredly a far cry from Woodstock, home of the CLI.

With the oft-repeated claim that the divorce of the theological and literary departments at the institute would produce some sort of moral calamity one recent graduate of the school had little patience. While literary and theological students had once been 'mixed up together like the members of one family,' he said, that situation no longer obtained in the late seventies. According to his assessment of the situation, a 'wall of separation had been rising between the students' in the two departments. This unwelcome development should not, he claimed, be entirely attributed to the recent construction of a building devoted exclusively to theological instruction. Rather, he suggested, the architecture merely reflected a division already formed in the student body.[21]

The delegates who came to Guelph that steamy day in July 1879, if they had been consulting their denominational journals at all, ought to have become reasonably well acquainted with the questions placed on the agenda of the Educational Conference. From the very beginning a brave effort was made to judge on its merits the question of the move and to leave aside for the moment the matter of financing, whether it be undertaken by the denomination as a whole or by wealthy members such as William McMaster. In the senator's absence, Dr Castle of Jarvis Street Church skilfully marshalled the arguments on behalf of the project. What he had to say at this point and later on in rebuttal to the defenders of the status quo at Woodstock revealed a great deal about his image of Ontario's future and of the Baptist role in that future. He began by trying to reassure the sceptical that 'we are not ambitious to have the institution in Toronto for our own sakes ... But I have a very strong conviction that, looking into the future, and considering the influence of the denomination upon that future, and the influence of city and town upon the men who are trained respectively in each, while I am perfectly willing to grant that the country churches for the future will need excellent men, a great need which I fear will be unmet will be for men to take hold of and control the great centres.'[22]

Then Castle reminisced about his own experiences as a student at the University of Lewisburg – 'Pennsylvania's Woodstock' (later Bucknell University) – remarking that he 'left it with all the conceit that is usually generated where a course of study is completed in a little town.' He continued: 'If there is anything to take conceit out of students it is getting out of little towns and out of their own colleges.' This conceit and the insularity that fed it would hardly, in Castle's view, equip the budding pastor for 'the age and the work before him.' It was plainly not enough for an institution to cope only with the present and foreseeable future of small-town Ontario. What was patently needed was a responsive pastorate for a community in the process of rapid urban and technological change. This kind of message, first addressed to the faithful in 1879, was to be employed again within a decade during the debate on the location of McMaster University.

Castle's candour, the plausibility of his arguments, and his fervent plea for a ministry 'trained under the very best intellectual circumstances' so that they might achieve the 'greatest possible grip on society,' doubtless changed a good many minds at the conference. Bolstering his arguments was the telling point presented by William Muir, the influential editor of the *Canadian Baptist*. Muir contended that the presence of a Baptist theological school in Toronto would reduce the danger of 'some of our young men taking their University course there and not returning to Woodstock for theology but [rather] going to the other side,'23 a trend already causing considerable concern.

Even before the merits of the move had been thoroughly discussed, Castle was pressed by some members of his audience to indicate flatly what kind of financial assistance had already been pledged by benefactors. Castle's rejoinder was that the 'parties from whom the large sum is to be had ... have a conviction that unless the denomination ... thinks well of the position and sees that there are advantages in it that cannot be had elsewhere, the [Canadian Literary] Institute should remain where it is.'24 As best he could, Castle was attempting to convince the conference that the denomination should not and could not 'be bought.'

All the same, the mention of money was bound to influence thinking and emotions. Most of those present were aware of the distressing financial straits of the institute and could not help but warm to Castle's comforting though vaguely worded assurances on the question of financing. It is not surprising that the committee's resolution favouring the move was finally adopted. It only remained for Castle to promise the delegates that the literary department of the institute would not be neglected. Further, the school's interests, though physically divided, were not to be spiritually disrupted. To this end he moved that in the event of the theological department's transfer to Toronto the CLI should receive from the denomination an endowment of 'not less than $50,000 at the earliest possible time.' When the fear was expressed that the move to Toronto might be hamstrung if the motion were construed to be conditional upon raising the endowment, the convention, 'breathing fire,' unanimously passed the resolution.[25] The Rev. S.A. Dyke subsequently took over the campaign to raise the endowment funds, 'no part of which' it was decided 'was to be used for current expenses but all to be invested to the best advantage and the interest alone to be available for use.'[26]

With these matters out of the way, Castle rose to cap the proceedings by reading a letter from McMaster announcing that the senator would personally donate $2,000 annually for three years toward the salary of Fyfe's successor at the institute. This well received act of munificence, a timely palliative to say the least, served appropiately to bring the conference to a close. As a reporter for the Woodstock Sentinel-Review, who probably thought the gathering might turn out otherwise, wrote: 'The discussion was lively, brilliant, and even exciting, but the best of feeling prevailed, and at its close it was remarked by many that they had never seen a meeting so distracted at first, and at the last closed in such a spirit of harmony and good will.'[27] Castle's shrewd sense of timing and skilful handling of the issues and the delegates combined with the formidable financial problems confronting the institute to bring about the results that he and McMaster had been seeking.

If some dissatisfied souls were still convinced that the denomination had been hypnotized by promises and bought by the senator's money, they may have been gratified by an article that appeared in the Toronto Globe two weeks after the Guelph meeting had adjourned. The article assumed, as so many delegates had done at Guelph, that McMaster had secretly made a firm offer of an enormous sum on condition that the theological department be moved to Toronto. The Globe, which after all was on McMaster's political side, seemed on the face of it to be using McMaster's promise as a form of political blackmail to extract money for equally worthy purposes from other would-be philanthropists in the country.[28] While commending the paper for its 'sensible and excellent' account, Castle hurriedly repeated in public the statement he had made so frequently at Guelph, that no specific sum had ever been guaranteed by McMaster or anyone else and that the decision to move to Toronto had been dictated not by an individual and his friends but by the denomination in 'full and solemn assembly.'[29]

Some of the delegates may well have scoffed at this last declaration after they had returned home and found time to recover from the euphoria that had enveloped the closing stages of the conference. One account, written in reminiscence twenty years after the event, asserted that 'a number of brethren were sincere in believing that Dr Castle and Senator McMaster should have used their influence and wealth in paying the Woodstock debt and in making it possible to develop the theological department of Woodstock College into a well equipped theological seminary.'[30] In part an exercise in afterthought, this statement may therefore be too ambitious a reconstruction of what actually occurred at the end of the conference. Another point raised by the same writer concerns McMaster's reputed reaction to the criticism of the removal scheme. Although there is no other documentary reference to the episode, the account relates that at the close of one argumentative session McMaster, who, of course, did not attend the conference, 'took Dr Castle aside and told him he was through, that he had decided not to go through with the Toronto Baptist College ... but to give the money to the Rochester Theological Seminary instead. Dr Castle [however] persuaded him to go forward with the Toronto enterprise.'[31]

Other observers did not underestimate the role that the senator's wife had played in the undertaking. After all, they reminded themselves and others, she had arranged for Dr Castle's pastorate at Jarvis Street Church and had urged Canadian Baptists to emulate the practices and achieve the unity of their American coreligionists. Was it not possible, they asked, that she had initiated the removal program? Mrs McMaster's influence on her husband's decisions on such matters may be nothing more than a myth, but as a factor in the situation it cannot be entirely ignored. Theodore Harding Rand, a prominent Baptist from the Maritimes who became the university's second chancellor, may have started the rumour in 1892 in the following contribution to the *McMaster Monthly*:

Some time after settling at Rathnally, her Toronto country home ... she suggested to the Senator that he give Rathnally ... for the purposes of a Theological Seminary. She renewed the suggestion from time to time, and never ceased to cherish the hope that beautiful Rathnally should be devoted to the preparation of young men for the gospel ministry. She obtained a partial promise that it should be as she wished. When Dr Castle came to Toronto on a visit, she enlisted his interest in the project, which finally resulted in the erection of McMaster Hall in Queen's Park.[32]

Rathnally, however, situated near Aurora, was more than a stone's throw from Queen's Park in the heart of the provincial capital. Although the senator may have honoured the supposed promise to his wife in principle, he obviously did not with respect to location. 'I well remember' a Baptist layman wrote with what could have been a reference to this matter 'when Senator McMaster thought of building the "Hall" *farther North*, he took Mr [Joshua] Denovan ... my dear old pastor ... to see the proposed site, & Mr.

Denovan said Bro. McMaster have your College *nearer to the University in the Park*, so that Students who may wish to take the Arts Course can slip across the Park ... & lose *as little time as possible*.[33]

More important than the actual location of the new institution was the need for accommodating in it the varied beliefs that still flourished in the denomination. According to one plausible account Senator McMaster's intention 'was not to minister to the need of a few narrow-minded sectaries but to the entire denomination with all its diversities of view.' 'If he had in mind any existing models,' the account concludes with a reference that calls to mind the thinking of Castle and Mrs McMaster, 'it was the great Baptist universities and theological seminaries of the United States.'[34] Possibly in keeping with this concept the Trust Deed, by which McMaster conveyed to the college the property he had purchased for it on Bloor Street, stated the doctrinal qualifications of prospective faculty in fairly general terms.

As anticipated, some of the 'narrow-minded sectaries' reacted unfavourably to the all-embracing statement. Brantford's John Harris, the prominent farm-implement manufacturer, who accepted an appointment to the Board of Trustees, did so with potent misgivings. 'I had great delicacy' he confessed in the summer of 1881 'in acting on the Board of Trustees because I had feared that I would be at variance with those brethren who pay too little attention to the theology of prospective appointments to the College.'[35]

Such statements revealed that a good deal of doctrinal accommodation was needed in the proposed institution. A strong echo could still be heard of that ancient conflict between the respective advocates of open and closed communion, not to mention the differing views of the pre- and post-millennialists. The pre-millennialists, who were particularly active in the Brantford district, were vocal supporters of the strict construction of Scripture and, more importantly, convinced of the need for proclaiming the imminent second coming of Christ. Some of them, like Elmore Harris (the son of the plough-maker), who would later precipitate a controversy at McMaster University, appeared to be firm advocates of the 'any moment advent.' The pessimism of this group, which believed that only Christ's return before the millennium would eradicate the world's depravity, had hitherto set them off sharply from the post-millennialists, who were just as convinced that utopia in the form of peace and harmony on earth could be achieved before the second advent.[36] In effect, the approach adopted by the Harrises was wholly Christ-centred and supernatural, while the post-millennialists were prepared to accord man a greater role in the act of rejuvenation.

Yet, as McMaster and Castle soon discovered to their considerable gratification, some of these otherwise irreconcilable elements had already begun to co-operate, if not with overpowering enthusiasm at least with commendable efficiency, in such vital fields as home missionary work and education, notably at the Literary Institute in Woodstock. It was the senator's hope that this growing accord might be institutionalized in the college he was planning for Toronto and be made to serve the Baptists of the 'entire Dominion of Canada.' But in order to maintain what harmony had been achieved and to inspire it elsewhere, McMaster, in organizing the executive structure of the new institution, resorted to what George Peel Gilmour later judged to be a 'more dangerous expedient than Fyfe's plan of subscribers and independent trustees.' He decided to have the 'Board of the College elected by and made responsible to the denomination.'[37] The result was a 'close corporation,' a self-perpetuating body that bore no resemblance to its predecessor at Woodstock.

The task of selecting trustees to serve on the Board was a painstaking one that called for all the tact, shrewdness, and diplomatic prowess McMaster and Castle could command. Not only did a multiplicity of attitudes and positions have to be taken into account in order to achieve effective representation but an effort would obviously have to be made to recruit trustees from centres boasting substantial Baptist populations. 'It would have been very unfortunate' McMaster wrote typically at one stage of the proceedings late in 1880

had the name of Mr [Henry] Moyle been overlooked, as he is what may be regarded as a representative man, being chairman of the Trustees of the [CL] Institute, & it may be regarded as a fortunate circumstance that Mr Elliot insisted upon his name being withdrawn as he is too pronounced with reference to the question of future punishment, his being a Trustee might have got us into trouble ... It will be quite enough, for us to carry Boyd on our back.[38]

The Honourable John Boyd, a University of Toronto graduate who had recently been named a Queen's Counsel, was to become a few months later the chancellor of Ontario. His worldly views, which demanded space in the senator's elaborate balancing act, clearly induced as painful a headache for the planners of the college as did the less sophisticated opinions for which the senator also felt compelled to make room on the governing body.

In any event, the first duly appointed Board of Trustees included, in addition to McMaster, Castle, and Boyd, William J. Copp, a Hamilton businessman, James Mill of St Catharines, Charles Raymond of Guelph, and Henry Moyle of Paris. They were joined by Thomas Shenstone and William Buck, two prominent manufacturers from Brantford, a city that deserved strong representation because of its comparatively large Baptist population and the interest it had consistently shown in theological education. Two well known Liberal politicians were also named to the Board: Alexander Mackenzie, the late prime minister of Canada, and John Dryden, an MLA. Both men had championed policies that Baptists had long considered their private preserve, the separation of church and state and the abolition of the clergy reserves. A member of Castle's Jarvis Street Church, Mackenzie had become a Baptist in his native Scotland after falling under the powerful sway of zealous adherents of the Haldane school.[39] The close association of the Mackenzies, Drydens, Browns, and McMasters with the Reformers suggests, as was once said of the Church of England and British Tories, that the Baptists were simply Liberals at prayer.

When Board appointments were being considered, Montreal was not neglected. The original springboard of Baptist endeavours in Canadian education and the home of affluent coreligionists was given four places on the Board, to be filled ultimately by A.A. Ayer, T.J. Claxton, A.H. Munro, and John Turnbull. If McMaster and Castle are included the Toronto contingent numbered five, the remaining appointees being Boyd, A.R. McMaster, the nephew and business associate of the senator, and Daniel Edmund Thomson, a prominent member of the city's legal fraternity and William McMaster's solicitor.

These exercises in consensus theology and regional representation were accompanied by the hope, already expressed by the senator, that the Toronto Baptist College would emerge as a national institution for the denomination, in the sense of furnishing theological training for the graduates of other Baptist institutions in Canada. In August 1883 that hope was redeemed in part when the Baptist Convention of the Maritime Provinces voted to adopt such a procedure. The subsequent appointment of Dr Daniel M. Welton of Acadia University to the chair of Old Testament exegesis in the Toronto college thus honoured, to quote the TBC's records, 'a pledge to our brethren by the sea' that should their students come to Ontario they would enjoy the instruction and sympathy of one who had been a leading advocate of ministerial education in Nova Scotia.[40]

Again, a faltering institution in Manitoba, Prairie College, founded by a dissatisfied teacher from the CLI, was closed down by the provincial convention but not before its seven students were encouraged to attend the Toronto Baptist College, described grandly as the 'One Baptist Theological Seminary for the Dominion of Canada.'[41] These developments were, to evoke Davies's earlier strictures against Jarvis Street Church, an excellent example of centralization, not to mention aggrandizement. 'What will do so much' the denomination's *Year Book*, asked rhetorically 'to consolidate and unify our churches in faith and practice, in aims and methods, as to have their leaders in the east and west and centre moulded under the same influence [and] inspired by the same teachers?'[42]

The cultural and spiritual metropolitanism of the kind envisaged by McMaster, Castle, and others seemed to complement the commercial hegemony that entrepreneurs of the senator's standing had long aimed at bestowing upon Toronto. The little towns, disparaged by Castle at the Guelph Conference in 1879, and the cities that unaccountably lacked ambition were clearly to become back numbers in the empire-building schemes and to lose out in the process of 'natural selection' that this expansion seemed to inspire. Just as obviously, Toronto's Baptist ambitions were not to be confined to that city and its Ontario hinterland. Although Acadia, for reasons to be noted later, was not integrated with the TBC in the manner anticipated by Castle and his colleagues, the overtures to that institution and the absorption of Prairie College manifested a territorial imperative that fitted well with Ontario's heartland mentality in the closing years of the nineteenth century.

On the college's opening day, 4 October 1881, John Castle, predictably named its president, sounded the keynote in his inaugural address. He talked at length about the advantages of 'the Metropolis,' whose population was then crowding the 100,000 mark: 'A school for the training of our ministry, having its seat in Toronto, the focus of the intellectual, educational, and commercial forces of the Province, is not a recent conception. Some of the wisest of our leaders ... saw clearly that the intense currents of city life, the multiplicity of its social, literary, and religious opportunities ought to be utilized in the training of the rising ministry.'[43]

Having exalted the setting, Castle proceeded to set the tone of the college's approach to the tasks at hand. 'We have not dared to prescribe' he began 'any definite attainments in secular learning as indispensable for entrance to the ministry...We may prefer Paul, the polished logician, the cultured and classical scholar, but Our Lord' he continued as if to pay some kind of tribute to Fyfe's earlier efforts at Woodstock 'used the rough, uncouth youth Peter before he used Camaliells, the apt student. And when the Master summons such again, whether from the farm, the anvil or the cobbler's bench, let not his church object.'

At this point Castle felt obliged to get to the heart of the matter: 'Nevertheless it is true that the ministry which creates stable, intelligent, enterprising churches – which moulds and controls public sentiment for Christianity, which maintains its hold upon our children and keeps them from drifting away from the faith of their fathers to other communions is a ministry trained in secular and sacred learning.'[44] The reference to secular together with sacred is significant; for there was little doubt in Castle's mind that the findings of the philosopher, the scientist, and the historian might have a role to play in making even more meaningful the message of the Scriptures. This was an allusion, albeit a faint one, to the need for fusing ancient Christian principles with the so-called New Learning, a practice some would later repudiate as dangerous to 'established truths.'

Yet all this talk of the advantages of 'the Metropolis' and of 'sacred and secular learning' had to be related to the admittedly modest proportions of the Toronto Baptist College in 1881. Undeniably, McMaster had provided well for it – an initial outlay of $100,000 and a pledge of an annual contribution of $14,500 – and its impressive building, suitably named McMaster Hall, was designed by the Toronto church architects Langley, Langley, and Burke in the Romanesque Revival styles. But even so, the college began its career on Bloor Street with a tiny three-man faculty, which included Castle, and a student enrolment of twenty.[45] Nor was anyone at this early date prepared to predict how much or how little the churches might contribute to the new enterprise. The only certainties seemed to be that some of the rancour at Guelph had carried over into the early eighties and that it was still sturdily believed in some quarters, though in fewer than before, that a 'book-trained pastorate' was suspect. And when small-town congregations, many of which had been put in their place in 1879, did make donations for educational purposes they were most likely to earmark their gifts for the Literary Institute,[46] which, after all, had twelve instructors and over two hundred students. Only time would tell how much support the churches would furnish the Baptist College in Toronto. In a sense, however, a donation to the CLI was a form of indirect offering to the latter, for the new institution would rely heavily upon Woodstock College – so renamed by statute in 1883 – for many of its early registrants. The Literary Department of the old CLI was already, in effect, being turned into a kind of preparatory school for the centralizing institute in Toronto.

In the meantime, curricula and standards were being formulated at the TBC. From the outset trustees and faculty realized that they would be coping with two sorts of students. On the one hand, there would be those, long familiar on the Woodstock scene, whose cultural opportunities had been desperately limited. This group, to quote the *Year Book*, 'still constitute[d] a large proportion of the [Baptist] ministry.'[47] On the other hand, there was a minority whose earlier educational enrichment readily fitted them for advanced work at the collegiate level. A uniform curriculum for all would therefore be inappropriate. Those who had already graduated from the

Literary Institute or a comparable public institution or who had taken courses at University College in Toronto would require something far more substantial than those who arrived armed only with enthusiasm and piety. For the latter, literary training was deemed a prerequisite. Ordinarily these students were encouraged to enrol in Woodstock College to remedy their academic deficiencies. In some instances, however, this was impractical, and for their benefit a number of literary courses were added to the curriculum of the TBC. If these students showed marked progress and, like their more fortunate confrères, wished to take regular collegiate work in addition they could register for classes in what the Rev. Denovan had called the 'University in the Park.' If accommodation were available, all those who did take advantage of this opportunity could reside at McMaster Hall. Since only nominal fees were charged by University College for its sought-after lecture courses in languages, mathematics, and metaphysics,[48] the courses offered at a reasonable tuition in the secular institution 'across the way' could readily be taken along with theological instruction at the TBC.

While these matters were being squared away, the administrative structure of the college was being erected. The original constitution laid down the duties and functions of the Board of Trustees and the faculty. The effect of the original Trust Deed had been to vest the property in the Trustees jointly, an exercise in 'close corporativeness' acknowledged in the constitution. A number of standing committees of the Board had immediately been named to deal with executive, financial, library, and instructional matters. The latter, the Committee on Instruction, discharged the responsibilities of a university senate, that is, 'to make itself conversant with the course of instruction and discipline ... and with the work accomplished by the students, and to attend the ... examinations of the College and to report thereon to the Board.'[49]

Within three years, however, this relatively simple arrangement had proven unsatisfactory for a number of reasons. In the first place, it had a structural flaw: in addition to their other duties, executive and financial, Board members had difficulty coping with academic matters. A division of labour seemed imperative, nothing short of the creation of a senate to deal exclusively with academic policies and practices.

But there were even more compelling political and financial grounds for this constitutional change. Although major regional sensibilities had been mollified by the nature of the Board nominations in 1881, many a Baptist church still felt shut out of the college's deliberations. And when this feeling took hold the purses invariably snapped shut. By 1884 it had become clear 'that the churches were contributing relatively little' to the venture in Toronto. There was also a conviction that room should be found somewhere in the college's administrative structure for representatives of Baptist constituencies elsewhere in the country. The establishment of a body to represent those who felt neglected and to acknowledge the presence of other Baptist conventions might kindle the enthusiasm of the far-flung Baptist denomination and entice larger offerings from its congregations. An administrative refinement undertaken in the cause of academic efficiency and standards was also aimed, therefore, at attracting more broadly based support from the denomination at large.

By the fall of 1884 a committee had completed the necessary spadework and the Board was prepared to seek a legislative amendment authorizing the creation of a senate. The legislation passed at Queen's Park in the spring of 1885, said the report of the gratified Executive Committee, vested 'the vital part of the control of the College in a Senate elected by the representative bodies of the denomination in the different sections of the Dominion and by the Faculties of our Chartered Institutions of Learning.' It was critically important that

our 'Close Corporation' has voluntarily resigned its most important functions to a body at once National and representative in its composition. We cannot doubt that this transfer of Power from the Board ... to an Elective Senate will convince our Churches that the College ... is fully their own property. It is to be hoped that with the joy of ownership and control may come also the deep sense of responsibility which will induce the utmost care and wisdom in the choice of Representatives, *and at the same time develop a generosity which will anticipate as well as supply all the wants of the College*.[50]

The expectations were too great. However much the change may have eased the burden on the overworked Board and furnished a more effective forum for the discussion of academic affairs, it seemed to inspire no appreciable increase in church offerings to the TBC. 'Pitifully small' they had been before; pitifully small they would remain. As it had in the past the institution continued to depend for its operation, indeed for its survival, on the munificence of individual benefactors, the most prominent of whom was, of course, McMaster himself.

As for the faculty, whose duties and responsibilities had also been defined in 1881, their situation was not markedly transformed by the constitutional revision four years later. As hitherto they were empowered to make recommendations for appointments, dismissals, and promotions, but after 1885 they would do so through the Senate, which in turn would channel to the Board along with its own recommendations those from the faculty upon which it was disposed to act.[51] Along with his advocacy of a senate, Castle had pushed for an innovation that was potentially far more portentous for the faculty, but one apparently enjoying its approval. What he wanted was a more definite and full abstract of doctrine than the one contained in the Trust Deed to which professors had initially been required to assent. 'For many reasons' he reported to the Board in the spring of 1884 'it was not deemed wise or fitting to prepare a new Abstract of Doctrine. We therefore submit the one which is used for the same purpose in the Constitution of the Southern Baptist Theological Seminary ... a Document which has been drawn up by one of the ablest and most conservative bodies of Baptists, and which has stood the test of criticism and trial.'[52]

One could read a tactical manoeuvre into this proposal. From the very beginning some members of the Board had been dissatisfied with the vague wording of the Trust Deed and had urged the drafting of a more explicit statement. The question arises: Had Castle been obliged to acknowledge this demand in order to obtain support for a senate? Or had he done so in order to attract the aid of conservative forces in the Maritimes and the Northwest for the college's program? Or was it an attempt to offset the impact of powerful ideas and concepts being generated on the theological left and to assure the Baptist faithful in Canada that no revolution was being contemplated in the college's curriculum?

Answers to these questions are difficult to furnish. Castle went out of his way at the Baptist Union Conference of May 1884 to assure his coreligionists that the Abstract of Doctrine was not 'the result of outside pressure' and those who thought so 'were grievously in error.' And yet his concluding remarks suggest that he anticipated some such pressure: 'in view of this published statement, should anyone hereafter raise a doubt as to the soundness of any one of the professors in regard to inspiration, or accuse any of rationalistic tendencies, what shall be said of him?'[53] In any case, Castle had already alluded to this matter in his annual report when he dwelt on the need for defining the 'moral, mental, spiritual, and doctrinal qualifications of the men to be employed [at] this period of uncertainty and shifting in the ... positions of some noted theological teachers, both in the Old World and the New.' In a similar vein the secretary of the Board had intoned two years before that 'if ever there was a time in the history of Christianity when the Ministers of religion had need to be thoroughly equipped with all the resources of the best and most liberal culture to enable them to meet the polished shafts of a refined and subtle infidelity, that time is now.'[54]

The polished shafts were being forged and dispatched in this instance by a number of the 'higher critics,' principally those who had already begun to apply the mechanics of scientific analysis to the study of Scripture in general and the New Testament in particular. In an age when the natural sciences, so recently liberated from philosophy and theology, were beginning to make whole regions of experience more explicable it was understandable that some scholars should wish to subject Biblical literature to the same kind of scientific scrutiny that had produced so many fresh insights into secular literature and historical sources.

German theologians and philosophers had been in the vanguard of this movement, and by the closing decades of the century their approach and techniques were being enthusiastically adopted by a growing group of American scholars. In their effort to establish the historicity of Holy Writ the higher critics sought to reconstruct the setting in which each book of the Bible was composed and to determine the motivation and purpose of its authors. Out of this kind of investigation would come, it was hoped, a relevant message for modern society. Thus was launched an academic process that would profoundly influence Protestant, and particularly evangelical, institutions in North America. On a number of crucial occasions the health, and in one instance the very life, of McMaster University was threatened by the virulence of the conflict that the higher criticism ultimately provoked.

Although this form of scholarship had not, in Castle's time, attained the formidable proportions it achieved a quarter century later, he and other custodians of the 'sacred heritage' were perturbed by its implications. They seemed less concerned about the validity of the scientific approach to the Gospels than about the concepts and attitudes of some of those who employed that methodology. As an approach it might, in their view, be safely combined with others to produce a more satisfying explanation of Biblical phenomena. After all, teachers wishing their theological students to be immersed in a stimulating and intellectual urban environment were hardly likely to frown on a new approach that might well enrich the fare to which prospective Baptist pastors were being introduced. But Castle and his colleagues feared that the methodology of the higher criticism threatened to become an end in itself, in effect a secular theology shaped exclusively by humanistic and scientific calculations and completely devoid of spirituality. They noted that some of the higher critics seemed to be moved by the urge to make the past wholly subservient to the need of the present. Indeed, by implying that the basic values of contemporary culture were more vital than those previously known and more reliable guides to further investigation the new Biblical critics seemed to be modernists-in-the-making. To the faculty of the Toronto Baptist College such a position was anathema and constituted a rejection of traditions without which, they fervently believed, no theology worthy of the name could possibly be preserved, let alone propagated.[55]

Castle was well aware of the hostility that had greeted the writings of such biblical scholars as Mark Hopkins and Noah Porter in the United States and of how the Bible Conferences of the seventies had demonstrated the power of conservative reaction to their pronouncements.[56] In view of his advocacy of a more conservative doctrinal statement in 1884 such lessons may not have been entirely lost on the astute president. At a time when it was vital to attract as much support as possible to the TBC the mollification of the Baptist majority commanded a high priority. In keeping with this endeavour Castle bent every effort to ensure that the students and graduates of the college gave a good account of themselves, especially while serving rustic pulpits.

Among the constitutional amendments that the president had proposed in the spring of 1884 was one stating that the 'aim and methods of the college ... are to raise up a practical ministry by making the Missionary Work of the students during vacation a part of the College Course.' Clearly Castle wanted to stress the missionary and pastoral labours of the students, 'both as a part of their training for their life work, and an important immediate agency for establishing new interests and fostering weak ones.'[57] In many of his statements Castle used the term 'workmen' to describe these student pastors, as if to assure unsophisticated urban congregations as well as rural ones that the men who came to them were not mere book-trained sycophants but were 'worthy of their hire' and could sympathize with their problems in a time of rapid social and industrial change. This would achieve the twin objectives of reassuring the conservative faithful and forging a link with the urban society of the future.

In these same months the president and his colleagues also busily cultivated the formal relationship with Woodstock College (the new name for the Literary Institute) and what Castle called the 'moral affiliation' with the University of Toronto. Indeed, it was his hope that a future appointment to the faculty of the college would be a 'son of both the Institutions ... a natural inspiring perpetual brotherhood.' Robert Fyfe, had he been alive, could not have put it better. This growing liaison with the university seemed to many the culmination of the process Fyfe had championed during the educational debates at mid-century. The view held by his generation was that it was far wiser to leave general collegiate training under non-sectarian state control than to have it presented along with theological instruction in a denominational institution. As one of Fyfe's contemporaries phrased it, admittedly twenty years later: 'I remember well the founding of McMaster Hall. I remember it was built on a piece of land purchased from the Toronto University, under, if I remember correctly, express powers conferred by the Legislature. It was built on a University ground as a theological institute, the idea and the avowed purpose being affiliation with Toronto University.'[58]

Whether or not this had in fact been the case, the important word appears to be 'affiliation.' Unquestionably, the term meant different things to different people. For the writer just quoted it clearly meant the sort of arrangement that the University of Toronto was pursuing in the eighties, the scheme of university confederation. By means of this device denominational institutions in the province, such as Trinity, Wycliffe, Victoria, Queen's, and the TBC, would federate with the university and surrender to it whatever instruction in arts they had hitherto offered. 'Any scheme for University Confederation to be acceptable to the country' one of its supporters argued 'necessitates the support by the Senate of a complete and undivided teaching faculty capable of giving instruction in all the subjects of the Arts curric^m of a great Univ^y. That it is, moreover, necessary to the success of such a scheme that there should be no [overlapping] of work between the confed^g Colleges and State Faculty beyond furnishing such tutorial assistance as their students may require in their attendance on the lectures of the State Faculty.'[59]

To others like John Castle, however, affiliation meant something else. This had first become evident early in 1884 when, at the invitation of Queen's Park, Castle and his counterparts at the other theological schools were invited to discuss informally the whole question of federation. On this occasion and at subsequent meetings of the group, Castle took the position that an association with the university need not rule out the possibility of a theological school's organizing a partial arts curriculum to supplement whatever students might take at the provincial institution. This was potentially a significant departure from the traditional Baptist stance. Moreover, it was one strongly backed by Professor Malcolm MacVicar, a recent appointment to the TBC faculty upon whom Castle appeared to rely heavily for guidance and advice. Since MacVicar's support was crucial, a brief examination of his career and his principles seems in order.

A native of Argyleshire, Scotland, the young Scot had accompanied his emigrating family to western Upper Canada in 1835, two years after William McMaster arrived in Toronto.[60] A Presbyterian, MacVicar had taken a number of courses at Knox College before venturing forth as a teacher, principally of young men anxious to qualify for admission to the embryonic University of Toronto. In this interval he unaccountably left the Presbyterians and attached himself to a Baptist congregation in the city where he may have come to McMaster's attention. If such a meeting actually took place, the future senator, who later came to confide intimately in this Baptist convert, may have been impressed above all by the sincerity of MacVicar's educational commitment and may even have been responsible for encouraging his fellow Scot to attend the University of Rochester.

In any event, after his graduation from that institution MacVicar launched on a lengthy career in the United States as an administrator in public education. His responsibilities ranged from principalships of collegiate institutes and normal schools to superintendencies of state educational systems. An enthusiastic teacher with formidable organizational skills, he made a significant contribution to the legislation that established New York's normal school system and was entrusted with planning the schools to be constructed under the program. In the fields of methodology and text book preparation MacVicar was equally active, particularly in mathematics where his 'illustrative contrivances' for demonstrating arithmetical relations received considerable acclaim. Just prior to his appointment to the TBC in 1881, while serving as principal of a normal school in Michigan, he was busily preparing an outline of a text on the philosophy of education.

After productively spending so much time in the public sector of education why, it might be asked, did MacVicar accept a post at a fledgling theological school, a milieu seemingly divorced from the one in which he had functioned for so long? An opportunity to return to an expanding Canada and to Toronto, his place of academic beginnings some thirty years before, may have accounted in part for his decision to pull up stakes in 1881. Probably as weighty a factor was the chance to apply his administrative and teaching talents in a new institution dedicated to preserving the Christian ethic in education, an opportunity long denied him in the American public school system. Moreover, the Toronto Baptist College was supported by an individual who clearly wanted the best for an educated Baptist ministry and was prepared to pay for it. In any case, it was a new challenge for an experienced educator able to thrive on challenges who had spent years promoting innovative techniques in the classroom. And while sizing up the situation at the TBC MacVicar had come out strongly in support of Castle's scheme to enlarge the institution's arts curriculum, an area in which he believed he could make a distinctive contribution. For one thing, he was eager to develop a philosophy curriculum, particularly on the apologetical side. In his subsequent courses for theological students MacVicar discussed, among other themes, atheism, materialism, and modern agnosticism. He seemed especially anxious to probe the relationship between science and religion, and by 1886 he was actually occupying a chair in the subject and teaching students to apply the scientific method in the investigation of religious truth.[61]

Meanwhile, in May 1884, at the annual conference of the Baptist Union in Brantford, MacVicar was permitted to present the case for an expanded arts curriculum at the TBC. Although a good deal of attention was directed to missions in the Northwest and related matters, he succeeded in having much of an afternoon session set aside for his submission. As others had before him, he underscored the need for higher education under Christian auspices. 'We need to complete our system of denominational education with a Literary College' he told the delegates at Brantford

which would come in between [Woodstock College] and our Theological College. The Professors in the Literary College should be men of God as well as men of learning and ability . . . They should be unreservedly consecrated to the training of the young men and women who are to be leaders and standard bearers in the state and in the churches . . . they should have special power in directing every form of investigation towards the development in their students of an exalted Christian manhood.[62]

MacVicar concluded by urging the location of such a college in Toronto 'upon the University grounds' and in association with other denominational schools and with the university. By this means — hardly the 'confederation' envisaged by the latter — the Christian factor would be preserved and the denominational institution would have 'all the advantages of a well equipped provincial university.'[63] If this scheme ever materialized, Baptists would, in effect, have their cake and eat it too. To be sure, they rejected the thought that their literary school should enjoy degree-granting powers, preferring these to be lodged with the university. Nor was there any suggestion at this stage that such a school should attempt in the foreseeable future to teach anything like the number and variety of courses that the university offered or planned to offer.

Apparently MacVicar's proposal and Castle's enthusiastic endorsement of it were warmly received at Brantford, and the conference gave them a moral mandate to pursue the matter with other denominational spokesmen and with provincial politicians. Certainly the TBC Board approved the scheme at a special meeting early in the new year. They were prepared to back the federation proposal recently made by the minister of education provided that MacVicar's points were taken into account and certain modifications accepted. These would have enabled the denominational colleges 'to make the fullest use of the advantages of federation without in any way sacrificing principles or methods of procedure that are held by any of the parties to be essential to acquiring a true education.'[64]

In the ensuing discussions the university Senate made a change in its requirements that thoroughly delighted Castle and MacVicar, for it seemed to reinforce their campaign for a stronger literary faculty at the TBC. The change would have enabled a ministerial student at any of the theological schools to substitute in the final year of his collegiate course a proportion of the subjects taught in his particular school, thus saving a full academic year in the combined university and theological courses. When this decision was announced in the spring of 1885 Castle rejoiced that 'whatever may come of the present agitation regarding University Confederation we have much to gain and nothing to lose by securing affiliation.'[65] This not only put the case mildly but demonstrated as well the substantial difference in Castle's thinking between confederation and affiliation. It doubtless occurred to him that it might be possible ultimately to substitute any proposed arts course at the TBC for its university equivalent in a manner comparable to that for theological ones. Not surprisingly, Castle welcomed this form of affiliation from which the Baptist institution patently had 'much to gain and nothing to lose.' So did William McMaster, with whom the whole idea might even have originated; in the summer of 1885 he was prepared to help finance the appointment of 'two new professors . . . in order to do effectively [the] new work' that would be required at the TBC.[66]

Looked at from another angle, MacVicar's submission at Brantford, with its emphasis on the need for developing in students an 'exalted Christian manhood,' may have struck some people as a vote of non-confidence in the spiritual integrity of the University of Toronto. Why was the latter apparently not deemed as acceptable a vehicle of secular subjects as it had been a generation earlier? Had there been in the Baptist constituency any suggestion of sympathy for the reaction gaining ground in the decade against the supposed godlessness of the university? In 1884 Castle and MacVicar might have been made painfully aware of that reaction in those Baptist congregations whose affections for some time they had been trying desperately to cultivate. Castle's tentative plan for an arts faculty at the TBC might have been a creature of external pressure from rural and working-class Baptists who might have resented the prospect of having their offspring subjected to the allegedly demoralizing influences of University College. If there was a pattern of conservatism in the measures proposed by Castle in the mid-eighties – the Senate, the abstract of doctrine, and the more humble role assigned to ministerial 'workmen' – then his scheme for a literary college might also conceivably be fitted into that pattern. Through confederation, as it was understood by its critics, the Christian ethic was feared to be in danger of subversion; through the sort of affiliation Castle and MacVicar sought, on the other hand, that ethic would stand a far better chance of survival, and the forces of secularism and rationalism would be kept in check.

But the form of affiliation favoured by the TBC ultimately proved unacceptable at the University of Toronto. The alternative, virtual integration with that institution, was equally unacceptable to Castle and MacVicar. At this point in the discussion another strong voice was raised against union with Toronto. Although he may have shared the others' apparent concern about the spiritual welfare of the university, Theodore Harding Rand was unmistakably disturbed, as were Castle and MacVicar, about the fate of the college's arts curriculum, particularly its offerings in philosophy, in a closer relationship with that institution.[67] Rand's reservations were echoed by the heads of other prospective parties to federation, with the result that, for a time, the whole scheme threatened to collapse. This in turn provided Rand with another argument for encouraging the TBC to remain aloof from the proceedings and to seek an independent course.

A Maritimes Baptist and Acadia graduate, Rand had come to the TBC in 1885 to fill the chair of apologetics and ethics. He had impressive credentials as a Baptist spokesman, an effective teacher, and an educational administrator. Indeed, it was probably his vaunted organizational ability that prompted Castle to seek his services just as, years earlier, the president had sought MacVicar's. There was a striking parallel between the two men's careers as educators, administrators, and advocates of educational reform. Where MacVicar had made his name in the American mid-west, Rand had established his claim for recognition in the Dominion's Atlantic provinces. Clearly, the Baptist College in Toronto was not going to lack qualified leaders and expertise in the teaching field.

In his native Nova Scotia Rand had campaigned long and hard, in a manner that would have warmed the heart of any Upper Canadian Baptist, for free, non-sectarian education supported by general assessment. Although this approach had not gone well in a community reared on an intimate alliance between pedagogy and the pulpit, the requisite legislation was passed by the Nova Scotian House in 1864. Almost at once the experienced Rand was called upon to administer it, a task to which he devoted the next six years of his life. Following his dismissal in 1870, apparently on political grounds – the Maritimes' version of the spoils system was still awesome – and after a brief sojourn overseas Rand returned in 1871 to take up a similar responsibility in neighbouring New Brunswick. The zeal with which he supported state-financed non-sectarian education in that province extended to his denial of public funds for Baptist institutions and to his battles with Anglicans and Catholics over the respective merits of state and church schools.[68]

While engaged in these emotionally charged activities on behalf of public education, Rand did not lose the esteem of the powerful Baptist constituency. Twice his coreligionists tacitly endorsed his educational efforts and presumably his theological soundness by electing him to preside over the Baptist

Convention of the Maritime provinces. Towards the end of his career there he left the public service to accept at Acadia University the chair of history and education, a new post tailored to his qualifications. According to one account, Rand's brief stay at Acadia was, like his term as a public official, a controversial one, so much so that he felt obliged to withdraw in the face of 'reactionary criticism.'[69] According to an official history of the university, however, Rand's decision to vacate his post and depart for Ontario and the TBC was deemed at the time to be 'highly prejudicial' to Acadia's interests.[70] This was borne out by one of Rand's students at Wolfville who told a committee preparing a compilation of reflections on the institution that he had always been impressed by the care with which Rand had attended to his teaching duties.[71]

No stranger to administrative challenges and criticism, reactionary or otherwise, Rand, like MacVicar, appeared to be very much in demand at the TBC in 1885. Apologetics and ethics may have been the field he was expected to till, but his organizational prowess obviously counted for as much as his academic competence, particularly at a time when significant decisions had to be taken with respect to the reorganization of the arts curriculum at the college. Rand was not at his post for long before he was attacking federation as a danger to the program that Castle and MacVicar had already charted. His commitment to that program came out clearly when he was approached early in 1886 to accept the principalship of Woodstock College following the resignation of Professor Newton Wolverton. In view of Rand's background this post seemed a more appropriate one than that to which he had initially been called at the TBC. The headship of a well established institution would likely appeal strongly to one who had grown accustomed to giving orders and implementing policy.

In appearance at least, the school in Woodstock was no mean one in the mid-eighties. A new building had recently sprouted on the campus to serve as a hospital and dining hall, and new facilities had been added to the older structures. According to a local Baptist pastor who lived through it all, the new architecture was planned as the first of a series of improvements with a view to equipping the college to meet the 'future requirements of a university.'[72] Indeed, the McMasters themselves had put in an appearance and officiated when the cornerstone of the Middle Building was laid.

But it was the spiritual as well as the institutional challenge implicit in the Woodstock offer that made it so attractive to Rand. There is some evidence to suggest that within a few months of his arrival in Toronto Rand had accepted the view that the provincial university was failing to provide a sufficiently moral environment for the teaching of its secular subjects. This was reflected in the condition he attached to his acceptance of the position at Woodstock

College. 'I assume' he wrote to its Board in May 1886 'that the institution may be freely developed to the fullest degree as a Christian school of learning ... as its future resources may permit. My convictions as to the soundness of this policy are altogether too strong to permit me to engage in the manner proposed in the conduct of the ... College if its future is not open to the widest practical expansion.' Rand's next comment was the crucial one: 'Dr [Samuel S.] Nelles [of Victoria] publicly stated last week at Cobourg that if there is anything better for modern society than a Christian university it is two or three of them, if the country can support them. This is so entirely my thought that it seems to me [that] no act of ours should in any way foreclose the future development of Woodstock College [as a university].'[73] The acceptance of Rand's condition and of a policy of expansion for the institution in Woodstock was the work of a joint meeting of the Boards of the TBC and Woodstock College. On the same day, 20 May 1886, Rand was relieved of his classroom duties in Toronto so that he might begin at once to serve as acting principal in Woodstock.[74]

The long-range development of Fyfe's school into another independent 'Christian university,' however, was at variance with MacVicar's hope that a literary college would be built upon the university grounds in Toronto, a proposal that was to survive the breakdown in negotiations for federating with the University of Toronto. The plans for Woodstock also threatened to violate traditional Baptist policy. Yet the scheme was doubtless inspired not only by misgivings about the godlessness of the University of Toronto but at least in part by financial certainties the lack of which in the past had precluded Baptist enterprises in higher education even if they had been philosophically acceptable. 'Poverty produces principles as wealth often does,' one observer wryly commented some twenty years later. 'The wealth of William McMaster discovered principles that we had never heard of before.'[75] In his letter of acceptance of the position at Woodstock, Rand had indeed mentioned a 'munificent offer' that the senator had made to the Board of Trustees, a prospective donation of $32,000 to the college provided the denomination raised an additional $56,000.[76] To this latter task both MacVicar and Rand devoted their efforts over the next several months.

In view of McMaster's reported pledge it is not surprising that the impression gained ground in Woodstock that he was as anxious as the others to promote the expansion of the school 'to the fullest degree as a Christian school of learning.' These developments produced an air of expectancy throughout the Baptist constituency; it appeared certain that their educational institutions in Ontario were about to enter a new and significant phase.

3
The founding of the university

Senator McMaster's munificence and Rand's initiatives combined to provide a groundswell for floating an independent Baptist university. Castle's powers of persuasion also helped the venture. A few months after Rand's acceptance of the Woodstock post, the president of the TBC told the Baptist Convention assembled in Paris that an association with the University of Toronto should not be arranged. The point that Rand and MacVicar had been making since the spring was stressed by Castle at Paris in October: that in the kind of federation Toronto had come to insist upon, a Baptist institution would lose a 'number of subjects [it] ought to have' and be reduced to a mere 'language school.'[1] Faced with this set of prospects, the Convention, on behalf of the denomination, decided to seek a university charter from the provincial government. This procedure, insisted upon by the senator, was a significant departure from the one employed to establish and manage the forerunners of the university, based as they had been on the support of trustees and subscribers. At the same time the trustees of and subscribers to Woodstock College undertook, according to an eyewitness account, to give up their management of that institution on the understanding that 'it be consolidated and developed' in the manner already proposed by Rand.[2] Deprived of its theological department in 1881 and of the leadership of stalwarts like Robert Fyfe, Woodstock now had an opportunity of becoming once again, as it had been for a generation, the centre of Baptist educational operations in Ontario and this time as something more than a preparatory school.

As Wallace Cohoe noted a few years later, however, no serious thought seems to have been given to the actual 'higher educational demands of

Western Ontario.' 'It seems strange' he continued 'that [the] matter [of location] was largely governed by wish psychology. There appears to have been no survey made as to [those] demands.'[3] Although, as Cohoe conceded, any kind of productive market research might have been beyond the capacity of that era, anyone who took the trouble to read the newspapers would have known that a venture in higher education had already fared badly in London, Ontario. The Arts Department of the University of Western Ontario had opened in 1881, but hard times and thin enrolments had closed it down again by the time MacVicar and Rand were working up enthusiasm for a revitalized Woodstock College.

Hard on the heels of the encouraging news from the Paris convention came a meeting of the Woodstock Board of Trustees on 19 October 1886 at which a special committee was struck to arrange a revision of the college's charter to permit its metamorphosis into a university. Two months later, to the gratification of the institution's supporters, the Charter Committee furnished a full draft of a 'university bill.' At the same time the Board of the TBC – the Senate had already been presented with the information – met to support the proposal and 'to consider the advisability of ... making an application to the Legislature ... by the Toronto Baptist College and Woodstock College for amendments of their respective Acts of Incorporation so as to vest the property and place the control and administration of [the] work of the two Institutions in a common Board and Senate.'[4] The meeting agreed that the 'blank in the draft Bill for the University be filled in with "McMaster,"' the first public association of the senator's name with the projected institution.

The enthusiasm of the founders was far from shared by all articulate and knowledgeable people in the constituency. Those who had complained earlier about McMaster's centralizing tactics again expressed such sentiments when they learned of the plans being hatched for Woodstock. Others pointed to the limited success of Trinity College, an earlier reaction against godlessness at University College. A large group remained convinced that the age-old principle of a division of educational labour remained the best formula for Baptists and that they should not attempt to duplicate the state's work.[5] But the enthusiasts for the other side had their way, and on 15 March 1887 a bill to unite the TBC and Woodstock College and to incorporate them as McMaster University was introduced at Queen's Park.

The forces assembled on behalf of the bill were both impressive and predictable; among other notables McMaster himself, Rand, Castle, and D.E. Thomson. By this time Castle came almost automatically to the task of explaining and exhorting and did so with all the vigour and plausibility that had marked his efforts to found the TBC some eight years before. At the outset he readily conceded that the proposal ran counter to the current fashion of federation and that he and his colleagues must do everything in their power to justify the project to the legislature. Castle started the ball rolling by noting, with as much modesty as he could muster, the success of Baptist institutions in the United States and the creditable showing of Baptists in Canada with such enterprises as the Canada Baptist College and Woodstock College. To the serious charge levelled by some Baptists and a variety of outsiders[6] that the founding of yet another university could only lead to 'cheapened degrees,' the advocates of the scheme retorted by pointing to the reasonably high standards set at Woodstock and the TBC. On the other hand, however respectfully received President Nelles's arguments had been about the need for more Christian universities, the head of the University of Toronto bluntly warned against the 'multiplication of Universities in a province like ours'[7] for fear they might encroach upon the funds available for his institution, a groundless concern in McMaster's case. Admittedly, some Baptist dissidents were prepared to accept the chartering of a separate university, but only in the expectation that it would ultimately accept the wisdom of federating with the 'University in the Park.'

Castle held a trump card, however, and after presenting his capsule history of Baptist educational achievements he played it with consummate skill. A manoeuvre that had helped to carry the day at Guelph in 1879 was executed again with finesse when Castle dramatically referred to certain unspecified funds that Senator McMaster had agreed to give an independent Baptist university. If this was a reference to the $17,000 he had been conditionally prepared to donate, the assembled legislators may have been excusably unimpressed. However, during the subsequent debate on the bill, according to a report in the *Canadian Baptist*,[8] a member of the government intimated that a considerably larger sum had already been allocated to the undertaking. Something in the neighbourhood of $600,000 had apparently been promised, an endowment that would have matched those of Queen's and Victoria combined, the other major denominational institutions then flourishing independently.

The minister's statement and the agreement subsequently embodied in the charter that the university would confer no degrees in arts until it received $700,000 in properties and securities point to only one conclusion. Senator McMaster was the only Baptist ready and willing to donate funds of this magnitude, and he had already suggested, to quote one study, that 'he would give more money [to the institution] than he had formerly promised.'[9] This was an understatement. Some three weeks after the University Bill had been introduced in the legislature McMaster drew up a new will leaving virtually his entire estate as an endowment for the projected institution. In the end the arguments marshalled by delegates from the TBC and the effort made to demonstrate the financial soundness and the academic respectability of the enterprise satisfied the legislators, and on 22 April 1887 the bill of incorporation received its third reading and was passed into law.

By stages, it would appear, William McMaster had openly come round to the support not merely of an arts college in some sort of loose affiliation with the University of Toronto but of an independent institution of higher learning. And reminiscent of the direction that Fyfe's enterprise had taken in Woodstock McMaster emphasized in his will the need for 'affording the best possible facilities for a thoroughly practical Christian course of education.' Contemporaries and later generations delighted in speculating on the extent to which the senator might have been influenced by others when he came to make his decision. As with the TBC, so with the planned university, the hopes and plans of John Castle must have played a crucial role. In the mid-eighties his persuasive advocacy of the step was powerfully buttressed by more recent recruits like Theodore Harding Rand and Malcolm MacVicar, both pillars of educational administration and Baptist lay endeavour. Indeed, MacVicar was long a confidant of the senator and, along with Charles J. Holman, D.E. Thomson, and Dr H.E. Buchan, was named in McMaster's will as a trustee of his estate.[10]

Some sceptics were convinced, and had little difficulty convincing others, that once again McMaster's spouse had been the deciding voice. As the late George Gilmour wrote, and he may well have been asked about this matter more than about any other: 'Old timers have assured me that it was substantially owing to Susan [Moulton's] advocacy that her husband gave his money to a university instead of a hospital.'[11] Wallace Cohoe was among those apparently most convinced of this. After all, he would argue, the senator's widow had provided much of the inspiration for the building of that Baptist showpiece in Toronto, the Jarvis Street Church, and for the appointment of its first incumbent, the esteemed John Castle.[12] On several occasions after the turn of the century Mrs McMaster had promised that she would 'state the facts [of the case] in my recollections of McMaster.' So far as is known, however, her recollections were never put down on paper. Apart from such recorded comments of hers as, 'I frequently proposed to him [McMaster] to duplicate what I would give to different causes [which] he usually did,'[13] there is no direct evidence that she exerted the influence on the senator that so many claimed she did in this matter of a bequest to the university. It is also just possible that McMaster, the business dynamo, had a mind of his own. There is good reason to believe, as Castle strongly hinted in 1887, that in an earlier will drawn up before he met Susan Moulton, the senator had proposed leaving a substantial sum to finance Baptist educational efforts.[14]

Before leaving the subject one other reconstruction ought to be quoted in full, if only to furnish an inkling of the problems that face an historian plagued by sources limited to the bizarre. 'Sir William McMaster' a book proclaimed years later 'gave McMaster College to the University of Toronto. [He] became interested in the education of women and feeling they deserved a fair chance as well as men ... he consulted the head officials of the Toronto University and also the Ontario University and proposed the matriculation of women. He was refused. "I will build and endow an institution of learning for women only," he said. Hence the founding of McMaster University of Toronto, Canada.'[15]

As for McMaster's bequest, its full magnitude, some $900,000, was not publicly revealed until after his sudden death on 22 September 1887.[16] The monumental irony of the situation struck even the most insensitive. At one stroke the university that McMaster had promoted was instantly financed but at the cost of his vigour, direction, and imagination. While his death released funds vital to the enterprise, the loss of his leadership was a hard blow. Although aged, McMaster was never infirm or senile and right up to the end had displayed the aplomb and inventiveness that had marked his long career in the country's financial world.

While his demise was being mourned the disclosure of his bequest forced an immediate discussion of two major questions: the possible federation of the institution with the University of Toronto, which some prominent Baptists were still doggedly promoting, and the physical location of the institution. To some people both questions had already seemed settled. Why organize a university at all if steps were to be taken with indecent haste to integrate it with the provincial university? As for location: had the whole campaign not been predicated on the solid assumption that the institution would be based on an expanded and rejuvenated Woodstock College? And if the latter were in fact built up in this way then would geography alone not rule out the feasibility of federation?

The independence of McMaster University had, in fact, been quite settled, although a number of people, including John Boyd, the chancellor of Ontario, spoke out vigorously against it. Boyd, whose inclusion on the Board of the TBC had caused McMaster some concern earlier, was convinced that federation would neither reduce the freedom of the new university to teach whatever it chose nor blight the moral environment afforded its students, two dangers that supporters of an independent McMaster had publicized to strengthen their case. Boyd wound up his argument by attempting to refute the claim that federation would have been at variance with the charter, the senator's will, and the principles of the Baptist constituency. Left unstated in Boyd's presentation was the implication that a McMaster University outside federation would sorely lack the intellectual stamina and stature to produce graduates the equal of those from the University of Toronto.

To these points the anti-federationists eagerly reacted. Led by Castle and Rand (MacVicar was out of the country when these proceedings began) they contended that only through independence could spiritual integrity and academic satisfaction be achieved. Understandably, Rand had always attached much importance to curricular content, and he intimated that in certain areas the University of Toronto was positively deficient. Statements of this sort did not enjoy the support of some voluble and sophisticated members of the denomination who felt that Rand's strictures were at the very least in poor taste and at the most downright inaccurate.[17] But one contributor to the debate remarked that McMaster had already been a victim of poor taste and cavalier treatment at the hands of the University of Toronto. Indeed 'the impression ... was that this rudeness had something to do with McMaster's decision to stay out of Federation and proceed to the acquisition of full University powers.'[18]

The important fact remains, however, that other articulate Baptists shared Rand's misgivings, valid or not, about the curricular situation at the neighbouring university. One such was James E. Wells, the writer and editor, who in the fall of 1887 spelled out the problem as he saw it in a letter to the *Canadian Baptist*. Wells came to this complaint after years spent bemoaning the cultural lag in Canada, the gulf he saw between the country's material progress and its meagre intellectual development, a gap that in his view had not been narrowed by the exertions of the University of Toronto. 'How many native-born and home educated Canadians' he had asked bitingly a decade earlier 'have widened the domain of Science, enriched the galleries of Art, found the clue to an intricate maze in history?'[19] During the debate over federation Wells had charged that at the University of Toronto

certain subjects of the highest importance are either wholly neglected or very indifferently provided for ... and which every educator must wish to see made prominent in McMaster. I might instance English Prose Literature and Political Economy, or rather Sociology in its broader aspect, two studies which most thinkers and educators will now admit should have a very prominent place in every course of liberal culture and which are almost neglected in Toronto University.[20]

The notion of introducing English studies as a formal discipline on its own would have appalled those who regarded a knowledge of one's literary heritage as part and parcel of a cultivated gentleman's cultural equipment, as an adornment not to be reduced to the indignity of a classroom 'subject.' The minuscule set of Canadian men of letters would probably have shared an English historian's recollection that 'such was our layman's pride that we thought it would be "low" to make ... English literature an examination subject ... It was not that we thought too little of [it] ... but that we thought it too sacred.'[21] Wells obviously did not share this view. He claimed, moreover, that through federation with the University of Toronto McMaster's functions would be limited to those 'of a mere language school,' one presumably fit only for grammarians, a group of academics that clearly failed to excite him. As to the neglect of political economy, there appeared to be some substance to Wells's accusations. Just a few years before, President Daniel Wilson of the University of Toronto had remarked that the appointment of a lecturer in that subject was understandably 'viewed with apprehension for fear of the introduction of Party Politics.'[22]

Wells's pungent comments on what ought to go into the making of a liberal culture graphically reflected the changing concepts of higher education then being entertained on both sides of the Atlantic. A heavy dose of educational utilitarianism had already been injected into curricular reforms by those who had imbibed freely of the writings of Herbert Spencer and Thomas Huxley. Launching an assault on the old curriculum, which had been heavily laced with classical studies, their disciples urged its replacement by more pragmatic courses designed to prepare students for an active role in the formulation and achievement of new social goals. They sought the introduction of programs that would not merely discipline but also prepare one for a full, active life in the task of bettering society. To this end, reformers – and Wells was a vocal one – sought to add to the traditional fare of education such fields of instruction as political science, economics, sociology, and a large array of subjects from the burgeoning natural sciences.

Then Wells launched into a lament that had long disturbed some Baptist educators: the prevalent 'cramming' brought on by what one critic had described as the 'evil genius of the competitive examination.' 'Originating possibly in the high standards of verbal and technical accuracy set up ... by the Provincial University,' so the charge ran, 'an unhealthy impulse' had ensured that 'straightaway Examinations would become the all important thing.'[23] Wells's ill-concealed fear, an echo of Castle's earlier one, was that should federation come about – to him an 'unthinkable' eventuality – the chief function of McMaster professors would be to cram students for Toronto examinations because the professors in the federated colleges would 'no longer be masters of their own subjects.' They would be 'degraded in spite of themselves' he asserted 'to ... mere tutorial drudges.'[24] This was strong, almost offensive, language. But significantly, it was endorsed by the phalanx of anti-federationists, both lay and clerical, who charged into battle to disperse the arguments of Chancellor Boyd and others who despaired of McMaster's future as an independent institution.

Whatever the validity of the rival arguments the McMaster Board of Governors thought it imperative that they be speedily submitted along with other crucial matters to the judgment of the denomination. Significantly, Guelph, the scene of Castle's triumphs in 1879, was selected as the site for this equally momentous convention in the closing days of March 1888. The deference to the constituency was no mere gesture; as already indicated, the founder of the university had specifically entrusted the institution to the judgment and deliberations of this large and democratically constituted body. This point was underscored by D.E. Thomson, the chairman of the Convention and one of the executors of the McMaster estate. 'Has the thought ever struck you' he asked in a manner calculated to put the seven hundred delegates in the best possible mood

how great a trust in his brethren is implied in the terms of his will and of the charter of this institution? It has no parallel. Without being imbued with the pessimism of a Carlyle on the subject of democracy, one might well hesitate to leave the administration of a great endowment, and the shaping of the policy of an institution of higher learning to the hands of representatives chosen by the individual churches. But, the founder, it is conceived, rightly judged that if there was a people on earth who might be trusted with such a power it was the Baptists, whose principles necessarily schooled them in the art of government.[25]

To no one's surprise the first matter on the agenda was the thorny question of federation. Attempts to defer a decision on the question or to thwart the scheme of independence were, to the gratification of Thomson and other founders, decisively defeated. A motion was then carried that '[the] University be organized and developed as a permanently independent school of learning, with the Lordship of Christ as the controlling principle.'[26] While the anti-federationists were probably justified in congratulating themselves on the scope of their victory they were soon enough reminded that there were still influential people in the denomination unhappy with what had been sanctioned. Although they had charitably refrained from turning the meeting into a divisive public debate they nevertheless worked off their resentment in private. Dr H.E. Buchan, for example, who had long served as secretary of the Board of the TBC, remained adamant in his opposition to a full-fledged university. In the spring of 1888 he saw no reason to alter the view he had expressed some months before in a letter to Castle: 'I scarcely think my presence will be specially needed at the . . . Charter Committee of McMaster University [for] though I heartily approve of every step in the direction of a thoroughly equipped Arts *College*, I am as much as ever averse to the *use of University powers* in any other Faculty than Theology – at least under existing circumstances.'[27]

Nor did other equally prominent and critical Baptists restrain their views in private. Among these were Hiram A. Calvin, the 'lumber prince' of Kingston, and George Holmes of Toronto, the province's master of titles. Although Calvin, to be sure, served briefly on the McMaster Board, he shared Boyd's view about the prudence of federation and shortly withdrew his executive expertise and financial support from the new institution. He switched his attention to Queen's, the local university, to which he dispatched not only sizable funds but also a son, D.D. Calvin, who in later years wrote a history of his alma mater and a chronicle of the family firm. For his part, Holmes backed the traditional argument, familiar to Fyfe's generation, that arts work as such was the state's obligation and ought not to be undertaken on any ambitious scale by a denomination, least of all by Baptists.

That there was some difference of opinion as to Fyfe's actual principles emerged in a letter written years later by D.E. Thomson to Chancellor A.L. McCrimmon:

The narrow view that the denomination should confine its educational work to the preparation of men for the Ministry ... is the one which dominated the earlier enterprises which ended in failure. The broad one ... that the education to be supplied under Christian influences should be for all classes ... was first advanced by Dr Fyfe and it is the one which has been steadfastly adhered to ever since ... He always insisted that we should furnish for our people educational facilities under Christian influences up to the limit of our ability.[28]

However Fyfe's original intentions might have been reconstructed and however unanimous the Guelph Convention might have appeared, the unpleasant fact remained that some affluent Baptists quietly denied vital support to McMaster.

But before this reaction could be evaluated by those who had won the day, the convention was plunged into a debate more disruptive than the one that had swirled briefly about the federation question. This had to do with proposed locations for the university. The possibility that Woodstock, once considered the first if not the only choice, might ultimately have to yield to Toronto was first rumoured in print nearly a year before in the pages of the

Canadian Baptist. The Rev Ebenezer W. Dadson, the paper's editor, had remarked that 'if there is any foundation for the rumour, *and we have every reason to believe that there is*, then the sooner the matter is settled one way or the other the better for the institution.'[29] Months before the question was formally placed on the agenda of the Guelph meetings it had been vigorously debated at local conventions and association meetings as well as in the denominational press.

The liveliest exchanges had occurred around the turn of the new year. Not surprisingly, Newton Wolverton, while still principal of Woodstock College, had assumed that Senator McMaster had had no qualms whatsoever about transferring to Woodstock the money he had initially set aside for an expanded arts program in Toronto. And certainly Rand, when he had accepted the principalship of the school, had, if anything, bolstered that impression. But Malcolm MacVicar immediately challenged Wolverton's reconstruction of events. Apparently a refutation from him would go far to satisfy well-wishers of the prospective institution, for they regarded a statement from MacVicar as 'decisive.' 'Besides being a most active member of the Charter Committee,' one wrote to him, 'you, of the four gentlemen appointed by Mr McMaster as his executors, are the one who was most intimate with him, and you are believed to be fully informed as to his views on these questions.'[30] To correct Wolverton's version of what had happened MacVicar took pains to point out that the decision to transfer the funds to Woodstock had been far from easy for the senator. He had agreed to do so, MacVicar disclosed, 'at the sacrifice of his own most cherished plans and purposes ... made to meet the strongly expressed views ... of brethren who had pressed upon him ... that unless he made the sacrifice Woodstock College would certainly have to be closed permanently ... The step ... cost him a severe struggle in view of his strong personal preference to concentrate in Toronto what he intended to do for higher Christian education.'[31] In other words, MacVicar hoped to make it clear that whatever the denomination really desired McMaster would ungrudgingly have accepted regardless of his own heartfelt preferences, in this case the establishment of the university in Toronto. The message must not have been unfamiliar to those who had sat through Castle's speeches at Guelph nine years before. But one question still had to be faced. Would not a good many people in 1888 be deeply influenced by what had been construed as the innermost wishes of a man whose generosity was going to make this whole venture in higher education feasible?

After supposedly setting the record straight, MacVicar and his associates took to the sidelines and let laymen battle the issue out with their opponents. Rand soon joined them: after all his talk of 'building up' Woodstock College, he had come round to accepting MacVicar's version of what McMaster had been up to all along. The upshot was Rand's resignation from the principalship of the school early in 1888.

In the meantime, the disputants battled with a vigour that recalled for many the tactics and arguments employed in 1879 over the removal of the Literary Institute's theological department. Notwithstanding the reasons for that earlier move, there were those who held that the theology faculty should again be uprooted and returned to its place of origin so that it might benefit once more from rural surroundings and from an intimacy with an expanded arts program at Woodstock College. Among the arguments persistently used against Toronto as a site for the university, the position defended by Dadson, Wolverton, John McLaurin, and Jones H. Farmer, who would briefly head the college following Rand's resignation, was that the queen city constituted far too great a distraction for a student body. Furthermore, to concentrate in Toronto would mean the emasculation of Woodstock, crippling financial losses, and the added expense of constructing new buildings in the provincial capital. Wolverton reminded his readers that many Baptists had already donated funds to the university on the understanding that it would be located in Woodstock. He warned that if Toronto were nevertheless selected as the site these funds might be withdrawn along with vital moral support. The warning was well founded. In the spring of 1888 the McMaster Board was obliged to return notes given by members of a number of churches because they 'declined to pay them on account of the removal of the Arts Department of McMaster University to Toronto.'[32]

In their rebuttal the advocates of Toronto dusted off, polished, and impressively exhibited the arguments that had made for victory at Guelph in 1879. Toronto's metropolitan stature, cultural assets, commercial hegemony, and its promise of even more productive growth were all cited by those who thought that the university should follow the example of the TBC. Toronto had indeed become a 'considerable city,' and its population, already impressive by Canadian standards when the TBC moved there, had during the eighties spurted ahead dramatically to 175,000. By 1890 its geographic size was nearing nineteen square miles.[33] Citizens who took pride in such matters were pointing excitedly to visible and welcome products of applied science and technology. Electricity had by this time been introduced, albeit on a flickering scale, to illuminate streets and run urban railways. The telephone had also arrived, and by the end of the decade there were no fewer than two hundred subscribers in the city, one of which was to be McMaster University, where a device was installed for the chancellor's convenience in 1888.

One prolific booster of Toronto unhesitatingly wrote at this time, 'not only does it occupy the centre of the Dominion of Canada, but the Centre of the Empire in the Western Hemisphere, as truly as London does in the

Eastern, as her contiguity to India, Australia, the West Indies, and all other British possessions, fully shows.'[34] As if this were insufficient the writer noted approvingly, and to the satisfaction of Toronto supporters among the Baptists who consulted his remarks, that as a 'city set on a hill,' Toronto 'has become the synonym of order, morality, temperance, and religion.' Who could possibly ask for anything more?

At least one prominent advocate of federation, John Boyd, also came out squarely for the Toronto site. This raised the suspicion in J.H. Farmer's mind that the chancellor desired expansion in Toronto as the prerequisite of federation, an object that might still be achieved in spite of the Convention's recent ruling on the matter. One supporter of the Toronto location was brusquely reminded of the dangers of this sort of equation. 'In the year 1887,' Allan M. Denovan wrote after the turn of the century,

when the question of [the] location of McMaster University was being discussed, I was an advocate of it being placed in Toronto, and in the way of argument I made the point then that were it here and should it desire at any time to federate with Toronto University it could do it a great deal easier than if it were at Woodstock. I remember one of those interested coming to me and asking me to drop that line of argument for if persisted in he thought the result would be that the University would be placed at Woodstock. I did as requested.[35]

The interested party who approached Denovan could have been a federationist or not, concerned respectively with tactics or with strategy. If an anti-federationist, he could have been any one of the group advocating Toronto for its own sake, people like the lawyers Charles J. Holman and D.E. Thomson and the businessman W.K. McNaught, all of whom had made good in the city's professions and marts of trade. To strengthen their case they noted that one library and one administrative structure in a congenial setting such as Toronto would be able to serve both arts and theology, a form of streamlining that would not only reduce expenditures but also provide the kind of concerted direction that society had come to expect from a first-rate institution.[36] Concern for efficiency as well as for standards was uppermost in the minds of this group and was clearly reflected in the debate at Guelph on the siting question.

The champions of Woodstock College understandably resented the imputation that their institution, however refurbished intellectually, would never achieve the excellence that critics like Holman and Thomson so highly prized. Apparently ministers in particular 'did a lot of talking' on Woodstock's behalf. But just as anxious to defend the old Literary Institute were those prominent citizens of Woodstock who had looked forward keenly to their town possessing a university. Invited to attend the convention, these citizens alluded repeatedly to a moral obligation to establish the institution in their community.

In the end, however, Woodstock was denied its university and Ontario society an opportunity to emulate (even if it had wanted to, which is doubtful) the American practice of locating small liberal arts colleges in pastoral environments. Yet, another kind of moral obligation was assumed and discharged by the McMaster Board when it announced that it would, in an 'equitable manner,' compensate the Woodstock subscribers and those congregations which had already offered financial support to the college's unsuccessful bid for university status.[37] At the same time statements contrived to carry as much reassurance as possible were made about plans to increase the efficiency of the college and to 'make it one of the best schools of its kind in Canada.' Sugar-coated though it was, the fate of the Woodstock institution as an effective preparatory school seemed for many to be sealed by the decisions taken at the Guelph Convention. The resulting demoralization may help to account for the marked lag in the activities of its Alumni Association after 1888.

Toronto's palpable attractions, the momentum already enjoyed there by the TBC, the persuasiveness of its leading Baptist promoters, and not least the open secret that Senator McMaster preferred it above all others as a site again helped to win the day. But no one, least of all the victors, remained long in doubt about the feelings of those rural and small-town congregations that lamented the decision to 'forsake' Woodstock. What made 'centralization' in Toronto particularly unpalatable was the related decision to remove the ladies' department from the college as well and to re-establish it as Moulton College in Toronto, endowed with the widow's wealth and comfortably ensconced in the senator's stately mansion. The Woodstock Alumni Association bitterly charged that in making this decision the McMaster Senate had acted 'in a wrong principle' by failing to consult the denomination's wishes.[38] In any event, the college ceased to function as a coeducational institution, and the emergent university started off by making additional enemies among rural congregations.

While fielding the complaints from the back townships and the Woodstock subscribers the victors at Guelph proceeded to the task of organizing McMaster University. The Board of the TBC had already wound up its business and officially passed out of existence when that institution was designated 'the Theological Department of the University.'[39] The defunct Board's place was taken by the new sixteen-man university Board of Gover-

nors all of whom, as required, were members of the Regular Baptist Missionary Society of Ontario or the Regular Baptist Missionary Convention, East
(Quebec). Shortly thereafter, and largely as a result of the organization of the
university, these two bodies united to form the present Baptist Convention of
Ontario and Quebec. This new association, like its predecessors, was empowered to elect Board members and to require them to report annually to
the denomination. The Board was carefully composed to include not only
avid supporters of the institution but also, doubtless to win them over, those
whose advocacy had been lukewarm or indifferent. Thus Hiram Calvin
found himself honoured with an invitation to sit on the Board, which he
shortly declined in favour of supporting the university serving the locality
where he had prospered as a timber merchant. But among those who eagerly
accepted the invitation to serve were such old standbys as D.E. Thomson, C.J.
Holman, William J. Copp, Thomas Trotter, Joshua Denovan, and John
Dryden. John Boyd, although hostile to independence, nonetheless received
and accepted an appointment. So did D.W. Karn, a former member of the
Woodstock delegation, who had sought to thwart the Toronto campaign but
who later expressed a desire to support the venture, wherever it settled, as a
worthy experiment in Baptist education. As had been the custom at the TBC,
Montreal and the Eastern Convention were given places on the new Board,
with A.A. Ayer again leading their contingent.[40]

The powers of the new Board, as laid down in the Act of 1887, were
substantially similar to those entrusted to the TBC Board: full administrative
and financial supervision of the university. Appointments and promotions of
faculty and the control and management of property and of the emoluments
of the university, these were by now the traditional preserves of such a body.
In the matter of a Senate the new institution could also call upon its predecessor for guidance. Predictably, all academic and curricular matters, together
with recommendations for appointments and promotions, were to originate
in the new Senate whose members, like the Board's, were to be drawn from
Regular Baptist bodies. Numbering forty members it was composed of the
governors and representatives of the old TBC, Castle, MacVicar, and Albert
Henry Newman, of Woodstock College, which as a preparatory school was
constituted an integral part of the university, and of the Alumni Association
of theology graduates. Provision was also made, as Castle had judiciously
ensured at the TBC, for the representation of sister institutions and other
Baptist constituencies in the Dominion. Thus Acadia University and the
Baptist Convention of the Maritime provinces, along with their counterpart
in 'Manitoba and the Northwest,' were given places in the boardroom of the
university.

The Senate held its first meeting even before the Guelph Convention had formally assigned the university to Toronto. Convened in the parlour of McMaster Hall on 18 January 1888, it was chaired by A.A. Ayer, who had made a special trip from Montreal for the occasion. Its minutes were carefully recorded by Professor Newton Wolverton, who was still entertaining the hope that Woodstock College would be selected as the nucleus of the university. Although committees were formed to devise curricula and set standards, much was plainly tentative about the Senate's proceedings in the early weeks of 1888. All present knew that basic policies would have to be decided at the forthcoming Educational Convention and until that was done certain critical matters, particularly those conditional on location, would have to be left in abeyance. Admittedly, an effort was made before the Convention met to name the first chancellor or chief officer of the university. On 30 March John Castle was strongly recommended for the post by a number of unidentified people, but he stated 'his own disinclination [for] the work of the Chancellorship.' Following his virtual withdrawal as a candidate the decision was taken the same afternoon to reconsider the matter 'in view of the importance of the step ... and as it was felt desirable that other members should have an opportunity of expressing themselves.'[41]

Once vital questions were resolved at Guelph the university's affairs could be arranged with greater dispatch. Accordingly, on 26 April 1888 the committee seeking a chancellor substituted Malcolm MacVicar's name for that of Castle whose failing health had ended his candidacy. MacVicar, the close confidant of the late senator and a leading backer of the university's independence and of its location in Toronto, promptly told the Senate that he would undertake the task. But he also sought to assure the institution that had lost out in the competition for university status that his acceptance of the chancellorship would be conditional upon the willingness of the Board and Senate to carry out the Guelph resolutions with respect to Woodstock College. Apparently the senator's widow had much to do with the plans that MacVicar proposed for the school in the summer of 1888. The chancellor urged that it 'be made an Institution where young men can obtain a first class general education, and at the same time have many of the advantages of a good practical School of Technology.' Mrs McMaster's suggestions and the interest she showed might have been signs that she wished to compensate for the much-criticized decision to terminate coeducation at the school.[42]

Like many of MacVicar's proposals this one survived only as a good intention. His tenure as the university's chancellor, though widely acclaimed, turned out to be disappointingly brief. He resigned in 1890 while still serving what was essentially a paper institution. But while he served he took an active part in every major policy decision. For example the question whether or not the chancellor ought to be a member of the teaching staff was debated at considerable length. It was finally decided in the fall of 1889, after a wearying series of motions, amendments, and sub-amendments, that he ought not to be so described but rather should be termed the 'head of the university having the general oversight of all its departments under the direction of the Board of Governors and the Senate.'[43]

The next matter for the Senate to settle was the status of the teaching staff itself, particularly its qualifications and responsibilities. Described in the charter as a 'Christian school of learning,' the university could appoint to arts positions only those who were 'members in good standing of an Evangelical Christian Church,' although appointments to the faculty of theology understandably were to be drawn exclusively from the membership of Regular Baptist Churches. It ought to have been quite clear to any observer that there was no intention to restrict arts appointments to members of the Baptist denomination,[44] a reasonably public fact consistently ignored by many within and without the denomination who invariably jumped to the conclusion that the faculty in arts was to be narrowly selected from Baptist ranks only. In fact, judged in terms of the society of late-Victorian Ontario there would have been few prospective academics within the Protestant community who were not members in good standing of some evangelical congregation or another. The Act of 1887 had also laid down that as far as the student body was concerned 'no compulsory religious qualification, or examination of a denominational character shall be required from or imposed upon [it] ... other than in the faculty of theology.'

With regard to academic standards the Act had also been quite explicit: no degrees were to be conferred in arts until at least five professorships and standards equivalent to those at the University of Toronto were firmly established. The first requirement was met before the institution opened its doors to the first class of students in the fall of 1890. Headed by Chancellor MacVicar, the list included Albert H. Newman, professor of history and church history, Daniel Welton, the Maritimer and veteran of the TBC who was responsible for Hebrew and cognate languages, Theodore Rand, to no one's surprise named professor of the science of education, Newton Wolverton, plucked temporarily from Woodstock College to instruct in mathematics, and Peter S. Campbell, a classicist.

When these appointments had been agreed upon in the spring of 1889 the Board and Senate felt free to plan for the opening of what they briefly called 'the College of Liberal Arts.'[45] On two occasions, however, attempts were unaccountably made by E.W. Dadson and R.G. Boville, TBC alumni representatives on the Senate, to have the decision reconsidered, but their objections were set aside and plans went forward to launch the institution on schedule by the fall of 1890.[46] Dadson and Boville might have been concerned about the effect a recent disaster at the University of Toronto would have upon the fortunes of the fledgling McMaster. In February 1890, just when it seemed possible that the new university might need access to some of the facilities of the older one, a devastating fire tore through the provincial university; it wrecked 'a large portion of the buildings ... totally destroyed the Library ... and partially destroyed the Museum.'[47] An examination of McMaster University records for the period, however, disclosed nothing to indicate that its administrators were affected one way or the other by the catastrophe across the park.

Instead, their attention seems to have been riveted on such matters as appointments, financing, and curriculum. In addition to the chairs already assigned, the Senate, with the Board's concurrence, made provision for six others in arts and seven in theology. Until such time as the university opened, arrangements were made for lectures in the Theology Department to be delivered by some of the newly appointed members of the Arts Department.

At first glance the courses planned at McMaster bore a striking resemblance to those already offered at the University of Toronto. This should have come as no real surprise except that during the debate on federation J.E. Wells and Theodore Rand had insisted that independence would enable the new institution to offer substantial courses in English Literature and political economy, disciplines supposedly neglected by McMaster's large neighbour. Did the proposed fields of instruction outlined in early McMaster calendars reflect this intention to compensate for the alleged deficiencies of its sister institution? No explicit reference is made to political economy in these documents, unless it was included in civil polity, a field assigned to Professor Rand. Nevertheless, the Senate Minutes and early McMaster examinations[48] reveal that political economy was certainly available before the university's first class was graduated in the spring of 1894. As for Wells's other complaint about the lack of English studies, considerable emphasis appears to have been given to English literature. Indeed, Wells himself, anxious to practise what he had long been preaching, spearheaded instruction in Shakespeare, the nineteenth-century poets, and English literary history, the latter in collaboration with a newly acquired colleague, D.R. Keys.

, In the interval, between Wells's outburst of 1887 and the inauguration of the English courses he had sought, the University of Toronto had made good its alleged shortcomings in this field. Although there had in fact been a chair of history and English literature at University College since 1853, the field was divided in 1888, presumably to provide for a greater concentration on prose literature. The new English chair was promptly filled by the great teacher W.J. Alexander,[49] whose *Shorter Poems* and *Short Stories and Essays* later served to arouse the literary interest of at least two generations of Ontario high school students. In 1889, a chair in political economy and a course in political science – President Wilson's fears of partisan strife having obviously subsided – were also founded at the University and conferred upon the British economist William Ashley.

Why were critics like Wells not aware of these scheduled curricular changes at the University of Toronto? That institution had for some time been advising interested parties that it would feel obliged, in the event of federation, to introduce new courses to satisfy the colleges concerned. If this was news to Wells he could be charged with failing to do his homework and unfairly criticizing the University of Toronto. On the other hand, he might have attached little importance to Toronto's pronouncements and, given his keen interest in the cultivation of 'Canadian brain power,' have been anxious to promote the establishment of as many and as varied institutions as possible. Or was Wells, like the Thomsons, the Castles, and the MacVicars, anxious to advance the interests of McMaster so that it might afford a Christian alternative to the secularism of the University of Toronto?

Whatever the answers to these questions, Baptist educators pressed ahead with new fields of instruction at McMaster. Steps were taken before the first convocation to add to the store of 'modern' subjects by introducing political history, as distinct from the purely ecclesiastical history that had long been the staple of institutions developed under denominational auspices. It had traditionally been assumed, as in the case of English literature, that a student sufficiently drilled in the classics and leisurely steeped in the richness of his heritage could quite easily master history on his own and would not think of subjecting it to the degradation of the classroom and the formal examination. But as classical studies became less and less popular, trained and enthusiastic historians demanded that their discipline be recognized as political economy had been. If the mysteries of Adam Smith merited time in the lecture hall, why not the historical study of politics and constitution-making? And so the subject was finally accorded a place on university curricula.

McMaster was to be no exception to the growing trend. By 1895 both constitutional history and ancient history were being offered, along with considerable work in the old course in church history, by Professor Newman, the first occupant of the history chair at the university. Not surprisingly he received assistance in his all-encompassing endeavours. P.S. Campbell, the classicist, D.R. Keys, the scholar in English, and William J. McKay, a future editor of the *Canadian Baptist*, all pitched in to aid Newman. A move that would have thoroughly delighted a disciple of Robert Fyfe was the approval in 1895 of a course in North American history, particularly on constitutional aspects. Francis Parkman's chronicles, which for some years had been pouring out at an awesome rate, the provocative treatises of Goldwin Smith, a favourite with many Baptists because of his stand on the virtues of the separation of church and state, and the sombre writings of political scientist Woodrow Wilson, these stood high on the list of texts prescribed for the new course.[50]

Philosophy, a discipline accorded a prominent place in the TBC's curriculum and the first chair established at the university, was entrusted in 1892 to George Burman Foster, an American clergyman and alumnus of the Rochester Theological Seminary. He spent the year before taking up his McMaster appointment doing advanced work in philosophy and theology at the universities of Göttingen and Berlin. His brief exposure to the higher criticism did not appear to influence unduly the content of his courses at McMaster or to ruffle the sensibilities of the people who selected him for the post. In their minds he doubtless exemplified that liberal culture which John Castle had once sought to deploy against the 'polished shafts of infidelity.' This exercise probably helped to create what one student of philosophy at McMaster has called that 'breadth of outlook and freedom from narrow denominational or theological restrictions that characterized the leaders of [the] educational enterprise.'[51]

Like his hard-worked colleagues on Bloor Street, Foster had such a full load of teaching responsibilities during his three-year stint there that he may have had little time in which to display those insights into religious humanism that ultimately came to inspire his later career at the University of Chicago and to arouse the concern of the orthodox after the turn of the century. In addition to giving courses at McMaster in 'mental science,' the history of philosophy, logic, and psychology, he was expected to offer instruction in English Bible and the Old and New Testaments to its arts students.

When Foster accepted Chicago's offer in 1895 to fill its chair of systematic theology the decision was genuinely regretted on all sides at McMaster, and especially by those who had regarded his efforts in philosophy as a means of giving leadership in the 'independent pursuit of truth.' In contrast to the abuse levelled against Chicago in the next decade for its alleged heresy and modernism, no hint of such complaints found their way into the university's records in 1895 when Foster submitted his resignation. As events proved, however, his connection with McMaster was not wholly severed; over the years he would instruct and influence a number of promising McMaster graduates who furthered their theological and philosophical studies at Chicago, most notably Douglas Clyde Macintosh and Albert Eustace Haydon. In the meantime, Foster's place at McMaster was taken by another American and Rochester alumnus, James Ten Broeke, a native of Vermont who had in 1891 obtained his PHD at Yale and then spent a year overseas at Berlin and Oxford. His career at McMaster would be as long as Foster's had been brief: in all he would spend thirty-seven years there as professor of philosophy, psychology, and ethics.

Nor in that age of Spencer and Huxley were the natural sciences left out of account. At the outset, certainly, the offerings were meagre enough. Provision had been made for a chair in natural science in 1889, but three years passed before it was officially filled by Arthur B. Willmott. Willmott, who had taught previously at Antioch College and lectured briefly at McMaster before receiving the appointment, was a Victoria alumnus who had done graduate work in mineralogy at Harvard.[52] From all accounts he made the most of the cramped physical and chemical laboratories he constructed in the basement of McMaster Hall. For the better part of three years he handled all the scientific subjects offered in the syllabus until William Piersol, a University of Toronto graduate, arrived in 1895 to take over the work in biology.

This state of affairs prompted Wallace Cohoe to remark years later that 'our Professor of Natural Science ... was the lone occupant not of a [chair], but of an incipient grandstand now more densely populated, [a] primeval condition [which] however enabled us to avoid that pitfall of ignorance known as overspecialization.'[53] This primeval condition, Cohoe went on, seemed to be a function of the complacency that characterized the attitude of the educated in the early nineties, particularly in the field of science. In chemistry the atom appeared eternal and unsplittable; in physics, all was consummated. Before the century closed, however, Ernest Rutherford had gone to work on the atom and scientific findings in other areas, exulted Cohoe, were opening up a 'new heaven and a new earth.'

Meanwhile, whatever McMaster might have lacked in scientific personnel and plant it appeared to make up for in environmental stimulus. Cohoe, the university's first MA in chemistry, had good reason to congratulate the institution's founders for selecting Toronto as its home. The decision had made it possible for undergraduates 'to see and hear ... great leaders of scientific thought' who from time to time made a point of putting the budding Ontario metropolis on their speaking itineraries.[54] He reported years later:

The experience was a great joy and a wonderful inspiration. During one of the summer vacations [1897] the British Association met in Toronto ... One [demonstration] that impressed me was the production of fluorine by Henri Moisson ... probably the first time this had been done outside of [his] own laboratory in Paris. That man of great accomplishment in the world of electricity, Lord Kelvin, was there. He dominated the whole meeting as he did the whole field of physics as it existed at that time.[55]

Theodore Rand was another who obviously enjoyed his association with the rising city, particularly with what one writer has called its 'social and semi-literary societies.'[56] A writer and compiler of romantic verse – *At Minas Basin*, a colourful portrait of the New Brunswick scene, and *A Treasury of Canadian Verse* would appear some years later[57] – Rand frequently lectured to literary luncheons and to 'cultivated ladies.' Such outings must have counted as pleasurable diversions from the tasks of teaching and administration. It was just as well, for a good deal of work had come his way, largely as a result of Malcolm MacVicar's abrupt resignation in 1890 as chancellor and as principal of the Arts Department.

Few hints have been found as to why MacVicar stepped down from the leadership of the university. It is true that another and potentially more challenging offer had presented itself at this time, one involving the supervision of the varied educational ventures of the American Baptist Home Missionary Society. This opportunity would readily appeal to a man who was 'continually pulling up old stakes and extending the boundaries.'[58] But chronologically this invitation from the United States came some time after his decision to relinquish the chancellorship. Indeed, MacVicar had been prepared to stay on at the university in the reduced capacity of a professor in the Theology Department. Had the pressures of leadership been too much for him? In the light of his earlier career this seems rather improbable. Had he clashed then with fellow academics or with members of the Senate or the Board? There is a faint suggestion of this in a brief reference by a future chancellor to MacVicar's directness and his ability to ruffle feelings.[59] In any case he decided to withdraw entirely from the McMaster community and to undertake a new educational career in the United States where, after all, he had spent his most productive years.

MacVicar's departure was shortly followed by other unsettling developments – the death of the ailing John Castle, who had retired in 1889, followed within a matter of days by that of Professor D.A. McGregor, also a veteran of the TBC and the newly named principal of the Theology Department. Thus, within the space of four years many of the university's founders had passed from the scene, a sequence of tragedies that had begun with the death of Senator McMaster in 1887. The cumulative effect of these setbacks, particularly MacVicar's decision in 1890, dictated a large-scale review of the entire administration of the university. The Charter had provided, in addition to a chancellor, for two principals to preside respectively over arts and theology. It had been felt for some time, however, even before the casualty rate assumed alarming proportions, that since both departments were housed in McMaster Hall and had been 'brought into the most intimate association' their administrations should be unified and placed under the chancellor, who could then discharge the duties of both principalships as well. Early in 1893 the requisite amendment was made to the Act of 1887 and this arrangement came formally into effect.

In seeking a successor to MacVicar the Board of Governors had initially gone outside the institution for a candidate. When the latter, a Dr Jesse B. Thomas, declined after a long period of delay, it was decided to bestow the post upon the energetic Theodore Harding Rand, who had made a creditable showing as acting chairman of the Arts Department following MacVicar's withdrawal. The question is why the experienced Rand had not been picked at once for the position. Had it been felt in 1890 that new blood was needed at the top? After all, MacVicar, Castle, and Rand were virtually synonymous with the TBC and had become fixtures on the scene. Or was there a possibility that Rand had been desired all along as a successor and that Thomas's appointment had always been considered a remote possibility at best? But in that case why did it take the Board two years to make up its mind about Rand? It might well be that the action was deferred in order not to offend Rand's opposite number in the Theology Department, Professor Calvin Goodspeed, who had temporarily assumed the duties of the late Principal McGregor. This motive was implied by a statement the Board and the Senate issued following Rand's elevation to the chancellorship in 1892. 'We would have it thoroughly understood' the administrators eagerly reassured the readers of their annual report 'that in deciding to unify the Faculties ... of the University there was no disposition ... to undervalue or depreciate the faithful, self-sacrificing, and efficient work performed during the past two years by Professor Goodspeed, as temporary chairman of the Theological Department.'[60]

Whether or not Goodspeed was mollified by these remarks will never be known, but one can speculate with some confidence about how Rand received the news of his appointment. Just six years before he had undertaken to direct the fortunes of Woodstock College on condition that it be raised up as quickly as possible to university status. Now in 1892, although the locale was changed, he was at last head of a chartered university, one, moreover, that had in its two brief years of existence doubled its faculty and trebled its student body to the comforting total of sixty-two. Before he was forced to retire through ill-health in 1895 Rand presided enthusiastically over the frequent meetings called to complete and refine the undergraduate curriculum, a process that went on simultaneously with the preparation of the first crop of baccalaureates.

When these sixteen hopefuls were graduated at the university's first convocation in the spring of 1894 a writer for a popular magazine was obviously impressed by the spirit of the participants: 'The enthusiasm shown by the students who sat massed in the body of the large assembly ... showed plainly that they were filled with a spirit of loyalty to their university. A stranger suddenly introduced to the scene must have been impressed with the fact that this infant among Canada's universities had already made good progress, and showed signs of possessing innate powers of development, which promised to bring it early to a commanding stature.'[61] Rand and his assembled colleagues would have been hard put to match this eloquence in their own report of the proceedings. Held in the 'capacious audience room' of Walmer Road Church, the colourful ceremony was enhanced by the academic costumes of the graduands. These students had long requested the adoption of a style of formal dress as a means of overcoming 'the disadvantage in their intercourse with students of other Universities' and of fostering 'a true McMaster esprit de corps.'[62] The arts men appeared for their diplomas properly resplendent in mortarboards of the Oxford style and black alpaca gowns lined with white satinette and trimmed with white fur, while the theology graduands, similarly capped, were robed in black gowns lined in lavender. Within months of the convocation an Alumni Society was organized and E.W. Dadson named its first president. As provided for in the Charter, representatives of the Society were appointed to the Senate, a procedure that filled all the prescribed places on that body.[63]

Looking back from the vantage point of the Walmer Road ceremonies and assessing the progress made in the short period since the launching of the university, Rand might have placed near the top of the list of accomplishments the appearance in 1891 of the *McMaster Monthly*. Taken over from Woodstock College where it had functioned intermittently for about a year,[64] the magazine served McMaster as a productive vehicle for faculty member and student alike, and by the time of the graduation exercises of 1894 it had won commendations from a Toronto journal for its 'readable' news department and 'well done editorial work.'[65] The début of the *Monthly* was applauded by the faculty as tantamount to the establishment of an academic chair, a contribution that would complement the formality of the lecture hall. Essays, odes, reviews, historical expositions, and a variety of political commentaries, together with fulsomely eulogistic biographical sketches of Baptist educators, all found prominent places in the early issues of this new university magazine. Its advent coincided with the initial celebration of Founders' Day, the first major social event at McMaster. Probably inspired by Rand, the day was marked by a dinner for faculty and undergraduates and a commemorative ceremony featuring an address on the senator's accomplishments. It ended with a distinctive Randian touch: an original poetry reading.

The appearance of the *Monthly*, the staging of the first convocation, and the hammering out of general and special courses were encouraging achievements for an institution barely five years old. But no one, least of all Rand, minimized the difficulties that faced it, some of which were sombre legacies of the decisions that had determined the location of the TBC and then the university itself in the city of Toronto. To the resolution of those difficulties, some philosophical, others financial, Rand and his successors would now have to devote their energies as the turn of the century approached.

4

In pursuit of goals

The question asked by the original trustees of the Toronto Baptist College had to be asked again in the nineties: Would the rural and small-town churches actively support the university, this ambitious urban venture in higher education? The answer in the days of the TBC had not been encouraging. Only the generosity of Senator McMaster and a corporal's guard of affluent Baptists had bridged the financial gulf excavated by the indifference, if not the hostility, of many congregations. Over-all, the churches' contributions to the university remained distressingly small. In some cases there was a feeling that Woodstock College had been betrayed[1] and that if money were to be released for educational purposes it ought to be given to Fyfe's old enterprise. Years later, sometime Chancellor Oates C.S. Wallace reminisced as follows in a letter that was in places, admittedly, uncomfortably self-pitying: 'there are . . . a few still living who remember what McMaster was in 1895 when I took over its administration, what "snags" had to be dealt with in the churches, what patience and tact were required to win the general and enthusiastic sympathy of many of the churches, how torturingly small were our revenues, how lacking was esprit de corps among students.'[2]

There was another problem too. However competent a MacVicar or a Rand might have been in academic and professional circles, urbane manners meant much less in the farmsteads, villages, and small towns in which so many Baptists still continued to live at the turn of the century. 'There is a large element of our denomination' D.E. Thomson could write as late as 1917 'that will respond to vigorous Anglo-Saxon language but which feels dazed when bombarded with the more accurate but less readily understandable language of the school man.'[3]

Disturbing considerations such as these had forced themselves on the thinking of McMaster's Board of Governors just when an executive change was about to be made at the university. In 1895 illness dictated the resignation of Chancellor Rand as it had Castle's six years before, a turn of events that opened the door to the appointment of the Rev. O.C.S. Wallace as his successor. Wallace's nomination seemed part of an effort to gain for the university the affection and esteem that Woodstock College had long enjoyed in the rural churches of the constituency. Combined with this was an attempt to assure these more humble congregations that the spirit exemplified by Fyfe could and would be fostered at McMaster. At a time when support from the churches was vital the selection of a chancellor whose whole career had been an inspirational one in the pulpit seemed eminently judicious.

A native of Nova Scotia, a graduate of Worcester Academy, Acadia University, and Newton Seminary in Massachusetts, Wallace had served pastorates in the American mid-west and New England before coming to Toronto in 1891 to accept a call to the Bloor Street Church.[4] At his new charge Wallace had made many friends among the congregation, particularly with youthful churchgoers who were impressed by his abundant energy and athletic prowess as a footballer and a tennis player. His ability to communicate with the young was a quality that both Board and Senate had prized highly when they sought a replacement for Rand. In spite of the latter's enviable organizational ability and classroom proficiency, he had often given students an impression of aloofness and rigidity. A man like Rand, grown accustomed to devising and managing administrative systems, fending off politicians, and arranging corporate academic affairs, was not likely to strike up a warm relationship with a student body. 'Founder's Night under Rand' Wallace Cohoe sulphurically recalled 'was a purely memorial service and could hardly have been more stiff and solemn had the corpse been present.'

Oates Wallace, on the other hand, enjoyed much support among the rising college generation who had thrilled to his sermons at Bloor Street Church. This was amply demonstrated in a letter sent him by a grateful undergraduate three years after his appointment as chancellor. 'When the report was first circulated ... concerning [Dr Rand's] resignation,' his correspondent reported, 'a group of the "boys" ... were discussing the question of his successor. The general opinion seemed to be that the Board of Governors would, as usual, go a long distance away for a Chancellor, which caused me to remark they would be very stupid to go out of the country for a Chancellor when O.C.S. Wallace is so near at hand. This remark was received with much approval by all.'[5]

Although the university had only once in its brief existence 'gone away for a Chancellor,' and that after MacVicar's resignation, to this student the practice had become a tradition. This was clearly an exaggeration, but the glowing reference to Wallace was not. If Wallace had tried to build an esprit de corps at McMaster he had succeeded, at least with 'the boys' represented in this group.

To Baptists concerned that their urban university not break faith with them some pointed references in Wallace's inaugural address of 1895 must have been welcome. The new chancellor stressed that 'young men and wo-men, while preparing for the great duties of life, need a clear vision of Christ rather than an alluring sight of the grandeurs and glories of the world.' This dismissal of Mammon, and presumably of the cultural delights of Toronto, was acclaimed by those who had long been exercised about the diversions with which the metropolis might tempt the unwary. Already one contributor to the *Monthly* had denounced the theatrical and athletic displays which threatened the moral welfare of students in particular and of the citizenry in general.

From time to time correspondents also made Wallace acutely aware of the 'offensive conceit noticeable in certain of our College men'; Wallace Cohoe would redfacedly recall his own 'insufferability' when he received his degree at the turn of the century.[6] Another disturbed Baptist, this one a working girl whose lapses into illiteracy add a poignant touch to her criticism, complained that 'i ... have often hurd our Minister ask for help for Students of Mack Master Hall i was passing the Hall Saturday Night I never seen such vulgar-ness in toronto as I seen coming out of the Hall that night unless you put a stop to it I am a fraid that MackMaster will not be thought much of.'[7] For all these correspondents Wallace had time. Tirelessly he sought to assure both the humble and the exalted that the university was not about to become a refuge for snobs and for those who failed to appreciate what the denomina-tion called the 'heart sweat of the people.' Some of his correspondents obviously appreciated his attempts to discourage the bad spirit at the univer-sity of which so many had complained.

In the opening remarks of his inaugural address Wallace had stressed that McMaster 'is not a Pharisee ... is not inclined to mock God and mislead men by a pretentious use of texts from which her heart is far away ... our legend is our creed − In Christ all things consist.' He was saying in a simpler way what Rand had stated four years before on the opening of the Arts Department. But he then proceeded to discuss a vital matter that had been stated differently by his predecessor in the office.

McMaster University exists for the teaching rather than the pursuit of truth. Much of the educational work of the present day is a menace to all that is holiest in faith and loftiest in morality because it is moulded in form and determined in spirit by the contrary of that principle . . . We are not now denying that there is truth to pursue, but we do most confidently and solemnly affirm that there is truth to teach. However vast may be the domain of the unexplored and the unknown, it is yet true that something is known [and is] ours by the . . . attestations of the ages [or] by the unequivocal revelation of God . . . Before such truths as have been abundantly proven or clearly revealed we dare not take the attitude of the . . . doubter and the agnostic . . . It is our aim to send forth . . . scholars whose opinions of truth and whose principles of conduct shall not be . . . a source and occasion of irreligion in the communities in which they live.[8]

This message doubtless gratified the faithful who had feared for the consequences of uninhibited scientific inquiry into the origins of man and the universe. But while the conscientious scholar might welcome the references to vigorous teaching and however much as a Christian he might try to understand Wallace's good intentions, he must have been disturbed by the implications of that provocative message. An acquaintance of Wallace, a college president in Iowa, was certainly disturbed and unhesitatingly expressed himself this way:

When once that spirit — that a 'university exists for the teaching rather than the pursuit of truth' — has laid hold of an institution its zenith has been reached. Like the perfectionists in character no advance is believed possible, no advance will be made . . . every truth that is not brought home to the individual conscience and judgment and there accepted as truth on its own merits is, to a student, a worse than useless incumbrance . . . I believe in the scientific method, the method that is used in *all* good schools at the present day . . . and which the sentence quoted opposes. There is a wide difference between the scientific search for truth and the agnostic search for ignorance.[9]

Wallace may well have agreed that there was indeed a substantial difference between the scientific search for truth and the agnostic search for ignorance but no one will know for sure because Wallace's correspondence contains no reply to the letter from Iowa, nor for that matter other letters of a similar nature. One can only wonder about the reaction from Wallace's colleagues like A.B. Willmott and A.C. McKay, both of whom were thoroughly steeped in the scientific method, the one a recent graduate of Harvard, the other a product of the University of Toronto. One wonders too how J.E. Wells, who had long lamented the lack of organized research, particularly in literary studies, might have responded to Wallace's statement.[10]

It is possible, however, that what Wallace really sought to convey in 1895 was reflected in the letters he shortly received from McMaster graduates who had gone on to postgraduate work at the University of Chicago. 'I tell you honestly' wrote one in 1897 'that it is not McMaster's intellectual training I value most; although I have always taken the greatest pride in your exceptionally efficient general course. But I count most valuable your nurture of true personality, your development of a generous and noble manhood. I believe that many Colleges plan their work with a view to pander to the utilitarian desires of students.'[11] A confrère, Robert Wilson Smith, who later occupied the biology chair at McMaster, took up this theme a month later: 'If I were asked to sum up a comparison of McMaster and Chicago in a few words I would say Chicago tends to develop intellect, McMaster to develop character, manhood.'[12] Both writers were agreed that they had benefited much from the general course and from their alma mater's preparation of her students for life and its challenges.

To Wallace and his colleagues this seemed a reasonably commendable objective for the institution they were directing. At one point Wallace's argument was that money should not be spent exclusively on the intellect but rather on every department of a student's personality, particularly on cultivating his commitment to his fellows and his awareness of the responsibilities that he must discharge in society.[13] Rand had once, in a barrage of verbosity, urged this as the ultimate aim of a university: 'the establishment in the individual of such a relation between his various faculties and powers as shall result in the consciousness of wholeness and unity, and to bring into co-operative activity ... all his energies as the free movement of a living and consciously harmonious organism.'[14]

Wallace's remarks by no means dampened the search for new truths or the questioning of old ones at McMaster in the evaluation of one graduating year. Speaking for his own class of 1901, Archibald T. MacNeill told Wallace that 'it is surprising how many of the boys passed through the crises of their lives. Almost every one of us was caught in that undercurrent of questioning and doubt, and that spirit of unrest that is so prominent in McMaster.'[15] One wonders whether this peculiar spirit of unrest was provoked by Wallace's apparent anti-intellectualism or, conversely, stimulated by his endeavour to prepare students for the challenges of life in the 'outer world.'

In any event, those who took the trouble to write the chancellor invariably spoke highly of the general course as well as of the tone of the institution. The preparation of that course had occupied the better part of four years, and it was advisedly described as a general one. Over the four years of instruction that led to the BA degree, students were required to take annually English, a modern language, Latin or Greek, natural science (biology or chemistry), and mathematics or physics. Beyond the freshman year these staples were augmented by mental science (psychology) in the second year, by a combined course in constitutional history and political economy in the third year, and by church history, education or metaphysics, evidences of Christianity, and Hebrew in the graduating year. Provision, however, was made for those students who obtained high standings in their first-year examinations to do a limited amount of work in the departments in which they had excelled.[16] This shortly led to the creation of special courses designed in large part for prospective high school teachers, the forerunners of the full-fledged honours programs that were formally established when the university was relocated in Hamilton in 1930.

The anxious Wallace, meanwhile, had some cause to congratulate himself and his colleagues on how McMaster's spirit and expanding curriculum were making life worthwhile for some of its most recent graduates. But he was eager to collect a broader sampling of opinion, for he began systematically to solicit the alumni's assessments of their undergraduate careers, and in 1901 he arranged the university's first Alumni Conference. The response to his inquiries ranged from the floridly rhetorical – 'Humanly the movement [at McMaster] is so wise that to shrink from . . . it would be a grave perversion of duty' – to the cryptically encouraging – 'Some people . . . think that Varsity and Queen's are the *only two* institutions on the surface of the earth . . . If McMaster is allowed a fair field she will need no favor.'[17] The unflattering references to sister institutions were to be expected from bumptious alumni. But, significantly, full credit was given to McMaster's 'general education,' which, it was claimed, afforded as good a point of departure for life or for further study as the curriculum at any other university. At least one writer was in a position to compare McMaster with the University of Toronto and at the same time to praise the former's embryonic Master's program. 'I am looking forward' Philo K. Dayfoot wrote in 1896 'to receiving the McMaster MA. I have never been satisfied with the MA which I took from Toronto University, because it only represented one essay (Henry VIII and the English Reformation).'[18] The McMaster records, however, contain no Dayfoot thesis; one wonders whether, if submitted, it amounted in fact to anything more substantial than what had been expected of its author at the University of Toronto.

Among the other bits and pieces of reassurance received by Wallace and his successor, A.C. McKay, were expressions of surprise when wandering alumni learned that their university was favourably regarded in places as far afield as Connecticut, Illinois, and Missouri. Particularly pleasing would have been one letter's endorsement of McMaster 'as in every respect better than Newton [Academy],' a reputable Baptist school in Massachusetts which Wallace himself had attended. 'I failed to see [there]' the writer continued 'the unity that exists at McMaster.'[19] On the professional side another correspondent, the primciple of a collegiate institute in London patently loyal to his alma mater, announced that McMaster 'gives the best course in Canada for the secondary school teacher...Especially in Hamilton & also in London...the McMaster course is most favourably thought of.'[20]

Brickbats, however, invariably accompanied the bouquets. One image of McMaster took generations to dispel. Nothing short of a lavishly funded public relations campaign could have made any headway against the notions that the university was just 'a little school for Baptists' and that there was 'no University worth considering but Toronto'. Admittedly, Dean W.S. McLay periodically tried to point out that McMaster was 'in no sense sectarian though it is a Baptist institution.' As he wrote in 1913: 'Among our professors [nineteen in all] are an Anglican, a Lutheran, a Disciple [of Christ], and three Presbyterians, and among our students are representatives of all denominations, including Roman Catholics and two Jews. In this respect we are only like other universities, but I mention the facts because those who are not acquainted with them are apt to imagine that McMaster is limited to Baptists, which is by no means the case.'[21] What proved even more disturbing than references to Baptist parochialism, particularly for those who had once championed McMaster's independence as a means of affording proper instruction in the new knowledge of political science, was the report that the University of Toronto appeared to be offering a more productive course in that discipline than McMaster.[22]

Wallace also consistently heard from the theology graduates, a group with whom he understandably communed with greater ease and assurance. But even in this milieu he was acquainted with unpleasant home truths from far and near. A correspondent in India bitterly complained in 1899 about the alleged failure of the old TBC to produce missionaries for the foreign, and particularly the Far Eastern, field. Before he ended on the hopeful note that Wallace's efforts might furnish such 'emissaries of world wide thought,' the missionary unloaded his grievances upon those who had led the TBC in the eighties:

I must confess that for some years my soul was prejudiced against the [TB] College. I believe it was because of the conviction that the men then there were narrow, selfishly ambitious academically, and extremely provincial in their conception of God's Kingdom. This was forced on me owing to their attitude against my coming to India or any man whom they particularly wanted at home . . . The founder [McMaster], the then President [Castle], and Dr MacVicar were...the chief offenders in the count.

But the tide, he added hopefully, is 'coming up . . . The men of the old provincial days when America's needs were everything and God existed solely as the patron and benefactor of the North American Continent, "the hinge of the ages," the last testing place of Christianity . . . these men are passing.'[23]

Echoing the complaints of some prominent Toronto Baptists, the missionary charged that MacVicar and Castle were more concerned about their academic careers and the insular needs of America than they were about genuine world evangelism. In any case North America, he implored, ought not to be regarded as the '*ne plus ultra* of Providence.' A few years later the same correspondent thought he had cause to cheer when he learned of the McMaster 'Band Movement,' that 'consecrated body of soul winners'[24] who went out preaching the gospel to farm folk, factory workers, and flagging congregations. Hailed by the Baptist in India as 'just one of God's culminating lines,' the members of the Band were dismissed by Wallace Cohoe as misguided misfits or, even worse, as potential troublemakers who had no clear idea of what they were supposed to be doing at university. While Wallace thought more kindly of the Band than Cohoe, he may be forgiven if he failed to warm to the missionary's prophecy that the Movement 'may lead to the closing of the [university] and the turning of the whole staff to the great work of winning souls.'[25]

Although Wallace was not eager to turn McMaster into a kind of storefront university serving far-flung Baptist mission stations, he admitted that a larger effort ought to have been made to evangelize India and China. That Asia had been comparatively neglected at McMaster was periodically borne out by the evidence. For example, of all the graduates of the TBC only six had ventured to the Indian subcontinent, while fully sixty-four and six respectively had taken up work in Canada and the United States.[26] But these statistics had been compiled by the editors of the *Monthly* to refute another charge levelled at the TBC and its successor by aggrieved congregations in Canada. These critics had assumed that the life style enjoyed by the occupants of McMaster Hall predisposed them to forsake the rigours of a Canadian pastorate and to seek 'soft ones in the States.' Not only this, the evidence in the *Monthly* demonstrated that of some sixty graduates working in the

Canadian field only seven enjoyed the supposed advantages that went with an urban pulpit. Unfortunately the magazine's account ended with the very sort of flippancy that so easily angered the people in the townships. 'Of course, McMaster has grown big enough by this time' it remarked 'to be easy game for gunners great and small.'

Pacifying a missionary in India did not, for obvious reasons, enjoy the priority at Wallace's desk that the appeasement of local congregations did. Nevertheless the complaints of a Baptist in, say, Stouffville and of a missionary on the other side of the world had some common ground; both felt that too much time and money were being spent on educational extravagances at the university and not enough on evangelization, foreign and domestic. As one Barrie churchgoer plaintively put it: 'the Mission interest is in extreme danger of being most effectively side-tracked and all because the education interest is . . . presented to the people in a systematic Common-sense way, while the Mission interest is . . . left to the plan or no-plan of Tom, Dick & Harry.'[27]

If, as Carson J. Cameron indicated in his short biography of Wallace, the chancellor made one of his tasks the restoration of the 'good feeling that prevailed among Baptists toward our educational institutions in the age of Dr Fyfe,' it was imperative that he convince the churches that McMaster had their interests at heart and was attempting to serve their needs. But it was a 'hard fight' and 'like a soldier on the battlefield' in the words of another observer 'he sometimes advanced on his knees.'

For every welcome writer who might have complained of the 'vulgar clowns . . . in Baptist pulpits' and urged the sending out of good McMaster men to fill them,[28] there seemed to be at least two who dismissed the need for McMaster and an educated ministry. 'The people of Caledonia' warned one pastor, 'do not want to see the face of anyone advocating an offering for [a] McMaster fund . . . the people don't want to hear anything about Education.'[29] And A.A. Ayer of the Board of Governors could report some years before from the reasonably civilized metropolis of Montreal that '9 out of 10 of all the additions . . . to our churches . . . are from the middle and lower classes . . . [and] are not very polished . . . and not very anxious to support the university.'[30]

In the midst of all this Wallace might learn one day that a Baptist printer had sharply reduced his annual donation to McMaster because it had unaccountably gone 'outside the denomination to get the calendar printed.' Another day the chancellor would feel obliged to take time out to ponder requests from those who obviously regarded him as the fount of all information. A student at a Tennessee business college, for example, wanted to know early in 1900 whether 'we are in the 19th or the 20th century?'[31] Another Baptist made this enquiry:

Please excuse me for ... trespassing upon your precious time ... Will you kindly inform me as to the best place to purchase a Baptismal Suit? What is the price of a good one, including all the charges? ... Are they generally large enough to go over your shoes and pants? ... The reason I ask so many questions is, I have the offer of a suit here, but the pants and rubbers are separate, just firmly cemented together ... The pants are quite small in the leg. I can use the suit but not without taking off my shoes. I have been offered this for ten dollars, payable in installments. The suit has been very little used. It is owned by an old Congregational Minister ... It is about as good as it ever was.[32]

Still other correspondents were upset about the meagre representation that Baptists had on school boards and teaching staffs of elementary and secondary schools. They repeatedly urged the university to correct a state of affairs described by one Baptist in these terms: 'There is always a great big chance of a Presbyterian clergyman being on the High School Board in any town, and I find that when making appointments they have as much breadth of mind as a sunbeam ... We are in greater need of Baptist teachers, lawyers [and officials] than of Ministers at the present time.'[33] Unfortunately the chancellor's replies to such communications have not survived.

Meanwhile, in order to establish a closer liaison with the churches and to educate those who were 'ignorant of the completeness of our equipment at McMaster,' Wallace in 1904 appointed his close friend Carson J. Cameron as the university's first field secretary. By the time Cameron completed his first tour of duty two years later he had probably become, next to the chancellor himself, the best travelled Baptist in Ontario and Quebec. The son of a Scottish-born pastor and a native of Peterborough, Cameron had taught school for a number of years before taking a year of arts at the University of Toronto where he was an award winner in classics. After McMaster opened he joined its pioneer class and was active in the university's varied societies. He served as well as business manager of the *Monthly* and capped his undergraduate career by being elected chairman of the student body. Graduating with both the BA and B TH degrees, Cameron accepted a call to an Ottawa Valley church, where, over the years, he persuaded a considerable number of young people to attend McMaster. His marked abilities and commanding personality led next to his appointment as associate superintendent of home missions, a responsibility that put him in touch with virtually every congregation in the constituency. Given his vital background and his thorough familiarity with the university's affairs, it would have been surprising had Wallace not picked him in 1904 for the task of advertising the university's facilities.

For the better part of two years, after which he returned to the home missions field, Cameron promoted the cause of Christian education in the 453 churches on his rambling circuit. Pages of his field notes have survived to indicate the exhaustiveness of his travels, to record the results of countless interviews, and to give samples of the educational messages he broadcast from the widely scattered pulpits that were, sometimes grudgingly, placed at his disposal. Cameron's biographer claims that during his stewardship some $75,000 was raised from congregations and individuals for a Forward Movement on behalf of the University.[34] But the agonizing hours he must have spent soliciting moral and material support for McMaster, the high emotional price he must have had to pay for whatever dividends he did reap, may be imagined after reading what his successor said that he in turn had been obliged to undergo. 'I will not vex your souls' Stewart S. Bates reported confidentially to the Senate a few years later 'by dilating upon how many letters must be written, how many visits and addresses made, how many excuses met, and how much pleading there must be, before ... money is obtained for Institutions, which are at the very heart of our denomination's life. May you never know how often your representative is made to feel that his coming is unwelcome, that he is a beggar for a poor cause, who must be given a few coins to be gotten rid of.'[35]

In spite of the prodigious efforts of a Cameron or a Bates, Baptists could still write in and complain that 'you people do not do enough personal advertising ... We ought to get in touch more with Baptist students *all over the land*.'[36] Clearly what was required was a well staffed public relations office and a team of educational salesmen continually perambulating the constituency. Just as clearly, such an elaborate operation was financially out of the question.

Yet to 'reach Baptist students all over the land' had, ironically enough, been sought nearly twenty years before by the founders of the TBC when they had urged Acadia University and the short-lived institution known as Prairie College to send their theology students to Toronto. In the interval this merger of Baptist educational efforts had remained in abeyance while the TBC struggled to establish itself and when plans went forward for the founding of the university. Part way through his regime, however, Wallace was reminded of the original ambition in a series of dazzling letters he received from an active Baptist layman and high school teacher on the west coast. 'I have great expectations for McMaster,' wrote A.J. Pineo from Victoria in the summer of 1899, 'situated as she is, centrally, and in the most populous and progressive city of our Dominion, surrounded by a legal constituency which stretches from ocean to ocean, it seems to me that she must always be the great source and centre of educational power and influence among the Baptists of Canada.' Although he noted that Acadia University, Manitoba College, and a proposed institution in British Columbia would be sufficient for their own localities, 'it is to McMaster' Pineo maintained 'that we must look for the unifying ... of the results reached by these more local institutions.' These he described grandiloquently in another letter as 'a chain of educational fortresses stretching across the Continent.' Pineo concluded on the hopeful note that out of such an arrangement would come opportunities for postgraduate work 'such as are now offered at [the larger American] universities.'[37]

The ambitious militancy of the scheme – this talk of Baptist strongpoints where Christian learning could be vigorously consolidated and extended – and the designation of McMaster as a kind of GHQ for the whole operation doubtless gratified the vanity and stirred the imagination of a good many eastern Baptists. C.J. Holman, for one, had always believed that McMaster was the 'greatest Agency the Denomination possesses and that we can do nothing that will advance more the denomination's interests and the wider cause of Christianity than by making the University the greatest possible success.'[38] David B. Harkness, another western Baptist, went even further than Pineo. In a burst of denominational and nationalist enthusiasm he proposed a Baptist University of Canada, a central body with which all existing institutions could affiliate. 'The great advantages of this [arrangement]' Harkness claimed 'would be the dignity which such a larger institution would bring to the affiliated colleges; the avenues provided for fuller fellowship between the educational men of various parts of the country.'[39]

This was exhilarating talk at the turn of the century and revealed a great deal about the pride and ambitions of these energetic Baptists in strategic parts of the country. Having succeeded in business or in the professions they were anxious now to help promote a system of education under denominational auspices that would provide coming generations of Canadian Baptists with first-rate institutions capable of preserving their spiritual legacy and of enabling their graduates to cope with the demands of contemporary society. The advocates of the plan belonged, they proudly believed, to a 'peculiar people' with the capacity to make unique contributions to Canadian life. What better way to achieve this end, they asked themselves, than to establish a chain of Baptist institutions clear across the country?

Soon enough the heady visions of the Pineos and the Harknesses were rudely punctured by harsh financial and geographical realities. While it was all very flattering that McMaster had been singled out as the showpiece of the program, the university would be expected to assume much of the expense of founding new sister ventures or sustaining old ones in the west. That expectation would have to be discouraged: 'since the work they now have in hand taxes the revenue of the University to the fullest limit,' the westerners were told, the university could not come to the assistance of Manitoba or British Columbia. This unwelcome answer only served to confirm the growing suspicion on the prairies and beyond the mountains that eastern Canadian Baptists were not concerned with their problems. McMaster particularly, said the westerners, was 'letting [our] work languish for the sake of making a good numerical show in Ontario.'

Ultimately, the Manitoba Baptists proceeded on their own and in 1899 organized Brandon College. Further west, in Pineo's country, coreligionists bravely started up Okanagan College, an undertaking in which Chancellor Wallace took a keen personal interest.[40] Although in 1911 and 1912 both institutions affiliated with McMaster, thus faintly redeeming the hopes of Pineo and Harkness, only Brandon survived. Okanagan College succumbed during the first world war after a series of crippling financial setbacks. Throughout, Pineo's scheme had depended upon McMaster's capacity to afford men, leadership, and resources, but, as the university's Board of Governors had stated more than once, they had enough problems to keep them fully occupied in Toronto. Moreover, an institution that in the summer of 1906 could not post a cheque to a faculty member because the 'Treasurer [was] away wandering in Muskoka [and was] not expected to return until the end of August,'[41] was not likely to have the administrative muscle to manage the affairs of a 'chain of Baptist fortresses' from one end of the land to the other.

No one was more aware than Wallace and his successor, A.C. McKay, of the enormity of the problems that faced McMaster within its own limited hinterland. The fostering of an esprit de corps, the pacification of disgruntled congregations, the acquisition of competent instructors, the recruitment of students, and, above all, the enlargement of the university's facilities, particularly in the natural sciences, all combined to tax the inventiveness of McMaster's administration in the opening years of the century. And invariably, whenever the call went out for increased revenue and financial support, there were Baptists who immediately raised the question of university federation. In their view McMaster ought to reconsider the decision of 1888 and, instead of exhorting funds from the denomination for underwriting needed improvements in the arts and science curricula, look once again at the advisability of confederating with the University of Toronto. According to these people the latter had made good the deficiencies in its curriculum of a generation before, the flaws that Wells and others had stressed as making necessary an independent Baptist institution. A.M. Denovan pulled few punches when he wrote the following lines to Wallace in 1904: 'McMaster [has struggled] in its own way to do University work against fearful odds. Poverty produces principles as wealth often does . . . and now the poverty of McMaster University has given rise to another principle, namely that a man who knows a little of everything and not very much of anything is much better than a man who is master of his subject.' After thus assaulting the reputation of McMaster's general course, Denovan concluded that, through federation, 'the difficulties of carrying on an education for which she is not thoroughly equipped and on account of which her graduates in specials at least come into the field handicapped for the race, will be removed, and . . . she will be able to do the [theological] work for which she is fitted thoroughly and well.'[42]

While others were not as blunt as Denovan, their question was substantially the same: Why maintain McMaster at expense when we have the state university in the park? For the science faculty in particular it was unpleasant to be told that no amount of denominational sentiment would prompt one father to dissuade his son from attending the University of Toronto where he believed he could secure better scientific equipment. Another opponent of independence, Dr Frederick Tracy, a prominent Baptist layman and an academic with psychology texts to his credit, argued that 'four years' membership in a small homogeneous college . . . [tends] to restrict the mental horizon and result[s] in something less than a truly "liberal" education.'[43]

To the argument about the restrictiveness of a small homogeneous college Wallace Cohoe might have been able to offer a rebuttal. He recalled that his own class at McMaster had a 'very close association with our Professors', and he was inclined to think that 'it was not a bad thing for us – that under this guidance we were obliged to do a great many things for ourselves which in larger institutions might have consisted in bottle feeding.'[44] The comments volunteered by fellow alumnus Charles Eldrid Burke a few years later would have provided some welcome ammunition for the anti-federationists at this time. 'During the last two or three years,' he wrote the chancellor in 1911, 'as I have come more or less in touch with the work of some of the bigger Universities I have been more and more impressed with the importance of the work done by the smaller univ's and colleges, and their place in the system of National Education is certainly receiving more and more recognition from the larger state institutions . . . [in California and] the middle West.'[45]

Some of Tracy's critics eagerly pointed out that he would predictably promote the advantages of the 'State university' in Toronto, having served on its faculty since 1893 in the Classics and Philosophy Departments. Nonetheless, some Baptists were impressed by the solemn assurances from this obviously devout coreligionist that his own experience in University College had convinced him that the institution was not the godless school that so many had scorned a generation earlier. They might not have been so impressed had they known that considerable dissatisfaction had recently been expressed within the University of Toronto itself with the behaviour and the qualifications of some University College faculty. According to the criticism, which an official report sought to deflate, 'one person was said fit not for university but a technical institution' and, moreover, 'wasted his time in military and social matters.' Another professor was ominously labelled a drinker and, either because or in spite of this, was 'not held in esteem as an economist by city business men.'[46]

In the meantime, still another prominent Baptist, a Maritimer, while admitting that he had an 'imperfect grasp of the situation,' told Wallace that if McMaster was all that anxious to maintain its independence 'it almost looks as if it would do best to hold exclusively by a strong Arts course, and let the science men go.'[47] But to let the science men go was understandably the last thing that McKay and his colleagues in the natural sciences were prepared to consider. By this date, apart from McKay, who had assumed the deanship in arts while continuing to lecture in mathematics and physics, the sciences at the university were represented by R.W. Smith and Wallace Cohoe. Smith, who returned to his alma mater armed with a Chicago doctorate in biology to succeed William Piersol, was the first McMaster graduate in arts to become a member of its faculty. 'He is living proof' a colleague wrote approvingly of him years later 'that one may believe in God and Evolution, and by his wise mediation of the truths of Science he strengthens the Christian faith of those who sit at his feet.'[48] For his part, Cohoe, named to take the place of A.B. Willmott who left the university in the spring of 1900, came back from Harvard to occupy the chairs of chemistry and geology and to undertake instruction in quantitative analysis and related electrolytic work.

Smith and Cohoe saw that for proper instruction in their disciplines a larger plant would have to be built on Bloor Street and additional staff taken on. 'It does not seem possible' Cohoe wrote in the spring of 1905 'that under the [existing] arrangement one could be expected to do the work outlined with justice to the student, much less find time to get up new work of extreme difficulty.' He noted mournfully that he was not really proficient to teach some of the subjects advertised and much might have to be swatted up.[49] Although a welcome new building, appropriately named Castle Memorial Hall, had been constructed in 1901 to house a library and an assembly hall, laboratory space was still at a premium. The complaints about crowded quarters which had been a nightmare for Wallace in 1898 had, if anything, become shriller in the interval. By this time McMaster's student population had climbed from the modest sixty of Rand's first year as chancellor to over 170, a fair proportion of whom were enrolled in science courses. The nagging question was raised again: ought the denomination to undertake the building of more spacious facilities for the work already undertaken or should the whole matter be reviewed and an overture made to the University of Toronto for affiliation on its terms?

Before the matter was definitively settled Wallace resigned from the chancellorship and from the university, after a lengthy tenure of ten years. A 'pulpit man' from the start, he wished to return to his first love while he was still responsive to the needs of congregations. When the university's third chancellor stepped down in 1905 he opened the door to the appointment of Alexander Charles McKay as his successor. The move surprised few. McKay had been lecturer, registrar, professor, and then dean in arts, a post created in 1903 to meet the growing administrative needs of the university. The new executive head of McMaster had thus, in the space of fifteen years, occupied nearly every position of leadership and responsibility in the institution. His brother, W.J. McKay, the classicist and editor, after J.E. Wells, of the *Canadian Baptist*, would furnish him invaluable assistance as a colleague both inside and outside the university. The demand for imaginative direction, the need for turning back the federationists, and, once that was achieved, the task of finding the men and the means to enlarge facilities and to safeguard standards, all contrived to make McKay an obvious choice. His elevation to the chancellorship left a vacancy in the deanship in arts, one immediately filled by Walter Scott McLay, the holder of the English chair and a graduate, like McKay, of the University of Toronto.

As it turned out, McKay's exertions and arguments, combined with the determination of the denomination's leaders, settled the question of federation in McMaster's favour at least for the foreseeable future. In spite of the impressive though rather timeworn arguments of Tracy and his fellow federationists and in spite of the odds that the university appeared to face, the decision was taken to continue on an independent course. To be sure, the federation question would come up again and would not finally be laid to rest until the university physically uprooted itself as an immediate neighbour of the University of Toronto and migrated to Hamilton a quarter century later.

For the time being, however, independence had again been successfully defended, but at a physical and emotional cost impossible to measure. The corollary – the expansion of McMaster's plant and its curriculum, especially in the sciences – had to be undertaken at once. But it was well known that

Baptist donors were already reeling from one Forward Movement and could meet only a fraction of the estimated $50,000 cost of building a projected Science Hall. It had already been reckoned in the spring of 1905 that apart from building and maintenance costs at least $11,000 would have to be spent over a three-year period on permanent equipment, with the expectation that physics and chemistry would consume the lion's share of this awesome outlay. There was the recognition, too, that salaries would have to be increased in order to retain qualified personnel; salaries already accounted for nearly two-thirds of the university's annual operating expenses, which in 1905 stood at some $43,000.[50]

In these circumstances it is understandable that C.J. Holman, as spokesman for the Board, should strongly urge the new chancellor to follow the example of other university heads and approach the philanthropists Andrew Carnegie and John D. Rockefeller for assistance. Holman recalled that Carnegie had recently donated a large sum to Acadia University for essentially the same purpose,[51] so why not, he asked McKay, have McMaster file a similar application? In the meantime, the lawyer, with his customary directness, wrote Thomas Trotter, Acadia's president, and learned from him how best to approach the Scottish-born industrialist for funds. Trotter, who was a firm believer in the expansion of the sciences and had encouraged the introduction of a B SC program at Acadia, was only too happy to oblige a sister institution. In Carnegie's case, Trotter advised brevity; in Rockefeller's, as complete a statement as possible. He mentioned another point: 'I am aware, of course, that some of your consitutency would deprecate taking aid from the Standard Oil King, but they might not object to assistance from Carnegie ... [The latter] is particularly interested in science, and in assisting the smaller colleges ... and ... your science building is just what would appeal to him.'[52]

Whatever scruples the university might have had about accepting money from Rockefeller were obviously swallowed, for he and Carnegie both received lengthy appeals, contrary to Trotter's advice, from Chancellor McKay and the Hon. John Dryden, chairman of the Board of Governors. What was perfectly clear throughout, however, was that the administration was prepared to go ahead with its plans regardless of the outcome of the negotiations with the American industrialists. The university trusted that if the latter and the denomination could not meet the demand then by some kind of minor miracle 'a few people of fair means among us' might do so. This information was candidly conveyed to both Carnegie and Rockefeller when the appeals for aid were mailed off to them in the late summer of 1906. Indeed, by that date tenders had already been called and construction begun on the project. By July, the registrar, Abraham C. Newcombe, could assure the vacationing

McKay that the 'offices are ringing with the clang of hammers [and] the Partitions are in place . . . the new building is rising fast . . . [and] you would hardly know the spot now.'[53] Those students for whom overcrowding had become an academic way of life were encouraged by the thought that they would soon have possession of the commodious Science Hall.

Early in the New Year good news was received. Rockefeller agreed to donate the requisite $60,000 – presumably Carnegie had bowed out of the picture – provided the Baptists of Ontario and Quebec raised a subscription of at least $5,600. This condition the university cheerfully accepted on behalf of the denomination. By the fall of 1907 the architect commissioned to design the Science Hall could volunteer this description of the new edifice: 'It makes no claims as to beauty,' he began ruefully. 'The stern decree of the Board of Governors left no option. It was to be a plain workshop or nothing, and plain workshop it is . . . All the rooms are lofty and well lighted, having almost a surplus of window openings . . . There is nothing in the building to burn except the fittings and furniture. The Basement has . . . a large apartment for [a] Museum.'[54] He went on to note a little more enthusiastically that the building housed spacious laboratories for physics, optics, chemistry, and biology, and, in addition, it was crowned with a small greenhouse, all this at a cost of $53,000. A future physics professor at McMaster had cause to congratulate McKay on providing a workshop as standard equipment for that department, complete with a lathe, motor, generator, and the requisite tools, all to be 'operated as required by student mechanics.'[55]

Professor Henry Franklin Dawes was clearly indebted to McKay's keen interest not only in theoretical and applied physics but also in technical education for its own sake. The task of preparing skilled machinists for the industrial society burgeoning outside the modest campus of McMaster University amounted almost to a passion in the chancellor.[56] The spokesmen for that society, the Canadian Manufacturers' Association and various municipal boards of trade, had for years been urging stronger provincial and even federal support for the improved technical education that would enable Canada 'to hold her own in the great industrial warfare now in progress amongst the nations.'[57] While McKay may have had his doubts about the propriety of industrial warmongering, he had none whatsoever about the work of the Toronto School of Technology, an institution in which he took an active interest. By 1901 it reciprocated by offering him its principalship. Described by the obviously impressed McMaster Senate as a 'very important, influential, and lucrative position,' it was nonetheless turned down by McKay. It remained clear, however, that he never lost sight of the need for promoting technical education, and ultimately he left McMaster to take the office first offered him at the turn of the century.

That move, however, was not even contemplated when McKay and his colleagues eagerly set about in 1907 to exploit the advantages that accrued from the completion of the new Science Hall. To begin with, more sophisticated courses had to be planned at both the undergraduate and postgraduate levels and new personnel appointed to the faculty. To provide recruits for research and executive positions in Canadian industry McKay drafted a course leading to the B SC degree. When his program was approved by the Senate in the spring of 1908 it excited a considerable response from highly qualified students who had hitherto been restricted to the general science course.[58]

As for new staff, a replacement had to be found for Wallace Cohoe who resigned in 1907 out of a 'wholehearted desire to put Chemistry to work' in the realm of manufacturing.[59] Robert McLaurin, one of Cohoe's most able students, who had done graduate work at Harvard, was among the first to apply for the vacant position with the promise that he would 'make that department hum.' But another applicant was finally selected, an older chemist with the resounding name of John Bishop Tingle. It would appear that for a time the chancellor had some doubts about Tingle's candidacy, but by the spring of 1907 they had been dispelled and he was agreeing with his dean, W.S. McLay, that 'we are making no mistake about him.'[60]

Professor Tingle's credentials appeared respectable enough. He had worked under Sir Henry Roscoe at Manchester and had been trained by equally reputable chemists at the University of Munich, where, in 1899, he obtained his doctorate.[61] Unquestionably, too, Tingle was a published chemist. After his first year at McMaster he had papers accepted for publication in prestigious American chemical journals and was preparing new editions of his previous works on spectrum analysis and carbon compounds. He insisted, moreover, that his students, many of whom he claimed had been 'very badly trained,' should conduct original research under his supervision.[62] Tingle also made arrangements with the Universities of Minnesota and Illinois whereby those institutions furnished his more promising protégés with lucrative doctoral fellowships. Apparently his recommendations counted for a great deal. Dean McLay conceded that 'one could rely [upon them] implicitly . . . for Professor Tingle is never inclined to say a word more than the facts absolutely justify.'[63]

Some of Chancellor McKay's teaching load, meanwhile, was taken over in 1906 by John L. Hogg, H.F. Dawes's predecessor. A Toronto graduate and a Harvard PHD with publications to his credit and seven years' teaching experience behind him, Hogg served as professor of physics until 1910 when he departed to occupy the newly established chair at the University of Saskatchewan. Judging from the record no one could have accused Hogg of belittling his discipline, one that had recently been stimulated by new theories and applications. 'It may seem . . . to you' the physicist wrote McKay on one occasion 'that I am asking too much for a Department which has so recently been made to occupy its proper place; but I regard the work in Physics to be more fundamental and more comprehensive, and more intimately related to modern life than any of the other science departments, and in saying this I do not, for a moment, wish to disparage any other department.'[64] Then in 1908 work in one of those other departments was strengthened by the appointment of Cohoe's classmate, William Findlay, a Chicago PHD, to the chair in mathematics.

These acquisitions freed the chancellor for policy-making functions and for planning new ventures. Anxious to meet yet another need of a dramatically changing and demanding society, McKay aimed at laying the foundations of a medical school at the university. Years before, indeed within two years of its opening, McMaster had been invited to affiliate with the Trinity Medical College,[65] which since its founding in 1850 had experienced a chequered career of religious strife and financial woes. Although the matter was briefly discussed in 1892 nothing came of the overture, and a decade later the Trinity Medical College was amalgamated with the University of Toronto.[66]

In view of Trinity's record of difficulties and its decision to join the 'state university' why, one might ask, did McKay seek to follow Trinity's earlier example and organize a medical school in conjunction with an independently supported university? Significantly, the first step – the appointment of a Senate committee to examine the feasibility of a medical faculty – was taken in the spring of 1905 just when McKay was vigorously turning back the federationists' campaign. A clue to McKay's motives came to light in a letter he received from a Fort William physician who had read about his intentions in the *Canadian Baptist*. The news had obviously come as a surprise because the physician confessed that he 'had no thought that there was any possibility of establishing a Medical department at the University.' He went on to quote the comments that McKay had made by way of explaining his decision: 'If each year we could bring under our influence a large number of students preparing for the medical profession it evidently is our duty to undertake the obligations involved.' McKay's correspondent obviously approved of this ideal: 'In my few years of practice in this western country I have realized more and more the disregard of a great majority of the medical men for God and His Truth . . . I should welcome a sphere where I could devote my energies or a part of them to such a work as you propose to establish.'[67] A number of similar letters soon reached McKay, some of which appear to have been written by self-seeking medical men who had unremunerative practices in remote sections of the country. And at least one presumably unemployed architect anxiously sought the commission for planning the proposed medical facility.

Not only this, but there were rumours, as grandiose as they were unfounded, that massive benefactions were about to be lavished on the project. Professor William Findlay wrote McKay from Winnipeg that he had 'quite a string of telephone calls from people ... asking for confirmation of the newspaper story that Rockefeller had given two millions to found a medical department at McMaster.'[68] While only wishing that the Rockefeller story were true, the chancellor began to receive unsolicited advice and suggestions from other quarters. One writer reported that a leading Toronto physician was about to urge McMaster to take over Grace Hospital in the city. 'The present lady superintendent' McKay was advised 'is Miss Paton ... a member of the Baptist Church [and] they have a chapel service of hymn singing ... every morning [while] the nurses in training assemble for worship, [a practice] that would harmonize with the McMaster ideal.[69]

But none of these projects, real or imagined, ever reached fruition. The pressure of other business and the enormous expense that would have been incurred were sufficient to stall consideration of a medical school at McMaster, and early in 1908 the investigating committee struck three years earlier was regretfully discharged. One could speculate that a grave internal disorder at the university had also played a critical part in shelving its plans for expansion. The controversy that erupted at this time over the alleged unorthodoxy of two faculty members consumed much of the energy and resources that McKay would have preferred to devote to academic pursuits.

5

Strife

The first inkling of serious trouble cropped up in 1904 when a replacement was sought for Dr Calvin Goodspeed following his retirement from the chair of systematic theology. To this point the university had been spared the sort of strife that had infected some American schools when the higher criticism and its ally, modernism, had collided with the conservative force that would shortly take the name 'fundamentalism.' But McMaster was not the only Canadian institution to come under fire early in the century. Such sister colleges in Toronto as Knox, Victoria, and Trinity also went through a time of troubles as alarmed and vocal defenders of orthodoxy dug in their heels to combat the spread of the heresy that Biblical scholarship had been propagating for some twenty years. The difficulties that broke out at McMaster toward the end of Wallace's administration and engulfed his successor's arose out of the suspicion that new appointments to the university were being drawn from the ranks of scholars who sympathized with the modernist position. The appointment that appeared to cause the most concern was that of the Rev. Isaac George Matthews who was accused by some of a serious lack of 'spirituality' and a disregard for the ideals of Professor Goodspeed.

Esteemed by the Senate as a 'tower of strength against immature and erroneous teaching,' Goodspeed had served the institution from the very outset and had seldom been reluctant to tackle the higher criticism from the lectern, the pulpit, and the editorial pages of the *Monthly*.[1] 'I am very grateful to Dr Goodspeed' one alumnus informed Wallace 'for his conservatism, because I get so much of the other thing, indeed one can scarcely pick up a periodical without meeting it.' And in Cato, New York, an aging Malcolm

MacVicar, the university's first chancellor, added his voice to those urging a rejection of 'untried views,' praying that 'God may raise up liberal friends that will make possible [McMaster's] continued growth as a *conservative Christian institution* of learning.'[2]

Equally grateful for Goodspeed's conservatism was the Rev. Elmore Harris, a Toronto and TBC graduate and pastor of Walmer Road Church. Still very much a pre-millenialist, he was well regarded in the denomination and was a respected member of the university Senate. His praise for Goodspeed only served to sharpen his distaste for Matthews's appointment, a distaste freely expressed when the newcomer's name came up for the Senate's consideration in the spring of 1904. 'I am quite clear about the quality of the new man with one exception' Harris observed 'and that is as regards his spirituality ... I am quite clear that in a Theological School especially, the personality of the man counts for almost everything. Of course I do not allude to a holiness which is mere cant and consists of phrases and sanctimonious looks, but I am sure you see the vast importance of a character like that of Abraham and Moses, who looked for a city which hath foundations.'[3]

On the face of it, Matthews's credentials seemed sufficiently respectable. A McMaster graduate in arts of 1897, a keen student of Hebrew and its cognate languages, and the holder of a master's degree from his alma mater, he had preached on the west coast and edited the *Western Baptist* before returning to McMaster to enrol and excel in its Theology Department. According to the *Monthly,* moreover, he had been the unanimous choice for the faculty position among his fellow graduates.[4] An examination of the *Western Baptist* while it was under Matthews's editorial direction revealed that, if anything, he was a formidable defender of 'spirituality' and a critic of anything that smacked of heresy as he saw it.[5]

Yet Harris still continued to have misgivings about Matthews, and in view of the clergyman's standing in the community they were bound to receive considerable attention. Long active on behalf of the Foreign Missions Board, Harris had, at the invitation of the Senate, been giving well received courses at the university for would-be missionaries since 1890.[6] For years he had also offered a series of special lectures on evangelistic methods, all of which he generously did without fee. His independent means as the son of the affluent John Harris, the implement-maker, and his desire to evangelize in the lecture hall made him a much sought-after extramural lecturer. Moreover, as president of the Toronto Bible Training School, he effectively twinned his pre-millenialist message with a call for the reassertion of the Bible's place in church and society. It is not surprising that Harris organized in Toronto a branch of the American Bible League, founded in 1903 for that express purpose.[7] Using these varied sounding boards he unhesitatingly voiced his displeasure with Matthews's lack of 'spirituality.'

It was widely held that Harris's preoccupation with the presumed dangers of the new appointment resulted in part from his dissatisfaction with the content of McMaster's arts course, the same course that had helped to produce the man that was the object of his concern. When federation with the University of Toronto happened to come up for discussion just at this time Harris urged the university to abandon independence and affiliate with its neighbours. Although he knew his critics would say that his judgment was coloured by the fact that he was a University College alumnus, he seemed to believe sincerely that only through federation could McMaster concentrate upon what ought to be its primary function – sound theological instruction – and safely leave arts work to the care of the state.[8] But once the decision was taken in 1905 to stay on the course of independence Harris ungrudgingly went along. Furthermore, it is difficult to square his supposed distrust of the university with his gift in 1906 of a thousand dollars toward the building of the Science Hall. 'I wish it were much more,' he had said in his covering letter,' [for] I am delighted with the way University affairs are moving.' Clearly Harris had been one of the 'few people of fair means' among the Baptists who were prepared to supplement the contributions of outside benefactors towards McMaster's expansion in the natural sciences.[9] Admittedly, a year later Harris was having second thoughts about his regular annual subscription to the institution, perplexed by 'uncertainty as to the position of one (if not two) of the professors.'[10] By this time others were sharing Harris's perplexity about the two professors, one of whom was assuredly I.G. Matthews. But who was the other one singled out for such careful scrutiny? All the signs point to George Cross, another McMaster alumnus, who had in 1901 been appointed to succeed Albert Newman in the history chair.

For his part, Newman, who had gone on to take a position at Baylor University in Texas, also expressed grave doubts about the propriety of McMaster's acquiring Matthews. Although he was forced to admit some months later that he had originally 'exaggerated somewhat the gravity of the situation,' Newman in the summer of 1904 went so far as to tell Wallace that in view of the 'great deal of ... unfavourable talk' regarding Matthews, 'it would be the better part of wisdom for you to ask [him] to resign ... I know that this would be somewhat humiliating to you; but I fear that if you persist in upholding this appointment ... it will be difficult for you to retain your office, or to administer the affairs of the University with success.'[11]

Newman ended with some points that for many critics constituted the crux of the matter. He snorted that the Senate's decision to permit Matthews a year and a half of study at the University of Chicago so that he might come to his tasks more fully qualified would still leave him sadly deficient. What was even more alarming to Newman was that 'no one can tell with what views he may return from Chicago.' Harris had complained about Matthews's dearth of spirituality, Newman about his academic shortcomings, real or imagined. But these flaws would become positively dangerous should Matthews ever be exposed to the University of Chicago, an institution that was anathema to Matthew's critics. In a pamphlet Harris later described Chicago with his customary directness as a 'Menace to Church and Society.'[12]

Unquestionably, the University of Chicago, founded at mid-century under Baptist auspices and revitalized in the 1880s with the aid of Rockefeller money, was in the forefront of the campaign in the United States to subject Scripture to exhaustive analysis and to adapt the church to 'modernity.' Under the leadership of President William Rainey Harper, the university's Divinity School attracted such Biblical scholars as Shailer Mathews, Ernest De Witt Burton, Shirley Jackson Case, Gerald Birney Smith, and George Burman Foster, the philosopher-theologian who had once lectured at McMaster. All were profoundly affected after the turn of the century by the changes overtaking American society and politics and by the nostrums prescribed for that generation. It was the era of muckraking, of progressivism, of the social gospel, and of reform at nearly every level of political activity. Out of this exciting milieu came the 'Chicago school's' commitment to examining the church's role and theology's function in a society undergoing rapid transformation. Given the university's Baptist heritage and its swift emergence as a leading institution in the United States, not to mention the presence there of Professor Foster, it naturally became one of McMaster's favourite graduate schools.

Shortly after assuming the chancellorship, Wallace had made a point of enquiring about Chicago from the considerable number of McMaster graduates who attended the institution. From one, a theology alumnus of 1894 who had admittedly spent only a brief time there, he received a mixed appraisal. The sentiments expressed are worth quoting because they came from a future McMaster chancellor and they could have provided some ammunition for those who would within a few years train their sights on Matthews and 'Chicago men' generally. 'Certainly [Chicago's] influence' Howard Primrose Whidden wrote in 1897 'is not what we, who have the ideals that McMaster cherishes, believe should be exerted . . . It is not exactly a hot-bed of Heresy, and yet pretty tall heretics have grown there and will continue to be grown there for some time. For a man who has thought through ... things a little, it is not a very dangerous place; but I am quite satisfied that I did not take my regular Theological Course there.'[13] 'President Harper' Whidden conceded 'certainly loves Jesus Christ and endeavors to be true to him in his work; but' he added cryptically 'whether or not he is is another thing.' Whidden must have softened his criticism of Chicago in later years since John Northway, the Ontario clothier imbued with the passion of the social gospel, regarded him as the theologian who best articulated his own liberal views.[14] Whidden probably came to share the view, expressed by an alumnus of Chicago who had initially reacted against its liberalism, that 'looking back [Harper and his colleagues] seem relatively *conservative* ... [and] did not conceive themselves as an elite vanguard advancing an extremely radical message ... It never entered their minds to leave the church of their Fathers; they generally sought continuities with the older nurture and culture ... they would seem to be "evangelical" liberals as distinguished from the extreme "modernists".'[15]

Whidden's early reservations about Chicago at the turn of the century shared time and space with far more blatant denunciations of that institution and its radicalism. What particularly disturbed some members of the denomination was what had also troubled the Castles and the MacVicars in the mid-eighties. They charged that those who endorsed the scientific treatment of the Scriptures were prone to evaluate the past in terms of the present's moods and attitudes. This 'present-mindedness' threatened to subordinate a reverence for past achievements for their own sake to the task of providing ready solutions for current ills. Out of this, the complaint went, had come an excessive concern with the problems of the 'here and now' to the distinct disadvantage of the 'hereafter.' This tendency seemed especially marked in those higher critics who followed the path, trod later by Northway, of the social gospel, the attempt to apply the Christian ethic to the resolution of the problems that abounded in a rapidly changing urban and industrial society. But to many, if not most, Baptists the establishment of the Kingdom of Heaven on earth, which seemed to be the object of the movement, would be a travesty if it were arranged by anything short of the second coming of Christ.[16] The apparent obsession with the present and its challenges, which social gospellers and higher critics seemed to share, could degenerate, it was argued, into a passing fancy, a faddish device by which pastors who despaired of the traditional preoccupations of the pulpit could seek popularity and applause.

One wonders whether Harris's and Newman's distrust of Matthews may have stemmed from the social consciousness that had appeared a few years before on the editorial pages of the *Western Baptist*. To be sure, there are only hints of the 'social passion' in Matthews's columns, but certain passages may have set Harris wondering about the wisdom of his appointment to McMaster.[17] This fascination with the present and the current agitated another Baptist clergyman who would years later turn the conflict between modernism and fundamentalism into a personal vendetta against McMaster University. Alluding to the degree to which the higher criticism and related approaches[18] had gained ground in North America, Thomas Todhunter Shields remarked that the 'New World view of things ... is too often rather like a photograph than a good painting, it is without atmosphere and perspective.' He continued: 'it is characteristic of youth that it seldom recognizes its obligations to the Past, and its passion for prophesying is out of all proportion to its historical accuracy ... It was "a new king over Egypt which knew not Joseph" who brought Egypt to ruin. The principle forever abides. The new kings who ignore the obligations to the Past are a menace to the peace & prosperity of Society everywhere.'[19]

The point was eagerly taken up in the early issues of the *Monthly*. Understandably, Albert Newman, a church historian, argued that 'so far as modern theologizing represents a weakening of the influence of the eternal verities of divine revelation, a substitution therefor of the products of the unaided human intellect, it would be a misnomer to speak of it as an exemplification of religious progress.'[20] When Newman talked and wrote in this vein he elicited a warm response from sophisticated and unsophisticated supporters alike. While the tutored believer questioned the amnesia-inducing properties of the higher criticism, the untutored opposed the new theology simply because it was an unwelcome substitution for the old time religion. 'I think that God's word is so plain' ran one typical opinion 'that the illiterate and poor ignorant mortals can find full salvation in it as well as the very learned DD & LDD, PHD &c. &c.'[21] Another complained that 'there is going on a vast amount of philosophic and linguistic talk about the Bible ... the answer should be *Preach the Word*.' And from back townships like Norfolk County came the prayer that 'our various colleges ... may ever teach ... the old [verities] of the Cross as revealed in the inspired word.'[22] When a copy of the resolution incorporating this prayer was duly dispatched to the chancellor, someone, perhaps the sender of the covering letter, obviously felt it to be inadequate, for he inserted in the original text the admonition that the colleges ought 'to be kept free of the ultra rationalistic spirit.'[23]

For Newman and his colleagues the ultra rationalistic spirit and the unaided human intellect had sought to discredit revelation. Next called in question were the authorship of the Old Testament books and the Jewish tradition as a guide to the reconstruction of what had transpired in Biblical times. It mattered little when a spokesman for the higher criticism maintained that the Old Testament lost none of its value through being subjected to such scholarly inquiry and that revelation was actually placed upon a firmer foundation. A contributor to the *Monthly* retorted: 'To us there is less difficulty in accepting the plenary inspiration of the Old Testament on the authority of Jesus than in accepting the inductive view of [the good professor] in the face of Jesus' testimony.'[24]

As far as the conservatives were concerned – those who in the sense conveyed by MacVicar thought that ancient principles ought to be conserved – the appointment of Matthews registered a victory for those who would tinker with truth as revelation. If they had any say in the matter there would be no place in pulpit or classroom for those who would place the dubious wisdom of the present before the accumulated verities of the past. That this assessment of Matthews and other adversaries might in itself have been dubious is beside the point, for that assessment produced a situation that profoundly affected the fortunes of McMaster University and hence must be evaluated as a factor in that institution's development.

If the criticism of Harris or Newman can be taken at its face value Matthews and the 'other professor,' George Cross, appear to qualify for membership in the group described by Howard Whidden as 'the pretty tall heretics' who flourished at Chicago. The question to ask, however, is how heretical the teachings and statements of the two academics were by the standards of that generation. It would be profitable to examine first the case of George Cross because, unlike Matthews, he was a full-fledged creature of Chicago and therefore may have been more suspect in the eyes of Harris and his sympathizers than anyone else. Cross had come to exemplify for them everything abhorrent in the institution. Even more disturbing, Matthews's intention to return to McMaster seemed to have been prompted in large part by Cross's appointment in 1901.[25]

In 1910, after the Harris attack had been repulsed, Cross may have unwittingly revealed a good deal about his own role in the crisis when he wrote to McKay that 'it is quite evident that the insurgents were after bigger game than Matthews.'[26] He probably had in mind the possible effects that Harris's campaign would have had upon intellectual freedom generally at the university. By attacking Matthews Harris might have hoped to discredit others who were less easily assailable: was the real quarry George Cross himself?

Cross's work at Chicago, which earned for him the PHD degree, was by his own description 'mainly along the line of historical-theological study.' It examined the extent to which Christianity had been forced at critical stages of its growth into a confrontation with alien religions and how it had overcome or adapted itself to their ideologies. Obviously the approach that Cross took to the subject – he experimented with the seminar method – and the insights that stimulated his work readily commended him to those who welcomed his taking the history chair at McMaster following Newman's resignation. A missionary in India expressed a widely held opinion when he wrote Wallace in 1901 that Cross 'will get nearer the boys and ... get more *history* into them [than Newman]; I think you fortunate in having a man so well fitted to take the Chair.'[27] It is altogether likely that Newman got wind of this unflattering comparison, one that understandably might have served to sharpen his attacks on the ideas that Cross presented in the lecture room.

But Newman was not the only one measured and found wanting by the yardstick of Cross's accomplishments. 'When I was a student,' reminisced the Rev. William A. Cameron a quarter of a century later, 'Bunty [Elias Miles] Keirstead was the professor [of systematic theology] ... He was about as well qualified for the position as I would be to lecture in Astronomy ... The situation for us was saved because of the presence of George Cross, who really gave us a course in Systematic under another name.'[28] Keirstead had always, particularly at Acadia, his alma mater, been more of an evangelist 'helping people to believe' than an effective teacher.[29] To further offset Keirstead's inadequacies the Senate in 1901 nominated Joseph Leeming Gilmour of Montreal, the grandson of the pioneer who had helped to found the Canada Baptist College, to the chair of pastoral theology and homiletics. One writer regarded Gilmour and Cross as equally valuable to McMaster, while the young Howard Whidden welcomed Gilmour's appointment on the ground that 'there will be very little trouble now with respect to McMaster graduates in Arts going to other schools for their theological training.'[30] However, his loss to McMaster was keenly felt in Baptist church circles in Montreal.[31]

Meanwhile, those who, like Newman, entertained such strong reservations about Chicago may have been surprised to learn that that institution had by no means provided answers to all the questions in the fertile mind of George Cross. This came out, among other places, in Cross's statement that 'I think a ... sojourn in one of the British Universities might have a broadening effect on one's view of life.'[32] The possibility that he may have had some doubts about Chicago's capacity to edify and enlighten never appeared to occur to his detractors. They seemed equally oblivious to the point made by a colleague of Cross's that students, whether postgraduates like Cross or undergraduates in Cross's classes, just might 'do ... thinking on their own account' and refuse to 'sit with open mouths while the professors carefully measure out doses of theology of the requisite strength and quantity.'[33]

What Cross measured out in the classroom or on the lecture circuit frequently met with a gratifying response. Thus a Baptist in Sault Ste Marie congratulated the university on having such an academic on its faculty. He added that a 'life-long Presbyterian of large intelligence said to me that Cross's lecture was the best thing that he [had] ever heard on [the history of Christianity's relations with other religions.] You may certainly count on the loyalty of North Ontario.'[34]

Other audiences, however, were not quite as enchanted by Cross's extramural addresses. Perhaps at his notorious lecture to Woodstock's Canadian Club in the spring of 1909 the subtlety of his approach required an appreciative audience 'of large intelligence,' or at least a newspaper reporter endowed with the same quality. Elmore Harris was sufficiently disturbed by the account he received to raise the matter with the theology faculty of the university. Harris may have had a conversation with Joseph Gilmour because that anxious professor wrote a friend in Woodstock that Cross had apparently advocated 'a desirable religion in the East that would perhaps drop some of the essential features of Christianity and . . . assume some of the good points of Oriental religions and produce an amalgam . . . religion that would . . . be something better than anything we have yet had.'[35] By return mail Gilmour's correspondent told him what he wanted to know, firmly assuring him that there was nothing to the story that had come back to Toronto.

Not only this, but Gilmour's friend resented the account of the lecture that had been circulated and regretted that McMaster was no longer to afford Cross a platform 'from which to speak to Canadians in his helpful and inspiring manner.' The rumour, which had been spreading for some weeks, that Cross was about to leave the university was thus represented in this instance as a deliberate attempt by the university to get rid of an undesirable faculty member. The facts would seem to be that by the time Cross appeared before the citizens of Woodstock he had already made up his mind to accept a challenging and more lucrative post at the University of Chicago.

This must have come as welcome news to Elmore Harris who had already registered his strong disapproval of what Cross was reported to have said. Indeed, Harris's reaction to the Canadian Club lecture underlay his formal accusation that Cross's colleague Matthews was teaching unorthodoxy at McMaster. This was the second time that Harris had so accused Matthews; a year previously, having raised the matter in the Senate, he had an interview with Matthews on the subject of his teaching but did not pursue it at the time.[36] Now, in the spring of 1909, Harris was returning to the attack and demanding a full enquiry into Matthews's instruction and explanations from

Cross about his Woodstock lecture. The reports palpably agitating Gilmour exercised the suspicious Harris, who wasted little time in writing the chancellor: 'I wish to say that the utterances of such sentiments *at all* at Woodstock [mis-reported or not] in the present heated state of the public mind is, to say the least, very ill-advised and extremely unfortunate. No one is at liberty in such a position as [Cross] holds to utter any sentiments he likes.'[37] Harris ended with a blunt threat: 'Unless a pronouncement is made by the University regarding the erroneous character of these opinions if correctly reported, or at least regarding the sad imprudence of speaking them at all, I cannot see anything before us but a determined opposition to the University in whose interests we are all so deeply concerned.'

For his part, Cross had already tried to clarify the situation. Echoing Gilmour's informant he stated that it was an 'utter falsehood' that he had advocated 'either in words or in intention a composite religion made of Christianity and other . . . religions.' He advised McKay that he had already informed Harris of the true state of the case and if that clergyman continued to circulate a false story then he, Cross, could 'only leave him to his own conscience.' Cross outlined what he had sought to convey at Woodstock: an 'historical description of how the present world crisis in religion . . . came about, not to attempt to prescribe a solution to it.' His account is worth quoting as an example of the approach that he took to his material:

I pointed out that the progress of missions had brought us into contact with ancient faiths and civilizations. This had occurred at least twice before in the case of the Graeco-Roman and the Teutonic peoples, and the result was such an amalgamation of Christianity with other religions that even to the present day we were suffering from the corruptions that resulted. The situation today was more serious because of the extent of the missionary propaganda and the antiquity of these oriental faiths . . . particularly in India.[38]

What had probably antagonized some of his listeners and coloured the reports that reached Harris's sensitive ears was Cross's comment that the 'problem for the theologian was how to conserve the true Christianity while at the same time admitting that there were elements of truth in other religions.' In a good many quarters any reference, however oblique, to the study of comparative religion was enough to spark apopletic debate. It was common knowledge, however, that Cross had obtained Senate approval two years before for a course comparing the 'essential truths of Christianity with the ruling conceptions of other great world religions and of the Christian Scriptures with the Sacred Books of other religions.'[39]

Some of those who urged this approach to the study of the world's religions, and Cross may have been among them, did so in the belief that the new knowledge released by anthropology and sociology on man's origins and political and social development would afford as many insights into his religious behaviour as the study of theology alone. The Darwinian notion of evolutionary progress and the material gathered by Sir James Frazer on primitive religions combined to inspire a re-examination of the bases of all religions. Out of this merger came the shocking possibility that Christianity might be only one of many meaningful forms of religious expression.

The secretary of the Baptist Foreign Mission Board nervously reported that people in the Ottawa district from which 'many of our best students have come' were alarmed at McMaster's curriculum, particularly by Cross's alleged elevation of alien creeds to the commanding heights occupied by Christianity.[40] It would seem, however, that this alarm was not reflected at the annual meeting of the Ottawa Association in the late summer of 1909. The bulk of its working hours was given over to the discussion, not of education, but of a projected Baptist Union of Canada.[41]

The same mail that brought the unhappy tidings from the Ottawa Valley also informed McKay of other alleged shortcomings in the university's conduct of its affairs. These too had denominational overtones and concerned the awarding of a Rhodes scholarship to a McMaster graduand. The aggrieved writer, who had clearly missed the point of the award, felt that his own son, rather than the actual recipient – regrettably a Presbyterian – should have received the honour. 'Leaving out my son's merits altogether,' he began, 'I think the interests and welfare of the Baptist denomination, as well as of McMaster University have been slighted by the giving of the scholarship to one not a Baptist. McMaster University is an institution founded by a Baptist, sustained and supported by Baptists, and it surely could not have escaped your observation that whoever would win the Rhodes scholarship would be immensely benefited.'[42] The knowledge that the writer was a resident of Simcoe, the heart of one of the most disaffected provinces in the Baptist constituency, made the contents of the letter even more disturbing.

At about this time McKay and his colleagues received the unwelcome news that at least one association, Elgin, was about to entertain a resolution against Cross's teaching. It was strongly suggested that a copy of the professor's letter to McKay, along with supporting correspondence from those who had cleared him of promoting a 'compound religion,' be speedily despatched to all concerned. The suggestion was acted upon, and if there was dissension in the Elgin Association the documents sent down to Aylmer alleviated it. When the delegates assembled there in late May 1909 they recorded their appreciation of Cross's 'distinguished service, ripe scholarship, and strong Christian character.'[43] A random check of the annual meetings of other associations disclosed no significant backlash against the university and its faculty. Indeed, where one might have expected some heated reaction, in the Oxford-Brant Association in which Woodstock, the scene of Cross's controversial lecture, was located, favourable references were made to an address given by Joseph Gilmour on the educational interests of the denomination.[44]

Scattered charges continued to come in, however, though not at a rate Elmore Harris might have appreciated. From Lanark one critic, who had long complained about the 'Higher Criticism as taught by Professors Cross and Matthews,' wrote grimly about widespread discontent with the teaching countenanced by the university. In a statement that would have meant a sleepless night for Wallace a few years before, the writer told the Senate in the spring of 1909 that it 'will be a sad day for McMaster when she gets out of touch with the . . . denomination.' It must have been a considerable satisfaction to the critic to learn that Cross, one of the objects of his concern, had already resigned from the faculty. Of the two supposed higher critics at McMaster, Matthews and Cross, the latter seemed to be regarded as the more dangerous because he was 'better posted on Chicago Un[iversity] views.'[45]

While this writer scarcely disguised his jubilation over Cross's departure, others, including a good many Board members, were visibly demoralized by it.[46] Some of Cross's supporters, like some of his critics, felt that he had resigned because of what Harris had called the 'present heated state of the public mind' and because of the criticism levelled against him. Certainly Albert B. Cohoe, a representative of the Evangelical Alliance in New Brunswick, thought so. He stated what a good many Baptists were thinking when he wrote that 'Dr Cross is just the man for Ontario . . . If you ever get a less conscientious and tactful man, a man less genuinely Christian and more extremely radical you will have a row in Ontario from which any man may devoutly pray to be delivered . . . Ontario cannot afford to lose him.'[47]

Most of Cross's colleagues at McMaster shared this sentiment. 'His call to Chicago is one of the gravest concern to McMaster' was Dean Jones Hughes Farmer's typically dejected comment, and Farmer was a graduate of the conservative Southern Baptist Theological Seminary. Whether or not Cross was the bigger game Harris was stalking in his campaign to discredit the 'new theology' there is no denying the fact that the university community regarded him as almost irreplaceable. Yet, as one of Cross's defenders put it: 'we feared that [he] was too big a man for a small university to keep always.' This factor and the growing hostility in Ontario to the sort of instruction that he and Matthews had offered at McMaster probably made the Chicago invitation a highly tempting one. Before his departure Cross set out to assure his colleagues, particularly the chancellor, that 'my general position was all that I could have expected and ... it would have been wrong to accept more at McMaster's hands.' A month later, while confessing to McKay how much he enjoyed Chicago's congenial atmosphere, he nonetheless noted the 'greatness of the change for my family and for me ... and the worth of the Canadian character and its possibilities in the way of influencing the life of this continent.' 'It is possible' he concluded 'that what little I can do in the world may, in the end, mean as much at McMaster as in Chicago.'[48]

Cross's resignation made life much more difficult for I.G. Matthews. He could now be singled out for the attack that Harris and other critics had been mounting against McMaster's unorthodoxy, and Cross's departure made the critics' task easier. The Baptist who had rejoiced over Cross's leaving for Chicago now looked forward to Matthews 'confessing his sins.' Specifically, he expected the professor to state 'in a manly way' whether or not he minimized the writings of Moses and at the same time 'exalted whatever came from a Babylonian source.' The Senate was urged, however, to treat Matthews gently, for it was hoped that in his heart he would respond and allow the 'dear old Bible' to silence 'every usurper in the form of a Babylonian myth.' Matthews had introduced two new courses with the Senate's concurrence in the session of 1908-9. The first, Hebrew legislation, dealt with the 'legal and priestly sections of the Old Testament and their relation to the common Semitic heritage'; the second, Hebrew Wisdom, concerned the 'rise of modern literature and its relation to religious and social conditions.'[49] To some sceptics the latter course smacked of that disturbing scientific effort to 'recapture the particular situation in which each book of the Bible was written,' a favourite object, they believed, of the higher critic.

However unorthodox or radical Matthews might have been in the eyes of conservatives like Elmore Harris, while he was at Chicago he obviously had not considered himself to be such, if his assessment of a fellow student is personally revealing. The student in question was Douglas C. Macintosh, a graduate of McMaster who forsook chemistry as a career and later distinguished himself as a theologian at the Yale Divinity School. 'As I judge [Macintosh]' Matthews once wrote to Wallace 'he is conservative of spirit ... it might be that he would not be named "orthodox" by some, but I have found him exceedingly spiritually minded, and this with his sound common sense will save him from the dangers of radicalism.'[50] In turn, Macintosh, who presumably had been queried about Matthews's progress at Chicago, assured the chancellor that 'he is doing very good work here ... and will I feel sure give good satisfaction in McMaster.'[51]

At the outset of the controversy in 1904 Harris had been particularly concerned with Matthews's lack of spirituality. Although Matthews had regarded that very quality as a virtue in his classmate Macintosh, Harris repeatedly returned to this theme as a shortcoming in Matthews. By the spring of 1908 he had pretty well convinced himself that Matthews's scholarship was eroding his capacity to reach the students on a spiritual level, to him a grave fault.

At a meeting of the Senate shortly after New Year's, Harris took another approach to the problem, raising the matter of the articles of faith which had been endorsed by instructors at the TBC in the eighties. He went on to recall for the benefit of his fellow senators that at the meeting in May 1908 a senator had disclosed that the university had, as far as he knew, no similar doctrinal basis, a deficiency the distressed clergyman wanted corrected at once. Obviously Chancellor McKay was taken unawares by this turn in the discussion, though he promised he 'would find out how the articles of faith had been dropped and let Harris know.'[52] In a burst of hyperbole, which he doubtless hoped would excite the desired reaction, Harris announced that 'we have no standard; anything in the world can be taught in the University.' He was not disappointed. His remarks were too much for C.J. Holman, who submitted that, if the TBC had had articles of faith, 'those articles came in to McMaster as part of the theology faculty.' Harris's rejoinder to this was that 'we ought to find out if in fact we have got a standard.' For good measure he stated that he knew of churches that would not allow the university's representatives to visit them because the congregations simply had no confidence in the theology faculty. Harris ended by remarking ominously that this deterioration in the relationship between the university and the denomination was a new situation.[53]

The concerned Holman lost no time hunting up the trust deed of the TBC and what purported to be a similar document for the university. While unquestionably there had been such a document governing the affairs of the college, there was, according to George Gilmour, no actual trust or deed given to the university by Senator McMaster 'outside of his will.'[54] In any event, Holman told McKay early in February that he had found everything 'exactly as [he] expected.' However, all the senator had charged the Board of 'vigilant men of business training and experience' to do in his will was to maintain the institution 'with true and faithful regard to the work of affording the best possible facilities for a thoroughly practical Christian course of education.'[55]

When Harris formally accused Matthews of unorthodoxy at a Senate meeting on 11 May 1909 this matter of a statement of belief was immediately reviewed. It was reported that neither Senate nor Board minutes incorporated any such statement, although reference was made to one adopted in 1885. This turned out to be one of the amendments that John Castle had made to the original constitution of the TBC in an effort to assure the denomination that the institution would be better protected against the 'polished shafts of a refined and subtle infidelity.' The annual report incorporating the amendment and Castle's accompanying statement were read out by the chancellor at the Senate meeting on 11 May.[56] Although McKay went on to say that while he had found no record of the statement having been presented to any professor in the college there was evidence that it had been endorsed by the faculty in 1884.[57]

Meanwhile, another committee, the crucial one, was appointed to look into the matter raised by Harris 'touching on the teachings of Professor Matthews.' Chaired by the chancellor its work was largely taken up with an investigation of whether Matthews as an instructor had contravened the statements in Senator McMaster's will and in the trust deed of the TBC. The same day that Harris had the satisfaction of seeing the investigating committee appointed, he presented a communication to the Board flatly stating his opinion that Matthews's usefulness to the University was at an end. In a historical review of the case which he prepared later, Harris substantiated George Cross's belief that the critics were after bigger game than Matthews. 'I have no personal feeling against Professor Matthews,' Harris claimed, 'the question is very much larger . . . than any one person.'[58] In his mind it was the destructive effect of Matthews's teaching upon the university and the denomination. The matter had come to a head when Harris was provided with what he claimed was a stenographic record kept by the Rev. Glyn Williams of a series of course lectures Matthews had delivered to Williams and his fellow students.[59] According to that record, a copy of which accompanied Harris's statement, Matthews had on several occasions remarked that the earlier chapters of Genesis were a 'little folklore . . . exactly in line with the folklore of every people under the sun.' Another disaffected student, the Rev. John Linton, complained some years after the event that there 'was hardly one lecture when Dr Matthews did not suggest discrepancies, exaggerations, errors and contradictions in the Old Testament.'[60]

The Senate's investigating committee deliberated for over two weeks, examined the evidence furnished by Harris – though he complained that he had received all too few invitations to attend the committee – and then heard from Matthews and those anxious to speak on his behalf. Several prominent Baptists, their nerves visibly on edge, wrote in urging that the false statements about the university be corrected, and that 'every member [of the Committee] ought to pledge himself to accept the decision and abide by it.'[61] It so happened that Williams, upon whom Harris heavily depended, had confessed to a falsehood of his own when he unreservedly withdrew his assertion that Matthews had denied that 'there was any revelation from God whatever in the Pentateuch.'[62] In all other respects, an embarrassed Harris hastened to assure McKay, Williams had rendered an accurate account, an evaluation understandably discounted in some quarters.

In the meantime, George Cross, who had kept in close touch with the proceedings, wrote from Chicago to congratulate the committee's chairman on 'having some *men* in Toronto.' 'This matter can end in only one way,' he concluded, 'the separation of the heresy-hunter from the work of the University ... I am glad the matter is coming to a head.' One can readily imagine how Harris might have reacted to Cross's closing observation: 'Harris has never been a genuine friend of the institution and never will be.'[63]

For the investigating committee matters reached a climax on 29 May 1909 when it submitted its report to a special meeting of the Senate. Briefly, it found that the charges of unorthodoxy against Matthews were not proved. The Senate and the public were assured that, though Matthews accepted many of the results of modern critical scholarship, he 'held firmly to the inspiration and supernatural character of the Old and New Testaments.' The university, at any rate, was satisfied that the spirit in which it had been founded had not been flouted by Matthews's teaching. The statement shortly issued by the institution is worth quoting in full, for it exhibited prominently the views of those who had sought to discredit the attacks of Harris and Williams. 'McMaster University' the statement read 'stands for freedom, for progress, for investigation.'

It must welcome truth from whatever quarter, and never be guilty of binding the spirit of free enquiry. As a Christian school of learning under Baptist auspices, it stands for the fullest and freest investigation, *not only in the scientific realm but also in the realm of Biblical scholarship* . Holding fast their historic position on the personal freedom and responsibility of the individual, refusing to bind or be bound by any human creed, rejecting the authority of tradition and taking their stand on the word of God alone as the supreme and all-sufficient rule of faith and practice, the Baptists have ever been ready to accord to all students of the Sacred Scriptures the largest possible measure of freedom consistent with loyalty to the *fundamentals* of the Christian faith.[64]

Almost as soon as the statement was released, letters came in from the expected well-wishers. Hearty congratulations, for example, were sent to McKay from McMaster men at Chicago: Harris Lachlan MacNeill, Andrew G. Campbell, Douglas Macintosh (Matthews's former classmate), William

D. Whan, Duncan J. Welsh, John B. Pugelly, Donald H. MacIntosh, and Daniel Buchanan. The good wishes from Harris MacNeill were especially well received. A member of McMaster's first graduating class with teaching experience in both Canada and the United States, he had taken a leave of absence from Brandon College to pursue doctoral studies at the University of Chicago.[65] Meanwhile, another alumnus exulted that the university's statement was a magna charta, a declaration of independence. Still another, at Harvard, wrote that 'the teachers [at McMaster] may now go ahead unhampered by – well! I guess I won't use any swear words – unhampered by any more such difficulties.'[66] An assumption common to all the congratulatory messages was that the outcome of the Senate's deliberations was largely owing to Chancellor McKay. One letter, addressed simply 'Dear Mac,' must have been particularly welcome. 'All Protestant bodies' A. Stevenson wrote from the United Kingdom 'should take the same stand [as McMaster] to be consistent with Protestant principles' . . . [but] they have not done it, not one of them – at least not one of the so-called orthodox bodies – and so all the more honor to McMaster.'[67]

Apparently one such orthodox body, the local Methodists, were having their own difficulties with modernists. 'Gloomy without and lurid within,' ran one newspaper report, 'the Toronto Methodist Conference [recently] had a memorable session . . . the pent up fire and fury was engendered by Rev. [George] Jackson's recent book on biblical criticism [and] the discussion led to a general attack on the teachings of advanced theological colleges.'[68] The Toronto World, commenting upon the problems facing McMaster's neighbour, Victoria College, reported that the 'great body of the members of the [Methodist] Church recognizes the necessity of keeping up with the march of knowledge; the minority which represents . . . the same spirit which denounced Galileo . . . must [not] be allowed to resort to crucifixion, however conscientiously they may be rooted in their darkness.'[69]

As far as the McMaster situation is concerned, one is tempted to compare the Senate committee's report with the inaugural statement delivered by McKay's predecessor to the university community some fourteen years before. The point made by O.C.S. Wallace that the university existed 'for the teaching of truth rather than the pursuit of it' and the sentiments expressed in 1909 must for Harris have seemed separated by an unbridgeable chasm. While some might have argued that only a difference of degree separated the two statements, Harris could be forgiven for reading them differently when he voted against the Senate report. Harris's main grievance was that the report was really two things: first of all, a whitewashing operation to clear an instructor and, secondly, an irritating and perhaps even hypocritical attempt to assure the faithful that all was theologically sound at McMaster University. Harris warned that the university ought not to be encouraged to believe that it could have it both ways. His discomfiture was shared by at least three other senators who joined him in voting against the report: S.C. Cook, Joseph Shenstone, and C.J. Holman, who had earlier made such an effort to unearth wills, trust deeds, and other documentation pertinent to the case. Holman and Shenstone would be heard from in due course.

Harris might also have been bemused to read the word 'fundamentals' in the closing sentence of the Senate statement. In the United States the term 'fundamentalism' was already becoming a political label for the defence of the status quo and a battle cry in the conflict with the modernists. In 1910 the American denominational world was greeted with the first volumes of *The Fundamentals: A Testimony to the Truth*, a series setting forth the aims and objectives of the movement. Some of them served as a warning that a hitherto more or less seemly exchange of opinions between civilized people was now to become a battle between well organized and fiercely armed combatants.

Throughout the Matthews affair and during the years when Cross's work had come under fire, Harris had kept abreast of the activities of those groups in the United States who had mobilized their energies to attack the new theology. Indeed it went far beyond this. When plans were laid for the publication of the widely heralded *Fundamentals* in 1910, Harris was one of three clergymen appointed to the editorial committee. That same year Harris contributed his own polemic to the debate, at least in so far as it affected the Canadian and McMaster situations. His foreword to a fellow cleric's denunciation of a modernist Chicago treatise on atonement was followed by a biting commentary on how the Matthews incident had been disposed of by the university Senate in the spring of 1909. Harris argued that the 'question is not *how* teaching is to be done ... the question is not Are the students to discuss these problems? That goes without saying.' For Harris the central question was 'How is the student left? Is he to be left believing or doubting? Professor Matthews ... can hold all the vagaries of the Higher Critics he pleases as to the Old Testament, and he is at liberty to proclaim them from the housetop, but he must not ask the Baptist denomination to give an endorsement to such views or to approve the inculcation of such views from his chair in the Theological Department.'[70] It was precisely at this point that the Senate committee's conception of the problem had diverged from Harris's.

But what of Matthews and the steps he took to defend himself? Like Harris, Matthews went into print to explain his position. His statement had the sort of modern tone that made critics like Harris complain so vocally. 'It is not sufficient' Matthews wrote 'that [the] teacher possess exact knowledge of the past only . . . he must be able also to reinterpret the message in terms of the present. A modern theological seminary ought not to be divorced from the world to-day – and what a world for a theologian to come to!'[71] In the *Baptist Year Book* he made even more explicit remarks, which some might have interpreted as a bow in the direction of the social gospel. He reminded his readers that the 'practical side of life is more and more appreciated' by students, and that 'the great needs of the workaday world and the adequacy of the Gospel to meet these needs is the thought which is foremost in the minds of most.[72] In words reminiscent of his editorials years before in the *Western Baptist*, Matthews rhapsodized about 'A world with a growing mastery of nature, knowing her laws and reading them as our ancestors never dreamed possible; a world studying the human family, understanding the basal principles of social development, peering into the mysteries of the human mind.'[73] The latter, a reference to the early work of Sigmund Freud, had, along with adventures in comparative religion, been causing endless anguish amongst the defenders of the Bible. If Freud were anywhere near the truth man's behaviour was governed, not by the workings of the rational, but by the irrational forces of his 'lower nature.' It followed then that man acted not by choice but by necessity, and therefore he could not in justice be held accountable for his actions and sins. In such a context, it was asked, how could traditional religious restraints continue to function with the vitality they had enjoyed in the past? Matthews, as it turned out, had little confidence in Freud's findings, but he unhesitatingly brought them to the attention of his students.[74]

On the other hand, the contributions of the natural and physical sciences made a much greater impression upon Matthews. For him they had changed 'our expression and sometimes even our interpretation' of Biblical events. He was careful to point out, however, that 'the fundamentals [again the word was used in a way that would have outraged Harris] of true religion ever abide unshaken.' Although he was accused of a rhetorical flourish in the direction of the verities, there was nothing dishonest in Matthews's qualification. He was also well aware, as was Harris, of the enormous responsibility entrusted to the teacher. The day following the Senate committee's report he confided to McKay, with a kind of left-handed compliment to Harris's agitation, that 'I see more clearly now than hitherto that the teacher has perhaps a more intensive influence [than the pastor], even though the immediate scope be narrower. More than ever can I give myself to the students and to the work of the class room, and perhaps also with a soberer sense of the full responsibility of the tasks.' 'Thus in more ways than one' he concluded significantly 'I feel good will come of the "investigation."'[75]

The pious hope that all was at an end in the days immediately following the release of the committee's report was disappointed. In the course of his own rebuttal Harris had intimated that the Baptist denomination might have something to say about the Senate's decision. Within a week of Matthews's rejoicing, a member of the committee, John G. Brown, learned this at first hand from a friend in Ottawa. The gentleman in question was 'rather expecting the verdict the opposite of that ... rendered,' an understandable expectation considering that his pastor was the Rev. Glyn Williams, whose testimony had been used against Matthews.[76] Other Baptists were not reticent about expressing similar bewilderment to the senators who had sided with Harris and voted against Matthews's exoneration. Two such, Holman and Shenstone, rose to the occasion in the fall of 1909 and had a statement read into the Senate minutes that 'the whole attitude of the University towards the Bible [is] of such far-reaching importance ... that [it] requires the fullest consideration possible.'[77] They subsequently succeeded in convincing their colleagues of the desirability of deferring a report to the Convention until the matter had been thoroughly considered by that body. A week or so later, Thomas Trotter, a prospective appointment to the chair of practical theology, regretted that McKay had to be 'pestered with a re-discussion of the Matthews case; but since it has to be, I shall hope that ... in the end it shall prove to have been ... a means of securing a ... more permanent understanding.'[78]

When the Senate next met on 15 November Holman and Shenstone were gratified by the acceptance of their resolution requesting the faculty in theology to present to the Senate a 'statement in general terms of the view which in their teaching they seek to work out of the attitude of the Institution towards the Bible.' At a Senate meeting on 2 December 1909 the theologians duly made their report, in the course of which they referred to the fruits of Holman's research – the trust deed of the TBC, the supposed continuance of its terms in the university's Charter, and the resolution of the Guelph Convention of 1888. Their report was a declaration that 'each member of the Theology Faculty ... according to their best knowledge and belief ... is teaching in harmony' with the principles embodied in these documents. They agreed, furthermore, that 'while complete freedom should be accorded in the investigation and discussion of facts no theory should be taught in [the] University which fails to give their proper place to supernatural revelation ... or which would impair in any way the supreme authority of the Lord Jesus Christ.'[79]

A few days before the faculty prepared their declaration Thomas Trotter had assured the chancellor that the 'critical method in things biblical is ... not only legitimate but in these days necessary.' Nonetheless, as an incoming faculty member he heeded the Senate admonition and agreed to abide by the terms of the Trust deed of the TBC. As he had remarked some months before, he could 'fellowship a liberal as . . . fully as a conservative, if he is a reverent, sincere seeker after truth, and is loyal to the deity and saviorhood of . . . Jesus.' It must have come as no surprise to McKay when Trotter told him in a flash of redundance that theologically he 'ranked himself as a liberal conservative.'[80] One only wishes that Harris's pungent comments on such a stance had been preserved for posterity.

The report of the theology faculty, which seemed to beat a retreat from the lofty ground staked out by McKay's committee, was unanimously adopted by the Senate. As the *Baptist Year Book* blandly put it: 'it brought to a happy conclusion a discussion which while instructive and helpful had caused much anxiety to the friends of our educational work.' The Senate's action, it was hoped, would be construed, not as an endorsement of any particular form of theological criticism, but only as an expression of 'that reasonable liberty which has always been cherished by our people as a sacred possession.'[81]

These comforting sentences obscured, however, some disquieting events which had taken place behind the scenes. The day before the theologians completed their report and declaration McKay received a highly confidential letter from a friend, the Rev. Bert W. Merrill, who happened to be the Rev. T.T. Shields's assistant at the Jarvis Street Church. In spite of the steps taken to mollify conservative opinion, Merrill wrote, it appeared that Harris was 'going to carry on his campaign outside the Senate altogether' . . . and to exploit 'a widespread feeling of unrest among our pastors'. Merrill claimed that Harris was being guided 'by some person who is much shrewder in conflict than the Dr himself.' This eminence grise remained nameless, but in another part of the letter reference was made to Shields, the clergyman who, a dozen years later, would make life exceedingly unpleasant for the university. A warm friend of Harris, Shields had already made arrangements for the former to address Baptist ministers in London on what McKay's correspondent called the 'history (?) of the controversy.' That Shields was actually directing the attack on McMaster is open to dispute, but there was certainly no question in Merrill's mind that he 'should not be prejudiced against McMaster any more than he is at present.'[82]

The disquiet that Harris and Shields could tap at this time would spread in the next decade and spill over to engulf the university in a flood of controversy that made the Matthews affair a mere trickle by comparison. But McKay and his colleagues had no way of foreseeing this and continued to hope in 1910 that the recent Senate action and the welcome words of support from alumni, laymen, and missionaries overseas would effectively put an end to the discord that had disrupted the university's affairs for some eighteen months.

And there was cause for hope. From southwestern Ontario, for example, came assurances that Harris's actions outside the Senate 'will only increase the distrust toward [him] that is now setting in so strongly in other quarters, as well as here.'[83] Word came in that Matthews was giving 'clear and winning addresses' in that area and that rank-and-file Baptists were pronouncing him devout and tactful. People at the university knew only too well that they would have need of all the good will or as one writer said 'all the brawn and muscle' they could muster before the Convention met in the fall. For it would be then that the failure or success of the Harris attack would be decided. It was imperative, therefore, that the university assume the best possible posture. It was tactically urged that Matthews be put 'on his guard' so that he would avoid disputable points in his addresses to congregations. Another strategist, either pulling the chancellor's leg or demonstrating an exquisite ignorance, suggested that Harris be named one of the stalwarts to promote the university's cause at the forthcoming Convention.[84]

In a more pertinent vein Professor R.W. Smith, obviously relishing the prospect of a battle, wrote from the resort country to stress the need for organizing the defences of the university: 'if we can avoid it there ought to be no appearance of variance in the Faculty; if all the [theologians] . . . support Prof. Matthews statement . . . the heresy-hunters . . . must accept it.' Another militant correspondent had already written to announce that an 'Old Guard, thank God, is still in good fighting form to break any staff aimed at the chancellor.'[85]

When the matter was brought to the floor of the Convention on 24 October 1910 a number of documents were either read out or made available for the six hundred delegates from the 317 churches in the constituency. The annual report of the Senate and the Board incorporating the declaration of the theology faculty was read out to the assembly by the chancellor. At the request of the Rev. T.T. Shields, copies of the statement prepared by Matthews for the delegates were distributed beforehand. After Matthews had delivered his address, to which the delegates gave close attention, the Convention turned to a discussion of the Senate's report. Following a series of amendments and subamendments the adoption of the report was moved and the Convention called upon to approve the statement 'touching the attitude of the University to the Bible presented to the Senate on [15 November 1909] . . . by the members of the Theological Faculty'; this after the Convention let it be known that it relied on the Senate and the Board 'to see that the teaching of the Institution is maintained in harmony therewith.'[86] The motion, much to the relief of Matthews and McKay, was carried by a large majority. For those, like Merrill, who were aware of an alliance between Harris and Shields it must have come as a surprise that Shields seconded the amendment that paved the way for the adoption of the report. In his own review of the episode some twenty years later Shields attributed his action to his youth and inexperience – he was in his mid-thirties – and to his less than intimate acquaintance with the circumstances of the case.[87] But according to Merrill's reconstruction of the situation Shields's memoir is open to grave doubts. Others advanced different reasons for his failure to back Harris in the fall of 1910, notably his anxiety that an involvement in any kind of notorious incident might jeopardize his pastorate at the prestigious Jarvis Street Church.[88]

At any rate, the Convention endorsed the Senate's actions of 1909 and Matthews's teaching was vindicated. As on previous occasions congratulatory messages were dispatched to McKay, augmented this time by greetings from well-wishers outside the denomination. Most of these letters simultaneously subscribed to conservatism and free inquiry and insisted that the 'ultimate verities' could be preserved in the pursuit of productive research in Biblical studies. A Presbyterian rejoiced that the 'effort to muzzle honest and reverent investigation of truth' had been frustrated.[89] Nathaniel Burwash spoke for himself and for Victoria College when he agreed with McKay that 'it is very important to conserve every essential element of Christian truth and at the same time to maintain that intellectual freedom which is absolutely necessary to the work with which we are engaged.'[90]

Harris, who continued to write about the question until his death in 1912 at a remote mission station in Burma, retorted that Biblical criticism of the sort encouraged by men who professed to be conservative would destroy the plenary inspiration of the Bible and ultimately the foundations of faith itself.[91] George Cross, who also continued to contribute to the discussion, repudiated this view, repeating that Harris and his supporters had not been after Matthews so much as the university's intellectual freedom. A writer from the west extended this theme when he argued that if Harris had succeeded in putting McMaster 'out of business' he would then have turned his 'guns on the heretics of Brandon [College].' 'But now' he concluded with relief 'we breathe easily.'[92] Less pleasant in the letters delivered to McKay's office was the abuse heaped on Harris and those who had supported him: 'pious skunks' and 'insane persons.' Even George Cross, who had tried to control his emotions throughout the controversy, went so far as to hope that 'no man [henceforth] will feel it to be necessary to placate ... Harris.'[93]

On the other hand, there were others who, even though they had gone along with the Convention's decision, still had misgivings. A Woodstock

Baptist who began by saying that *'there is more for my boys in a course at McMaster than in any other place on earth ,'* could add that 'I do not think the fears of [Harris] and these men were wholly groundless ... I think in all probability Professor Matthews taught some startling things in class at the beginning ... things that the denomination would not tolerate even now, and which perhaps he would not at present teach or suggest.' Editorials in the *Canadian Baptist*, he claimed, had progressively seemed to reflect a drift in the classrooms of McMaster that made him feel restless.[94] In an earlier statement Matthews had implicitly acknowledged the need for care in the presentation of concepts and theories, and it is highly probable that after the debates of 1910 he took pains to ensure that he was not knowingly abusing his prerogatives as a teacher.

In any event, a hopeful Dean McLay advised George Cross in the spring of 1911 that the 'situation is much more favourable than it was a year ago; perhaps, after all, the result of the whole difficulty will be advantageous to our denomination.'[95] This hope was shared by everyone at the university as they set about to deal with other dimensions of its operation.

6
Interbellum

The apparent resolution of the Matthews question provided McMaster with a long-deferred opportunity to take stock of other matters affecting its well-being and to tackle problems that had been accumulating for three years. Although they had not been entirely sidetracked by debate, they also had not, in the circumstances, commanded anything like the undivided attention of those directing the university's affairs.

For one thing, there was the perennial problem of staffing. George Cross's departure for Chicago in 1910 was not the only reminder of the difficulties a small school faced when it came to retaining highly qualified personnel. At about the time Cross was saying farewell, Edmund H. Oliver, who had been taken on as a history lecturer in 1905, left for the newly established University of Saskatchewan.[1] A serious situation was happily averted when W. Stewart Wallace, who had taken honours at Toronto's Trinity College and done graduate work at Oxford, was appointed in his place. In the following session the arts community was further strengthened by the acquisition of William J.A. Donald, a McMaster alumnus who had pursued advanced work in political economy at Chicago. Both men proved productive scholars.

In 1913 Wallace published a study of the United Empire Loyalists that had the great merit of presenting them, not as the forbidding heroes of legend or the objects of a cult, but as plausible people of all shades of opinion and background. Donald wrote the first comprehensive account of the emergent Canadian iron and steel industry and the way in which it had been governed by the Dominion's tariff policy.[2] A long-time incumbent of a McMaster chair also produced a well received volume at this time: in 1914 James Ten Broeke, who had succeeded George B. Foster as professor of philosophy in 1895, published *A Constructive Basis of Theology*, praised by George Cross as a 'distinct contribution to the prolegomena of theology.'[3] In the same period Joseph L. Gilmour prepared an historical account of Canadian Baptists for the multivolume production known as *Canada and Its Provinces*.

These exercises in research and writing – the arts analogue to the scientific work undertaken by Tingle and Hogg – were warmly commended by Chancellor McKay as a welcome antidote to the disease of controversy that had stalked the university in recent years. As he had characteristically reported in 1908: 'one great danger in a smaller university is that the Professors shall become merely teachers and will not cultivate that alertness and spirit of research which ... extend the boundaries of knowledge and which characterize the great modern university.'[4]

Another mark of a great modern university was surely a stimulated and responsible student body. But for some observers this was precisely what appeared to be lacking at the university in the early years of the century. Whether or not the crisis precipitated by Elmore Harris had unsettled the undergraduates is difficult to determine; but there was considerable concern about the supposed erosion of the ideals and decorum that had governed the student body in the university's first decade. An overseas missionary was appalled to learn that hazing might enjoy some support among the students. 'I must be an "old-fogy,"' he wrote the chancellor, 'for I detest hazing and have often referred to McMaster as an example of a college having a nobler ideal than the barbarous practice of subduing a man by brute force. Perhaps we are getting a different class of freshmen now than we used to get ten or fifteen years ago!'[5]

Although the practice was vetoed on the McMaster campus, other student activities caused misgivings. Stewart Wallace was distressed by the 'giving of college yells' and other forms of 'hoodlumism' in the chapel-building. He never hesitated to complain to Dean McLay that his colleagues were remiss in permitting such behaviour. The Oxford-educated historian doubtless contrasted it with the civilized deportment of those who had shared his own stimulating experiences in 'that sweet city with the dreaming spires.' On one occasion he reminisced in the *Monthly* about a typical day in the life of an Oxford undergraduate, presumably hoping to shame his Canadian charges into changing their habits.[6]

In one of his annual reports to the chancellor there is a suggestion that Wallace linked those habits with the effects of the university's much-praised general course. He complained that the course was so broad and expected so much work from the student that it produced a cynicism which in turn might be contributing to the disorderliness he deplored. 'I say frankly' he wrote 'that I hesitate to characterize such a program in the language which it seems to me to deserve ... it convicts McMaster University of low ideals of scholarship and of superficial methods.'[7] He would have scoffed at the non-committal comment made at the time by an officer of the Department of Education that 'in the case of the McMaster course ... [they] have far more subjects of general culture than are offered by the other Universities.'[8]

Wallace was obviously anxious to reduce the over-all number of courses and to introduce more specialization into the arts curriculum. Much to his chagrin, this object was successfully combatted. The dictates of both economy and educational philosophy ruled out a change that might not only prove costly but also attach too much weight to the specialist at the expense of turning out 'men and women of high character' with a broadly based education.

While Wallace had been campaigning for a restructuring of the general course, Donald had been urging the establishment of more student organizations and discussion groups. As if to refute his historian-colleague, Donald claimed that, whatever its limitations, the instruction he had received at McMaster, particularly from James Ten Broeke, had stood him in good stead at Chicago. Echoing the commendations received by O.C.S. Wallace a few years before, he informed McKay in 1910 that his supervisor there was 'highly pleased that I had more Philosophy, Ethics, Education &c than the average man and with the amount of training I have both in Economics and other studies.'[9] But while he might not have shared Wallace's disgust for the general course, Donald did see merit in enriching undergraduate education through promoting the organization of more student clubs on the campus. He conceded that the university's Literary Society did bring such political luminaries as Sir Wilfrid Laurier and Henri Bourassa, the French-Canadian nationalist, to speak to assemblies. But what Donald wanted was a social science club, a forum for airing the latest findings in that area of study and 'helping the students to come to some more definite conclusion earlier in their college course' as to what they might wish to undertake as a future career.[10] Donald believed such clubs would work a desirable improvement in student interest and morale.

Although a body faintly resembling Donald's project was formed on a casual basis no well structured program of student clubs was inaugurated in the years before the war. Apparently Wallace's concern about hoodlums and academic superficiality and Donald's plans to raise morale were not avidly shared by their colleagues. There seemed to be a consensus among faculty and students that the associations already on campus were sufficient to stimulate and gratify the social and academic appetites of the student body. These included, in addition to the Literary Society, the Debating Club, the Athletic Association, and the YMCA and YWCA chapters at the university. The latter organizations, frowned upon in the early nineties as too pompous and genteel and, moreover, a threat to the churches,[11] had by this time become thoroughly acceptable agencies of Christian endeavour on the campus.

One professor disturbed by student listlessness was Glenn Campbell. Even when the Debating Club had taken on the potentially explosive question that 'Free Trade between Canada and the United States would be detrimental to the best interests of the Dominion,' he complained of a lacklustre performance, this in sharp contrast to the heated parliamentary discussions on Reciprocity he had observed in Ottawa.[12] The apathy that distressed Campbell and other faculty members in 1911 stood out in marked contrast to the emotional commitment that had ushered in the century on the McMaster campus. At that time imperial and national questions had agitated classrooms and the editorial columns of the *Monthly*. The South African War had excited heartfelt support at the university for the Mother Country's cause in the fight to put down the 'tyranny' of the Transvaal Republic. Typical of those years was a student's glowing remark that the 'British Empire has not yet reached the zenith of its power ... the present stage is only one stage in the evolution which will ultimately cement one of the greatest empires of any age.'[13]

Where had all that emotional fire and sentiment gone? Campbell and others asked a decade later. A student's rejoinder in 1911 was that indifference and apathy on the campus resulted from a lack of certain facilities crucial to a well-rounded college experience. What particularly agitated the Athletic Association and some members of faculty was the disposal by the university in 1911 of its one and only playing field 'without any reference to the voice of the student body.' According to the secretary of the Athletic Association there was 'strong dissatisfaction accompanied by a decline in enthusiasm and interest in the various branches of college life which have resulted in a decided lowering of the moral tone of the school.'[14] Stung by the criticism, the Board shortly undertook to find an adequate alternative to the lost playing field. But this endeavour, like the campaign mounted by McKay for a new science building and medical facilities, collided with one formidable obstacle: the campus's severely taxed grounds. As the university's architect had bluntly warned in 1907, 'unless more land is obtained, two more buildings must positively be [the] limit – [the] elastic limit ... Today the Science Building occupies all the available land to the south-west of [McMaster Hall].'[15]

Before another three years had passed this warning had been heeded and serious discussions begun on the urgency of acquiring more expansive property elsewhere. Academic and professional growth of the sort sought after by McKay and his advisers and the student body's desire for playing fields worthy of a university combined forces to promote the active search for a new site. Alumni were particularly pérsistent. "The Esprit de Corps of which we boast and I think justly' wrote one 'must be diminished [through] the lack of ...an adequate Campus'. 'There [has been] an apparent apathy,' he continued, 'which I am inclined to believe will become still more apparent if the need for a new campus is not met.'[16]

By this time, much to the alumni's satisfaction, the university had acquired its present colours. McMaster's stalwarts had hitherto taken the field attired in sweaters of green and black, unaccountably deemed appropriate for undergraduates at a 'Christian school of learning under Baptist auspices.' But since, as an alumnus recollected, 'Italian labourers at that time had a fondness for work sweaters [of the same colours] it is not surprising ... that ... McMaster teams [were] dubbed "The Dagos" [by] competing supporters.'[17] This reaction in supposedly civilized academic circles to the thousands of southern European immigrants then flooding into Ontario led to the adoption of maroon and grey: not that those colours in combination had some special Anglo-Saxon quality, but a locally recruited artist recommended them for their washability and complementary characteristics.

With this momentous decision out of the way the university turned to the matter of obtaining a new campus where McMaster's resplendently attired teams could display their prowess. Because the price of land in McMaster Hall's immediate vicinity proved prohibitive, a new site was sought in North Toronto, about five miles from the original campus and fronting on Eglinton Avenue near Avenue Road.[18] The decision to reconnoitre this location was received by some alumni with mixed feelings. Morden Long, one of the university's first Rhodes scholars, wrote from Oxford that he was very glad to learn that McMaster was contemplating a move north that would result in 'an ever wider sphere of ... usefulness.' He added, however, that 'it seems hard to have to give up McMaster Hall, and Castle Memorial Hall, about which already so many associations have clustered.'[19]

For alumni like Long the esprit de corps forged on the playing field might be too high a price to pay for that other kind of loyalty inspired by the sentimental and academic associations with the architecture on Bloor Street. Another graduate was gratified by the decision to remain within Toronto's metropolitan limits and wrote approvingly when he learned that the executors of the McMaster estate had in October 1912 formally sanctioned the university's purchase of twenty-five acres at the Eglinton site.[20] 'Wealthy

Toronto Baptists' he was confident 'are abundantly able to provide the buildings and put you on easy street financially.'[21] The prospective purchase must also have improved morale amongst athletes and students generally. Dean McLay observed in the spring of 1912 that a 'fine esprit de corps has been evident ... the students have given a good account of themselves in various intercollegiate contests and have sustained the reputation of Alma Mater.' And two years later even stern Stewart Wallace was becoming 'more impressed with the ... earnest manner in which the undergraduates ... apply themselves to their work.'[22]

W. Sherwood Fox, an alumnus who later became president of the University of Western Ontario, wrote from Princeton that he had feared that McMaster might move to some 'outside point,' a possibility that had in fact been discussed at least as early as 1911 when nearby Hamilton had been singled out for special attention.[23] A minor crisis had been precipitated in 1909 when the *Monthly* boldly announced that a decision had been taken to move the university to that city. Apparently the author of the shocking article was, to no one's surprise, an audacious Hamiltonian, Alvin Ogilvie, who saw to it that his home town's press received advance copies of the report and did enthusiastic justice to its revelations. 'The excitement and unrest was not momentary,' one account claimed, 'for rumblings of the ensuing controversy persisted for some time.' As it turned out, Ogilvie's statement would be recalled a few years later when a group of Hamilton alumni seriously proposed the move he had facetiously promoted in 1909 and which had actually been discussed in 1911.

One person who had recently been involved in the university's theological troubles thought the Hamilton suggestion merited full consideration. 'I doubt if any university can expect to fill a truly desirable place in the life of the people of the country' George Cross wrote from Chicago 'unless it gathers about it the sympathy and support of some civic community ... Hamilton might do fine things for McMaster.'[24] Cross must already have come to the conclusion that Toronto's main commitment would always be to the University of Toronto or to the other more firmly established denominational institutions in the city. If the relatively youthful McMaster moved to a new urban environment it might come to humanize it and be associated with its cultural and social progress and in the process produce a dividend for the whole country.[25]

Toronto's 'ambitious neighbour' – the sobriquet Hamilton had been sporting for a generation – had exhibited encouraging signs of growth since the turn of the century. Its population, fifty thousand in 1901, had swollen to over seventy thousand by the time McMaster's Board of Governors began reviewing its assets ten years later. Older industries had been streamlined and new ones attracted to the city by its strategic location, its improvements in communications – notably the Toronto, Hamilton, and Buffalo Railway and the electric radials – and its offer of tax exemptions or reductions. In 1910 the Steel Company of Canada had made its début, a merger engineered by the financial wizardry of Max Aitken out of a number of iron and steel concerns organized in the city in the 1890s.[26] Although it could not match Toronto's central location and prodigious exertions in wholesaling and commerce it nonetheless appealed to those Baptists anxious to remove Mc-Master from the embrace of the University of Toronto and the spectre of federation. Moreover, Hamilton had at least six flourishing Baptist churches and a growing number of McMaster alumni who could be expected to canvass actively on behalf of the transplanted institution.

But the people who shared Sherwood Fox's views had the last word when the decision was made to discard the Hamilton proposal and to select instead the Eglinton site. 'Toronto is growing even more rapidly' Fox claimed 'and will soon be plenty large [enough] to harbor two universities without either overshadowing the other.'[27] In addition, comforting reports were being received of increased attendance and Sunday School enrolment in the Baptist churches in Toronto's northern suburbs, all within easy reach of the projected campus. Not only this, but some McMaster alumni in Hamilton held unflattering views of their own city. 'I have come to realize' a high school principal wrote in the summer of 1910 'that unless a man is in Toronto, there is practically nothing new for him.'[28]

During the negotiations over the purchase of the Eglinton site, Chancellor McKay, while sojourning in the United Kingdom, decided to tender his resignation. More than once he had been approached by the board of the technical high school in Toronto to serve as its principal. When the invitation was extended yet again in 1911 he seemed anxious to accept it. His motives may not be difficult to isolate. When his colleague and close friend, Dean W.S. McLay, first learned of his intentions – and he was apparently the first to know – he warned the chancellor of the 'irksomeness of working for the Board of Education and of being subjected to the persistence of Ward Politicians seeking favours.' 'On the other hand' McLay conceded, possibly touching the heart of the matter, 'you will doubtless have the satisfaction of being at the head of a technical school instead of being at the head of a theological college. *I remember what you have often said, that you were not born to be in the midst of theological controversy* and [I] can sympathize with your desire to escape from it.'[29] To this McKay replied: 'All that I really know is that I have an opportunity to leave the Chancellorship ... and [do]

evidently what you expected me to do . . . you are not surprised that I take it.'
Nor was A.T. MacNeill at Woodstock College surprised. After expressing his
regrets to McKay he added consolingly that there 'would be a good deal less
worry and that is what you are looking for just now.'[30] Understandably,
strong efforts were made to retain him and commendations flooded his office.
Typical was that offered by Professor Smith when rumours first began
circulating that the chancellor might resign: 'the changes made in the curriculum in the last five years have been most important steps in . . . the direction of
what modern education ought to be . . . and the credit for these changes is due
to you who initiated them.'[31]

There is good reason to suppose that the resignation of J.L. Hogg at this
time was influenced by McKay's decision. True, he was offered the physics
chair at the new University of Saskatchewan, which had already claimed the
services of historian Oliver; but even so, Hogg had more than once expressed
appreciation for the productive environment the chancellor had created at
McMaster, particularly for scientists, and he had hinted that that environment might be jeopardized if McKay left the scene.[32] In any case the chancellor had made up his mind to resign. When he accepted the post at the technical
school he embarked on a career that brought him considerable satisfaction
and earned him an enviable reputation as an administrator and teacher in the
expanding field of technological training in the province.[33]

McKay's decision to depart coincided with, indeed it may have been
partially inspired by, the establishment in 1910 of a federal Royal Commission on Industrial Training and Technical Education. This had long been
sought by the Canadian Manufacturers' Association as a means of investigating the vital needs of the nation's growing industrial plant. To their gratification and to McKay's the recently appointed minister of labour in Sir Wilfrid
Laurier's administration, W.L. Mackenzie King, fully shared the views of
those educators and industrialists who passionately believed that improved
technical education was the prerequisite for the proper economic development of the country.[34]

And yet the question has to be asked: could not McKay, if he remained the
executive head of a university with expanding scientific facilities, be in just as
strategic a position to inspire and direct the sort of technological instruction
that he undertook outside McMaster Hall after 1911? Or was there opposition among some members of the Board and the faculty to research and to the
growth of scientific and technical courses on the ground that they would
detract from the real work of such an institution — the preparation of people
for the time-honoured professions? The failure of the universities to address
themselves to the task of meeting the demands of an industrial society had

long been a complaint of businessmen and industrialists.[35]

J.L. Hogg's comments suggest that the Board did not properly appreciate the significance of the research that he and his colleagues in the natural sciences were pursuing at McMaster.[36] Of course, the young and eager physicist may have taken his own work so seriously that there was no need for anyone else to do so. While there might have been some indifference to what the scientists on staff were doing – in this respect McMaster was not exceptional – there is no evidence that McKay's plans for the expansion of chemistry or physics were ever seriously opposed. In some cases mystification might have been mistaken for indifference or even hostility. What one authority had to say about the situation in the 1920s applies with even greater force to the earlier period: 'Research' E.W.R. Steacie has written 'was a vague and rare thing done by university professors for reasons best known to themselves.'[37]

Dean McLay undoubtedly put his finger on the crucial motive prompting McKay's resignation when he reviewed the chancellor's unpleasant experiences with theological controversies. Years before, while instructing at the University of Toronto, McKay had been appalled when a pitched battle broke out in his classroom between arts and medical students representing respectively the agitated forces of faith and rationalism.[38] Although during the Matthews controversy no police had been called in to separate the combatants, as had been the case earlier in his classroom, the recent confrontation with Harris must have reminded the chancellor of how an academic atmosphere could be poisoned by a war over doctrinal questions. Much of his administration had been dogged and his emotional reserves drained by the disputes that had raged around Matthews and Cross, and he must have unashamedly yearned for quieter groves more suited to his temperament, training, and purpose.

No one, however, could have seriously accused McKay of abandoning the institution he had served in so many and varied capacities for two decades. When he left to take up his new duties in the fall of 1911 much of the strife had subsided, science instruction had been firmly established in functional new quarters, and arrangements for relocating McMaster seemed well in hand. The student body had increased to nearly three hundred, a jump of 60 per cent from the figure for 1905, and there were in 1911 proportionately more students engaged in graduate studies in both arts and theology. Moreover, during McKay's administration salaries had leaped by a third to some $38,000 to meet the needs of the university's twenty-one faculty members and administrative officers.[39]

The man chosen to succeed McKay had been closely associated with the educational work of the denomination at both the preparatory and university levels. Like his predecessor in office, Abraham Lincoln McCrimmon was a University of Toronto graduate. A gold medallist in logic and philosophy, he was an honours candidate in Professor Ashley's newly established course in political economy at University College. Following his graduation McCrimmon had served briefly as Chancellor MacVicar's secretary, then taught high school, and in 1892 accepted a position as classical master at Woodstock College. At that institution he worked his way up the administrative ladder to the principalship in 1897. Invited a few years later to groom himself for a lectureship in political economy at McMaster, McCrimmon enrolled in post-graduate work at Chicago. After he completed the requirements for the MA degree in economics and sociology he was in 1904 given the appointment at McMaster. When he was selected as McKay's successor he held the chair in political economy, sociology, and education and was being assisted in his efforts by W.J.A. Donald, the lecturer in political economy.

McCrimmon's appointment had enabled the university to introduce for the first time a distinctive and entirely separate course in political economy.[40] Hitherto it had been presented in double harness with constitutional history. The new course reflected some of the great social and economic concerns of that generation, trade unionism and labour economics, the emergence of trusts and other forms of modern capitalism, and the doctrines of socialism. Beatrice and Sidney Webb, John Atkinson Hobson, the leading anti-imperialist of that age whose tracts on the economic interpretation of imperialism formed a new gospel, and F.W. Taussig, the student of the American tariff structure: these were some of the impressive names on McCrimmon's reading lists after 1904.

Apart from political economy, the future chancellor was also expected to develop a course in the relatively new discipline of sociology. Not surprisingly, his approach reflected the assumptions and interests of Chicago's Sociology Department, the first such to be established as an independent academic unit.[41] In McCrimmon's day the Chicago approach emphasized studies in the history of social thought and social origins, and examinations of the family, social classes, and methods of social amelioration, all of which were embodied in his course.[42] Prominent on the textbook list was the recently published work of Thorstein Veblen, himself a one-time instructor at Chicago, the epoch-making *Theory of the Leisure Class*. Conspicuous by its absence was Herbert Spencer's formidable *Principles of Sociology*, still regarded in some quarters as the greatest work ever written in the field. There had been a tendency in Chicago and other American schools, however, to question Spencer's credentials as a scientific sociologist in the knowledge that sociology to him was a sideline or at best only one means among many of applying his famed evolutionary formulas.[43] Such an attitude did not please the serious-minded practitioners of the new craft who felt that it merited full time devotion and should not be treated like some kind of chore-boy to supposedly loftier academic pursuits.

That Spencer should have been shouldered aside by the new sociologists – as seems to have been the case in McCrimmon's course as well – did not sit well with his successor as chancellor, Howard Whidden, particularly when sociology was 'articulated [so] closely with ... Practical Theology.'[44] I am coming to be more and more anxious' wrote Whidden to George Cross in the twenties 'concerning the place of Sociology in a theological curriculum ... I am sure that if Herbert Spencer knew some of the things that some of the Austro-American school of economists and sociologists teach in our generation he would make a very uneasy turn in his tomb.'[45] In McCrimmon's time as an instructor at McMaster the trend that so disturbed Whidden had not yet assumed such disquieting proportions.

That sociology was closely connected with practical theology few would have questioned in that earlier period. Indeed, the need for a 'rural sociology' was much discussed; it involved the use of some kind of preventive social medicine in the countryside. 'Here is one way' a hopeful correspondent wrote in 1911 'in which McMaster could further endear herself to some of her most valued constituents. As the country is the source of life for the city, so it may be said that, as goes the country life, physically, spiritually, economically and every other way, so goes the city life. Prevention in the country by expert social leaders, the preachers, would often make cure unnecessary in the city.'[46] Before long McCrimmon himself was directing theses on the role that churches might play in resolving problems that affected the social structure of rural areas in south-central Ontario.

These academic pursuits and attainments were all very commendable and welcome in a chancellor-elect. But considering McCrimmon's stay in that 'sinkhole of hell,' as the University of Chicago was regarded in some circles, one might have expected his elevation to the post would not have been eagerly acclaimed. But there was no outcry against the appointment. Indeed, on every hand it appeared to be applauded. Dean McLay, the outgoing chancellor's close friend and confidant and, of course, a congenial colleague of McCrimmon's, had occasion to tell the latter after his first year in office how well he had conducted himself not only at the university but also among the rank and file of the denomination. 'Frankly,' wrote McLay, perhaps less than frankly, in the fall of 1912, 'there has been nothing like [the success you achieved with the delegates at the annual Assembly of the Convention in Brantford] ... I have served under your three predecessors and have fully appreciated their good qualities but ... not one of them ever did, or perhaps could do, what you accomplished [there].'[47] A.A. Ayer, who might have been concerned about the number of Britons and Americans being named to university posts in Canada, remarked matter of factly that the 'promotion of a Canadian is desirable in every way and especially when none better than the Doctor can be found anywhere.'[48] This was pale praise, however, compared with the plaudits that poured from the pens of others. One writer compared McCrimmon's potential influence with that of President Eliot of Harvard, while another thought him 'an Asqueth, Lloyd George & a Lord Rosbery combined,'[49] a mixture that would probably have destroyed the party system in the United Kingdom.

What accounts, one is tempted to ask, for such extravagant eulogies? McCrimmon had unquestioned teaching talents, promising scholarship, and considerable diplomatic finesse, virtues that may have warranted a reasonably enthusiastic reception, but the adulation he generated among his fellow academics and churchgoers bordered on hyperbole, almost on the frantic. Was it because the university and the churches desperately wanted to believe that they had found a worthy successor to the esteemed McKay? Almost as if to convince themselves that the large vacancy created by McKay's departure could be adequately filled they seemed to be telling themselves that McCrimmon's qualities would meet the challenges of leadership and administration to which his predecessor had so effectively responded.

On the other hand, what accounted for the friendly reception accorded McCrimmon by the conservative Baptists who had so recently shared Elmore Harris's doubts about the university's orthodoxy? A clue is provided by McCrimmon's concern about the allegedly aggressive way in which I.G. Matthews had addressed congregations in 1910 when his teaching had been under scrutiny. But a more conclusive answer may have been embodied in a letter the new chancellor wrote Harris shortly before the latter died on a tour of Baptist missions in Burma.[50] He began by offering an interpretation of the controversy quite unlike McKay's view of it. 'I hope that the days of strife are past,' McCrimmon wrote, 'now we have the overt understanding with our brethren teaching theology that at any time they cannot teach the views we hold they are to go elsewhere.' He then went on to praise Harris and to assure him that it was not 'flattering sycophancy' when he said that the clergyman's name would 'receive, and can only receive, the highest place among Baptists' and that it would be 'written in the annals of Baptist History.'

In a burst of rhetoric that had not been fashionable at the chancellor's desk for some years, McCrimmon next dwelt on what he conceived to be the prime motive for his appointment: 'the [selection] committee made me feel that for a time at least I was the man to unify the denomination and to inspire our leading men with the thought of larger things for us in the Kingdom of God; if we are wise now in what we say and do, the misunderstanding of the past will soon be buried, and while we may not see eye to eye in all things, the spirit of brotherly love will . . . direct us to our destined goal.' Small wonder that one impressed layman told him in the fall of 1911 that although 'at first I had the idea that you were non grata to our Conservative friends . . . I learned that you had their entire confidence and I . . . most eagerly joined the rest . . . in presenting your name to the Senate.'[51]

McCrimmon may well have been what the university and the denomination needed at this juncture: a man who could heal, or give the appearance of healing, the wounds remaining from the Matthews controversy, and at the same time who would be credible to academic and churchgoer alike. But all the protestations of respect, admiration, and relief that greeted McCrimmon's acceptance of the appointment notwithstanding, his chancellorship was viewed in some quarters as a stopgap measure, an interregnum separating the regime of the dynamic McKay and the desired advent of an equally forceful academic leader.

As it happened, McCrimmon was under no illusion about his awesome task, and he had, to be sure, devoutly wished that some one else be chosen. In his letter to Harris, McCrimmon touched on a point to which he would continually return throughout his administration: 'I assumed the duties at great risk to myself, contrary to the judgment of my physician.' A.A. Ayer, who was aware of McCrimmon's reservations, urged him to 'work it out as we businessmen do; make . . . the others . . . responsible for something – let them do the worrying and you the overlooking.'[52] Whether or not the new chancellor followed this advice at the outset, he assumed his new duties in the sincere hope of unifying the denomination behind the university. And in the early years he was successful. Those congregations which had only grudgingly accepted the Convention's decision of 1910 were by 1912 offering more wholehearted support to McMaster. Especially encouraging to Stewart Bates, the educational secretary, was that the Norfolk Association and Waterford, two parts of the constituency most noted for their hostility to Matthews and his supporters, were now falling into line. 'We shall win out,' Bates added, 'Christian education *must* succeed.'[53] Even McCrimmon himself began to dare hope at this time that the 'churches are moving towards better relations with the University.' Although echoes of the recent controversy would occasionally be heard,[54] the early years of McCrimmon's administration were spared the agony that had gripped the closing years of his predecessor's.

But large problems still remained. Among these was the need to relocate the campus on the site acquired in North Toronto. For some months after the purchase was actually made in the fall of 1912 reservations were expressed about the shape of the property. Consequently, negotiations were started to buy adjoining properties or exchange them for parcels of the site no longer considered suitable. Throughout, the Senate minutes record, the university was guided by a great deal of information collected from other institutions, including, presumably, the University of Toronto.[55] The latter and Trinity College were expected to purchase the original McMaster property on Bloor Street.

In any case, while the Board continued to juggle properties on Eglinton Avenue, definite plans for constructing buildings and laying out playing fields could not be implemented. This was a disappointment to O.C.S. Wallace who had urged a speedy removal to North Toronto and the construction of 'worthy buildings – no factories or warehouses or barns.'[56] Wallace was not the only one dismayed by the delay; his regrets were soon shared by faculty and students, and particularly by athletes and alumni. But in the circumstances little could be done to expand what the university's architect had once described as the campus's 'elastic limits.'

The project of reconstruction was then deferred indefinitely, first by a business recession in 1913 and then by a calamity that occurred half a world away in the late summer of 1914. The outbreak of 'the Great War' diverted people, resources, and revenues from the task of building up McMaster to that of preserving King and Country.

7

Armageddon

On a visit to Germany in the fall of 1910 a McMaster Rhodes scholar remarked on that country's state of military preparedness. 'During the last days of my vacation' Morden Long told Chancellor McKay 'I had the opportunity of seeing the semi-annual review of the Berlin and Potsdam garrisons. These are the guards regiments, the pick of the German army, and the sight of 25,000 of them mustered with the great 'war lord' himself at their head was certainly a very imposing demonstration of Germany's military strength and organization.'[1] Shortly before this letter arrived McKay had received a communication from George Parkin, a Canadian director of the Rhodes Trust and a leading imperial federationist in the United Kingdom. 'We are thinking very intensely about national matters in England just now,' Parkin had written. 'There is no doubt that the European situation is an exceedingly awkward one. Naval questions are being discussed all the time and it is evident that there is a very deep tone of anxiety running through the whole country. We shall have to make sacrifices if we are to maintain the same degree of security that we have enjoyed ever since Trafalgar in 1805.'[2] Germany's emergence as a major land power in central Europe with pretensions to challenge Britain's naval might and imperial pre-eminence had sent a shudder of horror through Parkin and other imperial federationists.

Meanwhile, readers of the *Monthly* were reminded of the formidable power of the British empire which Parkin had no wish to see eroded away. They were also told of the degree to which Europe generally had been militarized since the closing decades of the nineteenth century. A McMaster undergraduate holidaying in England reported on the elaborate military ceremonies that attended the funeral of Edward VII in the fall of 1910. She wrote of the massed soldiery 'whose territorial region stretched from London to Bombay, regiments which man the Northwest of Canada, or have their quarters beneath the Lion's head of the Cape, followed by the bronzed naval brigade.' But her readers were informed that the dead monarch had also been an honorary colonel of foreign armies whose representatives were conspicuously on hand for the occasion; 'A glittering array,' she marvelled, 'Europe in arms.'[3]

It was a prospect ill-designed to please a Baptist reared on the abjuration of violence and militarism. C.J. Holman, a long-time member of McMaster's Board of Governors, had doubtless spoken for many Baptists and university people in 1901 when he opposed the formation of school cadet corps: 'I have no measure of sympathy with this drilling of our public school children with guns even if the guns are of wood.'[4] Chancellor Wallace had gone further, complaining about the unwelcome military overtones of the otherwise inoffensive Boys' Brigade.[5] Most Baptists would probably have asked, as did one pastor, 'Is training in the Army of the Lord for the noblest work of which the human heart and brain are capable, less important than the training of men for fighting the battles of nations?' When a Canadian Defence League was formed in 1909 advocating military training in peacetime only the Baptists, of all the denominations called upon, refused to support its aims.[6] And when McMaster was invited along with its sister institutions in 1911 to 'be associated in some manner with the work of the Militia,' it responded by tabling the proposal out of respect for the feelings of the denomination.

Alarmed though Baptists might have been by the growth of militarism, few of them were prepared for the abrupt and violent shattering of peace in the late summer of 1914. After all, little wars and rumours of a larger one had been conversation pieces for years, and yet no catastrophe had occurred. Not even the bloody assassination of a foreign archduke in a distant country seemed sufficient warning that a general conflict was about to convulse Europe. Germany's invasion of diminutive Belgium, the act which triggered Britain's entry into the expanding hostilities, came, as the *Canadian Baptist* put it, like 'a bolt out of the blue.' 'We had become accustomed' the editorial went on 'to think that war was an impossibility with our peace[ful] society and its international ramifications.'[7]

The events in western Europe had a profound effect on both faculty and student body at McMaster. Any apathy still lingering there about the larger questions facing the civilized world was quickly dispelled by the crisis that threatened that world in 1914. Equal parts of rage, compassion, frustration, and venom were mixed in a poem that one undergraduate composed for the

Monthly. Bernard Freeman Trotter addressed it 'To the Students of Liège,' one of Belgium's ancient university towns and, incidentally, a strong point in that country's defences:

> In old Liège, when those dark tidings came
>> Of German honour callously forsworn
>> And the red menace that should bring the scorn
> Of ages on the Kaiser's name and shame
> And crown their city with a deathless fame,
>> The students wrote, they say, that summer morn
>> For their degrees, then joined the hope forlorn
> Of Liberty, and passed in blood and fame.
>
> O valiant souls! who loved not Duty less
>> Than Honor, whom no fears could move to shirk
>> The common task, no tyrant's threat subdue
> When Right and Freedom called in their distress –
>> Not vain your sacrifice nor lost your work:
>> The World's free heart beats high because of you![8]

Solicitude for a 'bullied country' was soon matched by a desire to rally to Britain's side once she declared war on Belgium's invader. But hours before that solemn act was performed W.J. McKay, the editor of the *Canadian Baptist* and brother of the recently departed chancellor, posed a rhetorical question: Is it war for Canada? The response was not in doubt. In company with many of his fellow Baptists and other evangelical Christians[9] McKay had been declaiming for years against the sort of violence that had just erupted in Europe and against the preparations that had made that violence possible; but he could see no course for Baptists and other Canadians except to support the mother country. Reminiscent of the sentiments expressed at the turn of the century, when events in South Africa had generated imperial loyalties in the Dominion, McKay concluded that 'if necessity thrusts Canada into [the war] we are glad to know that her loyal sons will not shirk any responsibility.'

Once war was formally declared by Britain on 6 August 1914, McKay was well aware that Canada's commitment to participate at her side would in many quarters be considered automatic. But he believed, as many others did, that Canada's intervention went beyond legalistic interpretations of her relationship with the United Kingdom. McKay put it this way:

We do not wish to close our eyes to [the war's] fearful din. For it is our war not Britain's alone to whom we give support in her struggle. It has been frequently said in the past, 'that when Britain is at war Canada is at war' but different interpretations have been put upon the saying . . . *But we will say it now and with but one meaning.* Canada must take the field for this is truly her war. A terrible strain must come upon the mother country and Canada must feel that strain too. Not so severely as if our country were the theatre of conflict, or near it by an ocean's width than we are, but feel it deeply we shall.[10]

The British empire, exalted by McKay and the *Monthly* as the hope of civilization and of 'all that is truest and best in our national life,' was deemed worthy of every sacrifice. Already the university had been imperialized so to speak when it was formally designated in 1911 as a colonial university in affiliation with Oxford. The same year the Congress of the Universities of the Empire, convened by imperially-minded academics in Britain, extended an invitation to McMaster to send a representative, an invitation accepted by McCrimmon personally.

The zeal and dedication released on the McMaster campus seemed to be an extension of the traditional evangelical militancy of the Baptists. Combat against anti-Christian forces at home and on foreign mission fields in time of peace was now to encompass a campaign to destroy the enemies of the British empire, the acknowledged safeguard of civilization and of Christianity itself. The bearing of arms, the training of cadets, and the raising of an army of Christian soldiers, once considered so abhorrent, were now justified by the enormity overseas. For Dean Farmer the message was clear: 'All our forces must be mobilized for the winning of the war into which Christ's commission has sent us.'[11] Not only this, there was always the comforting possibility, as some of the practical pointed out, that military drill might provide the hapless cadet with 'intellectual stimulus.'[12]

The 'barbarism' perpetrated by the Germans in Belgium and elsewhere, condemned by Bernard Trotter in poetic form, was censured by others in sermons, editorials, and open letters. Stewart Bates, the university's educational secretary, put Germany's behaviour down to the 'ideals and instruction presented in [its] schools.'[13] This theme was taken up by the Toronto *Globe*, which charged that the 'false ideals of life set up in German Universities, the ideals of domination and Mastership . . . perverted the mind of youthful Germany . . . and destroyed the sense of moral distinction alike for the state and for the private citizen.'[14] For the theological conservatives who had long been searching for the ultimate condemnation of the German scholarship that had spawned the paganism of the higher criticism, the war must have seemed heaven-sent. For these people the successful prosecution of the conflict against Prussian militarism would also destroy those ideas which had poisoned the fundamentals of the faith. A resolution passed by the Ottawa Association in the summer of 1915 summed up this feeling well: 'We as Baptists protest the stand of any nation that regards a sacred treaty as a scrap of paper; much more do we take a stand, firm and uncompromising, against a school of thought that regards the Bible in any other sight than the infallible word of God and the Gospel of the Grace of God.'[15]

Still others, particularly in academic ranks, saw in the war not so much a theological crusade as an ideological one aimed at destroying forces that threatened the democratic ethic. This theme also elicited a warm response in the humble churchgoer of the back townships who could boast that every Baptist congregation in the land was a democratic or autonomous community and that 'the sum total of these small democracies was a mighty democracy willed and ruled by God.' That mighty democracy, no one had to be urged, must gather up its strength to defeat prussianism.

Having asked and answered the question Why go to war? the university next had to decide how to fight it and support it. For faculty members like Stewart Wallace, enlistment in the armed forces was the answer. Until they could actually be mobilized, Wallace and other intended recruits had to be content with an arrangement that would have been anathema to most Baptists just a few years before. In October 1914 Wallace and two colleagues, R.W. Smith and William McNairn, investigated the merits of organizing an Officers' Training Corps on the campus. At a meeting of the student body it was enthusiastically decided to have the McMaster unit join the University of Toronto contingent already formed across the park. Within a matter of days one hundred men had enrolled in the McMaster platoon and were drilling under Wallace's direction. By the end of November they had already taken part, alongside platoons from Wycliffe and Victoria Colleges, in a widely heralded sham battle in North Toronto against a force drawn from University College. The hardened colonel who evaluated the proceedings dutifully awarded merits and demerits to both sides and philosophically concluded, 'All I can say, gentlemen, is that it's a fine day to be out, anyway.'[16]

While Wallace had been directing McMaster's brave boys on the no man's land of North Toronto, Professor Tingle was pondering the implications of the expanding world conflict, anxious 'to make my resources as effective for the common good as possible.' For a start, Tingle decided to drop his subscriptions to the *Monthly* and the Athletic Association and to devote that and other funds to the encouragement of rifle shooting, 'particularly amongst the students of this University.'[17] For his part, the chancellor, with assistance from his faculty, prepared public statements and brochures for schools and organizations on the origins and implications of the war. Predictably, his version of events said more about the patriotic prejudices of his generation than it did about the actions that had actually contributed to the holocaust that burst upon the world in 1914. Clearly, to quote the *Baptist Year Book*, 'a University under Baptist auspices with the traditions of freedom incorporated in its history,' could do no less than provide inspirational messages to aid in the successful prosecution of the war.[18]

Amidst the brave words and the messages of dedication there were, to be sure, misgivings and doubts. Some Baptists raised the question, particularly when it became plain that the soldiers were not to be out of the trenches by Christmas: 'Can it be that we have been mistaken in our ideas of God? Why should He have permitted the appalling catastrophe that has overtaken the world?' But others urged that in the circumstances a basic query of this sort ought to be buried under renewals of faith in what Canada and the Allies were doing on the other side of the Atlantic.

A question that would not go away, however, was the effect the war would have upon the institution. It was one thing for McMaster to acquit itself honourably during the emergency; it was another to ensure that it would survive the demands that might be thrust upon it. Visible signs of the war's intrusion on normality was the abandonment of such social institutions as Founder's Night and the Literary Society banquet. But this was only an irritant. Much more serious were the wartime postponement of a new Forward Movement and the extent to which enrolment and the revenue from fees were affected by the crisis.

Admittedly, Ottawa did not actively encourage enlistment from Canadian universities in the early months of the conflict. But a growing number of high school graduates were more disposed to enlist than to further their education; the roll of army recruits from McMaster grew, and by the fall of 1915 the university began to feel the pinch. Figures submitted by the chancellor were eloquent enough; only fifty-five new students entered the university that fall compared with seventy-three in the registration period of the previous year, an alarming drop of 25 per cent. By the following spring it was noted that no fewer than twenty-one undergraduates, representing 12 per cent of the student body, had enlisted in the country's armed forces. It was recorded too that this figure included five candidates in theology who had departed to join up with their classmates in arts.[19]

But the war apparently could not be blamed for another statistic that thoroughly upset the administration. Fully fourteen divinity students de-

camped for reasons other than having gone to war. Although no explanation
for this exodus appears to have been committed to paper at the time, it might
be speculated that some of them were so disturbed by the close association of
applied Christianity with the violence and slaughter overseas that faith in
their studies was gravely shaken.

The departure of students for the battlefield was understandably greeted
with mixed feelings. The problem was how to maintain enrolments to avoid
serious deficits, a problem that plagued the university for the remainder of the
conflict. The response of the faculty posed another problem. When Stewart
Wallace enlisted in the 139th Battalion in the spring of 1916 the university
not only lost the services of a historian but felt morally bound to paying at
least a fraction of his salary while he was on leave from his teaching duties,
even though he assured them that he would not complain if they were forced
to reconsider their generosity.[20] For a time the university also lost the services
of Professor Glenn Campbell who in 1915 volunteered to act as an interpreter
for the British and French governments. 'As [the war] does not promise to be
over for some time yet,' the *Monthly* brightly announced, 'he will likely find
plenty of opportunity to "Parlez-vous" for British Tommies.'[21]

Some fear was expressed that if the rate of enlistment among undergraduates and faculty continued to climb the university might be obliged to
close down temporarily. Certainly this was to be the experience of a number
of theological schools in the United States once that country entered the war.
Although McMaster never did shut its doors nor follow the example of some
American universities and become a virtual military school, military training
was introduced on the campus in 1915 on a voluntary basis and then in 1917
as a compulsory part of the regular curriculum. A general regulation was
adopted in 1915 that students who qualified for certification in military work
would be allowed standing in one subject in case this were needed to make up
a deficiency elsewhere in their program. Early in the following year it was
decided that enlisted students should be granted standing in the year in which
they were enrolled when they enlisted.[22]

Confronted with massive wartime problems, the Board and the chancellor
were forced to revise drastically the plans so hopefully hatched in the pre-war
years. The move to a new campus and the construction of new buildings,
already threatened by a crippling business slump in 1913, were deferred
indefinitely by the hard times that accompanied the first year of war and by
the university's declining income. As long as hope held out that the war would
be a brief one, shortages, deprivation, and the cancellation of time-honoured
festivities could be borne. But by the spring of 1916 it was quite clear that the
stalemate on the western front would only prolong the hostilities and the

university would have to make do with whatever resources it could wring from the Baptist constituency. To add to the gloom the year had opened with the disturbing news that enlistments during the current session had deprived McMaster of over a thousand dollars in tuition and boarding fees.

It was deemed imperative then that a large-scale effort be made to meet the financial crisis. A target of $20,000 was aimed at in the denomination, and D.E. Thomson, the Board chairman, drew up a plan for publicizing the university and its war effort. 'I am going to unburden myself of some crude impressions,' he warned McCrimmon. Promotional literature, he urged, should be 'livened up with pictures and personal touches about . . . the boys at the Front; picture of Dr Gilmour in his regimentals as Chaplain . . . picture of Mr Wallace . . . now enlisted. But above everything else, a succession of short, pithy, striking paragraphs showing the number of students and graduates of McMaster and Woodstock who have enlisted and the effect of this on the finances of the Institution . . . If we go into this thing we need to put life and snap into it.'[23] The fate of this brochure is unknown, but the bulk of Thomson's advice was heeded, judging from the gratifying success of the campaign. Even with this financial injection, however, the patient still had to be solicitously cared for as enrolment and income continued to slide over the next two years. The undergraduate registration figures for 1918, 115 men and 63 women, contrasted dismally with that for 1913, 204 men and 44 women.[24]

In the meantime, the glamour and nobility associated with the cause in 1914 was badly tarnished by the disillusionment and bitterness of those who had been enduring months of trench warfare in Flanders. 'It is most remarkable,' wrote a Canadian expatriate pastor who had entertained McMaster veterans in England, 'this universal and bitter hatred in the men, of war and of soldiering, and all things military – Militarism has lost its glamour.'[25] On the other hand, a preacher who had lost a son in action early in the war wrote vehemently to McCrimmon: 'May those fearless defenders of national honour and human liberty shoot straight and strike hard that soon the enemy may be smitten to the dust!'[26]

Such sentiments were often thankfully interspersed with news of the hopes and ambitions of McMaster's men in khaki overseas. These tidings helped to relieve the chancellor of the strain of bad ones and to mask the ugly facts of receding revenues and dwindling registrations. 'In London there is a mecca to which all McMaster pilgrims gradually find their way,' Gordon Philpott informed McCrimmon toward the end of the war, 'It is the home of the Rev. W.F. Price . . . I recently spent [my] leave there and met more and heard more McMaster than I have ever heard in the three years since I graduated . . . You are always sure of a welcome and . . . everything is merry . . . and the meals, which interest every soldier, rival even a literary [Society] banquet.'[27] Among recent graduates who regularly availed themselves of the Prices' hospitality was Harold Adams Innis, who had captured special scholarships in political economy and philosophy and who had already given some inkling of his future reputation as one of Canada's leading thinkers in the history of economics and communications. Another frequent visitor to the Price household was the congenial and courtly Frederick William Waters, a future professor of philosophy and psychology at his alma mater.

Price, in turn, kept the chancellor fully informed of his one-time charges. 'We have been very interested to note' he remarked

how they retain their affection for their Alma Mater and how the old esprit de corps still dominates them – they love to foregather and talk – *how they talk* – of the never-to-be-forgotten student days, that seem now so far distant. Many a tale of mad prank and escapade we hear and laugh over – But as they speak of the old times, and the men who figure in them there is often a catch in the breath . . . when they tell of this one and the other who has 'gone West' . . . Yet there is always a tone of pride – they died nobly, those boys, as many a wounded one suffered nobly, and all nobly fought.'[28]

For McCrimmon, echoes of the war and its issues were frequently sounded closer to home in the very corridors of McMaster Hall. In the spring of 1915, while perusing the letters from the trenches and dressing stations overseas, he received a tersely worded statement from Sir Robert Falconer of the University of Toronto. It recommended purging Fallersleben's *Deutschland uber Alles* from the requirements of Junior Matriculation German. In his reply the next day McCrimmon agreed with his colleague that 'it does not seem fitting that Canadian students should in the midst of this war be compelled to study the national song of the Germans.[29] Not only was the recommendation adopted but also, in the closing months of the conflict, the acting minister of education announced that his department would 'not continue to accept the courses of any of the Universities in which German is compulsory, and desires that in such courses Spanish be allowed as an option for German.' War hysteria had plainly come to cloud the judgment of those responsible for Ontario's educational affairs.

But the political denunciation of an academic discipline did not end there. As the war dragged on and hatred accumulated some critics were disposed to question the right of native-born Germans to teach their mother tongue in the classroom. A case in point was Professor Paul Mueller who had, before the war, divided his time equally between University College and McMaster.[30] In the fall of 1914 a public outcry was raised against him and others because of their German birth. When President Falconer refused to dismiss them he was subjected to a good deal of verbal abuse. According to Stewart Wallace, who by the time he related this was a member of Toronto's faculty, a compromise was eventually reached whereby Mueller and two of his German-speaking colleagues were given leave for the remainder of the session. When the session ended, however, all three submitted their resignations.[31] The story was also circulated that Mueller was refused a doctorate in psychology at Toronto on the grounds that he was an enemy alien.[32] The story seems plausible enough when one discovers that a former president of that institution, Professor James Loudon, in 1916 joined the newly formed Anti-German League of Canada, which proclaimed 'No More German Immigrants, Shipping, Labour, Goods [and] Influence.'[33] The cold explicitness of the proscription left little to the imagination.

But while Mueller was obliged to depart from University College he was retained as a lecturer at McMaster, a fact that Wallace, a former instructor at the latter, strangely fails to mention in recounting the episode in his history of the University of Toronto. On pedagogical grounds alone, Mueller's retention would appear to have been a wise decision. 'He is an exceedingly able teacher' Dean McLay had advised the chancellor in 1911 'and is much liked by the students . . . we will do well to retain his services.'[34] Professor Tingle, who could not have been in fuller agreement, had a special reason for prizing Mueller's expertise. At the chemist's urgent request, the latter could and subsequently did provide for instruction in scientific German. Without such, Tingle asserted, 'no person can do work at all advanced, beyond ordinary undergraduate courses' because he would be cut off from vital monographs and periodicals.[35]

Years later, at war's end, a faculty member at Toronto congratulated McMaster on its treatment of Mueller: 'In the midst of the wild madness of our time I am deeply thankful that *one* Institution at all events kept its head and was kind to unfortunate people who were not responsible for the harm done the world by the German Empire. I am ashamed by the part played by our Alma Mater in such affairs and am glad that McMaster was able to show the true Christian spirit.'[36] McLay replied that, 'we would, I hoped, have acted as we did, but lest we should assume greater merit than is rightfully our due' he went on to say that Mueller was kept on because of his excellence as an instructor.

Indeed, a move to promote Mueller to the German chair at McMaster upon the death of the incumbent, Professor Malcolm Clark, was deferred until the end of the war, 'out of respect' one official surmised 'for the condition of public opinion.'[37] Before his promotion was finally sanctioned Mueller had to be reappointed sessionally, 'subject to possible adjustment' the minutes of Senate ominously recorded 'which may be necessary if war continues.'[38] Although no such adjustment was considered necessary it must have come as a nasty surprise to Mueller when he learned in 1916 that the Ryrie Prize was inexplicably transferred from German 1 to a Biology course.[39] Taking into account the spirit of the time it is not surprising that a good many people forgot that Mueller had lived over a quarter of a century in North America, had taken out Canadian citizenship early in the war, and had sent a son to fight with the Canadian Expeditionary Force in Flanders.

While the war proved an embarrassment for Mueller and for those who sought to retain his services, it provided a welcome opportunity for the highly patriotic Professor Tingle to apply his talents to the nation's war effort. Training chemists for war service obviously furnished him a more meaningful role than the early self-imposed one of funding rifle-shooting for McMaster's undergraduates. Although his patriotic offer to investigate special problems for Britain's Ministry of Munitions was politely declined,[40] Tingle was highly pleased when some of his more able graduates were taken on by the Imperial Munitions Board, the agency empowered to promote the production of war materiel in the Dominion. Late in 1915 an eager Tingle received a report from one of his 'boys' at a Montreal plant that gives some idea of the nature and range of the work involved. 'They turn out [here] over 20,000 lbs daily of triton,' Mansen J. Bradley wrote his former mentor. 'Am just getting accustomed to the physiological effects of nitro-glycerine; although it is odorless it affects the nerve endings of the skin causing the blood vessels to greatly dilate and thus producing a terrific headache ... I am working alone and I like the work on explosives very much.'[41] The magnitude of the undertaking of which the Montreal operation formed but a part was disclosed in the information that 'this plant works in conjunction with E.J. Du Pont De Nemours Powder Co. of Wilmington, Del., The Easter Lab. Chester, Mass. and the Ardeer Co. of Scotland.'

Late the following year another graduate of Tingle's laboratory reported that the Imperial Munitions Board was building a new explosives plant near Parry Sound at a place appropriately called Nobel after the Swedish inventor of dynamite. It was to this operation that Tingle made his most dramatic contribution. Although there appeared to be no opening for him at Nobel in the summer months when he was not in his classroom there was a brisk demand for his protégés. His irritation over the former ('apparently the Dominion of Canada' he grumbled once 'is like the first French Republic; it has no need of chemists'[42]) was assuaged by the employment of such former students as Ora E. Dennis, George E. Grattan, and Samuel Lepofsky.

Obviously word soon got about that Tingle had at his command highly lucrative jobs in the 'destruction industry.' Not all the consequences of this publicity turned out to be happy ones for McMaster's professor of chemistry. Throughout the early months of 1918 he and Dean McLay were pestered by a parent anxious to combine patriotism with profit. He was, in short, desperate to have his son obtain 'chemical employment' in the summer months, preferably in an 'explosive Labratory where he could do good work for this country.' The dean must have mentally begun formulating his negative response to the request as soon as his eyes fell on the following parental remarks: 'I understand that in order to be qualified for such work it may be necessary for him to devote more time to Chemistry than he has been doing so far. I want him to have all the time he needs, even if this involves his missing some of his classes in other subjects ... I hope that you will understand the situation and be good enough to explain this matter to my son's teachers.'[43]

Tingle's own exasperation with such tactics was soon offset by an opportunity that came his way to put his small cadre of able female students to work. He had continually encouraged qualified women to consider a profession in the sciences, knowing that in the United States many openings had materialized for their services in analytic chemistry.[44] When enlistments after 1915 drained off a number of likely male candidates Tingle stepped up his campaign to engage more female students. He did not have to be told what Chancellor McCrimmon had asserted in his recently published The Woman Movement, that while 'the duty of motherhood is as permanent as the race ... woman should have the right to test her powers, to seek a generous culture, and fit herself for economic duties.'[45] The militant suffragette who had urged legislatures and municipal councils to grant women the vote before the war might have scoffed at McCrimmon's bland phrases in 1915, particularly his statement that granting women the franchise would not meet all their problems. But the vital role that women would ultimately play on a national scale in the war effort was anticipated at McMaster as early as 1916 in the scheme that Tingle drew up for the employment of his female graduates at Nobel. Tingle had been guided in part by what his male protégés had had to say about the idea. 'I fully believe' wrote G.E. Gratton late in 1916 'that there is no work in the laboratory which a fully qualified woman could not or would not do ... The work [on the whole] is easy, the building clean and well heated ... At present there are no women employed in the laboratory but I see no reason why — in the event of the shortage — they should not be employed.'

But he smugly issued a warning that unwittingly betrayed the dependence of this branch of Canadian industry on American technical personnel: 'Of course if any of the girls come up here they must not expect to meet fellows of the same type as McMaster men are . . . this refers mostly to the Americans whose moral standards appear much lower than any I have been accustomed to . . . and Americans predominate.'[46] Perhaps the remoteness of the locale, the solitude of the north woods, and the relative absence of female companionship placed a heavy strain on the 'moral standards' of that generation.

Although Tingle and Grattan were convinced of the wisdom of sending female chemists to Nobel, not all those in the profession shared their view. Later on Tingle conceded that there had also been considerable opposition to the idea from officials in charge of providing labour for the plants of the Imperial Munitions Board.[47] He noted too that for a brief period there was a strong movement on the campus against the scheme, but he named no names. It is just possible that McCrimmon might have demurred, but if he did it was to little effect. In the spring of 1917 the contingent of three 'hand-picked ladies' descended (in the care of one of their mothers) upon Nobel. Unquestionably they had been carefully selected by their mentor and instructor. Tingle confided to his sister how he had chosen 'the girls' – Marion Grimshaw, Ruth Baker, and Bessie Cooke: '[They] had a fairly well developed sense of humour with the exception of one who was instructed to develop it or drop out . . . Before it was decided that they should be sent into the munitions works I had a plain talk with them, the general fact of which was as follows: I told them they must promise not to get married until at least a year after graduation; otherwise to take up this work would be a simple waste of their time and mine.' He went on to inform them cryptically that 'they must accept no chemical favours from any man during the first six months of their work.' It was obviously essential that they 'remember that they were going to be paid men's wages and would, therefore, have to do men's work.' With what must have been considerable gratification he pointed out that they were the first women chemists in Canada and as such 'would be under special scrutiny for flaws to be detected.'[48]

Thus armed and conditioned, though with considerable trepidation, the women departed for Nobel. The fear that they might after all be rejected by their male colleagues was soon dispelled. Although Marion Grimshaw reported that 'several men in the lab are still opposed to us . . . we haven't . . . had to compete with any petty meanness that amounts to anything, so we aren't worrying.' Much to Tingle's relief, she concluded by saying that the 'rest of them seem to like us and make things pleasant for us.'[49]

The shortage of qualified male chemists, met in part by Tingle's recruitment of Marion Grimshaw and her classmates in 1917, deepened as a consequence of a political decision made in the fall of that year. The heavy casualties sustained by the Canadian Expeditionary Force in Flanders had convinced the federal government of the need for compulsory military service. The voluntary system which had worked reasonably well in the early years of the war was now failing to provide the reinforcements needed on the western front. But the plan to compel enlistment was viewed critically by a number of Baptists, including vocal members of McMaster's student body. According to one contributor to the *Monthly*, conscription would 'do violence not only to Baptist principles but to the most sacred inheritance of the British people, namely individual right ... Personal freedom is the great fundamental principle which underlies all our institutions.'[50] In the opinion of more militant Baptists, however, the introduction of compulsory military service, distasteful though it might be in ordinary circumstances, was the only means of ensuring the preservation of those principles.

Furthermore, the militants complained that Ottawa was not moving quickly enough in the matter. At about the time Marion Grimshaw and her friends were settling down in their new quarters at Nobel, Joseph Wearing of Peterborough was briefing McCrimmon on the state of the enlisting campaign in his locality. 'The truth is' he wrote 'that very little more can be done under the voluntary system and the trouble is that the government is shirking its responsibility and has not got the backbone to go ahead with the compulsion measure.'[51] Prime Minister Robert Borden, upon whom McMaster had conferred an honorary degree just a year before, was well aware, however, of the politically explosive nature of conscription. Accordingly he had sought to persuade Wilfrid Laurier and the Liberals to join with the Conservatives to form a coalition government as a means of making the measure more palatable to French Canada. In the end, however, Laurier refused the invitation and openly opposed any attempt to conscript the country's manpower. But a sizable number of his English-speaking colleagues defected to Borden's side, enabling the Conservative leader to form the Union Government and to lay plans for a military service bill.

The move met with the approval of many Ontarians, including a respectable number of Baptists, who at any other time would have been dismayed to see so many Liberals, the traditional defenders of their principles, consorting with those who traditionally had opposed them. McCrimmon, for example, had grown concerned about the response to the war of Catholics in general and of Quebec in particular. The conclusion that he and many others had reached was that French Canadians were simply not 'doing their bit' in the struggle to save the empire, liberty, and Christianity. The passions of war, which reduced so many complex problems to a comforting if absurd simplicity, made no exception of the French Canadian question. Quebec's apparent failure to match English Canada's contribution to the Allied cause made that community, in the eyes of some, as culpable as Germany, the enemy of everything cherished by all right-thinking Canadians. This view was a more bellicose descendant of the Anglocentricity that years before had inspired the following comment in the *Monthly*: 'We cannot help regretting' said a reviewer of Louis Fréchette's poetry in the 1890s 'the spirit of bitter hostility to much that is dear to the hearts of the majority of Canadians which pervades these poems. Unless the people of Quebec can forget such sentiments by learning to admire and love our free Canadian institutions and the spirit of evangelical Christianity on which they rest, a great united Canadian nation is practically impossible.'[52]

Meanwhile, conscription, it was argued, would for all its faults have the one great merit of ending supposed inequities and forcing ungrateful French Canadians to accept their responsibilities as Christian citizens living in a civilized community. At least one overseas McMaster soldier frankly argued this case. With obvious relish Gordon Philpott told his mother the following story about casting his ballot in the general election called to endorse the Union Government's Military Service Act.

Only today I had an argument with an English nurse in my ward. An officer came in to get my vote ... and I voted for Conscription. The nurse smiled very approvingly and said we should have had Conscription long ago. I replied that I wasn't voting for Conscription but against the French Canadians, and on a straight vote for Conscription would vote against it. She was horrified and said it was necessary to hold the Empire together.

This rejoinder gave Philpott the opening he wanted: 'I retorted' he wrote 'that if our freedom was to be sacrificed for the sake of holding our Empire together, it was better to break it up. I love the British Empire, but I love liberty more.' To this the nurse tearfully replied: 'That is your way — take all *England* can give you, then throw her over at the critical moment!'[53] Not surprisingly, this portion of the soldier's letter was cut out when it was handed over for publication in the *Monthly*.[54]

A more dispassionate and scholarly view of the situation was furnished by Harold Innis after he received news of the formation of the Union Government. 'In soldiers' camps and hospitals' he told McCrimmon 'we seldom hear more than one side of the question . . . Opposition literature has been success-fully stamped out and Unionist propaganda reigns supreme.' He ended on the note of understatement for which he had been renowned as an under-graduate: 'Conscription is of no slight importance to the [English].'[55]

Back home, few among the faculty appeared to share Innis's dry restraint on the question. Professor Gilmour, chaplain of the McMaster OTC, had feelingly referred to the election as the 'crisis of the hour' and urged his readers to focus on the one and only issue – the endorsement of the Military Service Act. Turning to what he called 'the war policy of Quebec,' he remarked that if it were supported by the country at large, 'those who have voted for it will have to stand ready after the election to show us what practical means they have at hand to sustain our national honour and to defend our country from the barbaric ways of the present German leaders. If any citizen cannot see his answer to this he had better pause to consider before he marks a ballot that he cannot revoke.'[56] Gilmour's statement was genteel compared to what T.T. Shields of Jarvis Street Church had written on the subject a few days before. A vote for Laurier, that dynamic and popular preacher had warned, would be a 'vote against our men who are crying out for reinforcements and therefore . . . a vote for the Kaiser.' This unequivocal equation echoed much press opinion on the matter.[57]

For his part, Professor Tingle, the coach of McMaster's explosives squad, made no effort to conceal his patriotic feelings and his reaction to people who lacked the good sense to share them. 'Today is election day,' he wrote a graduate in France on 17 December 1917, 'and it will decide whether Canada drops out of the war or continues.' To his disgust he had learned that 'practically all the McMaster students are to vote for Laurier,' a prospect that 'makes me very sick.'[58] Many of these students – though their numbers cannot even be estimated – were still as anxious as ever to support king and country but not to the point of abandoning traditional Liberal principles and enforcing compulsory military service. Not so Dean McLay, who was per-sonally committed to the Union Government and conscription. Yet even he realized that he might be asking too large a favour of O.C.S. Wallace when he sought his public support for the campaign in Westmount. 'Such an appeal signed by you' McLay assured the former chancellor 'would have weight in such a time as this.' Then he plunged to the point: 'If you could do this consistently with your views as to the relations of Church and State, I feel sure that you would be striking a blow for righteousness.' 'It seems to me' he concluded with an air of unreality 'that a word from one dwelling in the midst of the French would be of special influence in guiding wavering ones to a wise decision.'[59] This comment was inspired by the same kind of dubious reasoning that had governed the appointment of a Methodist clergyman to take charge of recruiting in the province of Quebec.

The mood, the speeches, the urgency of the situation had left the issue in little doubt. But no one could have foreseen at the end of 1917 that within a year hostilities would have come to end almost as abruptly as they had begun in the late summer of 1914, long before Canada's conscription program would have any appreciable effect upon the outcome. And the chancellor, who had supported conscription almost as zealously as his colleague, Joseph Gilmour, was obliged to learn in the interval that he could not have it both ways. He could not advocate compulsory military service and expect to maintain a respectable level of enrolment at the university. He knew that tribunals had been set up to screen likely candidates for exemption from military service, but he hoped that special consideration would be given prospective university students. After addressing an appeal to Borden himself 'on behalf of the cause of education,' McCrimmon was told politely but firmly that 'instructions have already been issued to the [military] tribunals for [the] purpose of securing uniformity in [their] decisions. It would scarcely be feasible to issue instructions in any other than a general form; to particularize would be to open the door to many undesirable demands from other quarters.'[60] As it turned out, exemptions were in fact granted a number of McMaster students, and in the end only three were actually 'drafted,' the term used in the record.[61]

Professor Tingle was confronted with another kind of problem. A champion of conscription, he was nonetheless pained to learn in the summer of 1918 that no action was to be taken by the Department of Militia and Defence with regard to the special treatment of students of chemistry. Tingle's fierce professional pride was put out when he learned that while it was important 'from the military point of view to have officers specially trained in Medicine and Dentistry' it was not considered so necessary in the case of chemists. The prospect that recruits educated for four years in the intricacies of scientific research were to be lumped together in the same training units with the untutored rank and file of society was wholly repugnant to him.[62] In his mind there was simply no explaining officialdom's apparent insensitivity to the productive role that applied chemistry could play in modern warfare.

Within weeks of these reflections Tingle died suddenly. Only fifty-one years of age, he had recently been elected a fellow of the Royal Society of Canada — the first time this honour had been conferred upon a McMaster faculty member — in recognition of his scholarly output and his practical contributions to the war effort. To Bessie Cooke, one of his Nobel crew, who had offered her congratulations, he had replied that the 'good wishes of my friends are in many respects the pleasantest part of it.'[63] Tingle's death seriously disrupted the solid work that he had set in train at the university and dictated an immediate search for a successor. But the severe wartime shortage of equally qualified people in Canada and Britain and, as McCrimmon was informed, the employment of 'literally thousands' of chemists by the United States in research and production virtually ruled out a replacement until the war came to an end. And a potentially awkward situation militated against the temporary appointment of the chancellor's son, a graduate student in the discipline. 'It might be somewhat embarrassing' a Board member wrote McLay 'if [he] were doing the work, when the Chair was being filled by the Senate.'[64]

A man whose name kept cropping up in the course of the search was Charles Eldrid Burke, a McMaster graduate and former instructor at Woodstock College who had pursued doctoral studies at the University of Illinois. In 1918 he was dividing his time between teaching at the University of Vermont and research work for industry. Although he was not McMaster's first choice, and in spite of the fact that Tingle once damned him with faint praise,[65] Burke was warmly recommended by a classmate who had already declined the offer. 'Dr Burke is a splendid McMaster man' wrote Stuart J. Bates from the California Institute of Technology 'who might be glad to return to Canada. He should suit McMaster admirably. He is alive and up-to-date and he thoroughly enjoys teaching both elementary and advanced.'[66] That Burke wished to return to Canada was obvious, but wartime demands again rudely intervened. As he told McCrimmon, he felt that because of the need for chemists like himself in wartime America he should stay with the 'Du Pont people until war's end.'[67] Indeed, he waited for the twenties to close before he made his move to McMaster. Tingle's place was ultimately taken by Professor William Oscar Walker, a Toronto graduate who had taught at Chicago's Armour Institute and Queen's University before coming to McMaster in the fall of 1918.[68]

In one important sense, however, Walker was not a replacement. Whereas Tingle's forte had been research, his successor's was teaching. Walker's ability as an instructor earned him the warm commendation of one of his students, who later achieved prominence as a chemist. But the momentum that Tingle had achieved in the field of chemical research at McMaster was visibly stalled until Burke's appearance on the scene in 1930.

McMaster was not the only institution agonizing over faculty shortages late in 1918. The University of Toronto made an urgent appeal for the services of H.F. Dawes, one of its own doctoral graduates, in its undermanned Physics Department;[69] like Tingle, McMaster's sought-after physicist had not been idle in the closing months of the war. During the summer recesses he had been actively engaged in efforts to separate helium from natural gas, and by the fall of 1919 he was convinced that 'we have the Americans, who have been doing so much shouting about their Helium work, effectively beaten.'[70]

The work being done by Dawes and the acquisition of Walker helped to stabilize the situation in the sciences, but the university was well aware that there were deficiencies in other disciplines. In the second year of the war the chancellor had plaintively called for an enlargement of the faculty so that full-fledged courses could be offered in political science and more extended ones in history and political economy.[71] Late in the summer of 1918, just when the university was turning to the task of finding a replacement for Tingle, it was also trying to strengthen its staff in the areas to which McCrimmon had given so much priority. By this time W.J.A. Donald had already taken full time employment elsewhere in the field of urban research, and the need to replace him and add others in political economy had become urgent. Donald himself tried to help out with suggestions but he knew that he was clutching at straws: 'I scarcely know what to say about a supply. Does [Duncan] MacGibbon intend to return? . . . Another possibility would be to take [Harold] Innis on? I doubt however whether Innis would be interested . . . It has occurred to me that if the University really got into difficulties over the department I might be able to help out by coming over for one day a week.'[72]

After graduating in 1908, Duncan Alexander MacGibbon had undertaken doctoral work at Chicago and been appointed in 1917 a lecturer at McMaster in political economy and sociology. After spending a session in the classroom he enlisted and went overseas, where he was attached to the Armoured Corps. 'I am encased while at work, in overalls, much greased,' he wrote the *Monthly*, 'and I have great difficulty in trying to keep my fingernails out of deep mourning, with indifferent success, while working on the tanks.'[73] When he did return to Canada MacGibbon elected to join Brandon College, while Harold Innis tackled graduate work at Chicago and then, after turning down an invitation to teach at Brandon,[74] accepted a position at the University of Toronto.

This meant that for the immediate future McCrimmon, already saddled with heavy administrative chores, was obliged to do the lion's share of work himself in political economy and sociology. It was a heavy burden for a man whose health was so precarious. In a sense he could be described as a war casualty. 'It is a difficult situation' he confided to D.E. Thomson in 1919 'when one finds that the abnormal tension of the war period has left him with a peculiar ... condition which makes the arrival of mail a nightmare and a hint of trouble the precursor of sleepless nights.'[75] And throughout, the chancellor was obliged to address himself to the perennial problems of staffing, financing, and declining enrolment that were plaguing all departments at the university.

At the same time he and his colleagues had to spare some thought for the state of affairs that the country and the university would have to face after the fighting stopped, an exercise that had commanded a great deal of Tingle's attention in the months before his death. When the chemist had pleaded for the special wartime treatment of his students or their exemption from military service, he had sought to publicize the Dominion's need for skilled researchers. 'As you may be aware,' he told a prominent politician in Ottawa in terms reminiscent of Chancellor McKay's earlier hopes, 'considerable effort is being made at present to waken Canadian manufacturers to the importance of research work in Chemistry. It is obvious that without such work Canadian manufacturers cannot hope to hold their own after the war.'[76] In some instances the awakening effort seemed to be paying dividends. 'We started our Laboratory work some years ago,' the future owner of a flourishing carpet manufacturing company advised Tingle in the fall of 1917. 'At that time, it met with much opposition from the Mill men, who were new to the idea of chemists. However, they are now more or less educated to the idea of enlisting the assistance of a trained mind, and we see no reason why ... our Laboratory work should not soon be established upon a firm basis.'[77]

Tingle had also hoped for a greater effort on the academic front. Urging the expansion of scientific programs at Canadian universities, he noted that there 'is no provision in Canada for work of PHD standard in any way comparable to the organized courses which are available in any one of the dozen universities in the United States.'[78] But in spite of the efforts of Tingle and his colleagues across the country, doctorates remained 'rare birds,' as E.W.R. Steacie recalled, 'so rare in fact that any one with the title "Doctor" was apt to find himself receiving unexpected medical confidences.'[79] Indeed, more than a quarter of a century would pass before Tingle's dream of a flourishing doctoral program became a reality at McMaster. And it came only after an interval punctuated by theological strife, economic depression, the uprooting of the university and its transference to Hamilton, and another global conflict which, even more than the first, stimulated large-scale industrial expansion and scientific research.

Tingle's image of the post-war world and the role that the trained scientist could play in its progress had analogues in the hopes entertained by other McMaster people as the war drew to a close. Some put it simply, like Wilfred S. Mallory, a future high school teacher of physics who married Marion Grimshaw, one of Tingle's Nobel crew; he looked forward in Germany to a 'happy homecoming and a civilized use of our powers.'[80] Others, like Harold Innis, stated it more emotionally. Overwhelmed by the years of carnage and bloodletting that had threatened to destroy the world, Innis offered this passionate statement to the *Monthly*: 'There runs a deep, vibrant note of determination, that such misery shall never again in this generation mar the lives of so many millions of men . . . and that the trenches of autocracy which have been taken at such cost shall be consolidated against all the enemies of democracy.'[81] During the four long years of war McMaster had paid its own price in dead and wounded; of the 237 graduates and undergraduates who had enlisted in the armed forces twenty-two gave their lives.

In the meantime many of the survivors overseas were taking practical steps to prepare themselves for 'civvy street.' Indeed, McMaster soldiers may have helped to pioneer the institution that shortly took the name, Khaki University. 'As you know' Gordon S. Jury wrote McCrimmon early in 1918 'we have quite a McMaster colony over here, and have been making use of the opportunity to get together. When Dr Gilmour was here and met us informally at a picnic lunch we decided to meet again as a discussion class. This group still meets. It also became a kind of pioneer in the educational work which has now developed into a "Canadian Khaki College."'[82] F.W. Waters enrolled in a related venture, which he called the University of Vimy Ridge and which, like the Khaki College, sought to prepare the veteran for civilian life with a program of technical and vocational education organized in the form of a 'field university.'[83] According to Stewart Wallace, these enterprises constituted a first for Canada, the 'recognition of the principle that the civilian soldier is entitled to something more than food and clothing and $1.10 per day.'[84] Among those enabled to resume their teaching careers while still in uniform were Duncan MacGibbon and William A. Kenyon. 'I think the Khaki u will be of the greatest value' MacGibbon assured McCrimmon 'in turning men back to the thought of college who otherwise would feel they could not study again.'[85]

While all this was very gratifying there were disturbing aspects for those who ministered to the theological requirements of McMaster. Although Armageddon had in some cases confirmed the need to preserve the verities of religion, in a good many others it had shaken the traditional faith; in still others, particularly overseas veterans, it provoked the abandonment of pastoral studies. 'While [my] religious interests will always be paramount,' one McMaster solider confessed in the summer of 1918, 'I do not now feel that I have a distinct call to the ministry.'[86] Concern about the religion or irreligion of the returning soldier, who was regarded so often with mixed admiration and apprehension, produced a flurry of contributions to the denominational press. The alarming notion entertained in some veterans' quarters that a man who conducted himself as a Christian without necessarily professing a faith in the Scriptures ought to be accepted as a Christian, left the *Canadian Baptist* little alternative. 'At the very outset' one of its editorials pronounced in the fall of 1917 'we desire to place upon record as knowing no method of salvation for soldier or civilian other than that laid down in the Word of God.'[87] Yet certain letters and articles that appeared in the *Baptist* were hardly calculated to inspire Dean Farmer and his colleagues. In a typical column, headlined 'The Churches after the War,' it was announced that the conflict had exposed the weaknesses of the denominational systems and that the time had come 'to cast denominationalism aside and ... put into practice those principles of love and liberty of conscience that we have professed to believe.'[88]

To this the university and the constituency replied that denominational forces, like nations, had not outlived their usefulness. Alluding to the new dispensation emerging on the international scene, their spokesmen pointed out that however much hope a League of Nations might hold out for a world victimized by national hatreds, there was still a need for reformed and revitalized nations to give life and meaning to that association. In the words of one pastor, a committed denomination like the Baptists had 'a very special contribution to make in this critical, plastic age, this age when men everywhere are seeking for the basic and the fundamental.'[89] For all the disenchanted, the doubters, the materialists, and those who would 'reduce spiritual things to mechanistic cause and effect,' McCrimmon wrote out a personal message in his annual report in 1919: 'Now is the time for Christian scholarship to make its influence felt. The development of man is the most important enterprise of humanity and that development deals with the many different elements of human life and demands a variety of institutions, including Baptist institutions.'[90]

The Baptists' traditional spiritual weapons, wielded through their churches and particularly through their university, were considered sufficient to deal with the unsettling and novel dimensions of the period that would follow the greatest holocaust in history. It was not mere rhetoric when an English pastor told an appreciative chancellor that when 'nations are everywhere receiving a mould, the university is a factor the importance of which it is difficult to exaggerate.' 'I am sure' he concluded 'that McMaster with her sane Christian view of life is to do good work for Canada and the Empire.'[91] With this hope McCrimmon and McMaster ventured into the post-war years.

8

Post-war hopes and fears

The return of peace revived hopes that the expansion and building plans held
in abeyance during the years of slump and war might now go forward. But the
university did not press its claims upon the denomination at once; in the
spring of 1919 it decided to postpone a request 'in order not to interfere with
the adoption of [church] budgets, and the special appeal of the Home Missions Board.'[1] They were well advised to do so. Three years before, at the
height of the war, spokesmen for that Board had implicitly criticized the
long-standing practice of having the University Ministerial Committee pass
on the fitness of pastors for the home mission field. Instead they had urged
that a special examining and stationing committee of the HMB be formed to
judge the capacity of men for the pulpit. McCrimmon had taken this
proposal almost as a personal slight, and certainly as a slap in the face for the
university. Although he was told that he was reading too much into the
proposal, clearly there were people on the HMB who were not exactly enthral-
led with some of the candidates being assigned to the churches in their charge
and who wanted an opportunity to do some judging on their own. The
dissatisfaction simmering since the Matthews case came to a boil in this
attempt to force McMaster to share its appointive powers with the denominational body.

The distressed chancellor pointed out that for twenty years the HMB had
without question accepted the decisions of the University Ministerial Committee. Now, without any warning, it was demanding that a 'different procedure be taken respecting [a candidate's] fitness for Home Mission Work.'[2] He
invited Board spokesmen to look over the personnel of the Ministerial

Committee, for 'then they would see that we have tried to make it representative' of alumni and non-alumni and of people who were not formally attached to the university. Even though a compromise of sorts was reached whereby a joint Ministerial Committee composed of university and HMB appointees was struck,[3] the exchange of 1916 thoroughly disturbed some members of the McMaster community. Their state of mind was not relieved by the insinuations made from time to time that pastors lacking a McMaster BA were too often left 'unhonoured and unsung' by the university and by prominent men of the church who could put the letters of that degree after their names.[4]

Doubtless that wartime confrontation accounted for the chancellor's impatience in the fall of 1918 with the churches' allegedly thin financial response to the university in its time of budgetary troubles. In an appeal he drew up at that time to the constituency McCrimmon had been about to express his impatience, but D.E. Thomson talked him out of it. The message was subsequently diluted to calling attention to the substantial increases in a number of congregational contributions to the university.[5] McCrimmon's irritation, aggravated by worry and overwork, was not soothed by reports that a 'great many of the denomination have said, not a cent would they contribute to McMaster till they were assured that the Inspiration of the Old Testament received its rightful place in the teaching there.' This was a far cry from the messages of good will that had accompanied the chancellor's début in 1911. And this parting shot came from one of his alienated correspondents: 'I wish to say that I resent the idea that it is indifference on the part of the denomination that is the cause of what you deplore [the lack of support for the university] rather, it is conscience.'[6]

Other forms of unpleasantness intruded in 1919 upon McMaster's plans to publicize its needs and to mount a Forward Movement. Echoes of the pre-war strife reverberated strongly throughout the constituency and the university when the central figure in that earlier crisis announced his resignation from McMaster. I.G. Matthews decided to take up a pulpit in New Haven, Connecticut, and part-time teaching duties at the Yale Divinity School. Although Matthews had placed many students in his debt ('His going is a great loss for what he made the Old Testament mean to me' said F.W. Waters.[7]) he was anathema to others like the Rev. T.T. Shields of Jarvis Street Church. And it was clear that Shields's view of the matter expressed the thoughts of many Baptists not only in his own congregation but elsewhere in the denomination as well.

Early in 1919 Shields laid it on the line in a letter to McCrimmon. He started off by claiming that he had seconded the crucial amendment that had resolved the problem in 1910 in the interest of avoiding 'a split in the

Convention' and on the assumption that henceforth the university would sanction no form of teaching that smacked of modernism. Whether this had in fact been the clergyman's motive for voting the way he did on that occasion matters little. What does is that in 1919 Shields intimated that Matthews's departure was, to say the very least, timely: 'while the date of [the] vacancy in the Chair of Hebrew and Old Testament Exegesis ... was more remote than I then expected, it has at last occurred.' With respect to that vacancy Shields now tersely addressed himself in his letter to McCrimmon:

Hitherto those of us in the Denomination (and I believe they are overwhelmingly in the majority) who hold the historic Baptist view of the Scriptures of the Old and New Testaments, have had no quarrel with McMaster University as a whole; but only with an individual professor. But if another man holding similar views to those held by the professor now retiring were deliberately appointed ... in spite of the Convention's conviction on this subject [as expressed in 1910] ... such an appointment would ... compromise the entire University ... and in such circumstances, acquiescence, or even neutrality, for a great multitude of people, in which I would certainly be included, would be absolutely impossible.

But, Shields observed, a safe appointment would rally the dissidents to the university, and it would be assured of a ready supply of students, particularly from the United States where the 'radical teachings of many theological seminaries are driving young men to the short course Bible colleges.'[8]

Just a month after Shields's letter landed on the chancellor's desk Dean McLay received another which provided a troubling footnote. An undergraduate wrote grimly about the emergent conflict between theology and arts on the campus. This he regarded as only partly due to the sharp reduction in the theology enrolment in the latter years of the war and the supposedly concomitant decline in the department's influence at the institution. Basically, he attributed the estrangement to the notion, entertained by some students who felt that formal theology had failed to explain the recent Armageddon, that a sound preparation in the arts alone was sufficient for the assumption of pastoral responsibilities. Thus the arts man who aspired to a career in the pulpit could virtually 'get his own theology' without benefit of formal instruction and direction. This was, admittedly, an extreme position, the letter went on, because not all the arts men subscribed to the idea that the 'course in Theology [was] more or less ... an extra to be taken if the other special course (Arts) permits.'[9]

Pitted against this extreme position, according to this undergraduate, was another one. The 'radical theolog' regarded the arts man as 'a spiritual derelict with no harbor light near which he can ride at anchor till the storm is past' and thought that his faith 'had been wrecked by his contact with [the higher criticism] and the theory of natural selection in Biology.' Between the two poles ranged a larger number of theological students whom the conflict left in the 'throes of an intellectual maelstrom.'[10]

It was this kind of 'intellectual maelstrom' that Shields believed was devastating the formerly Christian university of McMaster, a storm unleashed by George Cross and I.G. Matthews. Shields's publicly stated opposition to the retention or acquisition of anyone holding those theologians' views could not have come at a worse time for the university. For one thing, it had been about to embark on an ambitious Forward Movement to finance the expansion deferred by the war. This fund-raising campaign could easily be jeopardized by the sort of hostility that Shields might be capable of directing against McMaster. For another, the chancellor was nearly exhausted and ill-prepared for a battle with a potentially influential critic of the university. As a matter of fact, McCrimmon had requested a year's leave in order to restore, as he put it to Board Chairman Thomson, his 'nervous aplomb.'[11] Although readily sympathizing with the chancellor's plight, Thomson begged him to defer his departure from the campus in view of the problems that Shields had raised. McCrimmon reluctantly complied on the understanding that Deans McLay and Farmer would share more of his administrative responsibilities. He needed no reminder that Shields might be prepared to organize a crippling opposition to the vital Forward Movement unless the 'teaching matter and other problems were cleared up.'[12]

There was abundant evidence in the chancellor's correspondence that the Jarvis Street pastor's well articulated concern about the instructional health of the university was shared by many in the denomination and that if their concern were not taken seriously they might well respond to Shields's dynamic leadership. And he appeared ready and able to lead. The possibility that he deliberately sought to exploit the university's vulnerability in 1919 – its ailing leader and its need for financial aid – is open to question, but there seems little doubt that he was anxious to rally conservative forces to what McCrimmon had called his 'sturdy sponsorship of the orthodoxy of the Denomination.' That Shields had already formally taken up the cause of fundamentalism was no secret, for he publicly supported the World's Christian Fundamentals Association when it was formed in Philadelphia in 1919.[13] Seven years later he would have the pleasure of presiding over its annual conference in Toronto.

To probe Shields's motives for his actions in 1919 is beyond the scope of a study concentrating upon how the university reacted to his criticisms and tried to parry his attacks. And yet at the time those motives, which have been productively explored elsewhere,[14] were not sufficiently taken into account by those at the university who were the targets of his displeasure. Shields was disappointed in his bid to be named in 1919 to the vacant pulpit of the Spurgeon Gospel Tabernacle, a leading Baptist church in the United Kingdom, an appointment by which he had set much store.[15] Others had also been disappointed, but for a different reason: McCrimmon had wryly remarked in the late summer of 1919 that 'some people would not look upon [Shields's] transference to the [Spurgeon] Tabernacle as an unmitigated loss.'[16] At any rate, it has been suggested that Shields compensated for the denial of ambition overseas by focusing his energies upon the problems that he saw confronting Ontario Baptists and McMaster University.[17]

In addition, Shields had long harboured a resentment over the treatment his father had received at the hands of the Convention and the university. The complaint was that in spite of the elder Shields's ability and faithful service, he, unlike his son, had never been given a prestigious pulpit and had suffered the fate of so many unhonoured and unsung home missioners. The Jarvis Street clergyman came to the conclusion that his father and the other Baptist pastors unlucky enough to lack a McMaster degree had been consistently discriminated against in the constituency. The following anecdote, related five years after the episode it describes, suggests something of Shields's attitude towards the university and of the motives behind it. In a chat in a Brantford church basement in 1920 Shields reportedly disclosed that as a young man he had planned to attend McMaster until he heard a professor say that 'unless a minister had the McMaster stamp on him he would not get any of the bigger churches of the Convention'; he then made up his mind not to go to McMaster but still to 'have the best church in the Convention.'[18]

Some years later Shields would put the case against McMaster far more pungently. 'Non-McMaster men' he charged in *The Plot that Failed* 'were tolerated for the doing of rough work, even as the Chinese coolies were . . . on the Western Front in the Great War . . . To my personal knowledge certain of the Faculty of McMaster looked upon non-McMaster men as useful only for carrying meals to the graduates of [the] University.'[19] Shields complained that in spite of his own accomplishments at Jarvis Street he had never been invited to occupy commanding positions in the Convention's hierarchy. He learned too that the university had for a number of years hesitated to confer upon him an honorary degree, even though Temple University of Philadelphia had seen fit to do so in 1917. He was doubtless aware that in 1913 there had been 'outspoken opposition in the Senate to [an honorary] degree for the present pastor of Jarvis Street Church,' brought on, he surmised, by the role that he had played during the Matthews controversy in 1910 and by his failure to enrol at the university. In any case, early in 1917 C.J. Holman, a long-time member of Jarvis Street and one who had never taken kindly to Matthews's presence, began urging the appropriate committee to reconsider Shields for a degree.[20]. The Rev. John James MacNeill of Walmer Road Church had already been put forward, and Holman felt that his own pastor should be similarly honoured. The Board member's appeals were heeded, and the following year Shields shared the platform with MacNeill to receive an honorary doctorate. But his acknowledgment address was hardly designed to improve his relationship with the university because it amounted to a warning that he could not be buttered up in this way.[21]

The next move that the university made, this one with respect to the 'teaching matter,' was probably also regarded by Shields as another exercise in flattery. He ought to have been gratified by the appointment early in 1920 of the Rev. Henry S. Curr, a conservative English theologian, to fill Matthews's position, but he said little in public one way or the other about the appointment. On the other hand, Holman, Shields's champion, did. 'This is a step in the right direction,' the Board member commended McCrimmon, 'correspondents in the old land assure me that [Curr] brings ripe scholarship coupled with clear strong conservative views on Biblical questions and that is what the denomination has longed for . . . he is no "side-stepper" and has the courage of his convictions which in these days is a rare quality.'[22]

It had been a difficult task to fill the chair. 'I wish I knew someone whom I could recommend,' O.C.S. Wallace had written earlier, 'but men capable of good work . . . who might be regarded as safe teachers, are not easily found north of Mason and Dixon's line.'[23] In the absence of qualified Baptist candidates a number of people at McMaster had at one point considered the credentials of a Presbyterian theologian, even though his appointment would technically have violated the university's charter. Thomson, who was no happier than his colleagues with that prospect, nonetheless resigned himself to it. 'So long as his teaching were not specially objectionable to either Conservatives or Radicals' he told the chancellor 'I think there would be no real danger of anyone applying for an injunction on the grounds of his not being a member of the Denomination.'[24] Happily, Curr's appointment had made this overture an academic one. One can only wonder how Shields might have reacted to the appointment of a non-Baptist to the sensitive position that Matthews had vacated. However, considering his ability to commune with fundamentalists of other persuasions he might have preferred a Presbyterian conservative to a Baptist modernist.

Unfortunately the arrival of Professor Curr did not clear up for Shields the problems that he believed still plagued the university and the denomination it was supposed to serve. That McMaster's orthodoxy must still somehow be suspect, in spite of Matthews's departure, was confirmed for him when he perused the editorial columns of the *Canadian Baptist* in the fall of 1919. He found particularly offensive an editorial entitled 'The Inspiration and Authority of Scripture,' an anonymous and scholarly piece contributed by a guest editor, a traditional feature of the denominational paper. In the course of the article the reader's attention was called to the welcome degree to which the conflict over the authority of the Scriptures had ceased to agitate the evangelical churches of the United Kingdom. On the other hand, 'it is a singular circumstance that on this Continent a considerable number of Christian people, including a fair proportion of ministers, are still threshing away at many of those questions ... To some extent this is true among churches in Canada ... where some crude theological views still prevail.'[25]

Shields was convinced that the writer was an academic personally denigrating the views held by himself and by many of his fellow Baptists. He soon took the matter up with the paper and announced his plans to have the article's contents brought before the Convention scheduled for late October in Ottawa. The news of Shields's intentions circulated quickly. Although the university was not in the direct line of fire, McCrimmon received assurances that if conflict were renewed and '1910 staged again' McMaster could count upon the support of those anxious to 'wage battle for democracy in the Baptist Denomination.'[26] There was every indication that the paper's editor and the university's leaders would face heavy sledding at the forthcoming Convention.

The question is why Shields was able to precipitate a crisis at this time. When an undergraduate had remarked in 1919 that the problem posed by Shields could be traced to the actions of 'William Hohenzollern' he presented, in a half-truth, a large clue to the puzzle.[27] There is little doubt that the war climate in Canada, characterized by unrelenting appeals to patriotism, the denunciation of the enemy as Huns or worse, and the exaltation of the Allied cause as a latter-day crusade, made extremism a virtue and the simplistic explanation of complex subjects a respectable activity. The power of the fundamentalist, which traded on these attributes, was made all the more formidable by the passions generated in the war years. Those who lambasted the *Canadian Baptist*'s editorial policy or the university's teaching in those post-war months underscored the connection between the one kind of war and the other. They delighted in using the vocabulary of Flanders in their campaign to defend the faith – 'going over the top' against the modernist and 'meeting and defeating him in No Man's Land.' In this combative

John Gilmour   Robert Fyfe

William McMaster   Susan Moulton McMaster

John Castle

D.E. Thomson

Malcolm MacVicar

T.H. Rand

James Ten Broeke

J.L. Gilmour

A.C. McKay

W.J. McKay

W.P. Cohoe   J.H. Farmer

Science class, 1896. William Piersol (third from left) and A.B. Willmott (right) instructing

Chancellor O.C.S. Wallace addressing a class, 1904

R.W. Smith's biology class, ca 1900

William Findlay

George Cross

I.G. Matthews

Elmore Harris

J.B. Tingle

H.F. Dawes

C.W. New

A.L. McCrimmon

McMaster OTC platoon on parade

McMaster Hall (etching by Owen Staples, ca 1923)

McMasterrifics, 1923

Girls' field hockey team outside Wallingford Hall, 1923

H.P. Whidden

L.H. Marshall

W.S.W. McLay

T.T. Shields

Albert Matthews

John MacNeill

atmosphere a spokesman with Shields's charisma could evoke a warm response from those agitated or uncertain about the direction being taken by the denominational press or McMaster.

There was, however, another side to the coin. Many other Baptists had somehow survived the emotional strains of Armageddon with their capacity intact for taking a balanced view of problems. Both the reasonable and the not-so-reasonable were in a position to debate the issue that Shields raised at the Ottawa Convention at the moment when the annual report of the Publications Board was presented. His motion called upon the delegates to declare their disapproval of the editorial. He claimed, among other things, that in its representative character as the organ of the Convention the paper 'commends to its readers some new vague view of the Scriptures different from that to which the Convention declared its adherence in 1910, and upon which the denominational University is declared to be founded.'[28] Shields's motion was seconded by the Rev. William Wardley McMaster, the grandnephew of the senator and pastor of Hamilton's James Street Church, an act obviously designed to lend some weight to Shields's proposal. Courtesy demanded that the general editor of the *Canadian Baptist* be permitted to address the delegates before the motion was debated. Although W.J. McKay had not written the offending article in question, he was obliged to accept responsibility for whatever appeared in the paper. There were some in attendance who speculated that the guest editorial had been written by I.G. Matthews as a parting shot at his critics. Others claim it was the work of Joseph Gilmour, who had a penchant for Biblical analysis but seldom, in his capacity as a church historian, an opportunity to demonstrate it in the lecture hall.[29] But the actual author did not come forward at Ottawa to claim his controversial progeny.

Shields tasted a welcome triumph when the Convention formally disapproved of the editorial that had caused all the turmoil. However, a bow was made in McKay's direction, for which Shields had not provided in his motion, when a resolution was overwhelmingly carried expressing for the editor the Convention's affectionate regard and implicit confidence in his editorship. The degree of support which Shields received on the main question must have pleased him just as it alarmed some of McMaster's theologians. Gilmour provided a possible clue to the authorship of the article when he wrote McCrimmon and asked for assurance, which he duly received, that what he was teaching at McMaster was 'not breaking faith with the Denomination' as reflected in the Ottawa resolution.[30]

For a brief spell, the university dared hope that Shields would be gratified enough by recent developments to call off the controversy and enable the institution to solicit the kind of support needed to meet the tasks confronting it in the post-war period. To an extent their prayers were answered. In the New Year McCrimmon outlined in his annual report the financial proportions of the rebuilding task. First of all, there was an urgent need for enlarging the original endowment, indeed for doubling it. He pointed out that the sharp reduction in the dollar's purchasing power since the start of the war had had the effect of cutting income from the current endowment in half. Not only this, but another million dollars was needed for new buildings and equipment for the proposed Eglinton campus. Once again the denomination would be urged to contribute to a Forward Movement in order to achieve these objects.

From the faculty had come requests for increased salaries, a pension fund, and a foundation for more student prizes and scholarships. Commenting on the special faculty petition submitted at this time, Dean McLay alluded to the wartime ceiling on salaries and candidly stated that professors' incomes were much too low. He added, however, that the faculty were loyal to the institution and would abide by the Board's decision. In the end a slight adjustment was made in the salary levels to meet at least part of the faculty's request.[31] As for a pension fund, the Board had approved in principle the establishment of one early in 1918 and had actually assigned to it part of some legacies that had come the university's way, a move strongly backed by John Northway.[32]

Board chairman Thomson called for an immediate overture to the constituency. 'There are not lacking indications' he warned McCrimmon 'that a time of depression may soon overtake us ... Even without depression ... the constantly increasing burden of taxation will, no doubt, have a tendency to dampen generosity.'[33] To help the cause the chancellor, aided and abetted by Thomson, Holman, and McLay, went into print to publicize the university's virtues and the role it had played and would continue to play in the educational life of Baptists and of the country generally. The upshot was the publication in 1920 of *The Educational Policy of the Baptists of Ontario and Quebec*, the first comprehensive historical review of Baptist educational enterprises in central Canada. One of the main objects of the essay, however, was to clear up policy misunderstandings that might have deterred prospective donors in the past. One great misunderstanding was the 'spectre of federation.' Thomson had good cause to fear in the fall of 1919 that 'unless there is a positive substantial beginning everyone will hesitate to lead off and we are likely to be drifted into a discussion of the Federation question.'[34]

What must have upset Thomson was the attitude of his fellow Board member Albert Matthews. The financial house executive was undoubtedly questioning the policy of independence when he told McCrimmon that 'I do not feel myself to be sufficiently in agreement with the present educational policy of the University to warrant [my] accepting re-election to the Board.' 'I hold the highest possible regard' he added hastily 'for the sacrificial services of its leaders yet I am coming to think these very real sacrifices on their part are unnecessary.'[35] Matthews was ultimately brought round by members of the Board, notably by the dynamic Edward Carey Fox. An honour graduate of 1906, the son-in-law of former Chancellor McKay, and an executive with a major meat-packing concern, Fox had joined the Board in 1913.

But the standard arguments for federation were reiterated in many quarters. McMaster would do well, it was repeated, to give serious thought to affiliating with the University of Toronto, to concentrate upon theological instruction, and to avoid costly and unnecessary duplication. 'Why' the question usually ran 'do we need to keep up a big Baptist University?'[36]

Two years before, while the war had still been raging, Douglas Macintosh, now a firm fixture at Yale, had responded to a request from McCrimmon for an opinion on his alma mater's educational policy. After commending McMaster's general arts curriculum as so many had done in the past, as a 'good broad foundation' for graduate study, he asked a pointed question: 'Can not some form of affiliation be devised with [the University of Toronto] which, while retaining the plan of limited specialization ... would enable Baptists to make use of the courses and equipment of the great public school which their money is helping to support?' 'Efforts might then be concentrated' he concluded 'upon developing more fully the theological department ... and courses in philosophy of religion&c.'[37] Although Stewart Bates took exception to what he saw as Macintosh's gratuitous remarks, Dean McLay felt that the theologian's thoughtful comments deserved an equally thoughtful reply. McLay pointed out that on the broad question of federation he had an open mind: 'Though I am not convinced of the wisdom of such a policy I do not consider myself an opponent of it. At the same time I do not take the ground that the policy adopted thirty years ago must never be questioned or that a different policy may not be proposed... But until the proposal of federation is brought fairly before the people I must of course be loyal to the present policy.'[38]

On another aspect of the problem an alumnus who taught physics at the University of Western Ontario remarked a few years later that 'Denominational educational work seems to be so handicapped by the religious prejudices of the ignorant ... members of our denominations, that I have often questioned the advisability of so-called religious institutions ... A higher and better grade of morality in some important respects is being propagated from the more scientific institutions under State guidance.'[39]

While this unsettling view had few supporters, other reasons were cited by alumni for urging federation on their alma mater. In the spring of 1919 a special meeting of the Ottawa Valley Alumni Association marshalled a familiar contingent of arguments, ranging from McMaster's inability to compete with the University of Toronto to the reluctance of the denomination to give it adequate support. Reiterating Macintosh's wartime points, they looked forward through federation to a reorganization of the arts program and an improvement in the theological course. Towards the end of their brief, however, they weakened their argument when they incorrectly asserted that the alternative to federation – the virtual abandonment of arts and the maintenance of theology – 'had been the original intention of the founders of McMaster.'[40] It seems clear enough that the original intentions of those founders had been to establish a full-fledged and independent university, the sort of institution that the anti-federationists of 1919 were trying to maintain. But as one undergraduate who later served on the theology faculty said at the time, 'Many of our Baptist people are unaware that the McMaster endowment was for an Arts department.'[41]

It was just as clear that a good many Baptists, as the Ottawa group had contended, were not enthusiastic supporters of the university. This was hardly a new disclosure, of course, but a fact of life that had long caused anguish in the hearts of McMaster's leaders and had prompted some of them from time to time to contemplate the apparent security of federation. But the influential Carey Fox, the packing-house executive and member of the Board, was never among these advocates; throughout, he insisted upon maintaining the separateness of McMaster. However, with the Ottawa Valley alumni he agreed on one point that his fellow Board members were not prepared to accept. He was convinced that the new site in North Toronto ought to be abandoned as much too expensive and the money applied instead to salaries and equipment. In all other respects he disagreed with the critics of independence, most notably with their argument that federation would relieve the university's financial problems.[42]

To the varied briefs that McCrimmon himself received in the course of the discussion he replied with one basic counterargument. In his *Educational Policy* he maintained that the 'idea that the denomination would be saved large financial outlays through federation ... rests on the fallacy that McMaster is a rival of Toronto and in its liberal culture in trying to make the man it will have to duplicate the expensive equipment of Toronto.'[43] McMaster had not departed from its original aims; it still sought to pursue a course distinct from that of its secularized neighbour. As the chancellor grandiloquently remarked before a student assembly, 'The only way to be sure of advancing the interests of the race is to have your thinking ... linked up with the creative personality of Him upon whom the doctrines of individuals and nations depend.' For McCrimmon this was the 'secret of the genius of the Christian University.'[44] Left implicit was the premise that since McMaster had survived the war it ought to be able to prosper as an independent institution in time of peace.

To meet the charge frequently made over the years that a small school like McMaster did not warrant large-scale support the chancellor trotted out the virtues of such institutions, their 'solidarity of life' and their 'intimacy of touch.' These comments were closely associated with McCrimmon's closing remarks in his *Educational Policy*, where he sought to shatter the hardy notion that McMaster was 'a selfish little denominational project, smelling of musty mediaeval ecclesiasticism.' 'We are here' he stated 'to serve the Kingdom of God, not just to prattle about the great Baptist denomination.' These were strong, almost provocative words in view of the Convention's stress upon the denominationalism of the university the previous fall when it had backed Shields's attacks on the *Canadian Baptist*. It was almost as though McCrimmon was trying in print to compensate for the tactical defeat the more liberal construction of McMaster's purpose suffered on that occasion. Obviously the chancellor and the Board took pride in the knowledge that non-Baptists were eager to join the university's faculty because McMaster 'stands for something.'[45] This larger spirit, they hoped, would appeal to those liberally-minded Baptists who were anxious that their university serve as a model of a Christian university and attract people of other denominations to its faculty and student body. This was a more fulsome version of the statement made by Dean McLay a few years before when he had sought to dispel the myth that McMaster was 'just a little school for Baptists.'

Curiously enough, there was considerable concern expressed privately at this time about the number of non-Baptists on the faculty, a concern that sparked an effort to attract qualified Baptist candidates whenever vacancies occurred. This may have been a direct consequence of the Shields controversy the year before and undertaken to assure the constituency that Baptist interests and direction were not to be wholly jettisoned at the university. But many in the denomination at large really wanted, not just Baptists at the helm, but safe, conservative ones, a predisposition that gravely troubled, among others, the young George Gilmour.[46]

For his part, McLay seemed to reverse his field on this matter of appointments; what he had once extolled he lamented in 1920. In spite of the fact that in the interval the proportion of non-Baptists on the faculty had, if anything, decreased slightly, he told a Chicago professor that 'we now have so many of other denominations [on our staff] that we are making a special effort to fill

... vacancies with ... our own people.'[47] About one promising applicant for a Latin appointment who in every way but one filled the bill the dean complained, 'if only he were a Baptist.' When an equally qualified coreligionist was ultimately named to the post McLay was plainly delighted, grandly welcoming the new recruit 'as a member of the Baptist brotherhood.' The dean's pleasure was shared by McCrimmon and Thomson, who felt that 'we already have so many members of the staff who do not belong to the Denomination.'[48]

Within weeks of this statement the university was obliged to take on a non-Baptist to assist in the new political economy course after both Duncan MacGibbon and Harold Innis declined the offer. But at least the appointment of Humfrey Michell, an Englishman, satisfied one criterion for Thomson, who had inexplicably dreaded that an American might fill the vacancy. On the other hand, the appointment in the spring of 1920 of Chester William New to the history chair,[49] following the departure of Stewart Wallace for the University of Toronto, must have been doubly welcome. A theology alumnus and an ordained Baptist minister, he had fared well in his doctoral studies at Chicago and gained valuable classroom experience at Brandon College.[50]

The administration's anxiety to preserve the denominational balance of the faculty stood in marked contrast to the pride with which the mingling of Baptist and non-Baptist had been noted in McCrimmon's pamphlet. In public, the university professed to be a liberal, almost non-denominational, Christian university; in private, every effort was being made to preserve its distinctive Baptist flavour. The public stance almost seemed to be a repudiation of the hopes that McCrimmon had expressed at the war's end about the need for denominational institutions such as McMaster. This exercise in ambivalence was doubtless viewed in some quarters as an attempt on the university's part – and a clumsy one at that – to enjoy the best of both worlds: the financial support of those who would put educational enterprise above denominationalism and the confidence of the Baptist constituency in what it regarded as its own institution of higher learning. Or was the effort to re-Baptize McMaster, so to speak, nothing more invidious than an attempt to ensure for the foreseeable future a core of faculty members committed to the beliefs and principles embraced by the Convention?

In the meantime, the chancellor's *Educational Policy* was being dispatched to every corner of the constituency and particularly to affluent benefactors in the United States.[51] For the second time in a generation John D. Rockefeller was approached for aid, this time with facts and figures indicating how McMaster had helped to satisfy the staff requirements of American colleges and universities and to fill the pulpits of American churches.[52] This was no idle boast. Besides meeting Canadian needs the university had since the turn of the century been repaying the earlier American effort at Rochester and Colgate to train ministers and teachers for the 'northern provinces.' Almuni of the calibre of D.C. Macintosh and I.G. Matthews had reversed the process and were making important scholarly and pastoral contributions to Baptist life in the United States.

Matthews ended up at Crozer Theological Seminary, where he was joined by fellow alumni, Oamer Daniel Priddle, Reuben E. Harkness, and Stewart Grant Cole, the student of American fundamentalism. At Chicago Macintosh welcomed to its faculty such new McMaster recruits as Archibald G. Baker, Ernest J. Chane, Albert Haydon, and Charles Thomas Holman, all of whom became productive scholars. In turn Rochester and Colgate, which joined forces later in the twenties, acquired the services of Ernest W. Parsons, John F. Vichert, J.W.A. Stewart, James D. Morrison, and Thomas Wearing, the brother of Joseph Wearing, the Peterborough lawyer. In addition, a number of strategically placed pastorates in the eastern States were filled through the years by McMaster graduates in theology. Not mentioned in the appeal to Rockefeller was that this trend may have come about more by accident than by design, some McMaster men simply preferring the American theological climate to the Canadian one.

As it turned out, Rockefeller failed to respond to McCrimmon's glowing prospectus, and the five-year fund-raising campaign envisioned in 1920 had to be stretched considerably before anything approaching the finances needed to double the endowment and to provide for a new campus materialized. Only by 1928, six years after McCrimmon left the chancellor's office, had something of the order of a million and a quarter dollars been collected or pledged toward a total objective of $1,500,000.[53] Thomson's point in 1920 that post-war recession and increased taxation would siphon off funds ordinarily earmarked for Christian education had apparently been well taken.

Yet in other respects the decade of the twenties had opened auspiciously enough for the university. In the first full academic year of peace McCrimmon was happy to report that enrolment had reached the high of pre-war levels, a sudden and dramatic spurt that came as a most agreeable surprise.[54] Equally gratifying were the evaluations of student behaviour and morale in the immediate post-war years. Although Dean Farmer cautiously remarked in the spring of 1921 that 'we have much yet to make up before we shall have recovered from the rebound after the War,' there seemed to be a discernible improvement in religious interest and study effort among the students. The subsidence of these qualities, though vaguely alluded to during the war, had not hitherto been frankly admitted. A student spokesman was inclined to embroider Farmer's guarded statement and pronounce that the university had 'now reached the high standard of pre-war days,' a standard it will be recalled, that for some had not measured up to that of the 1890s.

Encouraging words also came from the representative of the female undergraduates. She attributed the 'very marked change in the women's spirit' to the acquisition of Wallingford Hall, the residence for female students on St George Street. Named after the English birthplace of its donor, William Davies, the residence had the 'wholesome effect of breaking up class cliques and throwing together girls of all years.'[55] The chancellor, whose work *The Woman Movement* had made him in the eyes of one Board member an authority on 'this burning question,'[56] had told the students when the new hall was opened that 'women are on trial. It is for them to establish traditions of the best women's residence in Toronto ... It is the mark of the intelligent woman to submit cheerfully, for the sake of others, to regulations which they may consider unnecessary for themselves.'[57]

Certain student festivities shelved by the war were vigorously revived in the first full year of peace. On the evening of 28 November 1919, the *Monthly* told its readers, Founder's Night 'was celebrated with all its prewar splendor and gaiety,' though the room decorated for the occasion somberly reminded visitors of the 'late lamented hostilities' with its exhibit of a winged victory, the roll of honour, and many rifles and shells.[58] There was also a noticeable revival in the activities of campus clubs and societies. The Men's Student Body, accustomed to the dwindling enrolments of the war years, was challenged to provide for the needs of a much expanded student body among whom were doubtless some 'flaming youth,' the hallmark of the period. Along with other new departures, the MSB inspired a popular group known as the 'McMasterrifics' which staged variety shows of sorts and made its own small contribution to the roaring twenties in Toronto. The Debating Society, which had long been active on the campus, also managed to get off to a flying start, along with the Literary Society, which resumed its pre-war practice of bringing in eminent speakers to address students and faculty.

Meanwhile, the faculty and the administration continued to wax and wane as new appointments were made, Baptist and otherwise, and as deaths, resignations, and retirements took their toll. In 1920 a symbolic link with the university's origins was severed by the death of J. S. McMaster, the senator's nephew and one-time business partner, who for years had served as treasurer of the institution. His place was immediately taken by Elven John Bengough, who had been acting as his assistant as well as registrar.[59] By the end of 1926 two old veterans, Professors Campbell and Keirstead, had been retired, and

Dr Joseph Gilmour, one-time padre of the Officers' Training Corps and professor of church history, was dead. Campbell's responsibilities were ably handled for two sessions by James Stevenson and William E. Gwatkin, who taught Latin and Greek respectively, until they in turn resigned in 1928. They were joined by another linguist, Pierre Briquet, who was placed in charge of French instruction. Professor Mueller, who had managed to survive wartime hysteria and continued to occupy the chair in German, completed the group engaged in the teaching of foreign languages. In 1926 Dean McLay received much-needed assistance in English when George C. Haddow was appointed a lecturer in his department. The work in philosophy was still being conducted by the popular, though aging, James Ten Broeke, whose years of service were recognized in 1924 when the university conferred upon him an honorary doctorate of laws.

The year before the arrival of the new classicists and the professor of French, McMaster had welcomed Lulu Odell Gaiser (who came to assist R.W. Smith in biology) and Kenneth Wiffin Taylor, an alumnus who would instruct in both history and political economy. A graduate of the University of Western Ontario, Professor Gaiser had undertaken doctoral work in plant pathology and cytology at Columbia University. Taylor's annual salary of $2,400, the chancellor disclosed, was to be paid by a friend of the university, who turned out to be Cyrus S. Eaton, another alumnus who had made good as an industrialist in the United States.[60] Following his graduation from McMaster in 1921, Taylor had gone to Chicago armed with the following testimonial from Dean McLay: 'He is one of the most brilliant undergraduates we have ever had, quite the equal in promise of such men as MacGibbon [and] Donald ... who have represented this University in Economics at Chicago ... He was a candidate this year for a Rhodes Scholarship.'[61]

Professor Chester New heartily welcomed Taylor's return to his alma mater in 1925. Described by one colleague as a 'bridge between History and Economics,'[62] Taylor could relieve New in many fields of instruction. Taylor later recalled that he was advised a week before classes started that he would be teaching ancient history and 'to bone up on British history from James II to Waterloo.'[63] The professor of history, whose services had been sought after by other institutions, had for some time been openly complaining about his work load and calling for more help. 'The subject itself is bigger than that of any other subject,' New claimed with all the impressive conviction that he could muster, 'there is more ground to cover ... I know that in a similar manner the science men have their laboratory work, but as they constantly emphasize that, it is perfectly legitimate for me to emphasize the ... matter of quiz sections and consultations which is also, I think, more exacting work.'[64]

New's aside about scientists and his belief that they should acknowledge that instructors in arts might labour just as strenuously and productively as they, may account for the following criticism that came one day from Professor Findlay, the mathematician. 'At this morning's chapel service,' he complained to the chancellor, 'Dr New gave another of his extended expositions or sermonettes and I wish to raise the question of the propriety of any professor taking advantage of the chapel period for such a purpose.'[65] How this problem was resolved was not recorded, but anyone who had the pleasure of listening to one of New's 'extended sermonettes' will conclude that the historian had the last word.

New appointments in theology also occurred: the mid-twenties saw the arrival of Nathaniel Parker and Laurance Henry Marshall. The former, a native of Mississippi, had been teaching in 'a small Bible school in the backwoods of Kentucky' when he was approached by Dean Farmer with an invitation to join McMaster's theology department.[66] He arrived barely two weeks before the fall term of 1925 began. The appointment of his colleague, the Englishman L.H. Marshall, to fill the late Joseph Gilmour's old chair, turned out to be potentially the most explosive one of the decade, for it raised the possibility of renewed controversy. Among those who would bear the brunt of that controversy was yet another new appointment, this one at the very top. In 1923 the university formally installed its sixth chancellor, Howard Primrose Whidden, to succeed the ailing McCrimmon, who retired from the post, but not from the university, after twelve years of service as its chief executive.

In spite of McCrimmon's efforts to adjust to the demands of administrative duties, they had always been unwelcome to him and had placed a heavy strain on his emotions. This disability he had frequently discussed with his colleagues, particularly during the war years. In the summer of 1920 he informed McLay that 'owing to the persistent character of my sleeplessness and the fiendish delight it takes in making me super-nervous over the most trivial ... matters it was thought best that no further University correspondence should be sent to me.'[67] Time off was finally granted him, and for the next few months most of the university's administrative chores were taken over by Deans McLay and Farmer. Plans were laid early in 1921 to sound out possible successors when McCrimmon declared his intention to retire in the spring of 1922. When that day arrived a Senate resolution prepared for the occasion touched on the frustrations that had stalked his regime, how the war had demolished plans to enlarge the university's plant, and how his failing health and the slow return of normal business conditions continued to stall expansion after 1918.[68]

The critical question in 1921 was who should be approached to assume direction of the university at this critical stage of its development. Some people fondly recalled the kind of leadership McMaster had enjoyed in A.C. McKay's heyday and longed for a new administration of that calibre. Inevitably, prospective candidates were measured against McKay's personality and qualities. In the process unflattering references were sometimes made to McCrimmon himself. After submitting for consideration the name of a leading educator in Alberta who had shared McKay's interest in technical instruction, one correspondent observed that '[William Grant] Carpenter would be the opposite of Dr McCrimmon. He would not contend with him for platform honours and would not preach sermons. He would be Dr McKay in this regard, and when his turn came he would deliver his address on Education . . . in the non-oratorical, concise, *simple* style of the accomplished teacher.'[69]

The candidate who ultimately came to be taken more seriously than any other was Howard Whidden. His credentials and experience appeared to warrant his being placed on a short 'short list.' Like Theodore Rand, the university's second chancellor, Whidden was a native Nova Scotian and a graduate of Acadia University.[70] After taking his BD at McMaster in 1894 he had proceeded, like so many of his contemporaries, to Chicago, where he had kept O.C.S. Wallace advised of the theological tone of that controversial institution. He next spent some time in Morden, Manitoba, where he first developed his interest in the problems of western Baptists. After returning briefly to Nova Scotia he enquired of Wallace about pastoral possibilities 'up your way.' 'The [Maritime] Provinces do not seem to catch my heart strings at all,' he confided to the chancellor, 'Ontario would certainly call forth better work from me.'[71] Within a few weeks of this entreaty Whidden was invited to fill a pulpit in Galt, and to do part-time lecturing in public speaking at McMaster,[72] duties he discharged until called to the faculty of Brandon College in 1900. His acceptance of the offer apparently disturbed his friends, 'who seem to think me a little "off" in my convictions regarding the work in the West.'[73] Three years later the itinerant Whidden resumed his pastoral career at the affluent First Baptist Church in Dayton, Ohio. But Manitoba and Brandon were not to be denied. In 1912 when the western college sought a president it called once again upon a Whidden eager to serve the institution. His administration at Brandon was punctuated by a stint as a member of Parliament and vocal supporter of conscription and the Union Government in the closing stages of the war. Within months of his departure from federal politics in 1921 he was being actively sought as a successor to Chancellor McCrimmon.

Whidden's candidacy was a high-powered one. Wallace Cohoe, like others, was very much impressed by his varied experiences and distinguished presence. The chemist accepted as axiomatic that Whidden's new career would be a successful one, given his administrative talents, his capacity to inspire urban congregations, and his connections with politicians and educators across the country. Indeed, Cohoe felt that Whidden, if appointed, would be the 'first educational statesman to head McMaster.'[74] Those in the constituency and at the university who used former Chancellor McKay as a yardstick for measuring candidates were gratified to learn that, like McKay at McMaster, Whidden at Brandon had engineered the construction of a science building and had encouraged research in the natural sciences. A small college, he would point out in an article in 1924, might not be able to produce a great astrophysicist but it should 'aim at turning out intelligent groups with an appreciation of some of the things that an astrophysicist can do,' and of the achievements of the modern scientific and technological world.[75]

The only question that remained was whether Whidden would give up his work in the west, to which he appeared to have a deep commitment, and accept the post in Toronto. Certainly, Carey Fox, newly named to the Executive Committee of the Board of Governors, hoped that Whidden would heed the call. Fox and Albert Matthews, recently appointed chairman of the Board following the death of D.E. Thomson,[76] had met Whidden almost literally half-way at the Lakehead to discuss the proposal late in 1922. Writing to Whidden shortly after those conversations, Fox observed that 'at the moment I can only repeat what I said at Port Arthur, if you become our leader I will follow and support you and I confidently hope the Senate will give you a unanimous invitation and that you will see your way clear to come.'[77] His abundant enthusiasm for the appointment came through clearly in an interview nearly forty years after the episode he described here.

At the Lakehead, Whidden likely discussed the plans for McMaster which a few months later he would spell out in a letter to a friend. He looked forward, among other things, to a relocation of the university, if this were at all feasible, and to a 'definite campaign for increased numbers of students from all parts of the constituency' based on 'a glowing McMaster message to each of the Baptist associations.' In addition, he hoped that the institution's place and the chancellor's would be firmly established 'in all important educational and inter-University gatherings.'[78] And, as he pointed out elsewhere,[79] he wanted a university that would, even while it was cultivating chemistry and physics and absorbing the findings of the new social sciences, continue to stress the ultimate verities of the ancient humanities. An institution ought not to be known just for its applied science, its vocational training, or its professional schools, Whidden argued, but for that 'indefinable something which trains and inspires mind and heart for adaptable constructive leadership.' This kind of talk was well designed to appeal to the expansive Carey Fox.

Yet Fox's hope for unanimity in the acceptance of Whidden was rudely frustrated. A strong voice was raised against it in one of the opening shots of a controversy that would rack the university for the better part of five years and recall for many those unhappy times when Elmore Harris had questioned the teaching of I.G. Matthews. Within a week of Fox's hopeful letter to the chancellor-designate, T.T. Shields openly dissented when it came time on 22 December 1922 for the Board to approve Whidden's appointment.[80] Some weeks before, Shields had virtually accused his fellow Board members of engineering a leak about the appointment in order to give undue publicity to the move and undermine legitimate opposition to it.[81] This development was unpleasant but not totally unexpected. For a considerable period Shields had been expressing his reservations about the affairs of the university, and it was well known that he was anxious to share them with the denomination. After enjoying a brief respite after the Ottawa Convention in 1919, McMaster now had to gird itself for what was threatening to become an all-out fight to challenge its men and its policies.

9

'O, it's a lovely war!'

About a year before Whidden was publicly courted by McMaster an ambitious tour of western Baptist outposts was planned by the Board of Governors. The objects of the mission appeared obvious enough. First of all, the university had been promising to send a deputation west ever since the turn of the century as proof that the leading Baptist institution in the land was as anxious to meet that section's need as it was to meet the east's. It was almost as if McMaster was out to fulfil at least part of A.J. Pineo's hope that the university might undertake the direction of an expanding system of Baptist institutions of higher learning. But there was a more important reason for organizing the expedition. For months McMaster had been kept informed of the growing disenchantment among Baptists in the west with its satellite, Brandon College, a strong echo of the resentment directed against the parent institution in the immediate post-war period. A good many western Baptists, like their coreligionists in the Ontario and Quebec Convention, were expressing their dissatisfaction with the alleged liberalism of both Brandon and McMaster. One western correspondent blamed it on the unsettled state of affairs that followed the war, remarking that 'it is so easy for people to be panicky in these days.'[1] At a time when the university needed all possible support, financial and moral, throughout the country, it was imperative to mollify and reassure the westerners. Equally important was the necessity of gaining as much backing as possible for the candidacy of Howard P. Whidden for the chancellorship of McMaster.

The missionary selected for the task was not McCrimmon, whose declining health and hard-pressed nervous system ruled out his undertaking the journey, but the industrious Dean McLay, to whom the chancellor had been delegating more and more responsibilities.[2] The vice-regal visit to the border-lands of the Baptist constituency was obviously as welcome as it was overdue. 'I am sure' wrote alumnus W.G. Carpenter from Edmonton 'McMaster men throughout the West will be pleased with the courtesy of the Board of Governors in making it possible for you to visit them in their fields.' Duncan MacGibbon, now well ensconced at the University of Alberta, was a trifle less polite: 'I think that to some degree in the past, McMaster has been just a little lax in keeping in touch with her graduates.' But he concluded on the hopeful note that 'nothing but good can come of [the] visit.' McLay in turn waxed ecstatic over his tour. Unquestionably much good will was fostered, and public relations were improved between the Baptist metropolis and the west, between the alma mater and the considerable colony of McMaster graduates beyond the Lakehead. By and large, however, McLay had been preaching to the converted on the prairies. As events proved, many a western Baptist would continue to question the propriety of supporting the university and its affiliate in Manitoba.

Within months of McLay's visit Brandon College was subjected to the sort of investigation that McMaster had painfully undergone before the war and more recently during the squabble over the editorial soundness of the *Canadian Baptist*. In response to the complaints from those who questioned Whidden's fitness as president and the school's orthodoxy, particularly the teaching of H.L. MacNeill, the Baptist Union of Western Canada appointed a commission to review the curriculum and instruction of the college's theological department. Whidden bravely prefaced its proceedings with the statement that every teacher at the school was 'loyal to the great principles of the Christian life and truth . . . and [taught] the divine Saviorhood and Lordship of Christ.'[3] This claim, however, was heatedly disputed by western fundamentalists and by their powerful eastern ally, T.T. Shields. Indeed, it was plain that Shields regarded the west and central Canada as integral parts of the same problem and the fight to preserve orthodoxy as one to be waged as vigorously in one section as in the other. As for his conception of the situation on the prairies, the Jarvis Street pastor left no one in any doubt: 'The condition of affairs in the West has been brought about by the administration of Brandon College under the presidency of Dr Whidden.'[4]

Back in Toronto, meanwhile, it was equally plain that McMaster's Board of Governors hoped for a favourable decision from the Brandon commission before the Ontario and Quebec Convention met in mid-October 1922, so that delegates could be told that all was well in the western constituency and that it was solidly behind Whidden and McMaster.[5] Although the commission failed to deliver in time to suit the schedule of the Walmer Road meetings, the latter had little difficulty dealing with the allegations that Shields meted out on that occasion. The Convention ended by denying his charge that Frank Sanderson, a Board member, had questioned the credibility of the Scriptures. It went on to deplore the method and substance of Shields's attack and to call upon the churches 'to continue their full moral support of the University.'6 When the Brandon commission finally did submit its report early in the new year its contents were as welcome as they were predictable; for they affirmed that the Baptists of western Canada were 'to be congratulated on having an educational institution in [their] midst of the character of Brandon College.'7

Shields's reaction to all these proceedings need not be imagined; they are part of the record. In a letter in 1924 he evoked wartime passions in language which he would employ in his long battle with McMaster, asserting that to 'aid and abet the destructive work of Brandon College is nothing short of treason to Christ and His gospel.'8 Regardless of how the commission might have ruled on the matter of Brandon's soundness in 1923, the fact remained that Shields's followers continued to command a sizable audience in the west that would have ruled otherwise. The testimony of George Hilton, who directed a popular men's club at First Church in Calgary, could not be ignored: 'I have been getting around our churches,' he reported in 1925, 'two of them wouldn't even recognize me because I wasn't a follower of Dr Shields. I have found a great many of his followers all over the province.' He then noted that William Aberhart, the Baptist evangelist from Ontario and future Social Credit leader in Alberta, 'has made some very bitter remarks about McMaster people & is stirring up all the trouble he can.' 'His attitude and methods' Hilton concluded 'are mighty proof that the "Devil is not dead."'9

On the eastern front the lines of battle were already forming between Shields's forces and those led by the university he would seek to discredit. That the Convention should have met at Walmer Road in 1922 was highly indicative of the way in which the battle was shaping up. It was to Walmer Road and its pastor, John MacNeill, that some evicted members of the Jarvis Street Church who could not tolerate Shields's personality or his theology had transferred their loyalty in the early twenties. Others organized a new congregation, Central Baptist Church, in Castle Memorial Hall on the university campus. Among the refugees who left for Walmer Road was the businessman John Northway, who had been influenced by what he called the 'evangelical liberalism' of Howard Whidden and Dean Farmer, the last-named a deacon in MacNeill's congregation.10 A dependable benefactor of Baptist institutions, Northway had shown a keen interest in Whidden's work at Brandon. For him a 'reverently critical analysis' of Biblical sources had not appeared to sap the traditional faith in fundamental truths, and nowhere, as far as he was concerned, was this more evident than in the teaching of the people whom he respected on the McMaster faculty. When they were vilified by Shields, Northway had no choice but to seek out a new congregation. The schism at Jarvis Street set the stage for the furore that arose over Whidden's appointment as chancellor of the university, with Shields adamantly opposing it and Northway as adamantly supporting the candidacy of his 'favorite' theologian.

There were some in high places at the university who hoped that steps could be taken to head off the gathering storm. Albert Matthews, who along with Carey Fox had urged Whidden to accept the chancellorship, hoped that by a display of good will on both sides a serious confrontation could be avoided. Matthews's hopes soared when Shields indicated that he was anxious, in spite of his misgivings, to maintain some kind of unity in the Convention and would seek an interview with the chancellor-elect to discuss 'matters educational.' Visibly distressed by the charges of unorthodoxy levelled at McMaster, a worried Matthews wrote Whidden early in 1923 that he agreed 'with Dr Shields's thought in regard to this matter [of an interview].' 'There seems to be a great opportunity' he added 'to unite all our people behind McMaster, and we should not let [it] go by.' He closed by regretting that on a recent visit to Toronto Whidden had not remained over another day so that he could have had a talk with the pastor of Jarvis Street.[11] Whidden weighed the possibility that Shields might be sincere in this overture, but he remained sceptical about the advantages of such an interview. Furthermore, he was convinced that whatever Matthews might wish to do to patch up the quarrel, the rest of the Board 'would not want to take orders from Dr Shields.'[12]

Others applied the cold water treatment directly to Matthews's proposal for high-level conversations. Dean McLay was one of them; the Rev. W.A. Cameron was another. 'For heaven's sake' Cameron implored Whidden 'do not hold an interview concerning University affairs with T.T. Shields ... without other people being present ... He has no scruples about twisting things to suit his own purpose.' Cameron then expressed surprise at Matthews's conduct: 'Now do not misunderstand me, for Mr Matthews is a simple minded Christian gentleman and is doubtless doing what he thinks best. At the same time he has no right, as chairman of the [Board], to enter into any agreement with ... Shields without consulting [other] members.' 'Your own good sense' he congratulated Whidden 'has saved the day.'[13]

Whidden's good sense amounted to proposing a compromise arrangement, one befitting a former politician, which would have had discussions take place, not in isolation as Shields wanted, but 'in conference with the Board and Senate or with a committee appointed by those bodies.'[14] And in such a milieu, Whidden made it clear, he had no intention of yielding to a demand for 'a new series of affirmations' from himself since he had already given one when he accepted the chancellorship. Whidden's suggestion for a change of venue was rejected by Shields in a letter addressed to Matthews. Shields seized the opportunity to review Whidden's connection with Brandon which 'has been under fire of denominational criticism.' Shields ended by regretting that he could not meet the object of this criticism face to face.[15] Although the clergyman gave the impression that if any kind of overture had been made by the university he would have been prepared to let bygones be bygones, no such overture was in fact made, and much to Matthews's chagrin the Baptist summit failed to materialize. The possible consequences of this Shields spelled out in the same letter. 'I am determined' he told Matthews 'to be more aggressive in the future in the cause of evangelical religion, and in the defence of the faith ... I simply desire it to be known that the men who stand for the things that I stand for are a factor to be reckoned with in this Denomination.' At this point Shields served notice of the withdrawal of Jarvis Street's support for the university on the grounds that the church lacked confidence in its administration and its teaching.[16]

A number of McMaster people had already taken Shields's threats to heart and they urged Whidden not to provide him inadvertently with more ammunition. 'I have no doubt in my mind' Dean Farmer wrote early in March 1923 'that the last Convention [at Walmer Road] was won by ... assurances that pledges and commitments to the ideals and purpose of the [University] Charter [would be] fulfilled.' 'The body of *solid conservatives* are with us now,' he reminded the chancellor-elect, 'and it would be dangerous to go back on the pledges.'[17] Whidden needed no such warning, but all the same he appreciated his dean's concern.

The university, in the meantime, laid plans to install Whidden as its sixth chancellor and looked forward to a pleasantly impressive ceremony. Among those invited to adorn the platform was the president of Brown University, the oldest Baptist institution of higher learning in North America, 'an institution' as Whidden remarked to Shields a few days later 'with a wonderful record.'[18] The invitation was duly accepted by the incumbent, Dr William H.P. Faunce. The university was then disagreeably surprised to learn that Shields utterly disapproved of the Faunce invitation, this after he had missed a number of legitimate opportunities to discuss it in both the Senate and the Board, a point that Carey Fox angrily brought to the attention of the Senate during a review of the episode early in 1924.[19] Indeed, at the time a number of people had remarked on the clergyman's poor attendance record not only in the Senate but also at meetings of the Home Missions Board, a dereliction that cost him re-election to that body.[20]

According to Dean McLay's account, one of Shields's aides actually presented his pastor's protest as Whidden came down from the platform on the afternoon of his installation. 'It was' he said 'like handing a man a bill on his wedding day.'[21] In statements to the press and in public addresses Shields damned Faunce as a modernist and, 'in a manner calculated to impair confidence in the University' as the Senate later criticized his tactics, he repudiated those responsible for honouring Brown's president, chiefly Whidden and Farmer.[22]

A few days later Whidden sent a letter to Shields assuring him that Faunce's degree had been recommended in good faith and had nothing to do with his supposed modernism; rather it had been conferred as a tribute to a distinguished sister institution. McMaster's new chancellor admitted that it had never occurred to him to examine any of Faunce's pamphlets, and he supposed that the Senate was as ignorant as he of the theological politics of the scholar in question.[23] Dean Farmer supported Whidden by remarking that conferring the degree 'did not necessarily carry with it endorsement of Dr Faunce's educational policies or theological views any more than it did in the case of the other recipients of honorary degrees.' It was quite apparent that neither Whidden nor Farmer had thought it possible that Brown's president might be a representative of what the dean himself had once verbosely described as 'that shallow but specious anti-supernaturalistic phase of modernism which rejects all miracle . . . and which has such a low estimate of the religious reliability . . . of the Scriptures.'[24]

The explanations offered by Whidden and Farmer, however, merely added fuel to the fire of Shields's resentment. Should not the university, he asked, enquire into the respectability of a candidate's credentials before they put their imprimatur upon him? Although Faunce, who obviously felt that he should make a move, assured both Whidden and Shields that he 'affirmed [Christ's] Deity in every public address where I have opportunity,'[25] he had, as Shields well knew, written disparagingly of those who still combated the evolutionary theory in the schools and the higher criticism in the universities.[26] For Shields this was sufficient for an indictment. The clergyman then proceeded to publicize the letters that had passed between himself and McMaster on the Faunce affair. The chancellor, who up to this point had not appeared to take Shields's strictures very seriously, suddenly seemed to realize that the university might well have a long and ugly fight on its hands.

'He has placed the matter' Whidden told a nervous Matthews late in November 1923 'where we shall have to act as an intelligent Senate . . . evidently the die has been cast [and] we must act without flinching and with a view to seeing this through.' A couple of months later he wrote in the same vein to an alumnus teaching in a London collegiate: 'I am sure our people generally will appreciate the seriousness of the situation.'[27] Some, however, did not at this stage share Whidden's sombre view and dismissed Shields's supporters as so many 'pesky mosquitoes.' Yet a few weeks later the same people would be gripped by despair, complaining that the university was ignoring the gravity of the problem. This ambivalence in attitudes – complacency at one moment, near panic at another – which came to characterize the crisis in McMaster's affairs has been noted by a student of the American situation in the twenties.[28]

A minor irritant for the university at this time was the apparent failure of the *Canadian Baptist* to do justice to the new chancellor's installation ceremonies. The editorship had changed hands since the death of W.J. McKay – some would say Shields's criticism in 1919 had hastened it – and the Rev. Lewis K. Kipp was now in charge. McKay's successor was brusquely ticked off by Dean McLay for his supposedly inadequate treatment of the convocation addresses, particularly Whidden's. Kipp was accused, for the most part, of cribbing what the Toronto *Globe* had had to say about the proceedings. Either he was too new to the game or, a distinct possibility, he shared Shields's reservations about Faunce and was reluctant to accord the installation the prominence that McLay obviously thought it deserved.

But Kipp's alleged dereliction of duty was as nothing compared to Shields himself and the support he seemed to enjoy in certain crucial quarters. A Baptist in Westmount, Quebec, for example, though he had some reservations about Shields's tactics, fully backed his objectives and 'the fundamentals for which he stands.' He thought that he detected a dark conspiracy in the Faunce matter and called for the 'traitor in the camp . . . to step out and let us know who he is.'[29] However, it was comforting for the new administration at McMaster to learn that they still had the support of at least some solid conservatives. Thus, O.C.S. Wallace wrote from Baltimore assuring Whidden that he was 'in thorough accord with the [recent] protest of the Senate . . . against the attitude [and actions] of Dr Shields.'[30] A Board member, James Ryrie, informed a pleased John Northway on that occasion that the Senate 'gave [Shields] the best dressing down he ever received with between 25 and 30 members to meet him . . . John MacNeill didn't spare him I can tell you.'[31] Another correspondent, a pastor in St Louis, Missouri, complained that Shields 'almost persuades one to be a Modernist; he has theology but lacks religion . . . he and his ilk are obsessed with conceit and lust for notoriety.' A friend in London, Ontario, could not resist having some fun at the university's expense. 'It was a great surprise to me to learn' he wrote Whidden 'that you and so many other McMaster men [are] such a bunch of unrepentent heretics. Please tell Professor Farmer that I hope he will improve his theology. As for your own, the only hope I can see is frequent and regular attendance at Jarvis Street.'[32] The comic relief was welcome.

Although it was hoped that the abusiveness of Shields's campaign would hurt no one but its author, the broadsides from his newly established *Gospel Witness*, Jarvis Street's official mouthpiece, did damage in places that the university was anxious to placate. Early in 1924, particularly after the Senate had all but censured Shields, his paper denounced 'that modernist group' that had led the university 'to the edge of the precipice,' that 'little group in the Senate' who attempted to subvert the faith and to 'poison the springs of our denominational life,' that 'small group' who told the Board of Governors what to do.[33] As one aggrieved Baptist in Ottawa, plainly an avid reader of the *Gospel Witness*, stated the matter: 'Since the Matthews affair came up . . . and as I have watched [the university's] course at the Ottawa Convention and at the Walmer Road convention of 1922 – and still later in connection with [this] Faunce affair – [the] feeling has become deeper . . . that instead of our University being our protector from the assaults of the enemy, Anti-Christ . . . she is leaving the protecting and the fighting to some force outside the institution.'[34]

For Whidden and his friends one comforting aspect of this otherwise unpleasant commentary was that it had been written, not by a person whose attitude toward McMaster had been soured by recent events, but by one who had long held, certainly since the far off days of pre-war Ontario, that McMaster had failed to keep a 'united front in the battle against error.' Little of the correspondence to Whidden or McLay suggests recent mass conversions to the position that Shields took in the early twenties. On the other hand, not all those genuinely upset by recent developments would have committed their grievances to paper; they might instead have maintained a silent vigil against the university and denied it vital moral and financial support. 'One poor pastor' reported a Baptist from Claremont 'declared that whenever he received a letter urging him to present the cause of Christian Education to his people he was thrown into a state of fearful agony due to a conflict between his love for McMaster and a tender conscience which peremptorily forbade him to advocate her support.'[35]

Meanwhile, Whidden was full of praise for the colleagues who had shared with him in the Senate and elsewhere the burden of repulsing the attacks on the good name of the University. He was thinking particularly of Deans McLay and Farmer who had consistently offered him guidance and reassurance. He was also grateful for Professor Joseph Gilmour's 'valuable work in connection with this whole Shields-Faunce matter.'[36] Much more than any of the others Dean McLay was convinced that Shields had shot his bolt and that when the Convention assembled in London later in the year he would be properly disavowed, as he had already been in the Senate, and would lose out in a bid for re-election to the Board of Governors.[37] As the year wore on others were not as optimistic as the dean of arts. By the summer these doubters were sharing their concern with the chancellor. The Rev. J.G. Brown, who had himself come under fire from Jarvis Street, was convinced that Shields's 'propaganda is winning more to his side than he is alienating and that at the London Convention he is going to launch a gigantic effort to capture the Convention, divide the body and deal the University a death blow.' 'What grieves me' he mournfully concluded 'is the number of McMaster men who have gotten to believe Shields.'[38] Many of these alumni, as a colleague, G.P. Albaugh, has pointed out, may have been products of the English theology course, a certificate program not leading to a degree. Billed in calendars as a 'substantial' course, it was designed for 'men of maturity and experience' who for one reason or another could not meet the more exacting admission requirements of the BD course.

At this point, though he might not have thought the situation quite as grave as Brown had pictured it, Whidden was at a loss to know how to handle Shields's assaults. He was well aware that McMaster had a formidable opponent on its hands, but if that opponent were answered in print 'he and his friends' Whidden warned 'would simply . . . have something else to try to pick to pieces.'[39] At least one Board member, however, was prepared to take Brown's assessment of the situation at face value and urged, as a means of countering Shields, that 'something be done . . . to challenge the attention of our people.' He suggested that a special educational conference be held on the eve of the Convention at which McMaster's virtues could be paraded conspicuously before the delegates. But Brown himself, along with others, questioned the wisdom of this proposal. Such a gathering, they noted, would conflict with a fundamentalist conference planned by Shields's group, and it was feared that they might make capital out of a one-sided presentation of the university's case. Brown maintained, acknowledging the risk of sounding 'ultra pious,' that 'our only refuge is in God.' 'We cannot fight Shields with his own weapons . . . [but one] thing that comforts me is that the University belongs to Christ and is very precious in his sight.'[40]

In the end, Whidden and his advisors planned to use the London Convention as a means of assuring the constituency that McMaster had made every conscientious effort to abide by the terms of the Charter and that at no time had appointments been made or teaching condoned in deliberate violation of that instrument. It was agreed that the university's report should embody an historical review of the senator's intentions and of the university's fulfilment of them: the establishment of a 'Christian school of learning . . . affording the best possible facilities for a thoroughly Christian course of education . . . with the Lordship of Christ as the controlling principle.' The delegates were also to be told that 'in our teaching of Science and Philosophy, while there must always be generous regard for truth found in any realm, we give supreme place to the Christian view of God and the world.'[41]

This public reaffirmation, though agreed upon, must have been distasteful to the chancellor who in 1923 had balked at doing this sort of thing in Shields's presence. While anxious to assure conservatives in the denomination that they had nothing to fear, he was, unless pressed to do so, reluctant to classify himself or McMaster as conservative. Writing to the vacationing Dean Farmer he remarked that he knew of several Baptist college heads in the Northern Convention who would be ranked by the best men in Canada as quite conservative and orthodox. He added: 'I do not like to use these terms but they have to be used sometimes for convenience sake to distinguish their bearers from "out and out" Fundamentalists.'[42] Whidden seemed to be trying to say that there were no liberals as such but only varying degrees of fundamentalists. And there were indeed different tendencies within the fundamentalist movement in the United States, ranging from moderate to ultra-conservative.[43]

Reluctantly endorsed or not, the prospective review and reaffirmation of the 'Purpose of McMaster University' prepared by Whidden's office was warmly received in many circles. One correspondent, who ended up seconding the adoption of the university's report at London, seemed to touch the root of the problem when he observed that many people firmly believed something was remiss at McMaster: 'They would welcome a strong restatement of [the university's] present theological position . . . for, after all, that is the storm centre in their minds.'[44] And that clearly was reason enough for the kind of statement that Whidden laboriously prepared for the London meetings.

To the dismay of the university's friends the Convention did not proceed nearly as well as the chancellor and McLay had hoped. The university's report was ultimately adopted, but McMaster was subjected to fierce criticism for having conferred the degree on Faunce. Although Shields eventually withdrew an amendment spearheading the attack on this front, he did so on the understanding that a similar grievance from the Toronto Association would be aired at a later session. What also disturbed those who had expected an easy time of it at London was that an unqualified vote of confidence in the university was defeated, narrowly to be sure, but defeated all the same. Furthermore, even when the Toronto Association's critical resolution was in turn withdrawn the university's supporters had to pay a price. The Convention was directed to appoint a committee to review the whole honorary degree question. It was staffed by the principal combatants: Whidden, S.J. Moore, and Dean Farmer for the one side, and Shields and the Rev. John Linton, the Jarvis Street pastor's principal associate, for the other. A slightly watered down version of Shields's original resolution was finally agreed upon by all members of the committee, including the chancellor. Whidden actually seconded the motion for adopting the resolution that 'this Convention relies upon the Senate to exercise care that honorary degrees be not conferred upon religious leaders whose theological views are known to be out of harmony with the cardinal principles of evangelical Christianity.'[45] The experience had a considerable impact on Whidden who the following spring admonished McLay not to contemplate the awarding of any honorary degrees that year 'for fear of making unwise moves.'[46]

Another setback for the university, and for McLay's powers of prediction, was Shields's triumphant re-election to the Board of Governors. I.G. Matthews had failed as miserably as the dean in forecasting the results of the Convention. 'I do not doubt for a moment' he had written McLay from Crozer Seminary on 29 October 1924 'that you are a good prophet re T.T. and the Ballot box today. He, as well as most of those of his kind on this side, have about run [their] course.'[47] Whidden, for his part, ruefully conceded that he and a number of his colleagues at the university had badly misjudged the situation. He was clearly rankled by the way in which he had been forced to negotiate with Shields on a resolution that implicitly questioned university policy and by Shields's reinstatement as a member of the Board. He was angered that Shields should 'evidently think the Senate was definitely rebuked ... and [be] rubbing it in.'[48] Notwithstanding all the letters of reassurance that came to his office in the aftermath of the Convention, Whidden could not erase the feeling that he had been put down. On this point the dean of arts at the University of Western Ontario, Sherwood Fox, bravely tried to set his mind at ease: 'I am quite sincere in saying that your personal attitude during the debate drew people to you and that your position is stronger than ever.'[49] Words of this sort from a fellow administrator at a sister institution probably helped to restore Whidden's well-being. At any rate, he resolved that he was 'not going to allow Shields to disturb our peace very much during the present Convention year.' It was a forlorn hope.

That peace was to be imperilled, though no one realized it at once, by the tragedy that struck the theology department within a month of Whidden's firm resolve. On 8 December 1924 Joseph Gilmour died, leaving a yawning vacancy in the chair of pastoral theology. For the better part of twenty years he had served the university as theologian and church historian and had recently been relied upon for assistance in the varied confrontations with Shields. To him the battle had been a life-and-death matter for the institution. 'My father had once said to Dr Whidden' his son George recalled years later 'that McMaster had only narrowly escaped being a glorified Woodstock College rather than a university, and his early death ... amid the gloom of temporary defeat of all he had striven for made me determined that no such danger would be perpetuated if I could arrange otherwise.'[50]

An immediate effort had to be made to replace the elder Gilmour, a difficult enough assignment at the best of times but doubly difficult in the charged atmosphere of the mid-twenties. J.D. Freeman, an English pastor and TBC alumnus who quickly applied for the position, was well known in the constituency, having preached in a number of Ontario pulpits before returning to the United Kingdom where during the war he had frequently entertained McMaster soldiers. Although another Englishman was ultimately selected for the post, Freeman volunteered the information, which must have endeared him to his Canadian correspondents, that he loathed the 'Jarvis Street beauty.'[51]

The candidate whom the university was most anxious to recruit was L.H. Marshall of Coventry. A graduate of Rawdon College of Leeds and the University of London, he had established for himself a solid reputation in English Baptist circles as both a teacher and a theologian, an admirable combination that seemed to fit him as a worthy successor to the late Joseph Gilmour. However, Marshall had also received extensive training at the Universities of Marburg and Berlin in dogma, philosophy, and Old Testament theology, an educational experience not likely to make him many friends among those in Canada who still suspected the soundness of German Biblical scholarship. In considering the appointment, the university appeared to be giving notice that they had no intention of permitting the growing controversy with Shields to impair their right to hire qualified people.

When Whidden dispatched letters to a number of leading Baptist educators and pastors in Britain inquiring after Marshall's fitness for the post, he prefaced his questions with a brief description of McMaster's purpose and her needs in this particular instance. 'You know' he explained with characteristic reluctance 'we are quite a conservative institution, though we do not desire to become reactionary in any sense of the word.'[52] But the meagre description could be misleading: conservative by what standards, the recipients of his queries might have asked themselves, English or North American? As the article that Shields had found so offensive in the *Canadian Baptist* had noted, many English Baptists, though certainly not all, had left behind them the sort of acrimonious theological discussion that was still convulsing their counterparts on this side of the Atlantic. What Whidden's letters really amounted to was not so much an enquiry about Marshall's qualities as a warning that if he accepted the position at McMaster he might not be able to enjoy the same kind of placidly productive career that could be had in the United Kingdom. On the other hand, the chancellor sought to assure Marshall himself that if he came out to take the chair he should not have cause 'for any great anxiety,' in spite of recent 'interesting experiences.'[53]

The responses to Whidden's letters were uniformly favourable to Marshall. Indeed, any reservations were directed at the McMaster situation. 'I urged [Marshall] to remain in England' one of his mentors told Whidden candidly 'because I felt sure that he would be up against the kind of thing depicted in the *Canadian Baptist* debate. And I knew Mr Marshall to be a very sensitive man who would never do his best in any atmosphere of suspicion.'[54] But another and more positive view of the post Marshall was to fill appeared in an English church magazine. Speculating on his motives for accepting it and McMaster's prospects, the editor of the *Christian World* wrote that 'perhaps it is his passion to keep the young generation in hail which has led [Marshall] to decide to go to Canada, for McMaster University is a school of theological arts and science buzzing with young life.'[55]

The day that Marshall's appointment was approved by the Senate, 25 July 1925, those members present had read to them a telegram from T.T. Shields who happened to be on a visit to Los Angeles. Briefly and predictably the Jarvis Street pastor lodged a protest against 'any important action during midsummer when some Convention-elected representatives were known to be so far away.'[56] It was another portentous move in a campaign that in intensity and rancour would dwarf previous conflicts between the university and the denomination. At the height of the crisis one Baptist claimed that Marshall's appointment, to a far greater extent than the incident over the Faunce degree, was being used by Shields as a pretext for a full-scale attack on Whidden. 'The course was predetermined and resolved upon,' the chancellor was told, 'that is evident from the nature and manner [of] the opposition.'[57] This assessment of the situation seems plausible in view of the abuse that Shields had heaped on Whidden at Brandon.

Shields made good use of his time during the remainder of the summer of 1925, an eventful summer for the cause of fundamentalism. The notorious

Tennessee 'monkey trial,' in which William Jennings Bryan had carried his fight against modernism and the teaching of evolution to the courts, had been eagerly followed by Shields and may have encouraged him to make the most of the McMaster situation.[58] The achievement of the Peerless Leader in focusing international attention upon the forces attacking the theology of conservatism must not have been lost upon the most vocal spokesman for the cause in Canada.

Pretext or not, Shields spared no effort in the *Gospel Witness* warning his readers about Marshall's modernistic tendencies and the university's deliberate flouting of its commitment to the Charter and the senator's will. This was not exactly new material, but it had a sharpness and directness lacking in the earlier alarums over Whidden's appointment and the Faunce affair. Homiletics and pastoral theology constituted a highly sensitive area of instruction, one that could have a profound effect upon those who passed through it, a point that Shields skilfully emphasized in his editorials, public addresses, and sermons. The *Canadian Baptist* replied on behalf of the university. As McLay wordily reported to Marshall, the paper sought to stress 'certain aspects of your thinking . . . in order to reassure the members of the churches, some of whom have been rendered slightly critical by interested propaganda from a certain source.'[59] Somehow Dean Farmer managed to portray Marshall as a wholly acceptable defender of everything that Baptists should cherish. Whidden, perhaps to hide his own bewilderment, privately described Marshall as 'conservatively progressive' and John MacNeill (Shields's other bête noire) as 'progressively conservative.' How Shields might have dealt with such tags and the thinking that inspired them can readily be imagined.

In the meantime, that clergyman prepared to confront the Senate with a suggestion that a committee be appointed to check out a story circulating in the United Kingdom that Marshall was guilty of modernistic teaching. Although such a committee was formed in September it refused to follow the matter up and instead reviewed the statements already made with respect to Marshall's appointment. It satisfied itself that in the circumstances no further investigations were required and that Marshall had a clean bill of health, a conclusion affirmed at a Senate meeting on 15 October 1925. This alleged whitewash of the new appointee provoked a series of scathing articles in the *Gospel Witness*. The war was to be refought, this time in the trenches of theological controversy. Marshall was charged with having been trained 'in all the arts of the Germans,' and described as an enemy that had to be 'brought out of his dugout.'[60]

It should be noted, however, that this fusillade came on the morrow of the Hamilton Convention, which had met at the Stanley Avenue Church from 16 to 22 October. Clearly the very ferocity of the attack had much to do with the outcome of that Convention. All of Wednesday 21 October had been given over to a discussion of the University Report, and Shields and his followers had used the occasion to seek an endorsement of his demand for a Senate investigation of Marshall's theology. This was, however, massively turned back by a resolution that moved the adoption of the Report, the reaffirmation of the declaration approved by the Convention of 1910, and a commendation for the Senate and the Board on their appointment of Professor Marshall, who having 'considered that Declaration [had] entirely accepted it.'[61] This was a sharp slap in the face for Shields. But worse was to follow. A resolution was carried that effectively condemned an editorial that had appeared in the *Gospel Witness* two years before 'impugning the fairness' of former Chancellor McCrimmon when he had served as president of the fateful Walmer Road Convention of 1922.[62]

In view of these setbacks it is not surprising that the Jarvis Street magazine so bitterly attacked the university and its supporters in the days that followed the Hamilton Convention of 1925. The vehemence of the assault prompted a reply in the *Monthly*. The writer, who was planning on a high school teaching career, delightedly went through each of Shields's articles and with an undergraduate's inspired malevolence demolished to his own satisfaction the writings of one who was 'not a University graduate' and who, therefore, had 'none of the spirit of the colleges.' Had Shields been so endowed, the indictment continued, he would not have been led into the same error that had hamstrung Elmore Harris, namely, the belief that McMaster students blindly followed their professors and 'could be led by the nose.'[63] The tone of the counterattack must have convinced Shields that his earlier condemnation of the arrogance of McMaster men had not been misplaced. In effect they still appeared to look upon those who lacked the university's BA as 'hewers of wood and drawers of water' for those who possessed it.

Meanwhile, many friends of the university had already heaved a collective sigh of relief at the outcome of the Hamilton Convention and quickly congratulated Whidden on his successes there. 'You have Shields on the run now,' exulted one correspondent, 'keep him there ... that Wednesday surely set him in his true light before the Convention ... and there is a real change of feeling in our churches towards him.'[64] A week later another writer reported the comforting news, which amounted to a mild sensation, that two deacons in his church who hitherto 'had been quite friendly towards Dr Shields had invited ... Professor Marshall to be our anniversary preacher early in the new year.'[65] Indeed, wherever Marshall preached he brought to the surface what one observer recently called a 'cadre of strong supporters among lay folk.'[66]

Others curbed their enthusiasm with caution because they knew that Shields's political decline had been consistently and grossly exaggerated in the past. 'There is [much] work ahead still,' warned a Brampton pastor, 'for [Shields] is unscrupulous and persistent.' However much Whidden might have appreciated the congratulatory messages, he had a sinking feeling that this last correspondent was on the right track. Within a week of the Convention's adjournment and while the university was being vigorously attacked in the *Gospel Witness* the chancellor told a minister in Brantford that 'we must consider carefully what are the wise steps to take at the present critical juncture.' 'The victory won at Hamilton' he emphasized 'must be conserved in every way possible.'[67] While he was seeking out those wise steps, disturbing evidence came in that certain congregations and individual church-goers were still anxious about the state of McMaster's theological health. Accordingly they were as eager as ever to listen to Shields who, as one of Whidden's informants said, 'gives a lead that people as a whole respond to.' Particularly dangerous in the eyes of a Perth clergyman was that Shields was not only continuing to appeal to those whom he described as 'subnormal and the untaught folk' – apparently Jarvis Street's staple audience – but was 'deceiving . . . the very elect.'[68]

To gather as much information as he could on congregational reactions, Whidden conducted an informal canvass in the constituency. The Rev. Evan T. Newton may be given some of the credit for this approach, for he had suggested to the chancellor early in November that 'some one will have to tabulate the churches into classes . . . safe or not safe.'[69] The subsequent survey, though not as comprehensive as Whidden would have wished, did probe some of the more sensitive regions in the denomination. Whidden was shortly greeted with news that embodied about equal portions of hope and despair. In Brantford, long a pre-millennial and conservative stronghold, a number of influential Baptists continued to sympathize openly with Jarvis Street and much preferred the *Gospel Witness* to the denomination's official paper. But a pleasant surprise in the midst of the gloom was that Simcoe, which had proven difficult during the Matthews controversy, seemed, ac-cording to one observant Baptist there, 'OK on the whole.' Ministers in Boston and Stratford, however, were singled out as 'determined Shields men.' And so it went: some associations reporting that all or virtually all was well, others that 'it would be an easy matter to divide the churches.' Still other congregations confronted a numbing dilemma, put into words by a clergy-man in Arnprior: 'while we cannot wholly endorse Dr Shields, neither can we endorse . . . Mr Marshall; there is the difficulty – we seem to be drifting in the direction of disintegration.'[70]

One pastor, not content with being a passive observer, decided to do a little manipulating of his own, this in Norwich, Ontario, where ultraconservatives had always been prominent. He reported with no small pride that he had discouraged the circulation of the *Gospel Witness* 'with the result that there is not one copy being regularly received, my object [being] to centralize the attention of our people upon Norwich rather than upon Jarvis Street.' What Whidden might have thought of these restrictive procedures has not been preserved in the records. Quite possibly the chancellor in his most pressured moments might have shared one minister's opinion that Shields's forces occasionally seemed to represent what H.L. Mencken denounced as the democratic pestilence which threatened to destroy enlightened society. 'In [my] opinion' the minister had written 'our denomination is too democratic and there should be some means by which these constantly recurring attacks should be stopped as it upsets the influence and the work of the University.'[71]

Short of launching the unthinkable – a full-scale attack on the Baptist democracy – what means, Whidden asked, could the university employ to put Shields in his place and preserve the 'influence and the work of the University?' Should McMaster continue virtually to ignore its voluble critic or should it attack him on his own ground? The silent reponse, as Dean McLay pointed out, had clearly not worked, for 'many timid and credulous souls misinterpreted our silence as a proof that something was wrong and that we were unable to meet the charges.'[72] In November the charges were more sharply pitched after Marshall preached a sermon in Hamilton. It had produced an excellent index of the polarization taking place in the struggle. Regarded by the university's supporters as the 'most admirable sermon in every way,' it was repudiated by Shields's friends as a perversion of what a Christian statement ought to be. Leading the attack was the Rev. Clifford J. Loney, the unhappy host of the recent Hamilton Convention and a firm ally of Jarvis Street. Although some dismissed Loney as 'sadly lacking in Christian charity and practical logic,' others warned that many Baptists still appeared to welcome such defenders of the faith.

Reports such as these clearly influenced the letter Whidden wrote to a Sarnia minister who had invited Marshall to speak in his church late in November. It amounted in a sense to a kind of retreat in the face of mounting criticism, indeed a reflection on the chancellor's appointment of Marshall, and hardly the sort of clarion call to action that some of the university's friends were already demanding. 'May I suggest that you take up with [Marshall]' Whidden wrote the Rev. Robert R. McKay 'the desirability of his including in morning and evening sermon some pretty positive statements regarding the Cross or the Lordship of Christ that will really convey to troubled minds what so many are expecting in these days.'

Realizing that not all Baptists might share or welcome his views about the way in which the Scriptures ought to be interpreted, Whidden noted that 'there is nothing in the sermon to which I cannot subscribe, but it certainly does not go far enough to satisfy people fond of clear-cut doctrinal statements.' That some Baptist congregations might have favoured clear-cut statements over anything else seems to have dawned on Whidden only after Marshall's appointment had been formally approved. But in this instance he was plainly trying to make up for time lost in acquainting Marshall with the Baptist facts of life in Ontario. 'Dr Farmer and I' he informed McKay 'are trying to get [these points] across to him without in any way hurting his feelings.'[73] The admonitions of those who had warned Whidden of Marshall's sensitivity to such pressure must have come back to haunt the chancellor in the closing weeks of 1925.

Early in the new year Whidden received other chilling news from a high school teacher in Hamilton. It related in detail what had happened in Loney's church when a number of student-pastors among Shields's following address-ed an audience of Baptists drawn from various congregations in the city. There seems to be an impression that people will not heed the bombastic criticisms of impetous youths,' alumnus Walter Clarke wrote.

But let me tell you that two hundred Baptist people ... were there [and] as far as I could judge the vast majority believed thoroughly every word that was uttered ... These young preachers were on *fire*, they used burning phrases that the simple, good, honest people like to hear about Jesus, the Bible, the power of God, the wonder of the resurrection ... Then they turned the classroom inside out so that these simple folks might see the dangers of criticism, both higher and lower. They babbled about manuscripts, texts, inspiration, miracles. How foolish, I grant you. But how powerful to arouse, to frighten, to cause apprehension and suspicion. And when it was all over, the general impression was 'McMaster is surely a place that needs cleansing.'[74]

The same correspondent claimed that the quarrel in Hamilton was threaten-ing to divide not only congregations but even families. 'Some Hamilton graduates [do] not go to Toronto' Clarke told James Herbert Cranston, the newspaperman, early in 1926 'because ... it would be as much as their life was worth if their people knew they were attending a meeting opposing Dr Shields.'[75]

The ominous reports from Hamilton helped to confirm a state of affairs that had already begun to give Whidden some sleepless nights. While many ministers who were kindly disposed toward the university seemed to be able to hold their own against Shields's 'young men on fire,' others appeared to be no match for them. Whidden betrayed his mounting concern when he planned a special survey of McMaster's arts and theology graduates. Whether or not he actually obtained answers to his queries is immaterial; what is revealing is the nature of his questionnaire. He was anxious to learn, for example, how many prospective theology students might have avoided McMaster and enrolled instead in Bible training schools.[76] He also wanted to know how many graduates might have dropped out of the ministry because of intellectual difficulties created by exposure at the university to 'somewhat radical ideas.' The chancellor then went on to ask: 'Is there anything in a little personal fear of mine that not a few of our men have lost their bearings ... because they studied here in the earlier or later periods when both sides of the question were not freely opened up? Do the majority of radicals belong to [the] period when Cross and Matthews taught here?'[77]

This was agonizing on a grand scale. It took no great perceptiveness to determine the direction of Whidden's line of questioning. Had Cross and Matthews somehow failed to produce pastors of conviction who could stand by their principles when confronted with opposition and doubt? Had a whole generation of clergymen lost their bearings and the commitment to the work for which they had been ordained? 'How can we ascertain' Whidden asked in another revealing question 'why so many of our graduates who have been in the ministry for a few years have gone into business or the teaching profession?' He furnished no statistics on the exodus to the secular world, but the trend was sufficiently noticeable to arouse concern in university and denominational circles.

One disturbing question remained. Stripped of their venom and unscrupulousness, were Shields's strictures against the university based on solid objections? Had McMaster, in fact, failed itself and the denomination by graduating pastors who lacked the courage of their convictions and were incapable of leading their flocks simply because they lacked a total dedication to their calling? And had this unhappy state of affairs been brought about by their having been trained by 'Chicago men?'

As best they could Whidden and his colleagues tried to put these questions out of their minds as they set about finding ways and means of responding to Shields's attacks. Ironically a Chicago man would have the last word when he furnished his explanation of McMaster's difficulties in the mid-twenties. In a letter to Whidden in the spring of 1926, Charles T. Holman, an alumnus of 1909, argued that if more Chicago graduates were in Canadian pulpits Shields would not be the problem that he was. But the promising expatriates, according to Holman, 'had found the door closed to them' after the Matthews controversy. He continued:

I think that the more liberal Canadian Baptists have allowed themselves to be frightened by the Chicago bogey altogether too much. The simple fact is, as everyone knows, that if the Baptists in the northern states were without the Chicago trained men the loss in intelligent and competent leadership would be incalculable ... And unless I am greatly mistaken the cause of intelligence in religion among Canadian Baptists has been greatly weakened because of an almost hysterical fear of Chicago men.[78]

That point had already been driven home by another prominent Baptist, this one no expatriate. Whidden had to concede, in a reply to Senator F.L. Schaffner, that 'unfortunately many of our brightest ... graduates who have done postgraduate work in the United States, have not been ... wanted in Ontario churches.' 'Quite a few of our men' he sadly admitted 'do not read widely, much less study laboriously.'[79] The message seemed unmistakable. If more pastors in Ontario could have matched Shields's astoundingly success-ful appeal to the emotions with an impassioned intellectualism, then, accord-ing to Holman and Schaffner, the Jarvis Street clergyman would have been no threat at all.

Not surprisingly, all this discussion and introspection, not to mention the pressures to which he was being continuously subjected, began to tell on the chancellor. He appeared visibly strained at a meeting in Montreal where he had been upset by the critical remarks of the Rev. John Linton, one of Shields's principal confederates. And although much of the routine work of running McMaster had been delegated to Deans McLay and Farmer, there was still much for Whidden to do on Bloor Street. Moreover, he was also expected to sort out the problems of Brandon College, which was at this time going through severe financial and administrative difficulties. While dealing with these matters as best he could and while trying to sublimate his own misgivings about the university, the chancellor turned to the task of meeting Shields's assaults.

This came not a moment too soon for some people. Walter Clarke, Whidden's candid Hamilton informant, had said late in January: 'If [Shields's] charges against [the university] are not true ... then it is the duty of those in power to protect the school from slander, lies, and insidious prop-aganda. If they do not take action soon the opportunity will be gone and a new governing body will certainly be elected at the next Convention.'[80] And a minister in Norwich, a community not exactly on the most friendly terms with McMaster, reported that if care were not taken some churches in the area would appoint delegates to that Convention who might 'make the situation critical.'[81]

At the outset of his own campaign Whidden corresponded with as many pastors as he could in order to determine the university's standing in the constituency and to give assurance that 'we are not anxious to impose our view upon any of [them].' This was no easy task because the chancellor had recently lost the services of Stewart Bates, the educational secretary, who had frequently served as the university's trouble-shooter. Perhaps because of this, the results of Whidden's canvass were inconclusive. But the information he did amass was incorporated in a publicity campaign to present the university's side of the case. The campaign was to be subsidized, not by regular funds, since this might confuse the denomination, but through an independent appeal, an arrangement that would try to raise $3,000 towards the goal of meeting the challenge of the *Gospel Witness*.[82] Yet Whidden was well aware that the university was also up against cynical or hostile segments of the secular press. An issue of this sort with great potential for newsworthiness was bound to appeal to the imaginative reporter and the reader hungry for tidings of battles and turmoil close to home.[83]

Steps would have to be taken to put the university's best foot forward in pamphlets and in the denominational and public prints. Plainly such headlines as 'Shields Calls McMaster Arts Men Hoodlums' could not be answered in kind. Rather, the university would have to counter with straightforward explanations of its educational policy and a step-by-step refutation of Shields's less inflammatory allegations. But at the use of one medium Whidden balked. Radio station CFGC in Brantford was prepared to offer equal time to the university, having already given the inventive Shields an opportunity to air his views, but the chancellor declined.[84] The ten-dollar charge for the service could not have governed his decision, but he may have decided that radio was a wholly undignified vehicle for the sort of exposition the university was seeking to promote. Another possibility is that Whidden feared his own public-speaking ability would not measure up to Shields's unquestioned prowess and believed that the debate had best be left to the printed page. Whenever Shields and Whidden did engage in public discussion the chancellor invariably came off second best, not so much in content as in delivery and timing.[85] Understandably, Shields, like his friend William Aberhart, the radio evangelist of Alberta, shrewdly employed the electronic wonder that revolutionized the transmission of information in the twenties. The episode provided a good example of Shields's ability to exploit the innovative and the radical in his campaign against the university.

Before he had sufficient time to evaluate the results of his own publicity efforts, Whidden was jolted by unpleasant incidents within the walls of the university. On 18 March 1926 a statement appeared in the Toronto papers over the signatures of purported 'Baptist ministerial students of McMaster University.' Briefly, it protested 'against the retention on the staff of McMaster University ... of one who ... is a self-confessed liberal evangelical.'[86] Marshall was not denounced as a modernist, the catch-all hate term in the fundamentalist glossary; he was tagged with the less offensive but still reprehensible label 'liberal evangelical.' A good many scholars and ministers, including Baptist ones in Toronto, who eschewed the sort of modernism that Dean Farmer had long repudiated, could still unashamedly use this term to describe their own theological position. But obviously, it was just as repugnant to ultraconservatives as modernist had been.

At any rate, no fewer than twenty-three persons signed the statement of protest, the 'noble 23' as they came to be known among the university's opponents. Whidden immediately questioned the legitimacy of the protesters, pointing out despairingly to a Kitchener clergyman that 'Fourteen of them will not be ranked as regular students even at the close of this year and only three have taken any lectures with Professor Marshall. At least two of them were persuaded to sign what they thought was a statement of student belief in the historical view of the Book of Jonah, not knowing that they were signing a protest, much less a protest that would be given to the public through the daily press. So it goes.'[87] The acknowledged leader of the group was James McGinlay, a Scottish-born student who had registered in the English theology course two years before. The protest followed hard on the heels of the successful evangelistic tour of those 'young men of fire' who had so alarmed Walter Clarke in Hamilton. By this time they were well known followers of McGinlay, namely William G. Brown, William S. Whitcombe, and A.J. Fieldus.

The university had known for some time that the gulf in the student body, first publicized by an undergraduate at the start of the decade, had widened as the Shields controversy assumed major proportions. Although only a small minority of the students openly supported activists such as McGinlay and Brown, there was no question that the silence of some others masked misgivings of one kind or another about the way the university was conducting its affairs. Dean Farmer referred understatedly to the 'unusual feature' of the session: the 'cleavage in the student body.'[88]

While the Toronto press was having a field day with the revelations of the noble 23, the constituency and the university were treated in the *Canadian Baptist* to an article by Professor P.S. Campbell openly attacking Marshall and his theology. Student dissent was one thing; the breaking of faculty ranks in the face of the enemy was another. Campbell's action raises an interesting question. How many of his colleagues might have shared the aging classicist's reservations about the new man in theology but hesitated to express themselves in public? Professor Curr might have felt the same way, but he left the university during the summer, just as the situation was approaching the critical stage. It was doubtless surmised in some quarters that his going had something to do with the troubles, because, according to the University Report for 1925, Curr had fully intended to return to McMaster when he embarked for Scotland in July. Then a cable was received from him some days later announcing that he had accepted the principalship of a missionary training college in London.[89] But the main reason for his departure seems to have been his reluctance to be used as a cat's paw by Shields's forces. Conservative theologian though he was, Curr had throughout remained on good terms with colleagues to the left of his position, and he had never taken kindly to the substance or techniques of Shields's campaign.[90] His loss was keenly felt by both sides. During his six years at the university the latter's critics had been hard put to find fault with this seemingly impeccable theologian, described by one western admirer as the 'most powerful force in McMaster University.'[91] A replacement was shortly found in Nathaniel Parker, a Baptist from Mississippi.

In the meantime the matter of student dissent and Professor Campbell had to be dealt with, and to do so the Executive Committees of the Senate and Board met jointly in late March. Their first proposals were to require one of the Stanley Avenue evangelists, W.G. Brown, to leave the university and to inform other student critics that their presence on the campus would be unwelcome in the next academic session. Where this decision was recorded in the minute book, however, pencilled marginalia show that it was overturned at a later meeting with a request that the minutes embodying the action be 'cancelled.'[92] Somebody must have realized that the explusions could easily have been misconstrued by the constituency and exploited by Jarvis Street for all their propaganda value.

Professor Campbell told the joint meeting when summoned before it that he had 'meant no unkindness or injury' by his article. He claimed that his only desire had been to protect McMaster against modernism, and that he had acted solely on his own initiative. The aged professor, who had been on the brink of retirement for years, had to be told by all present 'how such a letter played into the hands of McMaster's enemies.'[93] As for acting on his own, the assembled Senators and Board members might have been forgiven scepticism. It was common knowledge that Campbell had communicated with Shields on a number of occasions before his letter appeared in the *Canadian Baptist*.[94] Indeed, two years before he was hailed before the committee Campbell had been the subject of editorials in the *Gospel Witness* which had complained about the treatment to which the professor of Greek had supposedly been subjected at McMaster. 'For two years' a Port Hope minister claimed 'Dr

Shields had been sowing seeds of suspicion in [Campbell's] mind as well as in the mind of Dr Keirstead concerning the undoubted intention of the Board to cut off their heads.'[95]

What made the situation so awkward for the university was that the retirement of both professors had been deemed to fall due, indeed overdue, in the spring of 1926. Whidden fully realized what kind of political capital Shields would try to make out of their superannuation, but he could see no other way around the problem. On purely academic grounds it was considered unthinkable that Campbell should be kept on for another session. More than one distressed parent had sent Whidden a letter like the following: 'I knew of the weakness of the Greek department during Mr Campbell's regime' wrote Thomas A. Kirkconnell of Lindsay 'and sent my son to Queen's for his Classical course just on that account.'[96] The chancellor fully realized that the situation was a serious academic one.

The explanation for the retirement that Whidden gave Senator Schaffner nonetheless contained a statement betraying the other dimension of the problem that had brought Campbell before the committee: 'We did not think for a moment of superannuating him because he is a ramping fundamentalist.' A couple of months later Whidden gave Frederick C. Mabee a more composed account of the action taken: 'If we had not superannuated [Campbell and Keirstead] in April we would have done so for purely political reasons. We thought it only right to act honestly and consistently.' The university's decision, in other words, ought not to be interpreted as an attempt to punish Campbell for his literary lapses in the *Canadian Baptist*.[97]

Yet, predictably, this was how it was interpreted by Shields and his associates, and they immediately raised the question of Campbell's 'dismissal' at several association meetings. But if Jarvis Street expected a widespread denunciation of what the university had done it was disappointed. According to one account, Shields was decisively defeated when the Toronto Association dealt with the matter, a decision that turned out to be fairly typical when the issue was put to the test generally in the early summer. Yet these disappointments, like earlier ones, only served to convince Shields of the rightness of his cause and of the need to prosecute it with greater vigour. 'O, it's a lovely war' mused W.A. Cameron in a letter he sent Whidden from England in the summer of 1926. It had indeed all the makings of a 'lovely war,' and a playwright might well have appreciated the theatrical potential in the confrontation between Bloor Street and Jarvis Street, the posturing, the bravado, the bungling, the scouting expeditions, the propaganda, and the use of the Great War vocabulary, all of which made this appear a theological extension of the late hostilities in Flanders.

The battle entered a more critical phase in the spring of 1926 when Shields, rebuffed on one front, promptly attacked on another, heartened by being recently acclaimed one of the 'big guns' at a well attended fundamentalist convention in Washington.[98] Shields, in fact, appeared ready to challenge the university's right to retain the McMaster endowment and to demand that it be transferred to an institution of his making or choosing. The move may have been inspired by recent developments at Knox College in Toronto. A group of dissidents, claiming to be the 'continuing Presbyterian Church in Canada,' had successfully blocked an attempt in 1925 to have that theological institution become part of the projected United Church.[99] Could Shields and his followers, wondered nervous Baptists, similarly thwart the efforts of Whidden and his supporters?

The grounds for action against the university were, in Shields's view, fully justified. In its instruction and its conduct the institution was simply not subscribing to the terms of the McMaster will and the Charter that had launched it forty years before. Through correspondence and the highly effective medium of the *Gospel Witness*, Shields broadcast this message across Ontario in the spring weeks of 1926. Some of the university's friends were visibly disturbed by his strategy. Joseph Wearing of Peterborough was one of them. His instincts and experience as a lawyer made him fear that the wording of the will and the Charter might condemn the university to a losing battle. 'It is always a dangerous thing to leave money for denominational purposes' he wrote Whidden 'while at the same time setting out the doctrines to be subscribed to by those participating in the funds. The reason why this is dangerous is because the form of expressing these doctrines changes from time to time but the courts will hold to a rigid interpretation of the doctrines as they are worded in the bequests and will not take cognizance of any modern adaptation of these doctrines.'[100]

Wearing spoke for many on both sides of the dispute when he ended with the remark that Shields simply wanted 'to get hold of the trust funds himself.' However unlikely the prospect of Shields succeeding in such a manoeuvre seemed to many friendly Baptists, others close to the situation took it very seriously. A good illustration of both attitudes was furnished by correspondence that passed between John Northway and Dean Farmer in the summer of 1926. Farmer suggested that Northway's legacy to the university might revert if the institution were somehow taken over by Shields. The clothing manufacturer was touched by the dean's concern, but he assured him that Shields had already reached the summit of his power and was now going downhill,[101] another optimistic observation that failed to square with the facts. As it turned out, Northway's optimism was not shared by people like

Walter Clarke in Hamilton and Victor Evan Gray in Toronto. Indeed, for some weeks, as if to reply in kind to Shields, these men and other parties had been urging Whidden to initiate legal proceedings against Jarvis Street for libel and slander. The chancellor was told that 'Hamilton grads would strongly back such a plan' and that a 'court judgment would have mightier weight than debate and our adversaries would be properly PUT, to stay put.'[102]

Whidden, however, turned his back on these proposals. He reasoned that if McMaster should take such action and Shields did not follow through with his own, then again the clergyman could make political capital at the university's expense. If, on the other hand, Shields did take action himself and the university reacted to his initiative he could boast to the constituency that McMaster was attempting in 'pigmy fashion' to follow his tactical lead but on far weaker grounds. In the end, neither case was taken to court. But Whidden was so disgusted by the opposition of what he called 'fundamentalist congregations' that he contemplated an amendment to the Convention Act enabling that body to punish those churches and pastors who refused to accept the will of the majority. Obviously even he still hoped that the majority in this case would be on the university's side. Plans were drawn up to seek authorization from the forthcoming assembly to apply for this amendment. Then Whidden betrayed the fear that the majority might in fact be on the other side. What other consideration could account for the following question he directed to a lawyer friend: 'What is your judgment with regard to the possibility of an approach being made to Parliament by the Executive Committee of the Convention without first submitting it to the Convention?' 'I take it' he added 'there is nothing to hinder us legally from doing so.'[103] The strain was beginning to tell. The anti-democratic character of the proposal seemed to concern him less than the calculating afterthought that 'it would probably ... be poor tactics.'

Yet, short of taking Shields to court on charges of slander or ridding the Convention of 'undesirable elements,' the university's friends wondered what effective steps McMaster could take to defend itself at the forthcoming assembly in October. No one had to be told that the issue would be fought to a finish when the delegates came together to discuss the university's affairs. While Shields and his allies accelerated their attacks and spread out across the constituency to give sermons on the dangers of modernism at McMaster the latter's supporters were urging Whidden along a course charted earlier in the year. It involved the use of a relatively simple strategem: a case ought to be made out for labelling the dispute an artificial controversy, provoked not by basic doctrinal differences but by matters completely extraneous to any respectable theological discussion.[104] 'The main thing' as Joseph Wearing expressed it in late September

is to get the idea well established in the minds of the people that it is not a question of modernism or fundamentalism because there is no such question in the Convention but that the whole question is the personality of Dr Shields himself who can never be either appeased or satisfied and whose whole life has been filled with contention of one kind or another. I believe that the people are more and more getting seized of this fact and I think that it should be driven well home to them at this Convention.[105]

Another Baptist layman, who said that he regarded Dean Farmer 'almost [as] a saint,' probably expressed the thoughts of many who hitherto had not said much in the dispute; echoing Wearing's point, he remarked that 'what fundamentalism [is] or modernism is we are not very much concerned over ... The great majority of Baptist laymen ... look upon these two "isms" as something for the Theologs to argue over if they want to, though to us it looks like foolishness, a beating of drums and sounding of cymbals.'[106] And to a good many theologians, for that matter, it was not as contentious a matter as this layman made it out to be, but a subject more appropriate for a mild common room discussion than for a fierce public debate in an arena. As one former McMaster theologian recently remarked, a conservative like Curr had never been alienated by the evangelical liberalism of a Marshall.

Even so, right down to the wire, there was much 'beating of drums and sounding of cymbals' in the larger world of the constituency. Reports came in from such scattered points as Collingwood, Brantford, Ottawa, and Peterborough that Shields and his associates, W.G. Brown, James McGinlay, and G.W. Allen, were raising audiences to ecstasy and leaving their foes disgusted with broadsides like 'this hellish stuff that has come from the pit, that has got into Professor Marshall's head.'[107] An excellent example of the hearsay that characterized the controversy was furnished by G.E. Grattan, one of Tingle's old students. He reported that at an Ottawa rally for Shields a 'statement was made that Mr Albert Matthews told Dr Shields that [Chancellor] McCrimmon had stated that he doubted if Mr Sanderson had any God left.'[108]

In the end, the university pretty well kept its own counsel when it came to preparing for the Convention. The report composed for the occasion by Whidden and the Board included a section headed 'McMaster University four-square with Baptist principles' and began with the following statement: 'Surely we do not need to reassure our brethren assembled in the Convention that the people who administer the affairs of our University are loyal Baptists, desiring to conduct [those] affairs ... in harmony with our historic principles and well within the provisions of the Charter *when truly understood*.' Then the following words were added, reflecting the pressure exerted by those university supporters who wished to stress the artificiality of the dispute: 'But if it is necessary then we wish to reaffirm our position as above, and to declare our intention to keep constantly before us the vision and faith of the founder of McMaster University, the spirit and genius of our denomination, as well as *essential evangelical doctrines*.'[109] At a Senate meeting held on the eve of the Convention the Rev. Andrew Imrie, a Board member still concerned about the propriety of Marshall's theological position, expressed hope that something could be done to allay the denomination's suspicions. The not unexpected response was that 'no matter what action [was taken], there would be controversy in the Convention, if members of the Convention chose to precipitate it.'[110]

It was soon enough precipitated. On 19 October 1926, when the Convention's decks were cleared for a discussion of the University Report, the Rev. J.H. Brown, long an outspoken critic of Marshall, Whidden, and Farmer, launched the first attack. Once denounced by Dean McLay as 'fanatical, intolerant, and censorious,' Brown submitted a resolution condemning Marshall's theology and virtually calling for his dismissal. The university's backers countered by condemning the 'campaign of misrepresentation and slander carried on by the editor of the *Gospel Witness*' and by calling upon the Convention to affirm its confidence in the work at McMaster.[111] A no-holds-barred discussion followed, dramatically punctuated by speeches from pastors McGinlay and Whitcombe, two of the 'noble 23,' and a reply from the Rev. R.R. McKay on behalf of the university. The debate was carried over into the evening session, a stage in the proceedings enlivened by Marshall's witty and vigorously presented statement and by Shields's strongly delivered denunciation of that theologian's views and the policy that permitted their propagation at the university. It was the high point of the Convention. Fortunately Marshall carried the fight on his own and the university's behalf; he alone was a match, as it turned out more than a match, for Shields as a public debater.

In a pointed effort to discredit Shields as the vaunted upholder of Baptist traditions and the verities, Marshall reminded his audience that historic Baptist positions on such crucial matters as liberty of conscience and the freedom to seek the truth were actually being sapped by Jarvis Street's actions and utterances. Shields was portrayed as the embodiment of a radicalism that threatened to destroy those principles which had long sustained Canadian Baptists and their educational institutions. Marshall expressed the concern of people who had for years been alerting the denomination to the dangerous ends to which Shields's campaign appeared to be devoted. The theologian concluded with an unequivocal statement:

The bigoted intolerance that has been displayed is at complete variance with the historic Baptist position simply because it seeks to strangle that reasonable liberty which is the birthright of every true disciple of Jesus Christ. Dr Shields and his followers are a divisive and disruptive force in our denominational life, and it seems to me that it is essential that drastic action should be taken by this Convention that so miserable a campaign should cease.[112]

Then the hour approached when everyone knew a vote would have to be taken on the resolutions, indeed, on the issues that had been consuming the physical and emotional energies of the constituency and the university for the better part of four years, ever since the Walmer Road Convention of 1922. The vote was a standing one. When the scrutineers finished counting heads they reported that the university and its officers and instructors, including Marshall, had been endorsed by a vote of 708 to 258. It was an outcome that sceptics earlier in the year would have totally discounted and one that even a cautious optimist might not have anticipated. The Convention then went on to accept the University Report, including the assurance that McMaster was four-square with Baptist principles, and to administer other rebukes to Shields himself. When he was called upon to apologize publicly for his recent conduct, a motion subsequently withdrawn, Shields rejoined that 'I count it the highest honor of my life to have earned the displeasure of such a spirit as has been manifested here.' One of his supporters dismissed the Convention's actions as much like those of an assembly of 'bootleggers passing censure upon the provincial police.'[113]

Former Chancellor Wallace, who had been given the privileges of the floor of the Convention, summed up his impression of the proceedings. Well known for his solid views, he was 'impressed by the personnel of the majority. It included, as it seemed to me, nearly all the solid elements of the denomination. As the followers of Dr Shields gathered about him at the close of the meeting, to join in their singing and other emotional manifestations, I could not but be impressed with the inferior personnel of the group.'[114] Whidden was only too happy to receive a copy of this account, the original of which was sent to S.J. Moore, a Board member and an old friend of Wallace's. In a letter to the chancellor, Wallace rejoiced that the university was moving toward a 'real' conservatism, dedicated to the preservation of the genuine essentials of evangelical Christianity and shorn of the animosity and emotionalism that had retarded its progress throughout the decade.

To Dean Farmer it meant an opportunity for McMaster to deal with questions that had long been submerged by the controversy. As he stated in his annual report in 1927, an attempt ought to be made to 'harmonize in the student's thinking ... various opposing tendencies' that had come to characterize the volatile world of the twenties. Set against the move to substitute for Christianity a 'mere system of ethics' was, in the dean's view, an equally undesirable 'antinomianism' that ignored the basic virtues of honesty, truthfulness, and courtesy. And for those who wished to fight Unitarianism, with the 'heresy of emptying His humanity of reality,' Farmer had this message: that the 'truly Christian University [should] cleave fast both to His deity and His humanity in all humility and confidence.' Finally, while the worldliness of many a professing Christian had become a deplorable fact of modern life, a university like McMaster, warned the dean, ought not to forget, in its efforts to combat secular influences, that Christ 'mingled freely in the life about Him and expects us both to be in the world and yet not of it.'[115]

In his congratulatory letter to Whidden, Wallace also looked forward to McMaster improving its relationship with the constituency, a matter that had once meant so much to him as a harassed chancellor at the turn of the century. Wallace's welcome comments came hard on the heels of encouraging words from an entirely different source. During Whidden's 'week of conflict' he had received a comforting phone call from Arthur Meighen, his former political superior,[116] who just a few weeks before had lost out in his own struggle against Mackenzie King.

McMaster's victory seemed as complete as could be expected in the closing months of 1926. The forces commanded by Shields had failed to capture the Convention or to gain control over the university. But if the latter had in fact been their object, and if they had been successful, McMaster might have shared the fate that shortly overtook a Baptist institution in Iowa. Denounced for years as modernist and anti-Christian by disgruntled Baptists in that state, beleaguered Des Moines University had been refused financial support and in May 1927 submitted to a takeover by the Baptist Bible Union of the United States. The moving spirit behind this development was none other than T.T. Shields, the Union's president. Denied an opportunity to correct McMaster's state of affairs the clergyman turned gratefully to the task of transforming the school in Des Moines into a 'great Christian institution of higher learning ... absolutely free from the taint of modernism.'[117] To this end all faculty and staff were obliged to subscribe to the Bible Union's fundamentalist confession of faith. A good many faculty members who refused to do so either resigned or were summarily dismissed. Their exodus, combined with mounting student displeasure and differences between the opinionated Shields and his associates, resulted in a fiasco. The demise of Des Moines University in 1929 was highlighted by a noisy student demonstration against Shields's leadership, which culminated in a barrage of eggs directed at the administration building in which Shields had taken prostrate refuge while urgently telephoning the police.

Although McMaster was mercifully spared this kind of indignity, its constituency had nevertheless been seriously divided at the recent Convention. There were still prominent Baptists who publicly complained, as C.J. Holman did, that McMaster had disqualified itself by teaching views antithetical to those of its founder – after all, some 250 had refused to express confidence in the university. By this time Holman, the aging lawyer and sole surviving executor of the McMaster estate, had already resigned from the Board of Governors and was openly championing Shield's critical view of the university and his dubious efforts in Des Moines.[118]

Meanwhile, in addition to his activities in Iowa, Shields took initiatives in Ontario, launching his own Union of Regular Baptist Churches and his own educational institution, the Toronto Baptist Seminary, as a counterpoise to the Convention and the university. It was claimed that by the early weeks of 1927 no fewer than fifty-six students had enrolled at the seminary, evidence, as one enthusiastic Shields ally exclaimed, 'of the support of the Baptist Constituency.'[119] It was asserted that a fearful McMaster had attempted to block the chartering of the school, but Whidden hotly denied this. Unquestionably, Shields succeeded in enlisting the support of a considerable number of churches; indeed some put the figure as high as forty, out of a total of five hundred in the Convention. Typical was the Stanley Avenue Church in Hamilton, scene of the tumultuous Convention of 1925, which advised Whidden's office late in the following year that it no longer planned to contribute to Christian education as long as that meant the university. Also typical was that some members of the congregation who had broken with Shields and their pastor took up a collection of fifty dollars for McMaster.

Morover, some of the beneficiaries of Christian education at McMaster had already expressed reservations about it and continued to do so in defiance of the Convention. But the dean of theology could report in the spring of 1927 that the division in the undergraduate body 'has not had the same novelty about it nor has the feeling been so acute' as in the previous year. He then observed that the 'majority of those who signed the [original] protest ... have come to understand better the real issues.'[120] One of them plainly did not. James McGinlay, the acknowledged leader of the malcontents, never gave up his campaign on the campus, and as a consequence his registration was cancelled in the fall of 1927. Once again the Toronto papers were provided with a tasty morsel for their front pages.

Although the disruption might have been welcomed in some quarters because it led to the departure from the Convention of pastors and congregations who had long been thorns in the flesh, it was lamented in others for the possible serious effects on the university's standing in certain vital parts of the constituency. At least one pastor, while admitting years later to having received 'a great deal of good' from Marshall, remarked that it had been made painfully obvious to him that the professor was 'not in harmony with the beliefs of many of our people.'[121] And some congregations which elected with varying degrees of enthusiasm to stay in the Convention may still have shared many of the objections of those who departed. Shields may not have been too far off the mark when he claimed that 'there are many ... who privately acknowledge that they have no sympathy whatever with ... Marshall's views and that they strongly disapprove of the Convention's general attitude.' 'But they are confident' Shields concluded 'that there are better days in store! As yet they have reserved their fire! They are getting ready!'[122]

Nearly a quarter of a century later Chancellor George Gilmour seemed to concede the point when he recalled the events of the late twenties: 'it was felt wise [for] some time following the controversy, to play down the University's name in some sections, but now it is quite necessary to improve our relationships particularly in the area of London and west to Windsor.'[123] Sixteen years after the 1926 Convention had supposedly decided the matter, McMaster's educational secretary obliquely betrayed the difficulties it had caused the university in the long interval. He disclosed that at least one prominent member of a large Toronto congregation had withdrawn his support from the university, 'an indication that there are fires that still smolder [and] can be fanned into a flame.'[124] The university may have been spared a takeover by obscurantists in 1926, but parts of the constituency remained openly hostile to the university or were reduced to pained indifference to its interests. To this extent Shields could claim a victory against the institution that had been monopolizing his attention for the better part of a decade. Frustrated ambition, personal animus, a conviction that McMaster had become too arrogant, the belief that modernism in one form or another had indeed engulfed the university, all these had served to fuel Shields's fiery campaign in the twenties and to convince some elements in the denomination that his cause had been timely and just.[125]

The university, for its part, had held throughout the controversy that the results of recent scholarship and the basic tenets of the faith were not incompatible, that in fact they were complementary, an echo of the view expressed by moderate theologians. This was the public statement offered by the university, appended to such documents as the report submitted to the

Convention of 1926. But what then of the agonizing moments when Whidden wondered aloud whether the teaching of 'radicalism' at McMaster might have weakened the resolve of theological students? Was there some validity to the charges made against the institution by some of Shields's more moderate supporters? In the end, the chancellor convinced himself that the university had remained true to its founding principles and to Baptist beliefs and that the appointment of L.H. Marshall had not contradicted those principles and beliefs. But he could not choose to think otherwise.

On the other hand, those who had accused McMaster of modernism without necessarily endorsing Shields's flamboyant crusade must have felt their misgivings confirmed when they consulted an article Marshall contributed to the *Monthly* in 1930. 'No matter what the subject we study, we cannot afford to neglect German scholarship,' it began. 'In all the higher departments of life, as our own Carlyle said, "Germany, learned, indefatigable, deep-thinking Germany," comes to our aid ... In the department of theology, the "Queen of the Sciences" (and I am still old-fashioned enough to believe that live, scientific theology deserves to be thus exalted), her contribution is unique.' The next sentence must have been particularly unnerving: 'Whatever the vagaries of German radicalism and extremism may be, she has done a vast amount of illuminating and constructive work.' Marshall then extolled, with a side glance at the implications of the recent turmoil, the freedom enjoyed by the German academic. According to Marshall, he 'can advance any views he likes provided he can defend them before his peers in a sound, scientific, academic way.'[126] That was precisely the issue which had alienated so many of the denomination's rank and file. Did a sound, scientific, academic way of defending a position provide the religious stimulus that should serve as the mainspring of theological instruction at McMaster University? Fifteen years before, Elmore Harris had complained, not so much about I.G. Matthews's credentials, as about his lack of spirituality. Did Marshall, it would be asked again, lack the same vital quality?

While these questions were being raised, indeed even while Marshall had been preparing the article, he decided to resign from McMaster and return to England to take up a pastorate in Leicester. Those close to the situation claimed that he did so because he was denied the ultimate accolade, the deanship of theology, when it fell vacant after the death of J.H. Farmer.[127] According to the available documentation, however, the Board of Governors, at the urging of Whidden and his fellow theologians in an all-out effort to change his mind, did offer him that position.[128] Ironically, this overture followed the timetable Shields had prophesied before the Convention of 1926. His respect for Marshall as a person was amply displayed as well: 'If Professor Marshall remains in McMaster,' Shields had told congregations in

Woodstock, 'within five years he will be Chancellor, for there isn't another man in McMaster University that can measure with him as a man.'[129]

Marshall, however, rejected the Board's offer and officially tendered his resignation in late February 1930. To Whidden he offered an explanation testifying to the power that McMaster's critics still enjoyed in the denomination. 'In discussions of this question' Marshall wrote

I have been given to understand that even if it were desirable in all other respects that I should be appointed to [the deanship], the state of affairs in the denomination would make my appointment impossible – or at least inexpedient. If such is the case, I am bound to regard a situation of that kind as fatal to my continuance at McMaster in any capacity ... I shall be relieved of the uncomfortable feeling that I am occupying a position which lack of full confidence ... has virtually undermined.[130]

The university's triumph of 1926 seemed increasingly pyrrhic as the years wore on.

Yet Marshall did strike one hopeful note in his letter to the chancellor. In describing his decision as the best course for all, he noted that McMaster 'will begin the new chapter in her career free from any suspicion [and] ... dissension will get its quietus.' He was wrong about the liberation from suspicion, but he was correct about the new chapter, one about to be written by a decision more far-reaching than the one to which Marshall had painfully come. After years of discussing campus space and the need for a new site and endless negotiations for properties elsewhere, the university was about to uproot itself and move, lock, stock, and barrel, to the city of Hamilton, a transfer first suggested in the distant days preceding the first world war. Another dimension of the university's needs, as vital for many as the instruction carried on within its walls, was about to be met. But the enormous financial campaign that was mounted to subsidize the move encountered in many areas the hostility or the indifference of those whom Shields and his allies had succeeded in alienating. This fact of life was forcibly brought home to the university when the 'New McMaster Campaign' was launched in 1928.

10
Towards a fresh start

Somehow, over the years, the university had weathered the perennial afflic-
tion of financial stringency and survived the convulsions triggered by controversy. Through everything, it had continued to teach, graduate, and fail
students, to offer new courses, to make appointments, controversial and
otherwise, and to enlarge its original endowment. In the process it had
groomed products for the professional, academic, ministerial, and economic
marketplaces of the province and the country; by the close of the twenties
there were thirteen hundred names on the roll of living alumni. The university
had also addressed itself to issues agitating Canadian society in the post-war
years, particularly the temperance question, which had long exercised the
denomination and its educational institutions.

Characteristically, Whidden threw himself into public discussions with all
the vigour of his Union Government days. The movement in favour of the
Ontario Temperance Act found him solidly on the side of the angels of
sobriety. However, as chairman of the Dominion Prohibition Federation in
the early twenties he sought to achieve a greater urbanity and credibility for
the movement: 'the day was gone forever' he was quoted as saying 'when
temperance reformers could be classed as a collection of hysterical women
and spineless men.'[1] Whidden's tactics in this instance reminded friends and
foes alike of those he employed to defend the university and Biblical scholarship. The emotionalism and hysteria he had deplored in the campaign against
Marshall he would also combat in the temperance movement. This analogue
further embittered his relations with Shields, a volatile crusader who
mounted against the Barroom the same kind of ferocious attack that he had
directed against McMaster's modernism.

Whidden also frequently expressed opinions on such varied topics as the need for Anglo-American unity and the refinement of Canadian politics, and denounced, among other things, the 'abominable influence' Stephen Leacock's articles in the Toronto *Saturday Night* were said to be having upon 'our young business and professional men.'[2] Again, Shields might have been pardoned if he wondered why Whidden was not equally concerned about the abominable influence a Matthews or a Marshall might have had upon 'our young ministerial candidates.'

The chancellor also came out strongly in support of such new national publishing ventures as the *Canadian Forum*, one expression among many of the self-consciously nationalist spirit that gripped the academic community in the aftermath of the first world war, particularly at the University of Toronto. Understandably, Whidden lauded the recently launched *Canadian Journal of Religious Thought*, no mean publication for those days, which miraculously managed to survive for nearly a decade. He told an Acadia colleague that 'the more I come to look at our whole Canadian situation the more I am disposed to feel that such a Journal as this is needed ... [we] must not continue to be entirely dependent upon American magazines.'[3] Subsequently putting his pen where his mouth was, he contributed an article to the periodical,[4] as did L.H. Marshall and the ever-productive George Cross.

As for the institution that he guided, Whidden could note with satisfaction in the late twenties that there were two dozen on the faculty payroll and over four hundred students at varying stages of enlightenment recorded on the registrar's books. This kind of arithmetical exercise comforted those who could recall the enormous difficulties the university had been forced to surmount since the early years of the century and particularly since the war. But for others the situation was not nearly so reassuring. Student enrolment, admittedly impressive by wartime standards, had not increased appreciably since the early part of the decade when it had started to match pre-war registrations. And although well qualified people had been appointed throughout the twenties, others had left, and some of the vacancies created by those departures had not been filled by the time the decade came to a close. More critical evaluations of the university's affairs put the blame for this, in part, on the notoriety of the recent controversy and, perhaps in larger part, on McMaster's circumscribed life on the Bloor Street campus. Now that the Shields menace seemed laid to rest it only remained to solve the second problem by transplanting the institution in more spacious and friendly surroundings elsewhere.

As for the new faculty appointments, they were, by and large, replacements. Professors Gwatkin and Stevenson, who had been shoring up the work in classics, both resigned in 1928 in protest over what they claimed to be declining standards at McMaster. Clement H. Stearn, an English scholar in Greek who had been teaching at the Bishop Stortford School, was ultimately appointed to take Gwatkin's place. Until he arrived to discharge his duties in 1929 the work in classics was assumed by solicitous faculty members of the University of Toronto. Stearn accepted the McMaster post in spite of warnings that he ought not to become involved in a university so obviously prone to conflict.[5] But he was convinced by a number of well-wishers that he could expect a congenial teaching environment there and a good spirit in its common room.[6] Within a year of his arrival Stearn was able to welcome an opposite number in Latin when Edward Togo Salmon, a doctoral candidate at Cambridge who had done his undergraduate work in Australia, came to take Stevenson's place.

In the meantime, the arts appointments made in the twenties, with the exception of the decamped classicists, were still at their posts. Notable among these were Chester New, Kenneth Taylor, and Humfrey Michell, all of whom were helping to establish the university's reputation in history and political economy. Between them they launched a new semi-professional course to help prepare McMaster undergraduates for the study of law.[7] They were also busily establishing work at the master's level in their respective departments. In political economy the work had been facilitated by fellowships funded by Cyrus Eaton, the Cleveland industrialist.[8] John E. Robbins, a full-time graduate student in the department and the first holder of an Eaton fellowship, prepared a study on hydro-electric development in the British empire. The enthusiastic Robbins kept the chancellor fully informed of his research and of his correspondence with other budding scholars in the Commonwealth, particularly in Australia, where considerable progress had been made in the production of hydro-electricity in the twenties.[9] Nor were his mentors idle. In 1930 Taylor and Michell, in collaboration with Professor W.A. Mackintosh of Queen's University, brought out the two-volume *Statistical Contributions to Canadian Economic History*,[10] a reflection of their interest in a subject which had been incorporated in McMaster's political economy course as early as 1922.[11]

Michell also ventured into the hard-nosed world of business to experiment with a 'commercial service' in co-operation with interested parties at the University of Toronto. Although McMaster gave this system of business forecasting its informal blessing it was 'definitely understood' remarked a cautious Board of Governors in 1923 'that the University could not afford to take any financial responsibility in connection with the new enterprise.'[12] How accurately, if at all, the Michell Commercial Service predicted the disaster that struck the business community in the fall of 1929 has not been recorded.

While Taylor and Robbins were concerned about the emergent Commonwealth, Chester New was equally interested in determining who might have helped to inspire its origins in the nineteenth century. In the late twenties he was putting the finishing touches to his biography of John George Lambton, Lord Durham.[13] Known to generations of students who passed through New's course in Canadian constitutional history as 'My Durham,' it was the first major attempt to reconstruct the life and career of the colonial reformer who had sought to resolve the conflict between freedom and order on Britain's imperial frontier. The book was awarded a glowing review in the *Times Literary Supplement* and the Gold Medal of the Royal Society.[14]

The natural sciences, which New had once tried to put in their place, continued to be represented by W.O. Walker in chemistry, H.F. Dawes in physics, William Findlay in mathematics, R.W. Smith and Lulu Gaiser in biology, and William McNairn in geology. In addition to promoting work in semi-micro qualitative analysis, Walker, like Michell with his commercial service, ventured into the practical world with a gold-assaying kit, long a boon to geologists in the field.[15] Dawes, the physicist, was still held in high regard at the University of Toronto where, according to Dean McLay, '[John Cunningham] MacLennan, who has an international reputation ... has frequently expressed the hope that McMaster may enter Federation [so] that he may once more have Dawes on his staff.'[16]

Dawes and the biologist R.W. Smith, among others, recognized in the post-war years the need for improving the content and the quality of university work in the sciences now that high schools were coming into their own and giving courses that a few years before had been the staples at the post-secondary level. Thus, in 1924 Dawes inaugurated a new four-year course in physics, 'covering all the work in Physics and a considerable portion of the work in Math.'[17] Efforts were repeatedly made to encourage what a later generation would call interdisciplinary studies, particularly by Smith. He and others who collaborated in the experiment, however, were disillusioned by the lack of student response. 'I am disappointed that so few... enter the Special Science Course,' he dejectedly wrote the chancellor in the spring of 1927. 'This is the more regrettable because some knowledge of Chemistry and Physics is absolutely necessary to a proper knowledge of Biology. Very few of the students of Special Biology take any other science, except Geology, and hence if they wish to continue post-graduate studies in their special subject they must be severely handicapped.'[18] A related lament was that there seemed to be little desire on the part of science students to form a club of their own comparable to the Literary Society and the other undergraduate organizations which flourished on the campus.

But what Smith had ascribed to student indifference might have been their reluctance to accept the intensive direction to which the professor of biology subjected his charges. William Findlay, the mathematician, implied as much. 'It has been my ideal and endeavour' he advised Whidden 'to place, as far as possible, the responsibility for the students' efforts and for judgement as to their daily attainment upon the students themselves ... It would seem to me that this must be at variance with the ideals of others, that the students find themselves ... under a regime of coercion leaving little to their own free activity in the matter of studies.'[19]

Another problem that concerned McMaster's scientists and that would not be immediately solved by moving to Hamilton was the inability, through lack of manpower and resources, to satisfy the special requirements of the varied classes of science students at the university. A later report observed: 'We group them [future high school teachers, industrial personnel, and post-graduates in research] all together and with some slight variations give them practically the same work.'[20] The lack of specialization, deemed a virtue a generation before, was turning into a liability as the demands of society, reflected in the substantive changes in high school curricula and the growing complexity of technological and industrial growth, intruded themselves on the traditional research and instructional policies of McMaster and other Canadian universities.

In theology, meanwhile, following Dean Farmer's death and L.H. Marshall's resignation, the chancellor became the acting dean while a rigorous search was undertaken for a permanent one. Albert Newman, who years before had served the university as a church historian, briefly returned to do that side of the late dean's work. He was able to stop pinch-hitting in 1929 when George Gilmour, after serving for some months as a temporary instructor, was given a permanent appointment as a lecturer in church history, a move that made Gilmour a colleague of his brother-in-law Kenneth Taylor.

As for the student body – approximately four hundred strong in 1928, the year the New McMaster Campaign was formally launched – it had in recent years added to the small coterie of pre-war campus organizations. Although no science society had yet been formed, a Modern Literature Club, a more elaborate version of the old Literary Society reflecting the students' desire to be put in touch with the work of contemporary novelists and poets, was launched with the aid of Professor George Haddow of the English Department. E.J. Pratt, the narrative poet who had already attracted critical acclaim in both Canada and the United Kingdom, was one of the guest speakers brought in by the club, and he regaled his landlocked McMaster audience with his 'deeply felt perception of the sea,'[21] one of his favorite themes.

Another major departure, a constitutional one, was the organization in

1927 of the first Students' Council. Hitherto there had been no single agency for co-ordinating the activities of all the organizations on the campus. Made up of the combined executives of the Men's and Women's Student Bodies, the Council also provided places for the representatives of the other organizations: the editorial board of the *Monthly*, which now sponsored a literary M to match the athletic one, the Modern Literature Club, the Women's Literary Society, the YMCA and YWCA, the Evangelistic Bands, which still aimed at helping the churches in the community to bring about 'decisions for Christ,' and, finally, the Athletic Associations.[22]

The last-named were gratified when serious thought was given in the late twenties to the establishment at the university of a formal department of physical education that would devote itself, as one Senate discussion phrased it, 'to the benefit of ALL students, rather than for a few ... who may be on athletic teams.'[23] Some years before, the Board of Governors had shown its anxiety about the physical stamina of the student body by forming a committee, on which the enthusiastic Professor New served, to 'investigate the physical needs of the students.'[24] But as the promoters of a revitalized physical education program fully realized, more space as well as more money would be the prerequisites for its success.

As any graduate over thirty-five could recall in the late twenties, the Athletic Association had been the first to press for the enlargement of the campus. The need for expanded athletic facilities and for playing fields worthy of a university, however, had been matched in the minds of others by the need for an enlarged academic plant. Even while student organizations were burgeoning and constitutional refinements were making them more productive, the New McMaster, rumoured throughout the years, began to assume a sharper form for students as the decade drew to a close. 'Into the class of things which had a very vaporous-like existence when we entered McMaster as freshmen' an editor of the *Monthly* wrote in the fall of 1927

was what was known as the 'New McMaster.' We are not exactly sure when the vision of the new school first arose, the realization that the present equipment was inadequate and the site cramped must have come early ... But now this vision is taking shape ... A mountain appears and on a shelf of that mountain, overlooking a broad valley, new buildings. A large campus surrounds the buildings, which is but the counterpart of those dreams entertained by the various Presidents of the Athletic Association for years back.[25]

The citizens of Hamilton, the site in this passage, would have appreciated the careful reference to their 'mountain.'

In 1916, just five years after an earlier proposal to move the university to that city had been discarded, Chancellor McCrimmon received the first strong inkling that Hamilton itself might be anxious to acquire a university of its own. R.A. Thompson, who presided over the Collegiate Institute there, dropped McCrimmon the following note in the spring of 1916: 'I have been appointed to a Committee of the Board of Trade here to report on the advisability of establishing a University in Hamilton ... This act has been taken on account of a letter sent to the Board by Dr Wickett, a citizen of Hamilton. The only way I can see for our city to obtain a university is to establish a new one, or to prevail upon some one of the existing colleges to locate here.' 'Is there any possibility' Thompson asked 'of McMaster University considering a proposition to remove to Hamilton if proper arrangements could be made?'[26]

McCrimmon's answer has not survived, but judging by the pattern of subsequent events Thompson's letter was a significant one. Hamilton's Board of Trade, renamed Chamber of Commerce in 1920, once the war ran its course would help launch a campaign to bring McMaster to the city. The next important step in the story of the move was the organization in 1920 of an Alumni Association in Hamilton for the express purpose of backing the campaign. One of the cofounders of the branch claimed years later that he had been inspired to do so by the facetious story spread in 1909 by a bumptious McMaster student that the university had decided to move to Hamilton. 'Here seeing the building and expansion that was taking place,' Charles S. Robertson pointed out, 'I became more convinced than ever that [the] proposal had real merit.'[27] He went on to relate how he had talked the matter over with another graduate, Mrs. A.R. Lancefield, one day on the street and then had discussions with Dr Richard Guyatt 'as to the best possible plan to have the move seriously considered.' Curiously, Robertson could not recall discussing the subject with Principal Thompson who had first mentioned the idea to McCrimmon in 1916.

The upshot was the organization in the spring of 1920 of an alumni branch after 'a very enthusiastic meeting of a number of McMaster graduates of Hamilton and Dundas.'[28] 'Its infection' he hoped 'may have some effect on this community.' The Rev. W.W. McMaster, pastor of the large James Street Church in Hamilton, was named president of the new organization in the expectation that his name would carry weight in the campaign. Another booster of both the city and his alma mater was Lloyd D. Jackson who, as secretary of the alumni branch in Winnipeg, worked for the move throughout the twenties and in 1930 was named chairman of the nationally-organized Alumni Campaign.[29]

Within a week of Robertson's report on the mobilization of the Hamilton alumni, the Board of Governors was told that Trinity College might consider purchasing the McMaster buildings on Bloor Street should they be vacated.[30] Although it was agreed that it would be difficult to indicate just when they might become available, the Board's discussion plainly revealed that a move to some new locality was not entirely beyond the realm of possibility in the spring of 1920. It is almost impossible to determine, however, whether the Hamilton site at this time took precedence over the Eglinton property upon which so many expansionists had been pinning their hopes since its purchase in 1912. In July 1921 Dean McLay reported casually to Edgar J. Tarr, the prominent Winnipeg alumnus, that the Hamilton Association of Baptist Churches had recently spoken out in favour of a move to Hamilton.[31] This was a marked reversal in attitudes. In 1916 a leading Baptist in the city had told the chancellor that 'we would like to have you visit our church ... but just now is not the proper time.[32] Presumably this coolness lay behind the same writer's complaint that the 'Baptist people of Hamilton had never been honored by the University' when honorary degrees were handed out.[33]

By the time McLay told Tarr about the latest developments in the Hamilton situation, that city's Chamber of Commerce had already received vigorously worded letters from both the alumni branch and the local churches and was seriously considering 'getting behind the movement.'[34] A special committee was formed at the Chamber, chaired by Lieut. Colonel B.O. Hooper, manager of the Bank of Hamilton. After investigating the matter, this group recommended the establishment of a permanent committee to carry out the steps necessary for the presentation of a formal proposal to the university's Board of Governors. Up to this point the university had not expressed its intentions one way or the other, but merely noted the activities of its zealous alumni. As the Chamber well knew, if Hamilton interests wished to welcome McMaster to their midst high level and intricate negotiations would have to be set in motion.

In the meantime, members of the newly formed alumni branch in the city kept up the pressure on both Hamilton and the university. A.R. Lancefield, husband of the lady with whom Robertson had broached the idea of a promotional campaign a year before, gave the Hooper committee an historical review of the university's proposed move to North Toronto. He noted that since the purchase of the Eglinton site the property had been ringed with 'shacks and other unsightly buildings,' hardly a fit location, he pointed out to the local merchants, for a proud institution like McMaster.[35] These revelations were followed up in a few days by a resolution of the local Lion's Club that strong efforts be made by the city fathers to induce the university to locate in Hamilton. Another segment of the community, according to the enthusiastic pastor of James Street Church, was also anxious to embrace McMaster. The city's medical association was eager to establish a school in connection with the university, though no communication originating directly with the association appears in the documentation.[36] The clergyman breathlessly reported that the projected medical facility would 'have the assurance of all the financial help needed from the Rockefeller Foundation when the right time comes.'[37] The hopes entertained by A.C. McKay before the war were once again briefly revived in the heady atmosphere of the early twenties.

But the James Street minister's assiduous promotional efforts did not end with this. Within a month of delivering his report on the medical association's desires he brought out a brochure extolling Hamilton's advantages as a locale for 'his great uncle's university.'[38] Hamilton's reputation as a 'lunch-bucket town' had already been broadcast far and wide, to the discomfiture of those citizens who desperately wanted to cultivate a more glamorous image of their municipality. The flattering word pictures, the impressive data, and the formidable statistics that W.W. McMaster and his helpers marshalled for the university's edification undoubtedly pleased Hamiltonians and at the same time created some stir in the chancellor's office and at Senate and Board meetings. Those who for years had put up with the physical restrictions of the Bloor Street campus and feared that the North Toronto site was deteriorating might easily have been impressed with the multitude of possible Hamilton sites to which the Rev. McMaster drew their attention. Hamilton Bay, for example, was described as a kind of southern Ontario equivalent of the famous watercourses that dramatized the settings of Oxford, Cambridge, and Harvard. The 'Mountain,' Hamilton's share of the Niagara escarpment, McCrimmon and his associates were advised, could also afford 'wonderful opportunities as campus and parkland.'

Another advantage offered by Hamilton evoked the arcadian atmosphere of Fyfe's ancient enterprise in Woodstock. After praising the city as one of the foremost in Canada, 'already much larger than was Toronto when McMaster was first established there,' a resolution of the Niagara and Hamilton Association suggested sites for a campus that would 'always have the advantage of rural surroundings.'[39] Hamilton's convenient location, demonstrated capacity for growth, and rapidly improving communications – 'no city is so well served with electric Radials [and motor highways] as is Hamilton' – added to its attractiveness.[40] The city's population had by this time reached 120,000, an increase of nearly fifty thousand since the last census had been taken in 1911, the year the university had first surveyed the city's possibilities.

Having examined the scenic wonders of this emergent heartland in southern Ontario, the Rev. McMaster turned to the matter of Baptist demography. 'If a line were drawn north and south immediately west of [the city]' he observed 'it would divide our Baptist consituency of Ontario and Quebec into about two equal parts; in other words, our most accessible Baptist constituency lies wholly west of Hamilton and would be wonderfully advantaged by [a] move to Hamilton.' He estimated that nearly eleven thousand Baptists resided within a radius of thirty-five miles of the city, in contrast to but thirteen thousand for the more populous Toronto area. 'A McMaster in Hamilton' the pastor claimed 'would command all 11,000 not to mention all Hamiltonians,' freed as it would be from competition with a sister institution in the same community.

The latter point was crucial because many Baptists were concerned about the problem of university federation; besides providing an opportunity for growth, a move to Hamilton would make the chances of McMaster ever becoming part of the University of Toronto very remote indeed. Understandably, the point was not lost on interested parties in Woodstock. Within a month of the appearance of the Rev. McMaster's brochure, echoes of an ancient debate were sounded in an editorial in the *Sentinel-Review* that reminded its readers of the town's 'moral claims' to the university's affections. 'There was a time' the paper recalled in reviewing the events of the mid-eighties 'when many Woodstock people felt strongly in regard to the influences and methods by which the town had been deprived of an institution which it had come to regard as its own. But the old struggle has not been forgotten, nor has time softened the memories of it.'[41]

If McMaster were to be uprooted to escape strangulation or federation or both, Woodstock's citizens asked, why not remove it to the community that Fyfe and Rand had once prized? The writer of the appeal was probably well aware of the difficulties through which Woodstock College was then struggling in its uphill battle to compete with expanding and publicly supported high schools in the district.[42] Relocating the university in the municipality might be one means of offsetting the decline of the preparatory school and the impact that process might have on the town. But it was a plaintive appeal that few at the university were prepared to take seriously in 1921, and it was buried under the avalanche of literature on the merits of the Hamilton proposal.

As the fall of 1921 lengthened, the idea of moving developed further. On the eve of the St Thomas Convention it was announced in Hamilton that an official deputation from the city, together with representatives of its Chamber of Commerce, had requested and received an invitation to lay the matter before the delegates of the denomination. Among those named to the Chamber's contingent was William J. Westaway, a local businessman destined to play a vital role in consummating the actual move to Hamilton some nine years later. When the Convention assembled the Rev. McMaster busily introduced the visitors from Hamilton and presented the city's claims. In view of the active discussion that had been going on for almost a year, he proposed a resolution that the Convention affirm the wisdom of moving the university to Hamilton and authorize the Board of Governors to begin negotiations with a citizens' committee in the city to ascertain the sites and financial terms available.[43]

Before the resolution was put to a vote it was agreed that the deputation be permitted to speak and that the chancellor be allowed to present the University Report. Also on hand, but dwarfed by the sizable Hamilton group, was a tiny two-man delegation from Woodstock visibly anxious to make the points raised by their town's newspaper two days before. It was also reported to the Convention that certain businessmen in Toronto, not to be outdone by their counterparts in the Ambitious City and in Woodstock, had sent a telegram protesting 'any suggestion of removal of McMaster University from Toronto.'[44] These advances and protestations must have come as a flattering interlude in the discussion of the university's affairs on that fall afternoon. The Toronto cable prompted the wry comment from D.E. Thomson that 'now that they see there is some danger of losing the institution, Toronto people will be expected to show a little more appreciation than they have hitherto done.'[45] However belated their concern for McMaster, some Torontonians stressed the point made by the senator and John Castle many years before about Toronto's unquestioned cultural advantages. All of these, the argument went, would be lost to the university should it move to Hamilton, a veritable desert by comparison. The argument was dismissed in some quarters with an admission that would have disturbed Castle's eternal rest: the cultural loss 'would be more seeming than real, as it is generally admitted the museums and libraries [of Toronto] are seldom if ever taken advantage of by the student body.'[46]

Having heard out the deputations, the Convention turned to McCrimmon's report. On the subject of removal it reviewed the recent history of alumni activities in Hamilton and then alluded to a matter which had not hitherto been spelled out publicly. This was an assurance from the Chamber of Commerce that the 'presentation, as a free gift, to the Denomination of a suitable site for the University would be the very least that the citizens of Hamilton should be prepared to contribute towards the University's move to Hamilton, should it come about.'[47]

Although these advances were welcome, McCrimmon's report noted that the issues involved were 'so great that they would require very careful consideration and discussion before any action could be taken,' and certainly nothing could be decided before the Convention of 1922 had had an opportunity to discuss the project. Nevertheless the Board pledged to investigate carefully the overtures from 'communities other than Toronto.' Satisfied that his main objective was achieved the Rev. McMaster withdrew his resolution.

A few days later Evan Gray, a senior civil servant at Queen's Park and president of the General Alumni Association, set about with the chancellor's help to reconstruct the St Thomas discussions for the benefit of his fellow alumni across the country.[48] The responses were uniformly encouraging. 'When McMaster people have a few minutes together' wrote Edmonton's W.G. Carpenter in a typical statement 'it seems to be quite the general consensus of opinion ... here that it would be a very desirable thing for McMaster to move to the City of Hamilton ... [which is] a larger field of support and of influence.'[49] Wallace W. Charters, a faculty member at the Carnegie Institute of Technology, wrote to the same effect from Pittsburgh, along with other well placed graduates who made an effort to keep in touch with the university's affairs.

The same day that Gray inquired about the St Thomas decisions the ever-energetic minister of James Street Church was urging McCrimmon to open informal negotiations with Hooper's committee so that sites could be examined and sources of possible support canvassed 'as a background for the fullest consideration of the whole proposition.'[50] Some Board members duly paid a visit to the city, and lengthy tours and luncheon conversations were the order of the day. During the visit they were particularly impressed by the site at Carroll's Point overlooking the bay; unfortunately it turned out to be equally attractive to the planners of a new civic cemetery. The prospective competition for the site the university would not have found to its taste.[51]

The tours and the talks were all very welcome, but if the university were going to pursue the matter actively with the city it would have to settle one major problem. Given the denomination's historic position on the separation of church and state, a principle which had governed the nature of Woodstock's support for the old Canadian Literary Institute, how could it accept Hamilton's generous offers of civic aid? A 'general and earnest' discussion of this question took place at a Board meeting on 13 December 1921,[52] out of which came a number of inquiries that were sent to the standing committee in Hamilton. Even if such aid were acceptable, that committee was asked if it could take the responsibility of urging municipal action for obtaining a million dollars, through a bond issue, for the support of enlarged science departments. This was an area in which the Hamilton committee, familiar as it was with their city's growing industrial needs, had understandably shown an interest from the outset. But the next question was the basic one. 'Would it be possible,' Matthews and McCrimmon asked, 'should our Convention [in 1922] be unwilling to accept aid through municipal taxation ... to raise the above sum by voluntary subscription from the citizens of Hamilton and vicinity?'[53] The reply was not encouraging. Stated simply, the committee in Hamilton felt that sufficient funds could not be raised in this manner, though they came up with an alternative possibility whereby annual municipal grants might be made to cover the expenses of educating non-Baptist students at the university.[54]

After discussing this response several Board members concluded that before the move received any more attention the capacity of Baptists to finance a Forward Movement for that purpose ought to be put to the test. Others, who obviously felt that the Board's hands were being tied by the enthusiasms of the Rev. McMaster, urged that he 'be *asked not to* complicate the Board's decision in any way.'[55] His support of Shields's attack on the *Canadian Baptist* two years before might help to account for the sharpness of their criticism. On the matter of the separation of church and state there was again considerable debate both at this meeting and at subsequent ones of the Board and the Senate. At a meeting of Senate early in March 1922 when it was reported that Hamilton was prepared to offer a free site of some forty acres, Dean Farmer and T.T. Shields, in a rare public display of unity, strongly opposed acceptance of it. They did so on the grounds that it would be made through the good offices of the city and therefore would constitute a violation of a basic Baptist principle. Their position was immediately challenged by several other senators, including Professor New, who maintained that no violation would be involved in such an arrangement, although it was agreed by everyone that the receipt of funds directly from the city would be unacceptable.

The only kind of offer from Hamilton that the Board could conscientiously accept on behalf of the denomination would have to be of a voluntary character; 'any other would run the fire of denominational criticism.'[56] In the spring of 1922 the university was already under fire from Shields's attacks on its instruction, a matter thrashed out at the Walmer Road Convention later in the year. Most Board members had no desire to add to the controversy by proposing an arrangement with Hamilton that seemed to flaunt a fundamental Baptist tenet.

By this time a survey committee appointed by the Board to collect data and formulate ideas had submitted a report that included sketches and plans for both the Hamilton and North Toronto sites. The survey committee estimated that regardless of the site selected a minimum of $800,000 would have to be raised to construct a main building, two dormitories, a heating plant, and a dining room. If a science building and a gymnasium were to be added, though no formal plans for these were projected in the report, that figure would have to be boosted to at least a million dollars. With annual operating expenses, estimated at $50,000, thrown in, the report reckoned that only a doubling of the endowment could hope to meet the problem. Included in the estimates was the expectation, entertained by the Hamilton Committee earlier in January, that the city 'would ... help out with the education of non-Baptists' and would sell on favourable terms a suitable tract to accommodate the new campus.[57]

The possibility that voluntary public subscriptions might provide the funds acceptable to Baptist principles was heavily discounted at a sombre meeting of the Chamber of Commerce's Board of Directors in March. The recent slump in business activity and rising unemployment in Hamilton were cited as the main reasons for discouraging a drive for public subscriptions at that time, a point pressed home by W.H. Cooper, the head of a local construction firm.[58] The city that looked so promising as a university centre was, like its sister municipalities in the province, plunged into a post-war depression which diverted many public and private funds to relief and welfare measures. The Rev. McMaster, who had obviously ignored the injunction that he stop meddling in the matter, added to the gloom by noting that, good times or bad, the 'big men of Hamilton, or men of big means are not at all public spirited.'[59]

In spite of slumps and an alleged lack of public spiritedness among the wealthy in the city, plans went forward for a joint meeting of the Hamilton Committee and the Senate early in 1922. Tours, luncheons, and correspondence had previously been the principal means of acquainting the parties with each other's plans and hopes. Now in the solemnity of a Senate meeting a full range of vital matters could be thoroughly discussed. At the outset of the meeting McCrimmon and Frank Sanderson, representing the Board of Governors, took the opportunity of disclosing the financial value of the university for the benefit of their Hamilton guests. This was probably the first time that such a computation had been made and presented publicly by the university. Statistics were submitted indicating that McMaster's total assets came to approximately $4 million 'plus good will.'[60]

At this point in the proceedings S.J. Moore, another Board member, noted a different kind of asset, not easily measurable to be sure, but in his opinion important enough to be ranked with the 'big battalions' that money commanded. That asset, which could generate money, was what Moore called the 'heart interest [an earlier generation had talked about the 'heart sweat of the Baptists'] which our denomination has in this University, and because the denomination has that heart interest, it means in the future, whether the University remains in Toronto or goes to Hamilton, a very important amount in financial support.'[61]

The Hamiltonians were quick to respond. Controller Calvin Davis, the city's representative at the meeting, pointed out that civic aid to enable McMaster to move to Hamilton would be regarded there not so much as assistance to the university as a source of benefit for the municipality. Davis was followed by Dr J.K. McGregor, the founder of a clinic in Hamilton, who spoke out for the need of a medical school in affiliation with a transplanted McMaster. Towards the end of the meeting, which closed 'in a mood of exhilaration,' a joint subcommittee was formed of the Hamilton Committee and a group from the Senate to furnish continous discussions.[62] The hope was expressed that substantial progress on the matter could be made by the time the next Convention met in Toronto in the fall of the year.

Although the educational sessions of the Walmer Road Convention were dramatically taken up by Shields's charges against Sanderson, some time was allotted to a discussion of the removal question. Board chairman Albert Matthews urged the Convention to approve what the Board and the Senate had already done and to authorize them to continue negotiating with the city. It would appear that Dean Farmer's, if not Shields's, objections to the free land grant had by this time been withdrawn because those negotiations were to be pursued on the understanding that Hamilton would offer a free site in addition to encouraging voluntary financial assistance from its citizens. Finally, Matthews called upon the Convention to launch the fullest discussion of the proposal throughout the constituency, a recommendation that was adopted without amendment. The way seemed clear to promote the scheme with even greater vigour.[63]

One visitor to the Walmer Road meeting who understandably took a keen interest in the proceedings was Howard P. Whidden, already the object of a large-scale hiring campaign at the university. Of the proposed move Whidden seemed unequivocally in favour. He reminded Matthews early in 1923 that he had already told the Board of Governors 'rather definitely that I would not have any confidence in undertaking the work of the Chancellorship if there was no desire . . . to change from the present location on Bloor Street.' One of the reasons for this stand he had disclosed late in 1922: '[An] institution, ranked as a smaller University or "Christian College," can always render its best service and develop its finest type of individual life when it becomes a vital part of a given community that is not large enough to cause it to be almost entirely lost in the community as a whole. The history of Christian Education on the North American continent verifies this easily.'[64] Whidden was prepared to look at alternatives to Hamilton,[65] but years earlier George Cross had expressed much the same thought about that particular municipality.

It was not long, however, before the chancellor-designate was going over the ground in Hamilton 'in a purely personal and unofficial [way] in order to feel out the situation.' Until he was formally invested with the chancellorship it would have to be unofficial in any case. To this interregnum may be attributed in part the delay in the negotiations with the Hamilton people. As Whidden remarked in March 1923, his 'present job [at Brandon] is quite big enough to keep me busy from now until mid-summer.' Nevertheless he spent a great deal of time in the interval before finally assuming his new responsibilities dashing off memoranda and arranging meetings in connection with McMaster's affairs.[66]

What probably contributed more than the interregnum to the difficulties plaguing the move was the continuing nation-wide recession which had particularly adverse effects upon Hamilton's heavily industrialized economy. In these circumstances the alternatives to the Hamilton move were resurrected for discussion. The university could, of course, stay on Bloor Street with all that location entailed; it could federate with the University of Toronto, a proposal already demolished on at least three occasions; or, finally, it could move out to the Eglinton site. Apparently Albert Matthews, for all his sympathy with the Hamilton proposal, preferred North Toronto until the spring of 1926. The simple but effective reason that he gave was that the Eglinton property was available.[67]

Yet in spite of Hamilton's sobering situation in 1923 the Senate and Board concluded, after a full discussion of the varied alternatives, that moving there was still the best solution to the university's problems.[68] But four additional considerations were deemed basic to the project. First and foremost, Hamilton's financial assistance must still be on a voluntary basis. Reference was made to the astonishing progress made in nearby Buffalo, New York, where $5 million had been subscribed for a university by citizens and corporations.[69] The remaining conditions were that control of the university as provided in the charter be preserved; that the denomination increase the endowment fund through a Forward Movement and by selling its available university property; and that Hamilton's citizens raise sufficient funds for the construction of university buildings and student dormitories upon an approved donated site.

Essentially all these points were embodied in the message that the university presented for the Convention's approval in the fall of 1923. Even before they were endorsed by a large majority of the delegates, comforting word came from Hamilton in a letter from the indefatigable Rev. McMaster. 'You need have no fear' he assured Whidden 'that there will be lack of enthusiasm [here]. Hooper, Westaway...the Mayor [G.C. Coppley] are all red hot enthusiasts and quite willing to go ahead on the voluntary principle ... The Mayor stated this morning that it was a bigger thing for Hamilton than any industrial concern coming here could possibly be.' But the clergyman was still concerned about the need for influencing the large business men of the city,[70] an exercise made more difficult in an atmosphere of financial crisis. However, the effort was made. Invitations went out to Hamilton's industrial and commercial leadership to attend the reception planned for Whidden's installation in November 1923. The guest list (it is difficult to determine how many accepted the invitation) reads like a *Who's Who* of the city's élite, from S.H. Alexander of Wood, Alexander and James, a large wholesale house, to Allan V. Young, president of the Hamilton Cotton Company.[71]

One of those who did attend was R.B. Harris, publisher of the Hamilton *Herald*, who either wrote or inspired an editorial that appeared in the paper the day after the festivities in Toronto. Commenting on Premier Howard Ferguson's remark at the installation that McMaster would remain in Toronto's educational atmosphere, the *Herald* observed: 'It is the "educational atmosphere" of which the premier spoke that is stifling McMaster University. It is an independent institution, and it is being overshadowed ... and stunted by the state-aided Toronto University ... It must be transplanted to a place where it will have room to expand ... Its salvation depends upon its removal.'[72] Not to be left out, the rival Hamilton *Spectator* claimed some months later that there was potentially a rich market for a university in the city. Noting that 'University classes had been conducted by the University of Toronto here for three years,' the paper hoped that 'these classes may go on increasing until such time as McMaster or some other university establishes itself in Hamilton.'[73]

Some supporters of the move to Hamilton became positively lyrical. Thomas Wearing wrote from Colgate University in New York that 'Hamilton ... will mean infinitely ... more to me when the institution I love moves out of Toronto and along the lake to become the centre of higher education for the Canadian Hamilton and the lovely lower peninsula of Ontario.'[74] Heart-warming words, but hardly in accord with the harsh economic realities that continued to harass the proposal. Periodically, meetings were held and views exchanged between the city and the university,[75] but the campaign virtually ground to a halt in 1924. This created considerable anxiety in the mind of W.J. Westaway, who had rapidly emerged as the spark plug of the Hamilton Committee. In defiance of the forbidding financial environment he continued to hope that 'two or three key men' could somehow or other consummate the arrangement.[76] Yet the notion that everything seemed to depend upon the actions of certain Hamilton interests infuriated another member of the Hamilton Committee. What the Rev. John C. Williamson wanted in the summer of 1925 was for Albert Matthews to head up the drive to obtain McMaster for Hamilton. Williamson claimed that in spite of appearances the matter was not dead in the city and argued that all that was required was a 'capable financial general' to take charge and inspire with his leadership the many Hamilton businessmen who were still 'very keen' about the project.

There should not be undue patronage of what some Hamilton men consider 'key men.' To my mind this thing is big enough to bury under high drifts all the 'key men' we have in Hamilton. The idea seems to be in many minds that McMaster is 'angling' for what she can get from Hamilton. Surely this is not true ... Heaven forbid that McMaster should ever be guilty of bartering her prestige for the dirty money or social influence (questionable) of so called 'key men' ... who have had the idea they could buy a University ... The sooner McMaster gets that idea out of Hamilton's head the better.[77]

Williamson's pointed observations were not entirely lost on Whidden and his colleagues when the campaign was resumed with greater purpose in 1927.

In the meantime, while the attention of the city was diverted by its worsening financial straits, the university was embroiled in the protracted conflict with T.T. Shields. The battle did not consume all the university's time and energy, of course, but it made heavy inroads upon those hours that could otherwise have been set aside for a discussion of the removal question. At times, indeed, the trouble at McMaster impinged directly on the negotiations with the Hamilton representatives. Dean McLay's explanation to John Firstbrook of what happened in the voting for the university's Board of Governors at the Convention of 1924 shows this:

I am still sorry that the Convention did not recognize your long and highly useful service by re-electing you to the Board ... I am sure, however, that the failure of the delegates to do so was in no sense a reflection on you but the result of two circumstances, namely the nomination of a candidate from Hamilton and the resolve of Dr Shields and his supporters to defeat some one of the retiring Governors. At that

Convention the proposal to move the University to Hamilton had been strongly urged, and consequently Mr J.W. Gillies of the Hamilton Citizens' Committee [and president of Gillies-Guy Coal Company], though practically unknown to the delegates generally was supported as an expression of the favorable feeling of the Convention towards the Hamilton proposal.[78]

Had Gillies not been a candidate for this purpose, the dean assured Firstbrook, 'the efforts of Dr Shields ... would have been fruitless.'

Although McLay said that the proposal to move had been strongly urged, there were indications that the question had been eclipsed by external problems and internal difficulties. For example, from late 1923 until the closing weeks of 1925 no entries on the subject were made in the Senate minutes. And even when it was discussed Whidden seems to have become disenchanted with the Hamilton site and to have favoured a shorter migration to 'some newer part of Toronto.' 'There is nothing that quite appeals to me' he wrote Matthews in the summer of 1925 'as having the characteristics needed as the St Andrews College site at York Mills.'[79]

The next entry in the Senate Minutes announced, on 12 November 1925, the appointment of a new Committee on Location, a more active replacement for the original one.[80] People were already referring to a renewal of the Hamilton project. E.J. Tarr, writing from Winnipeg at this time, had put it precisely in these terms, noting with pleasure that the Hamilton move was again under consideration.[81] Although it might have been under consideration on Bloor Street, Whidden gloomily reported that Hamilton 'seems to be rather dead on the subject,' a remark made while deflating an argument that Windsor or Ottawa might prove desirable locations for a transplanted McMaster.[82] Had Hamiltonians been aware of the comment they might have retorted that the university seemed to be paying little or no attention to the matter either, engrossed as it was in its showdown with Shields in the first half of 1926.

During that period at least one other community sought to compete with Hamilton and North Toronto for McMaster's affections. Emulating its counterpart in the Ambitious City, Guelph's Chamber of Commerce sent a letter to the Board of Governors in the summer of 1926 listing the virtues of their community and urging them to give the town their fullest consideration.[83] The proposal was eloquently supported by faculty members at the Ontario Agricultural College. One of the latter thought that if McMaster became the College's neighbour an 'interchange of lectures would be found both practical and profitable to both institutions'; another, Professor O.J. Stevenson of OAC's English Department, wrote at the close of the year that 'most Toronto men think of the OAC as a small institution for the training of farmers, and almost everyone who visits the place is astonished at its size and the extent of the work that it is doing ... We have here a magnificent plant ... and there is a stretch of untapped country with the finest boys and girls in Ontario to draw from, to the north and west.' 'Hamilton' Stevenson concluded firmly 'does not begin to be in it as a place for a university, but Guelph is ideal.'[84]

For that matter, there were still citizens of Woodstock who felt the same way about their own community, the very people who had backed its forlorn submission on the removal question at the St Thomas Convention in 1921. Five years later, however, they were taking a new tack. As if to acknowledge Hamilton's victory in the competition and at the same time salvage the fortunes of Woodstock College, they suggested that it be transferred to the new campus planned for Hamilton. This sentiment was recalled years later by J.H. Cranston: 'I have felt that there was real room at Hamilton for preparatory departments, *especially for men.* Woodstock College used to provide plenty of ministerial students and they were generally of good quality.'[85]

To the suggestion that the school be shipped to Hamilton – though they recorded nothing so explicit on the topic – Whidden and his contemporaries might have reacted much the same way that Chancellor George Gilmour did a quarter of a century later. In the summer of 1950 he wrote the following to Charles Vining, a Woodstock alumnus preparing a history of the institution:

One point raised in your letter is whether Woodstock College could have been transferred to the new McMaster campus in Hamilton and continued, as Horton Academy continues on the Acadia campus. Quite apart from the dwindling patronage of the school, this would have been impossible. In Hamilton there is a boys' school, Hillfield College, which is governed by a board many of whose members are strong friends of the University. To have established here a rival institution would have been to forfeit the good will of the community.[86]

About a year later in another lengthy letter to Vining, Gilmour recapitulated the reasons for what Cranston called the 'abandonment' of the school in 1926. Declining enrolments and inadequate staff brought on by the severe competition with the province's expanding high school system precipitated a financial and academic crisis which, Gilmour claimed, no amount of ingenuity or pump-priming could have alleviated. Vining was also reminded that the 'vicious' Shields controversy had then been in full swing and 'must have given Dr Whidden and others almost no rest.' For good measure, Gilmour quickly sought to refute Cranston's impression that ministerial students of good quality abounded at Woodstock. He disclosed that he

himself had refused the principalship there in 1925 simply because he regarded it as a third-rate institution and a hopeless cause,[87] descriptions that
would have embittered many a Woodstock alumnus who could recall that it
had been briefly courted as the nucleus of a university forty years before.[88]

Woodstock College was officially closed in the summer of 1926, just when
the Hamilton relocation campaign was being eagerly revived. Whidden was
advised by the Board of Governors to request the school's principal to give
his staff verbal and confidential notice that their services would not be
required after 31 August 1926.[89] Thus, of the four institutions founded by
Baptists in Central Canada over the course of the nineteenth century – the
Canada Baptist College in Montreal, Woodstock College, successor to the
Canadian Literary Institute, Moulton College, the school for girls, and
McMaster University – only Moulton and the university continued to function after 1926. And many were convinced that the latter too would soon
cease to operate as an independent institution unless it uprooted itself and
made a new beginning in Hamilton.

By the date of Woodstock College's demise, Hamilton had again become,
in Whidden's view, 'thoroughly alive' on the transfer of McMaster, a development that, among other things, unceremoniously swept the Guelph
proposal aside. The return to Hamilton of something resembling prosperity
in the summer and fall of 1926 had reawakened the city's interest. And with
the worst of the Shields crisis over, thanks to the decisions of the recent
Convention in Toronto, the university could pay greater attention to the
scheme. Indeed, even before the Convention adjourned Matthews was credited in the *Globe* with having made a characteristically guarded statement
that 'we have not yet closed the door on the Hamilton proposition.'[90] About a
week later the Board of Governors put a more positive face on the matter,
doubtless at the insistence of the energetic Carey Fox, and recorded in its
minutes that there was a definite possibility of renewing the Hamilton
negotiations.[91] In the interval, Matthews, who now gave the appearance of
taking charge as the Rev. Williamson hoped that he would, accompanied
Whidden and John MacNeill on a motor trip to the city. The trio, in the
chancellor's words, 'quietly viewed the landscape o'er' and looked 'without
prejudice at two or three properties.' All of this, Whidden warned a correspondent to whom he divulged the information, was 'to be kept under your
hat' until a definite decision was made.[92]

The same period witnessed a concrete expression of Hamilton's revived
interest in the project. In mid-September the Hamilton Committee, which
had been operating intermittently in one form or another for five years, was
drastically reconstituted so as to include at least a few of those 'key men'

whom W.J. Westaway and W.W. McMaster had been trying to bag. Among them were F.I. Ker, the publisher of the *Spectator*, Norman Slater, the president of a steel-processing firm, Col. J.R. Moodie, the textile manufacturer, W.H. Cooper, the contractor, J.P. Bell, the general manager of the Bank of Hamilton, and F.M. Morton of the International Harvester Company. They were referred to at the time as an informal committee of friends, a kind of shadow board of governors working in close conjunction with the formal body at the university.[93]

To speed matters up, this committee on 23 November 1926 reopened discussions with the university and sought to assure it that the city was now prepared to settle down to the serious business of bringing the institution to Hamilton. Carey Fox, who seems to have played a key role in the plans to rejuvenate the scheme, took a prominent part in these talks alongside Whidden and Matthews. It was probably no coincidence that a few days later his brother Sherwood Fox, president of the University of Western Ontario, was telling Whidden that he would be happy to accompany the chancellor to Hamilton so that together they might evaluate possible sites. Western's head also promised that he would do what he could to convince the Hamilton Committee, if indeed it needed any convincing at this stage, what McMaster's arrival in their community might mean in terms of income, the 'kind of argument' he noted 'that would appeal to the businessmen of Hamilton.'[94]

On the strength of the discussions of 23 November the newly constituted Hamilton Committee sent Whidden an outline of the terms on which the university might be induced to move to Hamilton. One sizable modification of the plan accepted in 1923 was the recommendation that an amount of half a million dollars be raised as a voluntary gift by the citizens of Hamilton along with a free site of some fifty to seventy-five acres, this in lieu of the earlier proposal that the citizenry raise funds sufficient to house the university in a group of buildings on an approved donated site.[95] But, as Whidden noted, the first charge on the $500,000 would have to be the cost of a new science building, the future Hamilton Hall.[96] In his memorandum to the denomination Whidden commented that 'this is better than the earlier suggestion in that it does not unduly place us under obligation to the people of Hamilton.'[97] The other basic considerations upon which the university had insisted throughout were retained, he assured his fellow Baptists, in the Hamilton Committee's document.

After consultation with the committee the chancellor urged the university to launch its own campaign in the constituency to raise $1,500,000 for the undertaking. To say that Whidden was sanguine about this prospect is to risk understatement. Nonetheless, he was convinced that after 'four years' residence within the bounds of this Convention I am led to believe that we can with confidence expect . . . Baptists to contribute $1,200,000 for Christian Education (the other $300,000 to come from graduates and friends in the United States),' a hopeful reference to, among others, Cyrus Eaton.[98]

Whidden then proceeded to recapitulate in his memorandum the major reasons for the move. Cramped quarters, inadequate equipment, and declining endowment had by now become commonplace references in any such review, but the agony of the recent conflict added a sharper note to Whidden's presentation. He stated it simply enough: 'Because of the perplexing and trying experiences through which we have been passing it is particularly desirable that we make a fresh start at the earliest possible date.' The sum and substance of what would likely accrue from that fresh start he furnished in point form:

Re: Hamilton Proposal

1 / McMaster University needs a more definitely accessible local constituency. In order that through serving that constituency well it may be conditioned to serve its special denominational constituency in a larger way.

2 / Hamilton is the finest unserved community in Canada.

3 / Apparent losses through removal from Toronto would be made up by reason of many intensive gains.

4 / The history of our highly standardized Christian colleges in North America reveals the fact that the institution aiming at broad general culture for real service can do its finest work in a community of its own.

5 / The History of Christian Education shows that while removal to Hamilton *might* be led to mean the gradual shifting of emphasis from the program of a Christian University to that of a municipal or regional university, there is no reason whatever why this need result.

6 / A comprehensive program regarding the training of our future ministers and Christian workers can be shaped up with due recognition of Toronto's strategic position.[99]

Whidden's statements and the more vibrant relationship growing up between the university and the citizens of Hamilton did not, of course, preclude a hard-headed discussion of details. Supporters of a move to the Eglinton property were gratified when their favorite location was made part of a comparative study of construction costs undertaken by the Board in

January 1927. Although the estimates indicated that the cost of rebuilding the institution in North Toronto would not be appreciably higher than in Hamilton, $1,302,000 to $1,279,000, the Eglinton site would be denied the crucial half-million dollars already pledged by the Hamilton Committee. This would mean that if a move were made to North Toronto the objective of the denomination's Forward Movement would have to be doubled, an unpleasant prospect for those who had to direct the campaign.

One month after construction costs were computed a highly confidential conference was called at the university once again to examine thoroughly the varied alternatives open to the university and to prepare the constituency for whatever step might have to be taken. In all, thirty-five people attended, drawn from the administration of the university and its senior faculty, from the Board and Senate, and from the Baptist ministry and denomination at large. Any significant expansion on Bloor Street was clearly out of the question, a point accepted axiomatically by everyone present. Dean Farmer expressed a fear, however, that recalled McCrimmon's earlier statement about McMaster being an alternative to the University of Toronto: 'in a move out of Toronto we might lose that urge to keep ourselves free of too worldly and material entanglements – Varsity constantly reminds us of our raison d'être ... City control [in Hamilton] might gradually infringe upon our direct control – lower our ideals – and affect our theology department.' In response, the Rev. E.T. Newton reminded the group of Fyfe's faith in the future and warned them that 'we cannot hold ourselves in check because we can't see clearly what fifty years will bring.'[100]

Any confirmed federationists at the meeting would have been disheartened by J.H. Cranston's remarks. The *Star Weekly*'s editor had completely changed his own views about the desirability of federation with the University of Toronto and willingly seconded a motion that 'Baptist interests would best be served through an independent McMaster.' The group went on to endorse the move to Hamilton as the best means of guaranteeing that independence. The endorsement also had the effect of overcoming the objections of those who had worried about the expense of developing the property in North Toronto. Other motivations in support of the move were reflected in the Rev. Huson W. Wright's hope that it would afford an opportunity to show Hamilton that 'we stand for something more than baptism by immersion,' and in John MacNeill's assertion that 'we will meet the challenge and stamp Hamilton with the seal of our Baptist spirit and life.'[101] The matter was then taken up by the Senate and the Board. By early summer the latter had approved the recommendation for the removal to Hamilton and the disposal of the Eglinton property, provided that the step received the 'hearty approval' of the Convention scheduled for Toronto's Temple Baptist Church in October.

At that gathering much time was devoted to reading Jarvis Street Church out of the Convention, a move that anticipated the expulsion in 1928 of other churches that had given their sympathy and support to T.T. Shields's newly formed association. This procedure, endorsed at a closing session of the previous Convention, had required an Act of Parliament because it involved a basic amendment to the Convention's constitution. The application to Ottawa for this power had further embittered the conflict and provided local newspapers with an opportunity to capitalize on the irony of the situation and do some moralizing of their own. 'Acts of Apostles not Acts of Parliament should be the Final Source of Power,' read a headline in the Toronto *Evening Telegram*. The accompanying article denounced 'clerical leaders' who would 'load the dice for or against . . . anybody with the secular power.'[102] In spite of Shields's blistering attacks on the measure and the press's hostility and ridicule the necessary legislation was passed, and the Convention was enabled to exercise 'proper discipline' upon its membership. A reporter for the Woodstock *Daily Sentinel-Review* gave his impressions of the high and low points of the Convention: 'In contrast to the grim and determined attitude of the majority faction prior to the Jarvis Street Church expulsion, the challenges and disturbances from the opposition . . . were treated almost jocosely, and in most cases were muffled into subsidence with laughter.'[103]

On 17 October 1927, the university's report and the removal proposal it embodied were put to a vote and formally adopted. The way was now clear, after six years of chequered negotiations and lengthy consultations, for the relocation of the university. About a week before, steps had been taken to dispose of the property in North Toronto, a sale that brought $175,000 into the university's coffers.[104]

At the very close of the year Hamilton's citizens were greeted in the Christmas numbers of both the *Herald* and the *Spectator* by Dean McLay's historical review of the university's accomplishments and his account of what the city could expect of its new institution of higher learning. It was fitting that the task of exposition fell to McLay. He had been at McMaster for nearly one-third of a century and as dean of arts had, with the aid of Dean Farmer, tided the University over McCrimmon's recurring illnesses and the interregnum created by his forced retirement in 1922. As professor of English, McLay had over the years seen hundreds of students pass through his classes. Many of them, as he noted in his Christmas message of 1927, had gone on to do respectable, in certain cases distinguished, work in teaching, writing, and research at some of the leading universities in Canada, the

United Kingdom, and the United States. Granted, McMaster could not boast elaborate graduate facilities or professional schools of its own, but it would continue, as it had in the past, the dean was careful to point out, to lay the 'foundation upon which its graduates may build when later they choose a profession or enter business or public life.' The general education which an earlier generation had lionized but which in a rapidly changing environment was already beginning to be questioned, was still officially regarded as the university's major contribution to society.[105] McLay's remarks neatly supplemented the message that Whidden had incorporated in the memorandum prepared late in 1926 for the benefit of the denomination. In words that could have been written by Robert Fyfe, John Castle, or Malcolm MacVicar two or three generations before, the chancellor trusted that the university in its new locale would become 'an increasingly productive missionary enterprise within the life of the denomination ... and an increasingly effective instrument for the building of the Kingdom and the leavening of the nation.'[106]

11
Conclusion

Nearly a century separated the establishment of John Gilmour's pioneering Canada Baptist College in Montreal from the launching of the New McMaster Campaign, a period punctuated with controversies. Gilmour's enterprise had been buffeted by the conflict between open and closed communionists; Senator William McMaster's had almost been wrecked by a struggle ostensibly between modernism and fundamentalism. In this sense, as in others, the varied institutions that the Baptists of central Canada had nursed into existence reflected the theological and doctrinal issues that helped to shape not only their own denomination but much of western Christendom itself since the early years of the nineteenth century. McMaster University and its forerunners constitute a kind of collective case study of the effects of a wide-ranging theological confrontation on institutions of learning on the Canadian scene.

This question opens up another theme that runs throughout the history of Canadian Baptist education. By virtue of their being Baptists, the founders of the school in Montreal, of Woodstock College, or of the university could not help but be influenced, stimulated, or repelled by what occurred in the sprawling Baptist constituency of the Atlantic world. McMaster University had been founded primarily to meet the needs of Baptists in central Canada, but in the process its ideals, principles, and goals had been moulded by that larger community. John Harvard Castle, one-time occupant of the opulent pulpit on Jarvis Street, had brought to the Toronto Baptist College the hopes and formulas that had proven so successful in the campaign by the Northern Baptist Convention of the United States to enlarge the scope and improve the quality of its educational facilities. To this endeavour Susan Moulton, the senator's wife, had made no small contribution.

Out of the effort at the TBC had sprung the expanded arts program, particularly in philosophy, which had helped to justify the establishment of an independent McMaster University in Toronto. And to that institution had gravitated as faculty the polished products of the Northern Convention's colleges and seminaries, most notably that in Rochester. John Castle, Malcolm MacVicar, George Burman Foster, who would later build a controversial reputation at Chicago, and James Ten Broeke, his successor at McMaster in the chair of philosophy and ethics, were all alumni of Rochester. Still another element had been added in Castle's day at the TBC, the conservative influence of the Southern Baptist Convention, whose articles of faith had been enlisted to preserve that school from the worst effects of the 'infidelity' of modern scholarship. That ideological connection was never severed. Dean Jones Hughes Farmer, a graduate of the Southern Baptist Theological Seminary, and Nathaniel Parker, a representative of the Southern Convention, would both in due course be invited to bolster work in theology at the university, the TBC's successor.

These infusions from the large American provinces of the Baptist constituency contrasted sharply with the British impulse that had helped to bring to fruition John Gilmour's experiment in the 1830s. That venture had reflected the efforts of homesick Britons, with assistance from Baptists in the metropolis overseas, to train a native clergy of their own, free from American influence and practice. A generation later, following the collapse of the Montreal college and the announcement by Baptists in the old world that they could no longer sustain the work in North America, Robert Alexander Fyfe's 'national school,' the Canadian Literary Institute, had sprouted in Woodstock. Shorn, by and large, of the support of their British coreligionists but still reluctant to accept the authority of newly established American seminaries like Rochester, self-conscious Canadian Baptists thus set about to correct the mortification of having no institutions to call their own.

However, by the time McMaster University appeared on the scene Rochester had grown so impressively in influence and prestige that its generous offer to aid embryonic institutions in Canada was almost impossible to decline. Consequently the Canadianization set in train by Fyfe and his colleagues was leavened by the continentalist contributions that Canadian Baptists had hitherto tried to reject or to politely ignore. If William McMaster constituted a bridge between the Atlantic world of John Gilmour and the Canadian one of Robert Fyfe, his wife, Susan Moulton, helped to forge a link between Ontario's needs in the eighties and the capacity of the Northern Convention to fill them. From the endeavours in Toronto had emerged an institution that partook less of the English collegiate experience, which the University of Toronto sought to perpetuate in Ontario, and more of the spirit and structure of the American college or seminary.

William McMaster's personification of the connection between the old world and the new was also evident in the Canadian progeny of the Scottish immigrant who had launched the Canada Baptist College. They would make an impressive mark on the university the senator founded – Joseph Leeming Gilmour and George Peel Gilmour, though the latter's major contributions lie outside the scope of this volume. Joseph Gilmour's work at the institution, however, is a reminder as well of the extent to which McMaster was forced to comb every part of the Canadian Baptist constituency for new personnel. As often as not the satisfaction of the university's needs highly inconvenienced somebody else. A disgruntled observer of the cultural imperialism inherent in this recruitment process might have echoed the criticism once levelled by William Davies against Senator McMaster's showpiece on Jarvis Street: what the university was doing smacked altogether too much of a 'hateful spirit of aggrandizement and centralization.' Certainly A.A. Ayer of Montreal thought so when Joseph Gilmour was enticed away to Toronto at the expense of the denomination's enterprise in the St Lawrence Valley.

Communities even further afield had been periodically plucked for the institution in Ontario, a small reflection of the metropolitanism in which Toronto as a whole seemed to indulge at the turn of the century. Theodore Rand, Thomas Trotter, and Daniel Welton had all been lured away from Nova Scotia and Acadia University to professorial or administrative positions on Bloor Street. Again, the west had periodically complained, if not so much about raiding tactics – though the departure of Howard P. Whidden for McMaster was regretted in Brandon – then certainly about the university's supposed neglect of Baptist work on the prairies and the west coast. The question may have been asked time and again in the areas which McMaster had seemingly relegated to the status of mere borderlands: had the effort in Toronto been worth the price paid by the latter in the loss of direction and leadership?

Yet the recruitment and the support sought for the university were not exclusively continentalist and Canadian. The old world, which had helped to found the pioneering venture in Montreal, was ultimately invited to staff its distant successor in Toronto after a lengthy interval in which North Americans had, virtually by default, established themselves in positions of authority there. In theology the British names come readily: Henry S. Curr and L.H. Marshall. One had been eminently acceptable to conservatives, the other not, but both shared, apart from their nationality and religious adherence, one vital essential: a respect for theological diversity and reasoned debate. Their theology differed not so much in kind as in emphasis and frequently recoiled in the presence of the less sophisticated beliefs of their North American counterparts. Their instruction and pastoral activities added for a time a vital component to the doctrinal admixture and fund of personal commitment that came to characterize the academic scene on Bloor Street. But their terms at McMaster were relatively short, and both, along with the British influence they exemplified, departed as a consequence of the tension generated during the Shields crisis of the twenties.

The melding of these varied theological strains served for over a generation to help prepare students for advanced work in those institutions to which McMaster had traditionally sent its more promising alumni in theology: Rochester Seminary and the University of Chicago. A triangular web of relationships was thus established in which McMaster graduates moved freely between Toronto and the two American centres, with many ending up in the seminar rooms of Chicago after taking the first stage of their post-graduate work in Rochester. Then, as if to enable McMaster to repay its debt to those who had originally helped to sustain it, a considerable number had gone on to assume pastoral and scholarly duties in American churches and seminaries.

But as some observers pointed out, that obligation was discharged at the expense of the university's capacity to fend off attacks from the theological right. Had there been on hand, so the argument ran, more pastors of the calibre of those who left to occupy American pulpits, McMaster's crises would not have assumed the proportions they did. But why had these graduates become expatriates in the first place? A more challenging environment, especially in the churches of the Northern Convention, was obviously one spur. Another was the reluctance of a good many Canadian congregations to accept the credentials and the message of university-trained clergymen. As a consequence, it would appear, the more scholarly and progressive McMaster graduates forsook the Canadian field and embarked upon more gratifying careers in the United States.

This decision arose out of a basic dilemma haunting Baptist education in Canada from the very beginning, which runs as a counter-theme through this study. To a large degree the troubles that plagued the Canada Baptist College and its ultimate successor, McMaster University, may be attributed to that never-ending debate in the denomination over the merits of an educated ministry. Was scholarship a genuine substitute for 'heart sweat?' A great many in the constituency had consistently thought not, and their attitude had caused anguish in John Gilmour, Robert Fyfe, O.C.S. Wallace, and A.L. McCrimmon when they had set out to gain moral and financial support for the institutions which they headed.

The reluctance to trust the 'school man' stemmed from a variety of considerations. Many an uneducated layman suspected the approach and perhaps the orthodoxy of his more thoroughly tutored coreligionist. Moreover, if education is a function of class, was there a marked unwillingness on the part of working-class Baptists, who made up a sizable proportion of the constituency, to support the manifestly middle class aspirations of the university? Although a shared religious experience may have blurred social and economic disparities in the Baptist fold as in other Canadian Protestant denominations, it is always possible that class considerations accounted for some of the distrust shown the university and its policies. A working-class Baptist in, say, Hamilton's Stanley Avenue Church could not easily share his deepest feelings with Howard Whidden, the well placed professional and educational statesman who had moved so affably among the affluent Baptists of Manitoba and those prosperous citizens of Dayton, Ohio, who made up one of the most prestigious congregations in the Northern Convention. And finally, at another level of tension, what of the attitude of rural Baptists toward the urban ways that dominated the educational affairs of the denomination? Without further research into such themes as social stratification and the conflict between urban and rural communities in the Baptist constituency no definitive answers to such questions are possible.[1]

Yet when one reviews class and education as a factor in the frustration of Christian education under Baptist auspices, one is reminded that Elmore Harris and Charles J. Holman, prominent Baptists who opposed what the university seemed to be doing, were neither uneducated nor representatives of the lower class. Born into wealth and respectability and a Toronto graduate, Harris, for one, does not fit the unflattering description with which McMaster's opponents were tagged. Similarly, how can one account for the number of McMaster alumni who leaned toward T.T. Shields during the battles of the twenties? These were not 'sub-normal and untaught folk,' as one of Shields's bitterest critics had dubbed them. However, as noted earlier, some of those alumni who ended up on Jarvis Street's side may have been graduates of the English theology course, that less rigorous and less challenging academic program at the university.

On the other hand, a considerable number of the technically uneducated, so often scorned by their supposed betters, must have compensated for that deficiency with abundant native intelligence and common sense to judge by the majorities supporting the university in crucial votes on its educational policies. There were simply not enough university or high school graduates among the delegates to conventions to swing issues in McMaster's favour in the twenties.

Meanwhile, in spite of the difficulties that arose in the university's relationship with the denomination, and in spite of its own modest proportions and the drawing power of the University of Toronto, McMaster succeeded in attracting, and in a good many cases retaining, scholars of no mean standing. Some have just been mentioned: philosophers and theologians of the standing of George B. Foster, Joseph Gilmour, I.G. Matthews, L.H. Marshall, and James Ten Broeke. Other academics in arts and theology were equally respectable by any standards applicable to institutions of higher learning in the Dominion two generations ago: J. Bishop Tingle, W. Stewart Wallace, Henry F. Dawes, Chester W. New, Humfrey Michell, Thomas Trotter, and W.J.A. Donald.

Recently, a McMaster scientist who doubles as an administrator marvelled that Tingle, for example, would elect to teach and do research at a neophyte institution when he would have been more than welcome at established universities in Canada and the United States. What had attracted him and the others to McMaster? One can only speculate. Tingle and his colleagues were, of course, neither required nor disposed to commit to paper their reasons for favouring the place over all others. It may have been because the university, as McCrimmon said in 1920, 'stood for something' and provided a plausible alternative to the kind of higher education then being offered by its large neighbour. Nor should one leave out of account the inspiration and leadership of Alexander Charles McKay, which helped to bring to the campus those qualified academics who strengthened the faculty in the years before the first world war burst upon the scene. In turn, many of those academics, emulating their colleagues in theology, trained a small but distinguished cadre of undergraduates for promising teaching and research careers in Canada and the United States.

The degrees that McKay had earned at the University of Toronto, however, serve to recall that the institution with which McMaster, in its quest for independence and an alternative, had thrice refused to federate had from the beginning been closely associated with the venture on Bloor Street. Along with American seminaries and graduate schools, Toronto or its affiliated colleges had prepared people in arts who later assumed key positions at McMaster, notably McKay himself. Others included Walter Scott McLay, A.L. McCrimmon, A.B. Willmott, McMaster's first natural scientist, William O. Walker, a successor, and C.W. New, who obtained his first degree at Toronto.

But the association with the University of Toronto reached much further back than this. Robert Fyfe had taken time from his career to help strengthen the institution he thought best fitted to meet the professional and academic needs of Ontario and to furnish undergraduate instruction for the hopefuls trained at his Canadian Literary Institute. John Castle had fondly talked at one stage of the 'natural inspiring perpetual brotherhood' between the Toronto Baptist College and the provincial university. Although their organic confederation was not achieved in the 1880s, and in spite of Toronto's alleged godlessness, what Castle had called McMaster's 'moral affiliation' with its neighbour remained more or less a constant until McMaster moved to Hamilton. On a number of occasions this intangible relationship had produced a kind of academic reciprocity, as when, for example, University College men had come to the campus to fill in for classicists who had resigned and when H.F. Dawes had been dispatched to an understaffed physics laboratory at Toronto just after the first world war.

In any review of McMaster's early development still another factor must be weighed. It was expressed by one of Fyfe's contemporaries long before the university was contemplated. 'If we Baptists would not be left behind' he had remarked in the 1850s 'we must keep pace with the times we live in, with the progress of science and the march of intellect.' This was no mere rhetoric. From the very outset Baptist educational leaders had, almost without exception, sought to fashion curricula that would not only transmit the best of literary and religious tradition but embrace as well the latest findings in arts, theology, and the natural sciences. The William McMasters and the John Castles, like the Fyfes before them, had not wanted their institutions deprived of science, philosophy, history, political economy, and sociology, in effect, the curricular wave of the future. 'So as not to be left behind' could well have served as an unofficial motto for the university, as fitting in its own way as the authorized one: 'In Christ All Things Consist.' And to 'keep pace with the times' McMaster under Whidden's direction had laid its plans to move to a new location and launch yet another stage in its development, one as momentous as the original decision to promote an independent university in Toronto.

APPENDIX A

Toronto Baptist College articles of faith

[The following is an extract from the Trust Deed of the Toronto Baptist College setting forth the doctrines to which the faculty and the students were to subscribe.]

The Divine Inspiration of the Scriptures of the Old and New Testaments and their absolute Supremacy and sufficiency in matters of faith and practice; the existence of one living and true God sustaining the personal relation of Father, Son and Holy Spirit, the same in essence and equal in attributes; the total and universal depravity of mankind; the election and effectual calling of all God's people; the atoning efficacy of the Death of Christ; the free justification of believers in Him by His imputed Righteousness; the preservation unto eternal life of the Saints; the necessity and efficacy of the influence of the Spirit in regeneration and sanctification; the resurrection of the dead both just and unjust; the general judgment, the everlasting happiness of the righteous and the everlasting misery of the wicked; immersion in the name of the Father, the Son and the Holy Spirit; the only gospel baptism; that parties so baptized are alone entitled to communion at the Lord's Table and that a Gospel Church is a Body of baptized believers voluntarily associated together for the Service of God.

(Hon. Wm McMaster to Trustees of the Toronto Baptist College: Conveyance of the College Site in Trust, Revised and Approved. Dated 1st December 1880)

APPENDIX B

An Act to unite Toronto Baptist College and Woodstock College under the name of McMaster University

Whereas it has been represented by petition of the Toronto Baptist College and Woodstock College, two institutions of learning, carried on in connection with the denomination of Christians called Regular Baptists, that the Toronto Baptist College was incorporated by an Act passed in the forty-fourth year of the reign of Her Majesty Queen Victoria, for the training of students preparing for the ministry of the Regular Baptist denomination, with power to confer degrees in Divinity, and has, since its incorporation, been in operation in the city of Toronto; that Woodstock College was incorporated under the name of the Canadian Literary Institute in the twentieth year of the same reign; that by an Act passed in the forty-sixth year of the same reign, the name thereof was changed to Woodstock College, and that the work of education has been carried on in such institution at the town of Woodstock for the last twenty-eight years; that it would conduce to the success of the educational work of the said denomination to have the property and control of the said colleges vested in a board of governors, subject to the powers and rights of a senate as hereinafter provided, and to have the usual powers and privileges of a university conferred upon such board and senate, and whereas it is expedient to grant the prayer of the said petition;

Therefore Her Majesty, by and with the advice and consent of the Legislative Assembly of the Province of Ontario, enacts as follows:

1 / From and after the date hereinafter fixed for the coming into effect of this Act, the Toronto Baptist College and Woodstock College shall be united and form one corporation under the name of McMaster University, and shall be under the management and administration of a Board of Governors,

which, until the appointment of a chancellor as hereinafter provided, shall consist of sixteen members, who shall be elected as follows: twelve members by the Regular Baptist Missionary Society of Ontario, and four members by the Regular Baptist Missionary Convention, East, which said sixteen members shall hold office for four years, except that of those first elected by the Regular Baptist Missionary Society of Ontario, three shall retire at the expiration of one year, three at the expiration of two years, and three at the expiration of three years, from the date of their appointment; and of those elected by the Regular Baptist Missionary Convention East, one shall retire at the expiration of one year, one at the expiration of two years, and one at the expiration of three years. And upon the appointment of a chancellor, as hereinafter provided, such chancellor shall be ex-officio a member of the said board, which will then consist of seventeen members.

2 / Such appointments may be made by such society and convention before the coming into effect of this Act, and the persons so appointed, and their successors in office, are hereby constituted a body corporate and politic under the name of the McMaster University, with perpetual succession and a common seal, with power to break, alter, and change the same at pleasure, and by that name may sue and be sued, and be able and capable in law to take, purchase, and hold any personal property whatsoever; and shall also be able and capable, notwithstanding the Statutes of Mortmain, to take, purchase, and hold to them and their successors, not only all such lands, buildings, hereditaments, and possessions as may from time to time be used or occupied for the purposes of the said university, including any preparatory or academical department, and for residences of the chancellor, principals, professors, tutors, students, and officers, with gardens and lawns attached thereto, but also any other lands, buildings, hereditaments, and premises not exceeding the annual value of $10,000, such annual value to be calculated and ascertained with reference to the period of taking, purchasing, or acquiring the same; and to accept on behalf of the said university, or any department thereof, including any preparatory or academical department, any gifts, devises, or bequests of any property, real or personal, and they and their successors shall be able and capable in law to grant, demise, alien, lease, or otherwise dispose of all or any of the property, real or personal, at any time belonging to the said university, or to any department thereof, including any preparatory or academical department, and to invest the proceeds thereof upon such securities, or in such way as to the said board of governors shall seem best, and also to do all other matters and things incidental or appertaining to such body corporate; provided always that the real estate not required for use and occupation or for the residences of the chancellor, principals,

professors, tutors and students as aforesaid shall not at any time be held by
the said university for a longer period than seven years, and that any such real
estate not sold and alienated within seven years of the time when the same is
received by the said corporation shall revert to the party from whom it came,
to the corporation or to his or her heirs or devisees.

3 / The said university shall be entitled to receive and hold gifts, devises,
and bequests already made, or hereafter coming into effect, by any person or
persons, to or for the benefit of Toronto Baptist College and Woodstock
College, or either of them, as fully and effectually as if the said university was
named in such gifts, devises or bequests, instead of Toronto Baptist College
and Woodstock College, or either of them, subject, however, to all the trusts
in such gifts, devises, and bequests provided. And all persons shall have the
power, notwithstanding the Statutes of Mortmain, at any time to grant,
devise, bequeath, or convey by deed, will, or otherwise, any real or personal
property to the said university, either for its purposes generally, or for any
department thereof, or otherwise, as may be provided by such grant, devise,
bequest, or conveyance, and no gift to the said university shall be void by
reason of the grantor having reserved any interest therein, or the income
thereof, for the term of his life, or any part thereof; provided, that no gift or
devise of any real estate or of any interest therein in favour of the said
corporation, shall be valid unless made by deed or will executed by the donor
or testator, at least six months before his death. And it is hereby declared that
section 2 of the Act, passed in the forty-fourth year of Her Majesty's reign,
chapter 87, being the Act incorporating the said Toronto Baptist College,
shall be construed to have conferred the power and right upon all persons,
notwithstanding the Statutes of Mortmain, to grant, devise, bequeath, or
convey to or for the benefit of the said Toronto Baptist College, any real or
personal property in the terms in said section provided, as well as the power
to said college to receive such grants, devises, bequests and conveyances.

4 / McMaster University shall be a Christian school of learning, and the
study of the Bible, or sacred scriptures, shall form a part of the course of study
taught by the professors, tutors, or masters appointed by the board of
governors. And no person shall be eligible to the position of chancellor,
principal, professor, tutor, or master, who is not a member in good standing
of an Evangelical Christian Church; and no person shall be eligible for the
position of principal, professor, tutor, or master in the faculty of theology
who is not a member in good standing of a Regular Baptist Church, and the
said board of governors shall have the right to require such further or other
test as to religious belief, as a qualification for any such position in the faculty
of theology, as to the said board of governors may seem proper; but no

compulsory religious qualification, or examination of a denominational character shall be required from, or imposed upon any student whatever, other than in the faculty of theology.

5 / The board of governors shall have full power and authority to fix the number, residence, duties, salary, provision, and emolument of the chancellor, principals, professors, tutors, masters, officers, agents, and servants of the said university, including any preparatory or academical department, and may from time to time remove the chancellor, principals, professors, tutors, masters, and all other officers, agents, and servants of the university, and of all departments thereof, including any preparatory or academical department, and may also appoint the chancellor, principals, professors, tutors, masters, and all other officers, agents, and servants, provided that such power of appointment as to the chancellor, principals, professors, tutors, and masters shall be exercised only upon the recommendation of the senate, as hereinafter provided. And the said board shall have the control and management of the property and funds of the said university, and shall have power to adopt by-laws and regulations touching and concerning all or any of the matters aforesaid, as well as concerning the time and place of meetings of the said board and notices thereof, the officers of the said board, and their election and duties, and all other matters and things which to them may seem good, fit, and useful for the well ordering and advancement of the said university, including any preparatory or academical department, not repugnant to the provisions of this Act, or any public law in force in this Province, and the same to alter or vary from time to time in accordance with any provision for that purpose contained in such by-laws and regulations, and after the common seal of the university has been affixed thereto such by-laws and regulations shall be binding upon all parties, members thereof, and upon all others whom the same may concern.

6 / It shall be the duty of the said board of governors to keep proper records and minutes of all and every their proceedings, and to keep proper books of account of the financial affairs of the said university, including any preparatory or academical department, and to present a report of the work of the said university, accompanied by a duly audited financial statement, to each annual meeting of the said the Regular Baptist Missionary Society of Ontario, and the Regular Baptist Missionary Convention, East, respectively. Should the said society and convention unite, such report and financial statement shall be presented to such united society, and such united society shall thereafter have the right to elect the aforesaid sixteen members of the said board of governors.

7 / The board of governors shall elect one of their number to preside at

their meetings, and to affix the university seal, and to sign all its papers and instruments in writing, for or on behalf of such body corporate, as may be necessary.

8 / All real and personal property, rights, franchises, and privileges of Toronto Baptist College, and Woodstock College shall, from the coming into effect of this Act, be held and vested in the corporation hereby constituted, subject to all trusts attaching thereto respectively, and the said board of governors shall thereupon continue to exercise all the rights, powers, franchises and privileges, not inconsistent with the provisions of this Act, that prior to that time shall have been exercised or enjoyed by the said Toronto Baptist College and Woodstock College, or either of them, in as full and ample a manner as the same shall theretofore have been exercised by the said Toronto Baptist College and Woodstock College, or either of them, subject, however, to the powers and rights of the senate of the said university, as hereinafter provided; but all legal or other proceedings, prior to the coming into effect of this Act, taken by or against the Toronto Baptist College, or Woodstock College, may be continued under the same name or style of cause in which they have been instituted.

9 / Nothing in this Act contained shall be deemed to authorize the use of the lands and premises conveyed to the trustees of the Toronto Baptist College by the Honourable William McMaster, by deed bearing date the first day of December, 1880, for any other purposes than those set out in said deed, nor to otherwise alter or affect the trusts in said deed contained, otherwise than by vesting the rights and powers of the said trustees in the university hereby created.

10 / Sections 2 to 10, inclusive, and section 12 of the Act passed in the forty-eighth year of Her Majesty's reign, chapter 96, being an Act to amend the said Act incorporating the Toronto Baptist College, shall from the coming into effect of this Act be deemed to be repealed, saving all acts, matters and things lawfully done thereunder up to the time of such repeal.

11 / The senate of the said university shall be constituted as follows: a / The members of the board of governors; b / the principal for the time being of the faculty of Toronto Baptist College, and two of the professors thereof, to be elected by the said faculty annually; c / the principal for the time being of the faculty of arts, and two of the professors thereof, to be elected by the said faculty annually; d / five representatives of the graduates in theology, to be elected by the Alumni Association of such graduates in theology for a term of five years, except that of those first appointed, one shall retire at the expiration of one year, one at the expiration of two years, one at the expiration of three years and one at the expiration of four years; e / five representatives of

the graduates in arts, to be elected by the Alumni Association of such graduates in arts for a term of five years, subject to the like exception as to those first appointed; f/ two representatives of the teachers of the preparatory or academical department of Woodstock College, to be elected by such teachers annually. In addition to the senate, as above constituted, for the general purposes of the university, the following shall be members of the senate, so far as the work of the senate concerns Toronto Baptist College, with the same powers and rights as other members of the senate as to all matters pertaining to the said Toronto Baptist College; g/ eight members to be elected by the Baptist Convention of the maritime Provinces, to serve for such term or terms as the said convention may decide; h/ the president of Acadia College, and two of the professors of said college, to be elected by the faculty thereof annually; i/ two members to be elected by the Baptist Convention of Manitoba and the North-West Territories, to serve for such term or terms as the said convention may decide.

12 / The senate shall have the control of the system and course of education pursued in the said university, and of all matters pertaining to the management and discipline thereof, and of the examinations of all departments thereof; and shall have the power to confer degrees in theology now vested in the Toronto Baptist College together with the power to confer the degrees of Bachelor, Master and Doctor, in the several arts, sciences, and faculties, and any and all other degrees which may properly be conferred by a university; and shall have the right to determine the courses of study and the qualification for degrees, and the granting of the same; provided the course of study prescribed for matriculation into the said university shall in no essential sense differ or vary from that prescribed for matriculation into the University of Toronto, and in respect to any degree which the said senate has power to confer, the course of instruction and the scope of the examination for such degree shall be as thorough and comprehensive as the courses and examinations for corresponding degrees in the University of Toronto; and the senate shall make recommendations from time to time to the board of governors for the appointment of chancellor, principals, professors, tutors, teachers, and masters, and no such appointment shall be made by the board of governors except upon the recommendation of the senate. And the senate shall have the power to settle, subject to ratification by the board, the terms upon which other colleges and schools may become affiliated with the said university, but no such affiliation shall take effect unless and until the same shall have been approved by the Lieutenant-Governor in Council; provided, however, that the said university shall not have the power or right to establish, maintain, or be connected with any school or college in theology other than Toronto

Baptist College, nor the right to affiliate under any conditions with any other school or college in theology; and may from time to time make by-laws, statutes or regulations affecting any of the matters aforesaid, as well as regulating the holding of meetings of the said senate, and the conduct generally of its business, and defining the respective duties, rights, and powers of the chancellor, principals, professors, tutors, and teachers of the said university, and the same from time to time to alter or amend as may be provided by such by-laws, statutes or regulations.

13 / Save as to the chancellor of the university, who shall as aforesaid, be ex-officio a member of the board of governors, no member of any of the faculties of the said university, or of the faculties of any school or college being entitled to representation upon the said senate, and no member of the faculty of any affiliated school of college shall be eligible for election to a position on the said board of governors, or said senate, who is not then a member in good standing of some Regular Baptist church in Canada; and in case any member of said board, or any senator ceases at any time during his term of office to be a member in good standing of a Regular Baptist church in Canada, or removes from the Dominion of Canada, or in the case of a representative of the said missionary society, or any of said conventions, removing beyond the bounds of the society or convention which appointed him, or in case a representative of any of the said colleges or faculties severs his connection with the college or faculty from which he is a representative, he shall thereupon cease to be a member of said board or senate, as the case may be, and the vacancy caused thereby, or caused by the death or resignation of any member of the said board or of the said senate, shall be filled by the body which appointed such member or such senator.

14 / Five members, or such larger number as the board may fix, shall constitute a quorum of the board; and nine members, or such larger number as the senate may fix, shall constitute a quorum of the senate.

15 / All questions shall be decided by the majority of the members present at the meeting of the board or senate.

16 / The chancellor of the university shall be ex-officio a member of and the chairman of the senate. In the absence of the chancellor, or at his request, a chairman shall be chosen by the senate from among its members.

17 / The seal of the university shall be affixed to all diplomas whenever directed by the senate.

18 / The senate shall not confer any degrees in the faculty of arts until five professorships, at least, have been permanently established and adequately provided for in the faculty of arts, and five professors appointed to discharge the respective duties thereof, nor until this has been to appear to the satisfaction of the Lieutenant-Governor in Council, nor until it shall have been made

to appear to the satisfaction of the Lieutenant-Governor in Council that the sum of $700,000, at least, in property, securities, or money, is held for the purposes of the said university, including any preparatory or academic department.

19 / It shall be the duty of the board of governors to furnish from time to time, or when called upon, to the Provincial Secretary full and accurate information as to the curriculum of study in every faculty of the said university (excepting Divinity) the number of professors, lecturers or other teachers in every faculty, and the subject of instruction assigned to each of such professors, lecturers or teachers; the subjects in which examinations are held for degrees in arts or medicine, and on which such degrees are granted, and whenever called upon to do so to furnish full and accurate accounts in writing of the property of the university and the income derived therefrom in order that the same may be laid before the Provincial Legislature at any session thereof.

20 / The said university shall not have the power to confer any degrees in arts except after examination, duly had in pursuance of the by-laws and regulations of the senate respecting such degrees; but ad eundem degrees may be conferred by the said senate upon the graduates of any university approved of for that purpose by the senate, and such graduates shall have, after the granting of such degrees ad eundem, the same privileges as graduates of the university.

21 / No person shall be admitted as a candidate for any degree in medicine or surgery unless such person shall have completed the course of instruction which the senate, by by-law or regulation in that behalf, may determine, in such one or more medical schools, as shall also be mentioned in said by-law or regulation.

22 / The treasurer, or bursar of said university, shall be bound, before assuming office, to furnish security for the faithful discharge of his duties by good and sufficient sureties, to be approved of by the board of governors, to the amount of $10,000, or such larger sum as the board of governors may by by-law or regulation fix.

23 / This Act shall come into effect on the first day of November, 1887, and the first meeting of the board of governors shall be held on the eighth day of the said month of November at two o'clock in the afternoon, in McMaster Hall, Toronto, and notice thereof shall be published in the newspaper called The Canadian Baptist for two weeks prior thereto; and the first meeting of the senate shall be held at such time and place as the said board of governors may at such meeting appoint, and thereafter all meetings of the board and senate shall be held at such time and place as may be determined on by the said board and senate respectively.

Abstract of the will of Senator William McMaster

[What follows is a condensation of the last will and testament of Senator William McMaster, dated 7 April 1887. It is based almost wholly on the version that appears in Robert Hamilton, 'The Founding of McMaster University,' BD thesis (McMaster University, 1938), 74-7. For the sake of brevity some of the legal terminology in the original has been either rephrased or omitted. A number of its sections (x to xII inclusive) have been ignored altogether because they dealt with technical or irrelevant matters (for example, the provision for reimbursing the trustees for the expense of executing the will). Passages enclosed by quotation marks have been quoted verbatim from the document. For purposes of comparison a copy of the original may be consulted in the offices of the Canadian Baptist Archives.]

I / I bequeath to my Trustees all my property whether in Canada, the State of Michigan, or elsewhere: 1/ My house on Bloor Street and the grounds and outbuildings not including the adjoining lands on the rear or any additional lands which I may purchase. My wife, Susan Moulton McMaster, is to have the privilege of using all the household or personal effects until her death. 2/ The $40,000 of stock held by me in the Standard Publishing Company is to be turned over to denominational societies if such is not done before my death. The balance unpaid, being $12,000 which is already deposited, is to be paid by my trustees after my death. The dividends are to be paid as follows: one-fourth to the Society for the Relief of Superannuated Regular Baptist ministers and the widows and orphans of Regular Baptist ministers, the balance to be paid equally to foreign and home missions. The share to foreign missions is to be paid to 'The Regular Baptist Foreign Missionary Society of Ontario and Quebec,' and the share to home missions to be divided, three-fifths to 'The Regular Baptist Missionary Society of Ontario,' one-fifth to 'The Regular Baptist Missionary Convention East,' and one-fifth to 'The Regular Baptist Missionary Convention of Manitoba and the Northwest.' 3/ The rest of my real and personal property is to be sold, and after my debts are paid, $340,000 is to be bequeathed to my nephew and business associate, James Short McMaster, now of London, England, in the manner later pointed out, and the balance of the proceeds is to be held 'as an endowment for a Christian school of learning to be known as McMaster University, a charter for which and to unite Toronto Baptist College and Woodstock College under the said name has already been applied for.' Until the transfer of the endowment to McMaster University, the balance of the proceeds of my general estate shall from time to time be invested in such securities as shall seem fit to my trustees 'subject to the supervision of a committee on investments to be appointed by the Board of Governors of the said university.' Out of the income of such investments shall be paid the following sums: a/ to my wife $5,000 in gold per year during her life; b/ to my sister, Ann, $500 per year during her life; c/ to Malcolm MacVicar, professor in Toronto Baptist College, $400 per year during his life; d/ to The Regular Baptist Missionary Society of Ontario $2,000 per annum towards payment of the salary and expenses of a general home missionary superintendent so long as such is employed.

The balance is to be paid to the Board of Governors of McMaster University to be employed as they see fit, except that the Board of Governors shall assure Toronto Baptist College, as the theology faculty of the university, of at least $14,500 per annum. After the decease or refusal of moneys by my wife, sister, or Malcolm MacVicar, such sums are to go to the Board of Governors of McMaster University, and also the said sum of $2,000 is to go to the Board of Governors of the University at any time of the non-employment of a general home missionary superintendent.

II / As to the promissory note from my nephew, J.S. McMaster, for $340,000, falling due in six months, no interest shall be charged him, for the time up to my death. (This $340,000 is the bequest made to J.S. McMaster.)

III / If the conditions are not fulfilled by those institutions to whom the moneys are left, the moneys are to pass to my nephew, J.S. McMaster.

IV / I hereby appoint the said Malcolm MacVicar, Humphry Ewing Buchan of Toronto, physician, Charles J. Holman of Toronto, barrister at law, and Daniel Edmund Thomson of Toronto, barrister at law, as my trustees.

V / I desire that whenever a legal solicitor or council shall be necessary in order to carry out the trusts hereby declared 'in connection with the administration of my estate, the said Daniel Edmund Thomson shall so long as he lives and continues the practice of his profession be retained to act professionally in all such matters.'

VI / I will that my trustees shall have power from time to time to change or vary any investments 'in such manner as shall seem best for the purposes of the trust and may, in their discretion, retain any investment or investments made by me in my life time whenever and so long as they deem it advisable in the interest of the trust hereby created so to do, subject, however, in these respects to the supervision of such committee on investments as aforesaid.'

VII / A receipt shall be 'a sufficient discharge to my said trustees' for any payments.

VIII / I authorize my trustees to sell my lands and properties as they see best, and 'recognizing the uncertainty in view of its location of what may be the best time to dispose of [the] Rathnally land, I authorize my trustees to retain the same so long as shall seem to them wise or expedient, not exceeding the term of twenty years from my death, with power to lease or otherwise use or deal with the said house and lands in whole or in part from time to time as they shall see fit, the rents and profits derived therefrom ... to go into my general estate and to be held subject to the trusts herein declared.'

IX / 'I direct that my trustees may employ a proper person or persons' to conduct such sales as are necessary in regard to my estate.

. . .

XIII / 'Desiring not only that the control of the income of the endowment herein bequeathed for McMaster University shall be entirely in the hands of the Board of Governors appointed by the denomination but that ... the principal of such endowment shall be vested directly in the corporation of the said University and under the control of the denomination through the said Board of Governors, I direct that as soon as the assets of my estate shall all have been realized and the annuities to my wife, my sister, and the said Malcolm MacVicar shall have fallen in by reason of their death or refusal to act as aforesaid,' that the 'said fund shall belong entirely to the said university, subject only to a charge thereon of the said sum of two thousand dollars per annum in favour of the Regular Baptist Missionary Society of Ontario ... [The] principal ... together with all securities ... shall be transferred to the said corporation to be held as an endowment ....And I particularly request that the said Board of Governors shall at all times take special care and precaution both by proper provisions in their by-laws and by careful attention thereto to have the oversight of such investments committed to trustworthy, vigilant men of business training and experience, and to have all reasonable safeguards provided with a view to keeping intact such endowment. And I solemnly charge them and the Senate of the said University to maintain the said institution with true and faithful regard to the work of affording the best possible facilities for a thoroughly practical Christian course of education.'

Notes

BGM   Minutes of the Board of Governors, McMaster University
BYB   *Baptist Year Book*
CB   *Canadian Baptist*
CC   Chancellor's Correspondence, Canadian Baptist Archives, McMaster University
CLI   Canadian Literary Institute, Woodstock, Ontario
GC   General Correspondence, Canadian Baptist Archives, McMaster University
MM   *McMaster University Monthly*
RBRT   Rare Book Room, University of Toronto
SM   Minutes of the McMaster University Senate
TBC   Toronto Baptist College

Unless otherwise indicated, unpublished material is held in the Canadian Baptist Archives at McMaster Divinity College, Hamilton, Ontario.

CHAPTER 1: THE FORERUNNERS

1 This information and the following material on John Gilmour were culled from his unpublished manuscripts, 'Note and Lecture Book' and 'Diary, 1853-1864.'
2 J.I. Cooper, 'The Canadian Education and Home Mission Society,' *Canadian Historical Review*, 26 (1945), 47

3 J.I. Cooper, 'An old time rival of McGill,' *McGill News*, 27 (Autumn 1945), 8

4 Quoted in D.G. Creighton, *The Empire of the St Lawrence, 1760-1850,* 2d ed. (Toronto, 1956), 314

5 *Fifth Annual Report of the Canada Baptist College* (Montreal, 1843), 6-7

6 Cooper, 'An old time rival of McGill,' 8

7 GC, 1957-9, G.P. Gilmour to W.K., 27 Nov. 1957. On this point see *Minutes, 25th Anniversary of the Grand River Baptist Association, Beamsville, C.W.,* 21-2 June 1844 (St Catharines, 1844).

8 Walter Pitman, 'The Baptists and public affairs in the Province of Canada, 1840-1867,' unpublished M.A. thesis (University of Toronto, 1956), chap. 1

9 A.J. MacLachlan, 'Canadian Baptists and public questions before 1850,' unpublished B.D. thesis (McMaster University, 1937), 71

10 Cooper, 'An old time rival of McGill,' 9. See also Canada Baptist College File, W.K. Anderson to P.F. (?) Hunter, 4 July 1898.

11 CC, 1906, J.M. Merriman to A.C. McKay, 25 June 1906. See also 'Diary of J.M. Merriman' in the Canadian Baptist Archives.

12 CC, 1904, A.A. Ayer to O.C.S. Wallace, 29 April 1904

13 A.L. McCrimmon, *The Educational Policy of the Baptists of Ontario and Quebec* (Toronto, 1920), 5. See also MacLachlan, 'Canadian Baptists and public questions,' 42.

14 F.T. Rosser, 'Robert Alexander Fyfe,' *Dictionary of Canadian Biography*, 10, 1871-1880 (Toronto and Quebec, 1972), 295-6

15 J.E. Wells, *Life and Labors of the Rev. R.A. Fyfe* (Toronto, 1885), 182-3

16 W. Sherwood Fox, ed., *Letters of William Davies, Toronto, 1854-1861,* with a preface by Harold A. Innis (Toronto, 1945), 112

17 G.S. French, 'The Evangelical Creed in Canada,' in W.L. Morton, ed., *The Shield of Achilles: Aspects of Canada in the Victorian Age* (Toronto, 1968), 29-30

18 Wells, *Fyfe,* 71n

19 Montreal *Register*, 9 April 1846, quoted in Pitman, 'The Baptists and public affairs,' 102

20 CLI, Faculty Minutes, 21 Oct. 1879

21 Pitman, 'The Baptists and public affairs,' 121

22 *Scobie and Balfour's Canadian Almanac and Repository of Useful Knowledge* (Toronto, 1850), 42-3

23 *Christian Messenger*, 13 Dec. 1855, quoted in Wells, *Fyfe,* 289-90

24 Fox, *Letters of William Davies,* 51

25 William Kingston, *Western Wanderings, or, A Pleasure Tour in the Canadas,* 2 (London, 1856), 3-5

26 Wells, *Fyfe,* 305-6

27 CLI, Administration, 12-3

28 *Minutes of the Grand River Association (North), 25 and 26 June* 1858, 7 (emphasis added)
29 Charles Vining, 'History of Woodstock College,' *Woodstock College Memorial Book* (Toronto, 1951), 27
30 See J.S. Moir, *Church and State in Canada West: Three Studies in the Relations of Denominationalism and Nationalism,* 1841-1867 (Toronto, 1959), chap. 5.
31 Vining, 'Woodstock College,' 29
32 Wallace P. Cohoe, 'The struggle for a sheepskin,' unpublished ms., 5
33 CLI, Faculty Minutes, [?] Oct., 1879
34 Woodstock College File, C. Vining Corr., G.P. Gilmour to Vining, 29 March 1951
35 Wells, *Fyfe,* 357-8
36 Fox, *Letters of William Davies,* 63, 85

CHAPTER 2: WILLIAM MCMASTER AND THE TORONTO BAPTIST COLLEGE

1 A.H. Newman, 'What I know about Senator McMaster's plans and purposes in the founding of Toronto Baptist College and McMaster University,' unpublished ms., 2-3
2 TBC, Letters, Wm McMaster to Mrs R.S. Fyfe, 12 May 1881
3 D.C. Masters, *The Rise of Toronto,* 1850-1890 (Toronto, 1947), Chap. 4; and 'William McMaster,' *Canadian Banker,* 49 (July, 1942)
4 See T.W. Acheson, 'The nature and structure of York commerce in the 1820s,' *Canadian Historical Review,* 50 (1969), 406-28.
5 G.P. Gilmour Correspondence, Personal, W.D. McMaster to G.P. Gilmour, 16 June 1962
6 Edith M. Firth, ed., *The Town of York,* 1815-1834: *A Further Collection of Documents on Early Toronto* (Toronto, Champlain Society, 1966), 245n
7 H.A. Innis, Preface, in W. Sherwood Fox, ed., *Letters of William Davies, Toronto,* 1854-1861 (Toronto, 1945), vii. See also Victor Ross, *A History of the Canadian Bank of Commerce,* 2 (Toronto, 1922), Chaps. 1 and 2
8 Innis, 'Preface,' *Letters of William Davies,* vii
9 J.M.S. Careless, *Brown of the Globe,* 2, *Statesman of Confederation,* 1860-1880 (Toronto, 1963), 9
10 F.H. Underhill, *The Liberal Tradition in Canada* (Toronto, 1960), 15
11 Wallace P. Cohoe, 'The struggle for a sheepskin,' unpublished ms., 33
12 Careless, *Brown of the Globe,* 2, 261
13 C.B. Sissons, ed., *My Dearest Sophie: Letters from Egerton Ryerson to His Daughter* (Toronto, 1955), 318
14 Physics Department Box, H.F. Dawes File, Gilmour to H.F. Dawes, 13 March

1942. See also Reuben Butchart, *The Disciples of Christ in Canada since 1830* (Toronto, 1949), 147; and *McMaster University, 1890-1940* (Hamilton, 1940), 7

15 For a somewhat different view see Biographical Files, William McMaster, G.P. Gilmour to W.H. Cranston, 23 March 1962.

16 Fox, *Letters of William Davies*, 135. For another description of the edifice see John Ross Robertson, *Sketches in City Churches* (Toronto, 1886), 25-31.

17 MM, 1 (1891-2), 146-8

18 *The Tyro*, March, 1879, quoted in the *Christian Helper*, 15 June 1879, 14

19 CB, 17 July 1879, 1. See also Paul Rutherford, 'Tomorrow's metropolis: The urban reform movement in Canada, 1880-1920,' *Historical Papers, Canadian Historical Association, 1971* (Ottawa, 1972), 203-24

20 J.M.S. Careless, 'Somewhat narrower horizons,' ibid., 1968 (Ottawa, 1969), 8-9

21 CB, 10 July 1879, 1

22 *Christian Helper*, 15 Aug. 1879, 65

23 CB, 24 July 1879, 4

24 *Christian Helper*, 15 Aug. 1879, 65-7

25 Charles Vining, 'History of Woodstock College,' *Woodstock College Memorial Book* (Toronto, 1951), 37

26 CLI, Executive Committee Minutes, 4 Dec. 1879

27 *Christian Helper*, 15 Aug. 1879, 71

28 Toronto *Globe*, 2 Aug. 1879

29 CB, 7 Aug. 1879, 5

30 Newman, 'What I know about Senator McMaster's plans,' 1-2. See also *Minutes, 24th Annual Meeting of the Grand River Association, June, 1880* (Toronto, 1880), 7

31 Newman, 'What I know about Senator McMaster's Plans,' 2-3

32 MM, 2 (1892-3), 156-7

33 CC, 1904-5, E.O. White to O.C.S. Wallace, 16 March 1905 (emphasis in original). See also *Reminiscences of Joshua Denovan* (Toronto; 1901), 40, 102

34 Newman, 'What I know about Senator McMaster's plans,' 4. See appendix A.

35 TBC Letters, John Harris to H.E. Buchan, 18 June 1881

36 See Ernest R. Sandeen, *The Roots of Fundamentalism: British and American Millenarianism, 1800-1930* (Chicago, 1970), 5, 132 ff; and R.L. Whan, 'Premillenialism in Canadian Baptist history,' unpublished B.D. thesis (McMaster University, 1945).

37 Woodstock College File, C. Vining Corr., Gilmour to Vining, 29 March 1951

38 TBC Letters, McMaster to D.E. Thomson, 15 Dec. 1880

39 Dale C. Thomson, *Alexander Mackenzie: Clear Grit* (Toronto, 1960), 9, 10. See also SM, 1, 6 June 1892, 204-5.

40 TBC, Board Minutes, 22 Aug. 1883

41 BYB, 1885, 99
42 Ibid., 100
43 MM, 1 (1890-1), 151-9
44 Ibid., 154-5
45 See TBC, Executive Committee Minutes, 8-13
46 *Minutes, Grand River Association,* 1880, 7, 9
47 BYB, 1882, 86-7
48 *TBC Calendar,* 1881-2, 6
49 TBC, Board Minutes, 12 April 1881, 6
50 Ibid., Executive Committee Report, 28 April 1885 (emphasis added)
51 *Act to Amend the Act Incorporating the Toronto Baptist College, 2nd Session, 5th Legislature,* 48 Victoria 1885
52 TBC, Third Annual Report of the President, 29 April 1884
53 CB, 5 June 1884, 4
54 BYB, 1883, 75
55 John Dozois, 'Dr T.T. Shields (1873-1955): In the stream of fundamentalism,' unpublished B.D. thesis (McMaster University, 1963), 33-6
56 Norman F. Furniss, *The Fundamentalist Controversy,* 1918-1931 (New Haven, 1954), 10-11
57 TBC, Third Annual Report, 1884
58 CC, 1904, A.M. Denovan to Wallace, 12 May 1904
59 RBRT, Loudon Papers, Loudon ms., 1884 [?]. See also W. Stewart Wallace, *A History of the University of Toronto,* 1827-1927 (Toronto, 1927), chap. 5.
60 Biographical Files, Malcolm MacVicar (clipping from CB)
61 *TBC Calendars,* 1882 through 1886; F.W. Waters, 'A century of philosophy at McMaster University,' unpublished ms. (1970), 14-16
62 CB, 5 June 1884, 4
63 Ibid.
64 TBC, Board Minutes, 23 Jan. 1885, 49-51
65 Ibid., *Fourth Annual Report of the President,* 28 April 1885, 6
66 Ibid., Board Minutes, 28 July 1885, 56-7
67 See CB, 2 July 1885, 4.
68 C.B. Sissons, *Church and State in Canadian Education: An Historical Study* (Toronto, 1959), 232, 242, 315, 321; Katherine C. McNaughton, *The Development of the Theory and Practice of Education in New Brunswick, 1784-1900: A Study in Historical Background* (Fredericton, 1947), 197-200
69 George Herbert Clarke, 'Chancellor Theodore Harding Rand,' CB, 1 Oct. 1944, 1, 5
70 R.S. Longley, *Acadia University, 1838-1938* (Wolfville, 1939), 91
71 A.C. Chute and W.B. Boggs, *The Religious Life of Acadia* (Wolfville, 1933), 144

72 R.W. Sawtell, *History of First Woodstock Baptist Church* (Woodstock, 1892), quoted in Vining, 'Woodstock College,' 46

73 Woodstock College File, T.H. Rand to Board of Trustees, 12 May 1886. See C.B. Sissons, *A History of Victoria University* (Toronto, 1952), 180-1.

74 TBC, Board Minutes, 20 May 1886, 68

75 CC, 1904, Denovan to Wallace, 12 May 1904

76 CB, 21 July 1887. These figures seem to be at variance with those given in Robert Hamilton, 'The founding of McMaster University,' unpublished BD thesis (McMaster University, 1938), 29.

CHAPTER 3: THE FOUNDING OF THE UNIVERSITY

1 See CB, 18 Nov. 1886

2 R.W. Sawtell, *History of First Woodstock Baptist Church* (Woodstock, 1892), 35n

3 Wallace P. Cohoe, 'The struggle for a sheepskin,' unpublished ms., 34

4 TBC, Board Minutes, 23 Dec. 1886, 69-70, 71

5 Robert Hamilton, 'The founding of McMaster University,' unpublished BD thesis (McMaster University, 1938), 26-7

6 BGM, 4, 1945, G.P. Gilmour, 'Proposed Charter Revision,' 3. See CB, 11 Nov. 1886 and 26 May 1887 for reports of Methodist and Presbyterian dissatisfaction.

7 RBRT, Edward Blake Corr., Misc., Box 112, 56-91, to Oliver Mowat, 23 Dec. 1890

8 CB, 28 April 1887

9 Hamilton, 'The founding of McMaster University,' 35 ff

10 Ibid., Appendix B, 75

11 Board of Governors Correspondence, 1957, Gilmour to C.P. Fell, 13 May 1960

12 Cohoe, 'The struggle for a sheepskin,' 33

13 CC, 1906-7, Susan Moulton McMaster to A.C. McKay, 29 Dec. 1907 [?]

14 CB, 6 Oct. 1887

15 MM, 39 (1930), 168-9

16 T.H. Rand to H.E. Buchan, 22 Sept. 1887

17 CC, 1904, A.M. Denovan to O.C.S. Wallace, 19 May 1904

18 Ibid., 1902-3, Fred. Hamilton to Wallace, 24 Dec. 1902. See also MM, 2 (1892-3), 40.

19 J.E. Wells, 'Canadian Culture,' *Canadian Monthly*, 8, no. 6 (Dec. 1875), 461. See Millar MacLure, 'Literary Scholarship,' in C.F. Klinck, ed., *Literary History of Canada: Canadian Literature in English* (Toronto, 1966) 529-30

20 CB, 24 Nov. 1887, 1

21 G.M. Trevelyan, *A Layman's Love of Letters* (London, 1954), 7

22 RBRT, Blake Corr., Misc., Box 112, 56-91, from Daniel Wilson, 27 October 1882
23 CB, 2 July 1885, 4
24 Ibid., 4 Nov. 1887, 1
25 MM, 1 (1891-2), 101
26 CB, 5 April 1888
27 Buchan to John Castle, 19 Sept. 1887 (emphasis in original)
28 CC, 1916-17, D.E. Thomson to A.L. McCrimmon, 24 Jan. 1917
29 CB, 7 July 1887, 4 (emphasis in original)
30 Ibid., 15 Dec. 1887, 19 Jan. 1888, 4
31 Ibid., 19 Jan. 1888, 4-5
32 BGM, 1, 26 April 1888, 31
33 C.S. Clark, *Of Toronto the Good: The Queen City of Canada As It is* (Montreal, 1898), 2
34 C.C. Taylor, *Toronto Called Back from 1892 to 1847: Its Wonderful Growth and Progress* (Toronto, 1892), 148-9, 250. See also CB, 1 Jan. 1880, 4.
35 CC, 1904, Denovan to Wallace, 17 May 1904
36 CB, 26 Oct., 15 Dec., and 22 Dec. 1887
37 Ibid., 5 April 1888
38 Woodstock College Alumni Minutes, 29 May 1888. See also Woodstock *Sentinel-Review*, 17 Oct. 1921.
39 TBC, Board Minutes, 28 April 1887, 72-5; Executive Committee Minutes, 28 Oct. 1887, 46
40 BGM, 1, 1
41 SM, 1, 30 March 1888
42 Ibid., 21-2, 5 July 1888, 35-41
43 Ibid., 27 Nov. 1889, 110-1
44 This point was stressed in print by O.C.S. Wallace, the university's third chancellor, in 'History of McMaster University, Toronto,' *Canada: An Encyclopaedia of the Country*, 4 (Toronto, 1898), 232
45 BGM, 1, 22 March 1889, 76
46 SM, 1, 28 June 1889, 26 June 1890, 118, 139
47 RBRT, Blake Corr., Misc., Box 112, 56-91, Statement to minister of education, 15 Feb. 1890
48 See *McMaster University Examination Papers*, 1891-1895 (Toronto, n.d.).
49 See Claude T. Bissell, ed., *University College: A Portrait, 1853-1953* (Toronto, 1953), 76-83.
50 SM, 1, 19 Dec. 1895, 297-8; Faculty Minutes, 1892-1908, 96
51 F.W. Waters, 'A Century of Philosophy at McMaster University,' unpublished ms. (1970), 20
52 Faculty Minutes, 1892-1908, 3; SM, 1, 2 May 1893, 215

53 W.P. Cohoe (quoting from his McMaster commencement address, 1944) to R.P. Graham, 24 Oct. 1946
54 SM, 1, 13 May 1895, 266
55 Cohoe, 'The struggle for a sheepskin,' 59-60
56 MacLure, 'Literary Scholarship,' 533
57 O.C.S. Wallace, 'A hint for the very busy'; and Norah Story, *Oxford Companion to Canadian History and Literature* (Oxford, 1967), 24
58 A.L. McCrimmon, 'Malcolm MacVicar,' MM, 14 (1904), 194
59 Ibid.
60 BYB, 1892-3, 119
61 E.P. Wells, 'McMaster University,' *Canadian Magazine,* 3, no. 4 (Aug. 1894)
62 SM, 1, 30 Jan. 1894, 235
63 BYB, 1894-5, 128
64 See Minutes of the Woodstock College Monthly, 2-17, and Minutes of the McMaster University Publishing Committee, 20.
65 Toronto *World,* 22 Feb. 1892

CHAPTER 4: IN PURSUIT OF GOALS

1 GC, case 9, letter to O.C.S. Wallace, 23 Oct. 1899; Woodstock College File, C. Vining to G.P. Gilmour, 28 May 1951
2 CC, 1926, O-Q, Personal S-Z, Wallace to H.P. Whidden, 12 Nov. 1923
3 Ibid., 1916-17, D.E. Thomson to A.L. McCrimmon, 13 Jan. 1917
4 C.J. Cameron, *The Life-Story of Rev. O.C.S. Wallace* (Toronto, n.d.), 6-7
5 GC, case 4, R. Adams to Wallace, [?] 1898
6 Wallace P. Cohoe, 'The struggle for a sheepskin,' unpublished ms., 49-50
7 GC, case 4, 1897-8, Jane Jones to Wallace, [?] 1897
8 MM, 5 (1895), 100-5
9 GC, case 1, 1895-6, T. Proctor Hall to Wallace, 17 Dec. 1895
10 See CB, 8 July 1897
11 GC, case 4, 1897-8, Fred. Eby to Wallace, 9 Sept. 1897
12 Ibid., 15 Oct. 1897
13 BYB, 1894-5, 130
14 E.M. Saunders, 'Theodore Harding Rand,' MM, 2 (1892), 8
15 GC, 1901, 13 Dec. 1901
16 *McMaster University Calendar,* 1894-5 (Toronto, 1894), 21-6
17 GC, case 9, 23 May 1899, 9 Feb. 1900
18 Ibid., case 2, 13 April 1896
19 CC, 1908, 12 June 1908
20 Ibid., A.M. Overholt to A.C. McKay, 12 March 1908. See also Walter S.W.

McLay, *Concerning McMaster University for Parents, Teachers and Students* (extracts from a paper read at the First Alumni Conference at McMaster University, 20 Dec. 1901).

21 CC, 1906-7, J.A. Hilts to McKay, 6 July 1907

22 Ibid., 1901, W.W. Charters to Wallace, 23 Dec. 1901

23 GC, case 9, 1899. The writer was probably the Rev. W.L. Laflamme of the Cocanada Mission in India.

24 CB, 21 April 1904, 9. See also *Hamilton Spectator*, 21 March 1907

25 CC, 1904-5, Laflamme to Wallace, 9 Feb. 1905

26 MM, I (1891), 85-6

27 GC, case 9, S. Sheldon to Wallace, 28 Oct. 1899

28 Ibid., Fred. L. Fowkes to Wallace, 6 Feb. 1900

29 CC, 1906-7, A.S. Cross to C.J. Cameron, 11 Dec. 1906

30 GC, case 2, 1 May 1896

31 Ibid., case 9, 14 Jan. 1900

32 Ibid., W. Bunt to Wallace, [?]

33 CC, 1908, E.E. Wood to McKay, 20 March 1908

34 C.B. Schutt, *Rev. C.J. Cameron: A Biography* (Toronto, 1935), 6

35 CC, 1913-15, S.S. Bates' Annual Report to the Senate, 1914

36 Ibid., 1906-7, J.C. Cornwell to McKay, 25 May 1907

37 GC, case 9, A.J. Pineo to Wallace, 19 Aug. 1899, Oct. 1899

38 CC, 1906-7, C.J. Holman to McKay, 17 May 1907

39 Ibid., D.B. Harkness to W.J. Scott, 8 April 1907

40 See K. Imayoshi, 'History of Okanagan Baptist College, 1907-1915' (1953), and W.E. Ellis, 'Organizational and educational policy of Baptists in Western Canada, 1873-1939' (1962), unpublished B.D. theses (McMaster University).

41 Senate Letterbook, No. 12, 22 Aug. 1906, 78

42 CC, 1904, A.M. Denovan to Wallace, 12 May 1904

43 F. Tracy, 'A statement on McMaster University,' 1-4. See CC, 1904, 11 Aug. 1906.

44 Cohoe to R.P. Graham, 24 Oct. 1946

45 CC, 1911-12, C.E. Burke to A.L. McCrimmon, 13 Sept. 1911

46 RBRT, Loudon Papers, Report on Conditions and Efficiency, 10 Feb. 1905

47 CC, 1904-5, Thos Trotter to Wallace, 25 Jan. 1905

48 McLay Corr., 1923-5, An Address, 1925

49 CC, 1904-5, Cohoe to Wallace, 22 March 1905

50 BYB, 1905, 199

51 R.S. Longley, *Acadia University* 1838-1938 (Wolfville, 1939), 109

52 CC, 1906, Trotter to McKay, 7 Feb. 1906

53 Ibid., A.C. Newcombe to McKay, 12 July 1906. See also Senate Letterbook, No. 12, 19 Sept. 1906, 107.

54 CC, 1907-8, Edmund Burke to McKay, 3 Oct. 1907

55 Annual Report, Physics Department, 1942-3
56 BYB, 1908, 132
57 Robert M. Stamp, 'Technical education, the national policy, and federal-provincial relations in Canadian education, 1899-1912,' *Canadian Historical Review*, 52 (1971), 405
58 CC, 1907-8, F.H. Jeffery to McKay, 13 June 1908
59 Wallace P. Cohoe, 'The young professor,' unpublished ms., 59
60 CC, 1906-7, W.S. McLay to McKay, 25 April 1907
61 R.P. Graham and L.H. Cragg, 'Department of Chemistry at McMaster University,' *Canadian Chemistry and Process Industries* (Sept. 1947), 1-2
62 Tingle Corr., J.B. Tingle to W.A. Noyes, 11 Feb. 1908
63 CC, 1912-13, McLay to S.M. Byrd, 1912 [?]
64 Ibid., 1909, J.L. Hogg to McKay, 4 Jan. 1909
65 SM, 1, 4 May 1892, 201; 25 June 1892, 209
66 See G.W. Spragge, 'The Trinity Medical College,' *Ontario History*, 58 (1966), 63-95.
67 CC, 1907-8, O.C. Withrow to McKay, 25 Dec. 1907
68 Ibid., Wm Findlay to McKay, 1 Jan. 1908
69 Ibid., J. Macintosh to McKay, 27 Dec. 1907

CHAPTER 5: STRIFE

1 SM, 2, 2 June 1905, 492; MM, 4 (1894), 229
2 CC, 1904-5, J.E. Hawkins to O.C.S. Wallace, 6 April 1905; ibid., 1904, Malcolm MacVicar to Wallace, n.d. (emphasis added)
3 Ibid., 1904, Elmore Harris to Wallace, 3 May 1904
4 MM, 14 (1904), 24
5 See, for example, *Western Baptist*, Sept. 1901, 4-5.
6 MM, 21 (1912), 237
7 Ernest R. Sandeen, *The Roots of Fundamentalism: British and American Millenarianism*, 1800-1930 (Chicago, 1970), 196-7, 201-2
8 CC, 1915-16, D.E. Thomson to C.J. Holman, 2 Nov. 1915
9 Ibid., 1906, Harris to A.C. McKay, n.d.
10 Ibid., 1906-7, Harris to McKay, 16 July 1907
11 Ibid., 1904-5, A.H. Newman to Wallace, 12 Jan. 1905, 31 Aug. 1904
12 'The University of Chicago: A menace to church and society' was the title Harris gave to his introduction to a review by E.J. Stobo in 1910 of a recently published Chicago work entitled *Biblical Ideas of Atonement*. The review was printed in pamphlet form in Toronto.

13 GC, case 3, 1897, H.P. Whidden to Wallace, 21 Jan. 1897

14 Alan Wilson, *John Northway: A Blue Serge Canadian* (Toronto, 1965), 198

15 C.H. Arnold, *Near the Edge of Battle: A Short History of the Divinity School and the 'Chicago School of Theology,'* 1866-1966 (University of Chicago, 1966), 26-7

16 John Dozois, 'Dr T.T. Shields (1873-1955): In the Stream of Fundamentalism,' unpublished BD thesis (McMaster University, 1963), 13-15

17 *Western Baptist*, March 1901, 2, 4; May 1901, 4; Oct. 1901, 1

18 Richard Allen, *The Social Passion: Religion and Social Reform in Canada, 1914-28* (Toronto, 1971), 154

19 McLay Corr., T.T. Shields to McLay, 14 Nov. 1917

20 MM, 8 (1898), 56-64

21 GC, case 1, 1895-6, A.T. French to Wallace, 15 Oct. 1895

22 *Proceedings, 20th Annual Meeting, Norfolk Association of Baptist Churches, June 11-13, 1907* (Delhi, 1907), 6

23 CC, 1906-7, A.E. Culver to McKay, 29 June 1907

24 MM, 5 (1895), 223-4

25 GC, 1901, I.G. Matthews to Wallace, 14 Oct. 1901

26 Ibid., 1910-11, George Cross to McKay, 27 Oct. 1910

27 Ibid., 1901, H.E. Stillwell to Wallace, 25 Nov. 1901. See also T. McC. Dadson, 'Professor George Cross,' MM, 19 (1909), 3-5.

28 L.H. Marshall File, W.A. Cameron to Whidden, 27 Dec. 1934

29 A.C. Chute and W.B. Boggs, *The Religious Life of Acadia* (Wolfville, 1933), 144

30 CC, 1906-7, Whidden to McKay, 29 Oct. 1906

31 Ibid., 1904, A.A. Ayer to Wallace, 18 April 1904

32 GC, case 5, 1898, Cross to Wallace, 7 April 1898

33 CC, 1910, R.W. Smith to McKay, 18 July 1910

34 Ibid., 1906-7, D. Spencer to McKay, 3 July 1907

35 Ibid., 1909, J.L. Gilmour to C.S. Pedley, 1 May 1909

36 SM, 2, 12 May 1908, 90; 13 May 1908, 122

37 CC, 1909, Harris to McKay, 29 March 1909

38 Ibid., Cross to McKay, 5 May 1909

39 SM, 2, 14 May 1907

40 CC, 1909, J.G. Brown to McKay, 1 June 1909

41 *Minutes, 74th Annual Meeting, Ottawa Baptist Association, 1909* (Ottawa, 1909), 4-6

42 CC, 1909, A.W. Smith to McKay, 20 May 1909

43 *Proceedings, Elgin Association; Minutes, 50th Annual Meeting, May, 1909* (Aylmer, 1909), 7

44 *Thirteenth Annual Report, Oxford-Brant Association, June, 1909* (Brantford, 1909), 4-5

45 CC, 1907-8, F.S. Weston to McKay, 5 Dec. 1907

46 BGM, 1, 11 May 1909, 335-6

47 CC, 1908, A.B. Cohoe to McKay, 4 June 1908

48 Ibid., Cross to McKay, 17 May, 21 June 1908

49 *McMaster University Calendar*, 1908-1909 (Toronto, 1908), 76-7

50 CC, 1904-5, Matthews to Wallace, 9 Feb. 1905

51 Ibid., D.C. Macintosh to Wallace, 30 March 1905

52 Ibid., 1908-9, A.J. Bengough to McKay, 29 Jan. 1909

53 Ibid.

54 GC, 1955-6, H, G.P. Gilmour to W.H. Harmon, 1 June 1956

55 Robert Hamilton, 'The founding of McMaster University,' unpublished BD thesis (McMaster University, 1938), Appendix B, 76-7

56 BYB, 1885, 101; SM, 2, 11 May 1909, 146-7

57 TBC, Third Annual Report, 29 April 1884

58 Elmore Harris, *Concerning the Attacks of Prof. Matthews on the Bible* (Toronto, 1910), 3

59 BGM, 1, 11 May 1909, 327

60 John Linton, *The McMaster Controversy: A Message for Ontario and Quebec Baptists* (Toronto, 1926), 12

61 CC, 1909, B.W. Merrill to McKay, 26 May 1909

62 Ibid., J.G. Brown to McKay, 1 June 1909

63 Ibid., Cross to McKay, 17 May 1909

64 SM, 2, 29 May 1909, 154-7 (emphasis added)

65 I.C. Morgan, 'Harris Lachlan MacNeill: A biographical sketch,' in J.R.C. Perkin, ed., *Summer in His Soul: Essays in Honour of Harris L. MacNeill, Theological Bulletin* (May 1969), 5-6

66 CC, 1909, T.H. Marshall to McKay, 3 June 1909

67 Ibid., A. Stevenson to McKay, 6 June 1909. See Stevenson's 'The New Protestantism' in the *Varsity* (30 Jan. 1886), 130, a critique of the Canadian clergy's supposed 'bondage in a theological Egypt.'

68 Woodstock *Daily Express*, 13 June 1910

69 Toronto *World*, 15 June 1910; C.B. Sissons, *A History of Victoria University* (Toronto, 1952), 233-9

70 Harris, *The Attacks of Prof. Matthews*, 14-6

71 I.G. Matthews, *An Address before the Convention of the Regular Baptists of Ontario and Quebec, 1910* (Toronto, n.d.), 4

72 BYB, 1909, 134

73 Matthews, *An Address*, 4

74 SM, 2, 29 May 1909, 154-7

75 CC, 1909, Matthews to McKay, 30 May 1909

76 Ibid., Brown to McKay, 1 June 1909
77 SM, 2, 21 Oct. 1909, 165
78 CC, 1909-10, Trotter to McKay, 30 Oct. 1909
79 SM, 2, 2 Dec. 1909, 172-5
80 CC, 1909-10, Trotter to McKay, 2 Sept., 26 Nov. 1909
81 BYB, 1910, 136
82 CC, 1909-10, B.W. Merrill to McKay, 29 Nov. 1909
83 Ibid., 1910, Gilmour to McKay, 3 June 1910
84 Ibid., James Ryrie to McKay, 29 Aug. 1910
85 Ibid., R.W. Smith to McKay, 18 July 1910; James Grant to McKay, 1 Dec. 1909
86 BYB, 1910, 50
87 T.T. Shields, *The Plot that Failed* (Toronto, 1937), 39
88 Dozois, 'Shields,' 63-4
89 CC, 1911-12, W.G. Wallace to McKay, 25 Oct. 1910
90 Ibid., Nathaniel Burwash to McKay, 26 Oct. 1910; Sissons, *Victoria University*, 238-9
91 CC, 1911-12, C.J. Holman, quoting Harris, to A.L. McCrimmon, 7 March 1912
92 Ibid., 1910-11, A.P. McDiarmid to McKay, 2 Nov. 1910
93 Ibid., Cross to McKay, 27 Oct. 1910
94 Ibid., W.C. Weir to McKay, 16 Nov. 1910
95 McLay Corr., McLay to Cross, 14 March 1911

CHAPTER 6: INTERBELLUM

1 He later wrote *The Winning of the Frontier* (Toronto, 1930), a history of missions in western Canada which ironically paid little attention to the considerable Baptist enterprise on the prairies.
2 W.S. Wallace, *The United Empire Loyalists* (Toronto, 1913); W.J.A. Donald, *The Canadian Iron and Steel Industry: A Study in the Economic History of a Protected Industry* (Boston, 1915)
3 F.W. Waters, 'Professor James Ten Broeke: A former student's tribute,' CB, 11 Nov. 1937, 6
4 BYB, 1908, 138
5 CC, 1908, J.F. Ingram to A.C. McKay, 6 Jan. 1908
6 W.S. Wallace, 'An Oxford day,' MM, 19 (Dec. 1909), 106-9
7 Annual Reports, History, Wallace to W.S. McLay, 10 April 1911
8 CC, 1910, John Sneath to McKay, 13 Jan. 1910
9 Ibid., W.J. Donald to McKay, 11 Sept. 1910
10 Ibid., 1911-12, Donald to A.L. McCrimmon, 21 July 1912
11 MM, 1 (1891), 173-7

12 Ibid., 20 (Oct. 1910), 32
13 Ibid., 9 (March 1900), 277-8
14 McLay Corr., Copy of a resolution of a general meeting of the Student Body, 28 Feb. 1911
15 CC, 1907-8, Edmund Burke to McKay, 30 Oct. 1907
16 McLay Corr., Calvin Harris to McLay, 5 April 1911
17 G.P. Gilmour File, C.S. Robertson, 'From Green and Black to Grey and Maroon,' 1
18 BGM, 1, 10 May 1910, 351
19 CC, 1910-11, Morden Long to McKay, 28 Oct. 1910
20 McLay Corr., J.D. Freeman to McLay, 29 May 1912
21 CC, 1912-13, Freeman to A.L. McCrimmon, 11 Nov. 1912
22 McLay Corr., McLay to McCrimmon, 9 April 1912; Annual Reports, 1914, History, Wallace to McLay, 29 April 1914
23 CC, 1912-13, W.S. Fox to McCrimmon, 11 Nov. 1912; GC, 1951-2, Gilmour to W.C. Murray, 4 Nov. 1952
24 McLay Corr., George Cross to McLay, 18 March 1912
25 See J.M.S. Careless, 'Somewhat narrower horizons' *Historical Papers, Canadian Historical Association,* 1968 (Ottawa, 1969), 8-9
26 See William Kilbourn, *The Elements Combined: A History of the Steel Company of Canada* (Toronto, 1960), Chap. 5
27 CC, 1912-13, Fox to McCrimmon, 11 Nov. 1912
28 Ibid., 1910, R.A. Thompson to McKay, 1 June 1910
29 McLay Corr., McLay to McKay, 17 May 1911 (emphasis added)
30 CC, 1910, A.T. MacNeill to McKay, 26 Feb. 1910
31 Ibid., 1909-10, R.W. Smith to McKay, 30 June 1909. See also W.S. McLay, 'Alexander Charles McKay,' MM, 21 (Nov. 1911), 49-57.
32 CC, 1910, J.L. Hogg to McKay, 20 June 1910
33 Tingle Corr., Tingle to N. Davies, 8 June 1915
34 Robert M. Stamp, 'Technical education, the National Policy, and federal-provincial relations in Canadian Education, 1899-1912,' *Canadian Historical Review,* 52 (1971), 415
35 Michael Bliss, ' "Dyspepsia of the Mind": the Canadian businessman and his enemies,' in David S. Macmillan, ed., *Canadian Business History: Selected Studies, 1497-1971* (Toronto, 1972), 185-7
36 CC, 1910, Hogg to McKay, 25 Aug. 1910
37 J.D. Babbitt, ed., *Science in Canada: Selections from the Speeches of E.W.R. Steacie* (Toronto, 1965), 24
38 RBRT, Loudon Papers, James Loudon, 'On hustling and hazing,' 1895
39 BYB, 1911, 132

40 SM, 2, 3 May 1904, 452
41 H. Becker and H.E. Barnes, *Social Thought from Lore to Science*, 3d ed., 3 (New York, 1961), 979-80
42 SM, 2, 15 May 1906, 18
43 Becker and Barnes, *Social Thought from Lore to Science*, 3, 796
44 CC, 1909-10, T. Trotter to McKay, 12 Oct. 1909
45 Ibid., 1925, C-F, H.P. Whidden to Cross, 24 April 1924
46 Ibid., 1911-12, F.E. Lumley to J.H. Farmer, 26 Oct. 1911
47 Ibid., McLay to McCrimmon, 24 Nov. 1912
48 Ibid., A.A. Ayer to D.E. Thomson, 29 Aug. 1911
49 Ibid., H.W. Piercy to McCrimmon, 24 Oct. 1912
50 A draft of this letter is in CC, 1911-12, 15 Nov. 1911
51 Ibid., Stanley Hughson to McCrimmon, 16 Nov. 1911
52 Ibid., 1910-11, Ayer to McCrimmon, 7 Sept. 1911
53 Ibid., 1911-12, S.S. Bates to McCrimmon, 20 Aug. 1912 (emphasis in original)
54 McLay Corr., J.R. Turnbull's correspondence with I.G. Matthews, various dates, 1915
55 SM, 2, 28 Jan. 1913, 331; 14 Oct. 1913, 351
56 CC, 1912-13, O.C.S. Wallace to McCrimmon, 28 Oct. 1912

CHAPTER 7: ARMAGEDDON

1 CC, 1910-11, Morden Long to A.C. McKay, 28 Oct. 1910
2 Ibid., 1909, G.R. Parkin to McKay, 1 April 1909
3 Katie W. Armstrong, 'In memory of Edward the Peacemaker,' MM, 20 (Oct. 1910), 6
4 GC, 1901, C.J. Holman to O.C.S. Wallace, 23 Dec. 1901
5 Ibid., J.C. Tibb to Wallace, 12 Dec. 1901
6 Carl Berger, *The Sense of Power: Studies in the Ideas of Canadian Imperialism, 1867-1914* (Toronto, 1970), 237-8
7 CB, 31 Oct. 1918, 8
8 MM, 24 (Oct. 1914), 1
9 See Michael Bliss, 'The Methodist Church and World War I,' *Canadian Historical Review*, 49 (1968), 213-33
10 CB, 13 Aug. 1914, 8 (emphasis in original) See S.R. Ramlochan, 'The Baptists of Ontario and World War I,' Graduate research paper, McMaster University (1973), 5-10.
11 Biographical Files, Dean J.H. Farmer
12 BYB, 1915, 160

13 Ninth Annual Report of the educational secretary (1915-16)

14 Toronto *Globe*, 20 April 1916

15 *Minutes of the Eightieth Annual Meeting of the Ottawa Baptist Association*, 1915 (Ottawa, 1915), 20

16 MM, 24 (Dec. 1914), 99-100. For the later activities of the OTC unit see 'Canadian Officers' Training Corps, University of Toronto Contingent, McMaster University Platoon: Contingent Orders, 1916-17.'

17 Tingle Corr., Tingle to Athletic Association, 6 Oct. 1914

18 BYB, 1915, 155

19 SM, 2, 9 May 1916, 437; CC, 1915-16, Reports on Enrolment, 1915-16

20 BGM, 1, 9 May 1916, 441; CC, 1916, W.S. Wallace to A.L. McCrimmon, 23 Feb. 1916

21 MM, 24 (April 1915), 258

22 BGM, 1, 4 May 1915, 430

23 CC, 1916, D.E. Thomson to McCrimmon, 2 May 1916. See Special War Contribution File, June 1916.

24 BYB, 1918, 136, 143

25 CC, 1918-19, W.F. Price to McCrimmon, 15 June 1918

26 Ibid., 1916-17, J.D. Freeman to McCrimmon, 11 Dec. 1916

27 Ibid., 1917-18, G.M. Philpott to McCrimmon, [?] 1918. Other samples of this kind of literature are in Letters from Overseas Soldiers File, 1915-18.

28 Ibid., 1918-19, F.W. Price to McCrimmon, 15 June 1918

29 Ibid., 1915, McCrimmon to Sir Robert Falconer, 6 March 1915

30 McMaster Faculty Appointments File, Paul Mueller

31 W. Stewart Wallace, *A History of the University of Toronto, 1827-1927* (Toronto, 1927), 191-2

32 McMaster Faculty Appointments File, Mueller

33 RBRT, Loudon Papers, 1916

34 CC, 1910-11, McLay to McKay, 4 May 1911

35 Annual Report of the Chemistry Department, April 1911

36 McLay Corr., John Squair to McLay, 2 June 1919

37 German File, E.J. Bengough's statement, 27 March 1939

38 SM, 2, 4 May 1915, 416

39 Ibid., 9 May 1916, 447

40 CC, 1916, Comptroller of Munitions to McCrimmon, 20 March 1916

41 Tingle Corr., M.J. Bradley to Tingle, 20 Dec. 1915.

42 Ibid., Tingle to P.V. Rosewarne, 20 April 1917

43 McLay Corr., 20 March 1918

44 For the impact of the first world war on United States manufacturing see Williams Haynes, *American Chemical Industry*, 2, *The World War I Period: 1912-1922* (New York, 1945)

45 A.L. McCrimmon, *The Woman Movement* (Philadelphia, 1915), Chap. 25
46 Tingle Corr., G.E. Grattan to Tingle, 16 Nov. 1916
47 Ibid., Tingle to N.W. Rowell, 4 May 1918
48 Ibid., Tingle to Lillian E. Tingle, 21 March 1918
49 Ibid., Marion Grimshaw to Tingle, 19 Nov. 1917
50 MM, 26 (Nov. 1916), 51
51 CC, 1916-17, Joseph Wearing to McCrimmon, 3 March 1917
52 MM, 3 (1893-4), 224
53 CC, 1917-18, Philpott to his mother, [?] Jan. 1918
54 MM, 27 (April 1918), 284-7
55 CC, 1917-18, H.A. Innis to McCrimmon, 15 Dec. 1917
56 CB, 13 Dec. 1917, 8
57 Ibid., 10 Dec. 1917; J.T. Copp and T.D. Tait, eds, *The Canadian Response to War,*
   1914-1917 (Toronto, 1971), 45-7
58 Tingle Corr., Tingle to R.R. McGregor, 17 Dec. 1917
59 McLay Corr., McLay to O.C.S. Wallace, 5 Dec. 1917
60 CC, 1917-18, R.L. Borden to McCrimmon, 20 Nov. 1917
61 SM, 2, 12 Feb. 1918, 41
62 Tingle Corr., Tingle to John Demaray, 12 Dec. 1917
63 Ibid., Tingle to Bessie Cooke, 12 June 1918
64 McLay Corr., F. Sanderson to McLay, 8 Aug. 1918
65 Tingle Corr., Tingle to W.A. Noyes, 21 Mar. 1918
66 CC, 1918-19, Stuart J. Bates to McCrimmon, 17 Aug. 1918
67 Ibid., C.E. Burke to McCrimmon, 9 Sept. 1918
68 R.P. Graham and L.H. Cragg, 'Department of Chemistry at McMaster University,' *Canadian Chemistry and Process Industries* (Sept. 1947), 2
69 CC, 1918-19, Toronto Physics Department to McCrimmon, 27 Sept. 1918
70 Ibid., 1919, H.F. Dawes to McCrimmon, 12 Sept. 1919
71 Ibid., 1917, A report from McCrimmon, [?] 1917
72 McLay Corr., W.J. Donald to McLay, 8 July 1918
73 MM, 28 (Oct. 1918), 28
74 CC, 1920, Innis to McCrimmon, [?] May 1920
75 Ibid., 1919, McCrimmon to Thomson, 12 Aug. 1919 (draft)
76 Tingle Corr., Tingle to N.W. Rowell, 4 May 1918. On this and related points see *A*
   Science Policy for Canada, 1, A Critical Review: Past and Present (Ottawa, 1970),
   25-9.
77 Tingle Corr., C.V. Harding to Tingle, 13 Oct. 1917
78 Ibid., Tingle to Rowell, 4 May 1918
79 J.D. Babbitt, ed., *Science in Canada: Selections from the Speeches of E.W.R.*
   Steacie (Toronto, 1965), 24
80 CC, 1919, W.S. Mallory to Faculty, 2 Jan. 1919

81 MM, 28 (Dec. 1918), 106-9
82 CC, 1917-18, G.S. Jury to McCrimmon, 2 Jan. 1918
83 Ibid., F.W. Waters to McCrimmon, 27 Feb. 1918
84 W. Stewart Wallace, 'The Khaki University of Canada,' MM, 28 (Dec. 1918), 97-100
85 CC, 1918-19, D.A. MacGibbon to McCrimmon, 30 Nov. 1918
86 Ibid., John W. Davis [?] to McCrimmon, 24 July 1918
87 CB, 1 Nov. 1917, 8
88 Ibid., 13 Sept. 1917, 3-4
89 CC, 1917-18, Robert Segsworth to McCrimmon, 6 April 1918
90 BYB, 1921, 143-4
91 CC, 1920-21, R.E. Freeman to McCrimmon, 10 Oct. 1920

CHAPTER 8: POST-WAR HOPES AND FEARS

1 See Minutes of the Committee of Forty of the Inter-Church Forward Movement, 20 May 1919.
2 CC, 1916, A.L. McCrimmon to C.J. Cameron, 16 March 1916
3 Ibid., D.E. Thomson to J.H. Farmer, 21 Sept. 1916
4 Ibid., J.H. Hunter to McCrimmon, 10 Oct. 1917
5 Ibid., 1918-19, Thomson to McCrimmon, 1 Oct. 1918
6 Ibid., 1916, Mrs Christina Stewart to McCrimmon, 5 March 1916
7 Ibid., 1919, F.W. Waters to McCrimmon, 15 April 1919
8 Ibid., T.T. Shields to McCrimmon, 3 May 1919
9 McLay Corr., L.C. Kitchen, 'Arts vs Theology' (1919), 1
10 Ibid., 2-3
11 CC, 1919, McCrimmon to Thomson, 12 Aug. 1919
12 Ibid., Thomson to McCrimmon, [?] Aug. 1919
13 See Stewart G. Cole, *The History of Fundamentalism* (New York, 1931), 233-6. Cole was a McMaster alumnus.
14 See John Dozois, 'Dr. T.T. Shields (1873-1955): In the Stream of Fundamentalism,' unpublished BD thesis (McMaster University, 1963)
15 Ibid., 65
16 CC, 1919, McCrimmon to Thomson, 12 Aug. 1919
17 John Pattison, 'The fundamentalist-modernist controversy in the Baptist Convention,' Graduate research paper, McMaster University (1973), 28
18 CC, 1923-5, M-N, E.T. Newton to H.P. Whidden, 7 Dec. 1925
19 T.T. Shields, *The Plot that Failed* (Toronto, 1937), 10
20 CC, 1916-17, C.J. Holman to McCrimmon, 22 Feb. 1917

21 *Maclean's Magazine*, 15 July 1949, 51
22 CC, 1920-1, Holman to McCrimmon, 4 March 1920
23 Ibid., 1919, O.C.S. Wallace to McCrimmon, 24 March 1919
24 Ibid., Thomson to McCrimmon, 30 July 1919
25 CB, 2 Oct. 1919
26 CC, 1919, J.E. Anderson to McCrimmon, 20 Oct. 1919
27 Kitchen, 'Arts vs Theology,' 3
28 BYB, 1919, 26
29 Interview with Professor H.W. Lang, 7 Aug. 1973, McMaster University
30 CC, 1919, J.L. Gilmour to McCrimmon, 17 Nov. 1919
31 BGM, 2, 18 Feb. 1920, 46-7
32 BGM, 2, 18 Feb. 1919, 10; 18 Feb. 1920, 46-7; Alan Wilson, *John Northway: A Blue Serge Canadian* (Toronto, 1965), 191, 218
33 Rockefeller Box, Thomson to McCrimmon, 29 May 1920
34 CC, 1919, Thomson to McCrimmon, 11 Nov. 1919
35 Ibid., Albert Matthews to McCrimmon, 23 Oct. 1919
36 Ibid., A.L. Huddleston to A.J. Madill, 2 May 1919
37 Ibid., 1917, D.C. Macintosh to S.S. Bates, 12 May 1917
38 McLay Corr., McLay to Macintosh, 22 Oct. 1917
39 CC, 1926, R-S, J.W. Russell to Whidden, 3 Feb. 1926
40 Ibid., 1919, V.E. Gray to Board of Governors, [?] 1919
41 McLay Corr., L.C. Kitchen to McLay, 7 June 1919
42 SM, 3, 8 May 1919, 98
43 A.L. McCrimmon, *The Educational Policy of the Baptists of Ontario and Quebec* (Toronto, 1920), 30
44 CC, 1920-1, 'An address to students,' 21 Sept. 1920
45 McCrimmon, *Educational Policy*, 31
46 G.P. Gilmour, 'A president's eye view, 1941-1961,' unpublished ms. (1963), 4
47 McLay Corr., McLay to R.J. Bonner, 19 Feb. 1920
48 CC, 1919, McCrimmon to Senate Committee on Vacancies, n.d.; Thomson to McCrimmon, 18 June 1919
49 BGM, 2, 14 April 1920, 52
50 McLay Corr., Morden Long to McLay, 15 Jan. 1921
51 Ibid., McLay to G.H. Clarke, 4 Dec. 1920
52 Ibid., McLay to D.E. Thomson, 25 Jan. 1921. See Gaylord P. Albaugh, 'Themes for research in Canadian Baptist History,' *Foundations*, 6, no. 1 (1963), 52.
53 BGM, 2, 13 Dec. 1923, 230-4; 3, 15 June 1928, 57
54 Chancellor's annual report, 1919-20
55 McLay Corr., Various annual reports, 19, 23 April 1921
56 CC, 1915-16, Thomson to McCrimmon, 10 Nov. 1915

57 Ibid., 1920-1, 'An address to students,' 21 Sept. 1920
58 MM, 29 (Dec. 1919), 119
59 BGM, 2, 21 Oct. 1920, 61, 63
60 Ibid., 18 May 1925, 275
61 McLay Corr., McLay to dean of the Graduate School, Chicago, 28 Feb. 1921
62 Interview with Dean N.H. Parker, 21 Oct. 1964, McMaster University
63 Interview with Mr. K.W. Taylor, 14 Jan. 1965, McMaster University
64 CC, 1923-5, M-N, N Misc., C.W. New to Whidden, 22 Aug. 1924
65 Ibid., 1923-5, C-F, F Misc., William Findlay to Whidden, 13 Oct. 1925
66 Interview with Parker
67 See *McMaster Alumni News*, 6, no. 5 (4 May 1935).
68 SM, 3, 19 Oct. 1922, 205
69 McLay Corr., 1923-5, G.H. Clarke to McLay, 18 Sept. 1922
70 A.B. McLay, 'Howard Primrose Whidden (1871-1952),' *Proceedings of the Royal Society of Canada*, Series 3, 46 (1952), 103
71 GC, case 3, Whidden to Wallace, 2 Aug. 1897
72 SM, 1, 20 Dec. 1898, 9 May 1899, 358, 363
73 GC, case 3, Whidden to Wallace, 16 April 1897
74 Wallace P. Cohoe, 'The struggle for a sheepskin,' unpublished ms., 43-4
75 H.P. Whidden, 'What is a liberal education?' *Canadian Journal of Religious Thought*, 1 (1924), 39
76 BGM, 2, 8 Nov. 1921, 103
77 CC, 1926, O-Q, Personal, D-L, E.C. Fox to Whidden, 16 Dec. 1922
78 Ibid., 1923, Whidden to W.A. Cameron, 24 March 1923
79 Whidden, 'What is a liberal education?' 39
80 BGM, 2, 21 Dec. 1922, 186
81 Ibid., 7 Sept. 1922

CHAPTER 9: 'O, IT'S A LOVELY WAR!'

1 CC, 1919, H.H. Bingham to A.L. McCrimmon, 20 May 1919
2 McLay Corr., A.L. McCrimmon to McLay, 24 July 1920
3 C.G. Stone and F.J. Garnett, *Brandon College: A History*, 1899-1967 (Brandon, 1969), 97
4 CC, 1926, S, T.T. Shields to A.F. Baker, M. Wolverton, and G.R. Maguire, 1 March 1924
5 Ibid., B-C, H.P. Whidden to W.G. Carpenter, 10 Aug. 1922 and 2 Oct. 1922
6 BYB, 1922, 40
7 Stone and Garnett, *Brandon College*, 97-8

8 CC, 1926, S, Shields to [?] Orchard, 1 March 1924

9 Ibid., 1923-5, G-L, George Hilton to Whidden, 18 Dec. 1925

10 Alan Wilson, *John Northway: A Blue Serge Canadian* (Toronto, 1965), 199-201

11 CC, 1926, M-N, Albert Matthews File, Matthews to Whidden, 14 Feb. 1923

12 Ibid., 1923-5, M-N, Whidden to John MacNeill, 20 Feb. 1923

13 Ibid., W.A. Cameron to Whidden, 28 Feb. 1923

14 Ibid., 1926, M-N, Matthews File, Whidden to Matthews, 9 March 1923

15 Ibid., Shields to Matthews, 23 March 1923

16 SM, 3, 20 Jan. 1924, 253

17 CC, 1923-5, M-N, J.H. Farmer to Whidden, 8 March 1923

18 Ibid., Whidden to Shields, 24 Nov. 1923

19 SM, 3, 20 Jan. 1924, 247-53

20 McLay Corr., 1923-5, McLay to W.S. Elliott, 4 Feb. 1924

21 Ibid.

22 SM, 3, 20 Jan. 1924, 247-53

23 CC, 1926, S, Whidden to Shields, 24 Nov. 1923

24 Ibid., Farmer to Whidden, 9 Jan. 1924

25 CC, 1923-5, M-N, Whidden to S.J. Moore, 10 Dec. 1923

26 See William H.P. Faunce, 'Freedom in school and church,' *World's Work*, 45 (1923), 509

27 CC, 1926, M-N, Matthews File, Whidden to Matthews, 29 Nov. 1923; ibid., 1923-5, M-N, Whidden to E.A. Miller, 18 Jan. 1924

28 Paul A. Carter, 'The fundamentalist defence of the faith,' in John Braeman, R. Bremner, and J. Brody, eds, *Change and Continuity in Twentieth Century America: The Twenties* (Ohio State University Press, 1968), 185-6

29 CC, 1926, S, J.A. Paterson to Whidden, 22 Jan. 1924

30 Ibid., O.C.S. Wallace to Whidden, 14 Dec. 1923

31 Wilson, *Northway*, 204

32 CC, 1923-5, M-N, M Misc., Duncan McDermid to Whidden, 30 March 1924

33 *Gospel Witness*, 17 Jan. 1924, 19; 31 Jan. 1924, 36; and 24 April 1924, 24

34 CC, 1923-5, C-F, F Misc., A.B. Foster to Whidden, 12 March 1924

35 Ibid., File on Educational Representatives in the Associations, E. Orsborn to Whidden, 4 March 1925

36 Ibid., 1923-5, G-L, G misc., Whidden to G.P. Gilmour, 15 Jan. 1924

37 McLay Corr., I.G. Matthews to McLay, 29 Oct. 1924

38 CC, 1923-5, B-C, B Misc., J.G. Brown to Whidden, 24 Aug. 1924

39 Ibid., Whidden to Brown, 6 Aug. 1924

40 Ibid., Brown to Whidden, 8 Aug. 1924

41 BYB, 1924, 174-5

42 CC, 1926, E-F, Dean Farmer File, Whidden to Farmer, 6 March 1924

43 Carter, 'The fundamentalist defence of the faith,' 182
44 CC, 1923-5, M-N, N Misc., Rev. H.C. Newcombe to Whidden, 24 Sept. 1924
45 BYB, *1924*, 43
46 McLay Corr., 1923-5, Whidden to McLay, 12 March 1925
47 Ibid., I.G. Matthews to McLay, 29 Oct. 1924
48 CC, 1923-5, B-C, B Misc., Whidden to Rev. L. Brown, 19 Nov. 1924
49 Ibid., 1926, E-F, W.S. Fox File, Fox to Whidden, 8 Nov. 1924
50 G.P. Gilmour, 'A president's eye view,' unpublished ms., 4
51 McLay Corr., 1923-5, Rev. J.D. Freeman to McLay, 18 Dec. 1924; CC, 1925, G-F, Freeman to Whidden, 26 Oct. 1925
52 CC, 1926, G-M, Marshall File, Whidden to C.E. Wilson, 17 June 1925
53 Ibid., Whidden to Marshall, 17 June 1925
54 SM, 3, 25 July 1925, 290-1
55 CC, 1926, G-M, L.H. Marshall File, clipping from *Christian World*
56 Ibid., Shields cable to the Board of Governors, 13 July 1925
57 Ibid., M-N, MI-MZ, Henry Moyle to Whidden, 12 April 1926
58 See Norman F. Furniss, *The Fundamentalist Controversy 1918-1931* (New Haven, 1954), 4-9; Stewart G. Cole, *The History of Fundamentalism* (New York, 1931), 308-10.
59 McLay Corr., 1925-6, McLay to Marshall, 20 Aug. 1925
60 *Gospel Witness*, 22 Oct. 1925, 4, quoted in W. Gordon Carder, 'Controversy in the Baptist Convention of Ontario and Quebec, 1908-1929,' *Foundations*, 16 (1973), 365
61 BYB, *1925*, 42
62 Ibid., 43
63 F.F. MacNab, 'An unfortunate necessity,' MM, 35 (Oct. 1925), 3-9
64 CC, 1923-5, G-L, E.C. Gosnell to Whidden, 5 Nov. 1925
65 Ibid., 12 Nov. 1925
66 Interview with Professor Lang, 7 Aug. 1973, McMaster University. Lang had been Marshall's pastor at Central Baptist Church, located in Castle Memorial Hall on the university campus.
67 CC, 1923-5, C-F, Whidden to C.R. Duncan, 27 Oct. 1925
68 Ibid., 1923-5, R, File on Special Verbatim Report Pamphlet, J.G. Van Slyke to Whidden, 10 Nov. 1925
69 Ibid., M-N, E.T. Newton to Whidden, 7 Nov. 1925
70 Ibid., 1926, G-M, K Misc., E.P.H. King to Whidden, 23 Jan. 1926. See also the Rev. Silas Lamb's autobiography, *Profile* (Hamilton, 1973), 47.
71 CC, 1923-5, R, H.E. Robinson to Whidden, 25 Nov. 1925
72 McLay Corr., McLay to Mrs Myrtle Manson, 3 May 1926
73 CC, 1923-5, M-N, Whidden to R.R. McKay, 27 Nov. 1925

74 Ibid., 1926, S, Walter Clarke to Whidden, 28 Jan. 1926
75 Ibid., Clarke to J.H. Cranston, 30 Jan. 1926
76 McLay Corr., 1923-5, J.H. Hunter to McLay, 11 Nov. 1923
77 CC, 1926, M-N, MCL-MCZ Misc., Whidden to J.O. MacLachlan, 9 Feb. 1926
78 Ibid., G-M, H Misc., C.T. Holman to Whidden, 9 April 1926. See G.P. Albaugh, 'Themes for research in Canadian Baptist History', Foundations, 6, no. 1 (1963), 52-3
79 CC, 1926, S-W, SA-SH Misc., Whidden to Sen. F.L. Schaffner, 29 May 1926
80 Ibid., S, Clarke to Whidden, 28 Jan. 1926
81 Ibid., G-M, K Misc., O.E. Kendall to Whidden, 21 Feb. 1926
82 Ibid., Whidden to Gideon Grant, 19 Feb. 1926
83 See Toronto Globe, 22 March 1926.
84 CC, 1926, W-Z, H.J. White to Whidden, 19 April 1926
85 Interview with Lang
86 See Toronto Globe, 18 March 1926.
87 CC, 1926, W-Z, W Misc., Whidden to J.R. Webb, 26 March 1926
88 Annual Reports, Dean J.H. Farmer, April 1926. Indeed, fifty-eight of the seventy-five students residing in McMaster Hall had petitioned for Brown's expulsion.
89 BYB, 1925, 169-70
90 Interview with Lang
91 CC, 1923-5, C-F, D Misc., O.E. Daniel to Whidden, 9 Sept. 1925
92 Senate Executive Committee Minutes, 27 March 1926, 1-4
93 Ibid., 1 April 1926, 3-6
94 See Toronto Globe, 26 March 1926.
95 CC, 1926, M-N, MA-MH, T.E. Meldrum to Whidden, 27 March 1926
96 Ibid., K Misc., T.A. Kirkconnell to Whidden, 12 Nov. 1926. The son in question ultimately joined McMaster's English Department. See Watson Kirkconnell, A Slice of Canada: Memoirs (Toronto, 1967), 9-10, 137.
97 CC, 1926, SA-SH Misc., Whidden to Schaffner, 29 May 1926; M-N, MA-MH, Whidden to F.C. Mabee, 27 July 1926
98 McLay Corr., 1925-6, Ll. Brown to McLay, 16 April 1926.
99 Interview with Lang. See Acts and Proceedings of the 51st General Assembly of the Presbyterian Church in Canada, 1925 (Toronto, 1925), 158-60
100 CC, 1926, W-Z, W Misc., Joseph Wearing to Whidden, 24 March 1926
101 Wilson, Northway, 206
102 CC, 1926, various entries under appropriate initial
103 Ibid., S-W, T Misc., Whidden to A.J. Thomson, 6 May 1926
104 McLay Corr., Mrs Zavitz, 'To the women of the churches,' 10 Feb. 1926
105 CC, 1926, W-Z, W Misc., Wearing to Whidden, 29 Sept. 1926
106 Ibid., G-M, H Misc., M.G. Hay to W.A. Cameron, 23 Oct. 1926

107 Toronto *Globe,* 13 Sept. 1926; Peterborough *Evening Express,* 25 Sept. 1926.
108 CC, 1926, G-M, G Misc., G.E. Grattan to Whidden, 24 Sept. 1926
109 BYB, 1926, 165
110 SM, 4, 14 Oct. 1926, 23-4
111 BYB, 1926, 35-6
112 See *Proceedings of the Educational Session of the Baptist Convention of Ontario and Quebec held in First Avenue Baptist Church, Toronto, October 19, 1926* (Toronto, 1926), 64-83.
113 Carder, 'Controversy in the Baptist Convention,' 57
114 CC, 1926, S-W, O.C.S. Wallace File, Wallace to S.J. Moore, 9 Nov. 1926
115 Annual reports, Dean J.H. Farmer, April 1927
116 CC, 1926, M-N, MA-MH, Whidden to Arthur Meighen, 10 Nov. 1926
117 For a full account of the episode and its aftermath see George S. May, 'Des Moines University and Dr T.T. Shields,' *Iowa Journal of History* (July 1956), 193-232.
118 See Charles J. Holman, *The Denominational Crisis. A Protest and an Appeal* (Toronto, 1926).
119 University Reorganization File, Charter Revision 1944-5, Thomas Urquhart to W.W. Denovan, 28 Dec. 1928
120 Annual Report, dean of theology, 1926-7, 2
121 Hamilton *Herald,* 23 Oct. 1935
122 *Gospel Witness,* 30 Aug. 1928, 1-2
123 GC, 1951-2, I, Gilmour to Stuart Ivison, 13 April 1951
124 Annual reports, 1941-2, H.E. Bridge to Gilmour, 4 May 1942. See also *McMaster University, 1890-1940* (Hamilton, 1940), 14
125 For a sympathetic account of Shields's motives and actions see Leslie K. Tarr, *Shields of Canada: T.T. Shields, 1873-1955* (Grand Rapids, 1967), Chap. 11.
126 MM, 39 (1930), 323-7
127 Mrs Ruth J. Braund (L.H. Marshall's daughter) to author, 19 Aug. 1975; interviews with Lang and Parker. Mrs Braund maintains that he was 'passed over' for a Canadian-born candidate, John MacNeill.
128 BGM, 3, 9 Jan. 1930, 95-6
129 CC, 1926, S, Extracts from Dr Shields's speech, 10 Sept. 1926
130 Marshall File, Marshall to Whidden, 7 Dec. 1929

CHAPTER 10: TOWARDS A FRESH START

1 CC, 1923-5, Prohibition File. For illustrations of the earlier campaign see MM, 3 (1893), 132; CC, 1909, Thomas Wearing to A.C. McKay, 27 May 1909.
2 CC, 1923-5, M-N, M Misc., H.P. Whidden to D.N. McLachlan, 19 April 1924

3 Ibid., Whidden to J.H. McDiarmid, 22 Nov. 1924
4 H.P. Whidden, 'What is a liberal education?,' Canadian Journal of Religious Thought, 1 (1924), 36-9
5 Classics File, C.H. Stearn, Stearn to Whidden, 2 July 1928
6 Interview with Dr C.H. Stearn, 6 Oct. 1964, Hamilton, Ont.
7 SM, 3, 9 March 1922, 173
8 Interview with K.W. Taylor, 14 Jan. 1965, McMaster University
9 Package #5, Economics-Michell, J.E. Robbins to Whidden, 22 Jan. 1930
10 Annual report, Political Economy 1930-1 (newspaper clipping)
11 SM, 3, 8 March 1922, 173
12 BGM, 2, 20 Sept. 1923, 214
13 Oxford, 1929
14 For a recent discussion of the historiography of this subject and the place that New's study now occupies in it, consult Ged Martin, The Durham Report and British Policy: A Critical Essay (Cambridge, 1972).
15 Interview with Dr R.P. Graham, 14 Apr. 1973, McMaster University; R.P. Graham and L.H. Cragg, 'Department of Chemistry at McMaster University,' Canadian Chemistry and Process Industries (Sept. 1947), 2
16 McLay Corr., 1924-6, McLay to F.W. Sweet, 26 Dec. 1924
17 SM, 3, 8 May 1919, 97-8; 12 May 1924, 263
18 Annual reports, 1926-7, R.W. Smith, Biology
19 Ibid., Wm Findlay, Mathematics, 25 April 1927
20 BYB, 1933, 148
21 A.J.M. Smith, ed., The Book of Canadian Poetry: A Critical and Historical Anthology, 2nd ed. (Toronto, 1948), 255
22 McLay Corr., 1923-5, I.H. Eberle to McLay, 16 April 1923
23 SM, 4, 26 Nov. 1929, 106
24 BGM, 2, 15 April 1924, 248
25 MM, 37 (Nov. 1927), 71-2
26 CC, 1916, R.A. Thompson to A.L. McCrimmon, 22 March 1916
27 G.P. Gilmour File, C.S. Robertson, 'From Green and Black to Grey and Maroon,' 2
28 CC, 1920-1, C.S. Robertson to McCrimmon, 5 May 1920
29 SM, 7, 7 Oct. 1955, 8-9
30 BGM, 2, 10 May 1920, 59
31 McLay Corr., McLay to E.J. Tarr, 7 July 1921
32 CC, 1915-16, J.J. Ross to McCrimmon, 13 Jan. 1916
33 Ibid., 1917, Ross to McCrimmon, 2 April 1917
34 Hamilton Chamber of Commerce [hereafter Chamber], Board of Directors' Minutes, 3, 1921-2, 14 June 1921

35 Ibid., 4, 1921-2, 26 July 1921
36 BYB, 1921, 142
37 Removal to Hamilton File, 1927, W.W. McMaster to F. Sanderson, 25 Aug. 1921
38 *McMaster University at Hamilton* (Hamilton, 1921)
39 Removal to Hamilton File, Items, Copy of a resolution passed unanimously by the Niagara and Hamilton Association of Baptist Churches, 1 and 2 June 1921, Welland, Ontario
40 See Jacob Spelt, *Urban Development of South-Central Ontario*, 2d ed. (Toronto, 1972), pp. 211-12
41 Woodstock *Sentinel-Review*, 17 Oct. 1921
42 CC, 1918-19, C.T. Holman to McCrimmon, 23 May 1918; McLay Corr., McLay to N.S. McKechnie, 2 Feb. 1921; BGM, 2, 14 May 1923, 208
43 BYB, 1921, 36-7
44 Ibid., 37-8
45 CC, 1921-2, Thomson to McCrimmon, 31 Oct. 1921
46 Chamber, Directors' Minutes, 3, 1921-2, 15 Nov. 1921
47 BYB, 1921, 142
48 CC, 1921-2, V. Evan Gray to McCrimmon, 26 Oct. 1921
49 Ibid., W.G. Carpenter to McCrimmon, 20 Jan. 1922
50 Ibid., McMaster to McCrimmon, 26 Oct. 1921
51 Chamber, Directors' Minutes, 3, 1921-2, 15 Nov. 1921
52 BGM, 2, 13 Dec. 1921, 115
53 CC, 1921-2, Board chairman and chancellor to Hamilton Committee, 15 Dec. 1921
54 BGM, 2, 10 Jan. 1922, 121-2
55 Ibid., 122
56 SM, 3, 9 March 1922, 179; 16 March 1922, 180-5
57 Removal to Hamilton File, 1927, Items, Report of Survey Committee, Jan. 1922
58 Chamber, Directors' Minutes, 5, 1922-3, 2 May 1922
59 Removal to Hamilton File, 1927, McMaster to McCrimmon, 30 March 1922
60 SM, 3, 4 May 1922, 187-90
61 Ibid., 'Stenographic report of S.J. Moore's remarks at conference with Hamilton deputation, 4 May 1922'
62 SM, 3, 4 May 1922, 187-90
63 BYB, 1922, 41-2
64 CC, 1926, M-N, Albert Matthews File, Whidden to Matthews, 12 Dec. 1922
65 BGM, 2, 12 Feb. 1923, 192
66 CC, 1923-5, C-F, C Misc., Whidden to W.A. Cameron, 24 March 1923; McLay Corr., 1923-5, Whidden to McLay, 2 June 1923
67 SM, 4, 17 May 1926, 16
68 BYB, 1923, 129-30

69 Removal to Hamilton File, 1927, Report of Hamilton Committee, 29 March 1923
70 CC, 1923-5, M-N, M Misc., McMaster to Whidden, 16 Oct. 1923
71 Ibid., Installation File
72 Hamilton *Herald*, 24 Nov. 1923
73 *Hamilton Spectator*, 13 Sept. 1924
74 CC, 1923-5, G-L, Thomas Wearing to Whidden, 24 Nov. 1923
75 Chamber, Directors' Minutes, 9, 1924-5, 13 May 1924
76 Removal to Hamilton File, 1927, Hamilton Removal Proposal, W.J. Westaway to Whidden, 27 May 1924
77 CC, 1926, M-N, Albert Matthews File, J.C. Williamson to Matthews, 5 June 1925
78 McLay Corr., 1923-5, McLay to John Firstbrook, 17 Dec. 1924
79 CC, 1926, M-N, Albert Matthews File, Whidden to Matthews, 15 July 1925
80 SM, 4, 12 Nov. 1925, 2
81 CC, 1926, S-W, E.J. Tarr File, Tarr to Whidden, 9 Nov. 1925
82 Ibid., C Misc., Whidden to O.U. Chapman, 20 Jan. 1926
83 BGM, 3, 24 June 1926, 1
84 McLay Corr., 1925-6, O.J. Stevenson to McLay, 29 Dec. 1926
85 University Reorganization Correspondence, 1944-5, J.H. Cranston to G.P. Gilmour, 21 Nov. 1944
86 Woodstock College File, C. Vining, Gilmour to Vining, 27 June 1950
87 Ibid., 17 April 1951
88 See Charles Vining, 'History of Woodstock College,' *Woodstock College Memorial Book* (Toronto, 1951), Chap. 6.
89 BGM, 3, 17 May 1926, 297
90 Toronto *Globe*, 20 Oct. 1926
91 BGM, 3, 2 Nov. 1926
92 CC, 1926, G-M, H Misc., Whidden to Dr J.A. Huntley, 25 Oct. 1926
93 Interview with Taylor.
94 CC, 1926, E-F, Sherwood Fox File, Fox to Whidden, 27 Nov. 1926
95 Removal to Hamilton File, Westaway to Whidden, 15 Dec. 1926
96 CC, 1926, M-N, MCL-MCZ Misc., Whidden to J.B. McLaurin, 20 Dec. 1926
97 Removal to Hamilton File, 'Memorandum re location and proposed Forward Movement of McMaster University,' 4
98 Ibid.
99 Removal to Hamilton File, 1927, Hamilton Removal Proposals, 15 Jan. 1927
100 Ibid., Hamilton-McMaster Memo, 28 Feb. 1927
101 Ibid.
102 Toronto *Evening Telegram*, 5 April 1927, quoted in W. Gordon Carder, 'Controversy in the Baptist Convention of Ontario and Quebec, 1908-1929,' unpublished BD thesis (McMaster University, 1950), 66
103 Woodstock *Daily Sentinel-Review*, 18 Oct. 1927

104 BGM, 3, 10 Oct. 1927, 35-6
105 Hamilton *Herald*, Christmas number, 1927
106 Removal to Hamilton File, 'Memo re location and Forward Movement'

CHAPTER II: CONCLUSION

1 A promising beginning has been made by W.E.W. Ellis in his 'Social and religious factors in the Fundamentalist-Modernist schisms among Baptists in North America, 1895-1934,' PHD thesis (University of Pittsburgh, 1974).

A note on sources

The bulk of the manuscript material used in the preparation of this history is housed in the Canadian Baptist Archives, McMaster Divinity College, or in the Office of the Registrar, McMaster University. The Archives is a valuable national repository for documents not only on Baptist affairs in the country but on Canadian social and religious history generally. The manuscript resources examined in this repository were as follows: the voluminous correspondence of four of the six chancellors who served during the period covered in this study, O.C.S. Wallace, A.C. McKay, A.L. McCrimmon, and H.P. Whidden; the letters and memoranda of Deans W.S. McLay and J.H. Farmer; the correspondence kept by Professor J.B. Tingle, the chemist; the annual reports of department heads; the minutes of McMaster faculty meetings and of the executive and staff meetings of the Canadian Literary Institute and the Toronto Baptist College; the minutes of the Alumni Association and of the board of the *McMaster University Monthly*; and the proceedings of various local associations of Baptist churches. At the Registrar's Office an assortment of miscellaneous records, the minutes of Senate and Board meetings, and the letterbooks relating to their deliberations were consulted.

Abundant and illuminating though these resources are, it is regrettable that there is little or no archival material for the administrations of Malcolm MacVicar and T.H. Rand, no correspondence from other department heads comparable to Tingle's, and virtually nothing of a documentary nature on William McMaster, the founder of the university. A request to see the records of the Canadian Imperial Bank of Commerce in the hope that they might shed some light on the senator's educational plans was turned down with the explanation that no material bearing on the subject resided in that collection.

Of other repositories visited – the Public Archives of Canada, the Department of Public Records and Archives of Ontario, the Rare Book Room of the University of Toronto, and the Hamilton Public Library – only the last two produced data genuinely relevant to this study. At the Rare Book Room the papers of Presidents Blake, Loudon, and Falconer offered much helpful information on the federation question and curricular matters. The Hamilton Public Library made available the records of the Hamilton Chamber of Commerce and newspaper scrapbooks dealing with the university's move to that city. A letter of inquiry was sent to the archivist of the Rochester-Colgate Divinity College, but assurance was given that there was nothing there not already on file at the Canadian Baptist Archives.

A certain amount of oral history was also gathered through interviews with C.P. Fell, E.C. Fox, G.P. Gilmour, R.P. Graham, George Haddow, Harold Lang, H.L. MacNeill, Boyd McLay, Marget Meikleham, N.H. Parker, C.H. Stearn, H.S. Stewart, and Kenneth Taylor. Printed sources included the *Baptist Year Books*, which furnished thorough annual reviews of the work of the denomination and its institutions, the *Canadian Baptist*, the denominational paper, and its arch enemy, the *Gospel Witness*, and the *McMaster University Monthly*. Of the newspapers consulted, those from Hamilton and Toronto understandably provided most material. An examination of the footnotes to the text will indicate how extensively they were used and the degree to which other papers were employed.

As to secondary works on the history of Canadian Baptists and of the university: considerable reliance had to be placed on unpublished theses. One of the best is Walter Pitman's 'The Baptists and Public Affairs in the Province of Canada,' a Toronto MA thesis (1956) that deals admirably with the earlier phases of Baptist educational policy. Also useful were a number of McMaster BD theses, notably Robert Hamilton's 'The founding of McMaster University' (1938), John Dozois' 'T.T. Shields: In the Stream of Fundamentalism' (1963), and W. Gordon Carder's work, 'Controversy in the Baptist Convention of Ontario and Quebec, 1908-1929' (1950). Scattered pieces, such as O.C.S. Wallace's contribution in *Canada: An Encyclopaedia of the Country* (Toronto, 1898), Joseph Gilmour's essay in *Canada and Its Provinces*, 11 (Toronto, 1913), the pamphlet brought out by A.L. McCrimmon after the first world war, *The Educational Policy of the Baptists of Ontario and Quebec* (Toronto, 1920), and, finally, the short history prepared by a committee in 1940 to mark the fiftieth anniversary of the university's opening, *McMaster University, 1890-1940* (Hamilton, 1940), all sorted out in a general way the main lines of Baptist educational policy and practice in

Ontario and Quebec. G.P. Albaugh's thoughtful 'Themes for research in Canadian Baptist history' (*Foundations*, 6) is a sobering reminder, however, of what remains to be done in the field as well as a useful review of the available literature. An extremely helpful item of a different sort is the *McMaster University Alumni Directory* of 1930, which lists to that point not only graduates and honorary degree holders from McMaster but also the alumni of Brandon College.

Anyone who wishes to place the university against the backdrop of developments elsewhere can ill afford to ignore such works as W. Stewart Wallace's *A History of the University of Toronto* 1827-1927 (Toronto, 1927), C.B. Sissons's *A History of Victoria University* (Toronto, 1952), Ernest Sandeen's *The Roots of American Fundamentalism* (Chicago, 1970), Norman Furniss's *The Fundamentalist Controversy* (New Haven, 1954), and Stewart Cole's *History of Fundamentalism* (New York, 1931).

Full references to the other printed sources, monographs, biographies, and articles that were used may be found in the footnotes to the text.

Index